THE LONGMAN COMPANION TO
THE FIRST WORLD WAR
EUROPE 1914–1918

LONGMAN COMPANIONS TO HISTORY

General Editors: **Chris Cook and John Stevenson**

The following *Companions to History* are now available:

THE LONGMAN COMPANION TO

The First World War

EUROPE 1914–1918

Colin Nicolson
University of North London

An imprint of **Pearson Education**

Harlow, England · London · New York · Reading, Massachusetts · San Francisco · Toronto · Don Mills, Ontario · Sydney
Tokyo · Singapore · Hong Kong · Seoul · Taipei · Cape Town · Madrid · Mexico City · Amsterdam · Munich · Paris · Milan

Pearson Education Limited

Edinburgh Gate
Harlow
Essex CM20 2JE
England

and Associated Companies throughout the world

Visit us on the World Wide Web at:
http://www.pearsoneduc.com

First published 2001

ISBN 0-582-28983-1

British Library Cataloguing-in-Publication Data
A catalogue record for this book is available from the British Library

Library of Congress Cataloging-in-Publication Data
Nicolson, Colin.
    Longman companion to the First World War: Europe, 1914–1918/Colin Nicolson.
        p.   cm. — (Longman companions to history)
    Includes bibliographical references and index.
    ISBN 0–582–28983–1 (pbk.)
    1. World War, 1914–1918.   I. Title: First World War.   II. Title.   III. Series.
D521.N48   2000
940.3—dc21   00–047881

10 9 8 7 6 5 4 3 2 1
05 04 03 02 01

Typeset by 35 in 9.5/12pt New Baskerville
Produced by Pearson Education Asia Pte Ltd.
Printed in Singapore

CONTENTS

PREFACE

The First World War was a cataclysmic watershed in the history of the European continent. Although it lasted only four years, and was entered into with a surprisingly naïve recklessness, the war ended Europe's pre-eminence as the wealthiest and most dynamic region on the planet, leaving it impoverished, demoralised and fragmented. By 1918, the five Empires that had dominated the lands between the North Sea and the Persian Gulf – British, German, Austrian, Russian, and Ottoman – had either disappeared completely or suffered mortal wounds. Millions of Europeans had been killed or disabled in battle, or from the diseases and deprivations that the war brought in its wake. Age-old patterns of trade had been disrupted, and poisonous and fanatical forces unleashed that would ravage the continent for half a century. New nations, with fresh-drawn but disputed borders, volatile ethnic compositions, and unfulfilled territorial ambitions were thrust prematurely into existence in the forcing house of war. On the other hand, the war accelerated scientific, social and political changes that would have taken far longer to work through had it not been for the irresistible imperatives of national survival that it posed.

In the 1920s and 1930s historians became shock-troops in the battle to justify or undermine punitive reparations against Germany, and many dedicated their lives to determining the origins of the conflict. Subsequently, the strategy and tactics of the generals, the social, economic, political and cultural impact of the war, and its seminal importance for almost every subsequent 20th-century development, provided rich seams for historical investigation. Nearly a century after the war ended, new research and interpretations flow unremittingly from the printing presses. Books about battles and campaigns alone would fill a small library. Another would be required to house the ever-growing collections of memoirs and personal accounts of the conflict. Pity, therefore, the humble historian who is asked to be your companion through this ever-expanding metropolis of learning. Inevitably, hard choices had to be made about which aspects of the war to cover in such a small compass. Thus, I have chosen to emphasise the impact of the war on the European continent, where almost all the fighting took place. Events elsewhere are only covered in so far as they affected Europe. Purely military history is not covered in any detail, in deference to the vast number of excellent reference works already dealing with this subject. Instead, I have chosen to concentrate upon somewhat less accessible areas: the long-term and immediate causes of the war; the anatomy of the crisis that unleashed it; attempts to end it; above all, its political, social and economic impact on the states that fought it, and upon the new nations that unexpectedly sprang into being as a result of the revolutionary forces that it unleashed.

AUTHOR'S ACKNOWLEDGEMENTS

I would like to thank my wife Doula for her forbearance in sharing me for so long with this project. I am also indebted to my long-standing colleagues and friends at the University of North London, Professor Denis Judd, Dr Kathryn Castle, Dr Kathy Lerman, Dr Ben Fowkes, Dr Patricia Mercer, and Dr Roland Quinault, for giving me access to their collective historical knowledge. It is gratitude more keenly felt because, all to often, I expected them to field obscure factual questions on their historical specialities, delivered in the most unlikely places and at the most inconvenient times. It is a tribute to their patience and the depth of their knowledge that they very rarely dropped the ball.

PUBLISHER'S ACKNOWLEDGEMENTS

We are grateful to the following for permission to reproduce adapted copyright material:

Map 1 from *The Oxford Illustrated History of Modern Europe*, Oxford University Press (ed. Blanning, T.C.W. 1996); Map 2 from *The Great Powers, Imperialism and the German Problem 1865–1925*, Routledge (Lowe, J. 1994); Map 3 from *The Partition of Turkey*, University of Oklahoma Press (Howard, H.N. 1931); Map 5 from *The First World War: Germany & Austria-Hungary 1914–1918*, Arnold (Herwig, H.H. 1996); Maps 6 & 7 from *History of the First World War*, Cassell & Co (Liddell Hart, B.H. 1970); Map 8 from *Europe Since 1870: An International History*, Weidenfeld & Nicolson (Joll, J. 1976).

Whilst every effort has been made to trace the owners of copyright material, in a few cases this has proved impossible and we take this opportunity to offer our apologies to any copyright holders whose rights we may have unwittingly infringed.

LIST OF MAPS

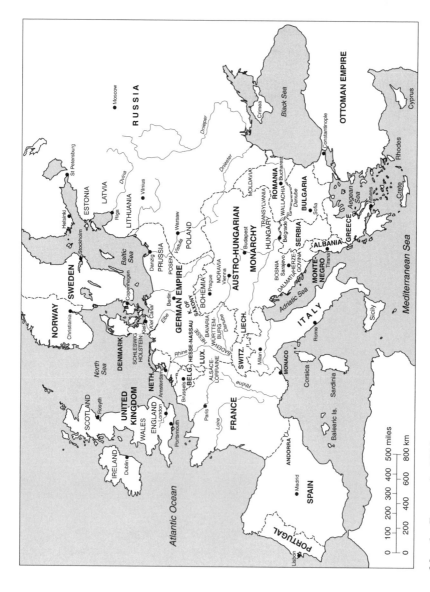

Map 1   Europe in 1914

Map 2   The European Powers in Africa: 1914

Map 3   The Balkans in 1914

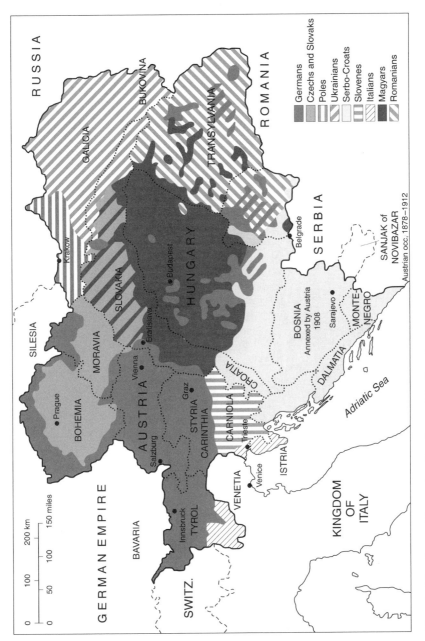

Map 4   The Austro-Hungarian Empire and its Peoples

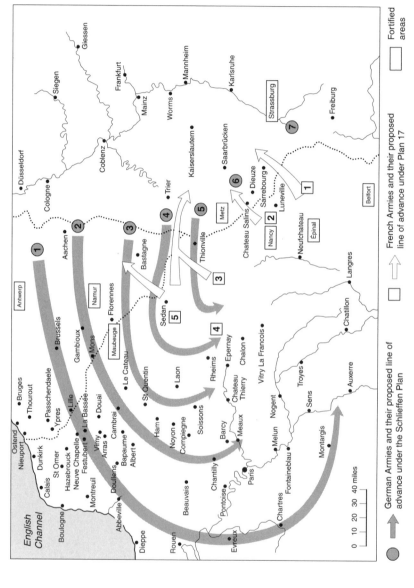

Map 5   French and German War Plans in 1914

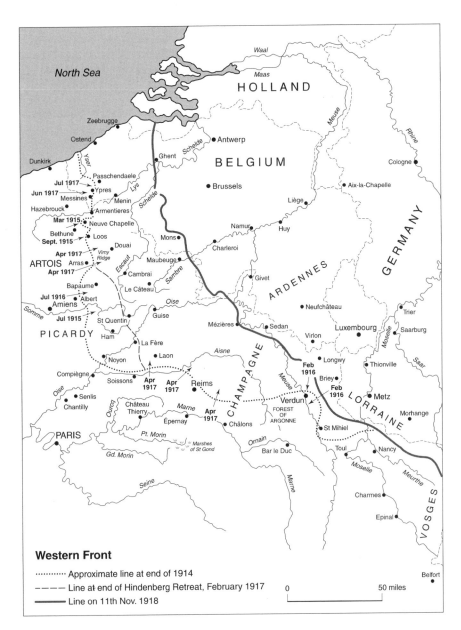

Western Front

·········· Approximate line at end of 1914

— — — Line at end of Hindenberg Retreat, February 1917

———— Line on 11th Nov. 1918

0   50 miles

Map 6   The Western Front: 1914–18

.... Eastern Front at the Armistice
of Brest-Litovsk
(15 December 1917)

———— The Eastern Front after the
Treaty of Brest-Litovsk
(3 March 1918) with Russia
and, east of Homel, the
territory occupied following
the German invasion of the
newly independent Ukraine

– – – – 1914 frontiers

0   150   300 miles

Map 7   The Eastern Front: 1914–18

Map 8   Europe in 1919

ALLIANCES AND AGREEMENTS

INTRODUCTION

By July 1914, Europe had become divided into two armed camps: the Triple Alliance of Germany, Italy and Austria-Hungary, with their associate Romania, confronted a Triple Entente consisting of France, Britain and Russia, with their protégé Serbia. These competing power blocs were bound together by a series of agreements that had evolved over a long period. Most of them were originally signed for defensive purposes, and were entered into as *temporary* solutions to specific security needs. None was intended to last more than a few years. But a series of international crises between 1898 and 1912 drove the partners closer together, solidified the Alliances and made it difficult to disentangle them. Increasingly, military ties reinforced the Alliances, and the war plans of the Powers were based on their relationship with their Alliance partners. By 1914, the Alliances had become both essential guarantees of security, and pledges that could drag nations into war to support the quarrels of others.

1.1   THE AUSTRO-GERMAN TREATY (7 OCTOBER 1879)

This agreement (sometimes called the Dual Alliance) remained in force until 1918. It was the first and longest lasting of the agreements that divided Europe into armed camps. Originally, the Treaty formed the cornerstone of 'Bismarck's system' that was intended to give him a lever to hold back Austrian ambitions in the Balkans, and was balanced by a parallel German commitment to Russia. After Bismarck fell in 1890, Germany's agreements with Russia were allowed to lapse, and the Austro-German Treaty took on the character of an anti-Russian alliance. The obligations it placed on both countries were central to the unfolding of the events of July 1914.

Main terms

- If Russia attacked either of the two signatories, the other would come to its assistance with all its strength.
- If either signatory was attacked by a Power other than Russia, the other would maintain benevolent neutrality.
- However, if Russia aided that other Power, the initial commitment would apply.

Development by 1914

At times, such as during the Bulgarian Crisis of 1885 and the Balkan Wars of 1912–13, the Alliance helped Germany to restrain Austria. However, in order to retain the loyalty of her only ally, Germany sometimes supported reckless and ill-considered Austrian adventures. Thus in 1909 Germany extended the Alliance to support an Austrian *offensive* policy in the Balkans. In 1908–9, Germany backed Austria in the Bosnian Annexation Crisis, and most irresponsibly of all, issued to Austria the 'Blank Cheque' of July 1914. The Alliance inevitably led on to a close *military* relationship: after 1908, the two Powers co-ordinated their war plans closely, and Germany's Schlieffen Plan depended on Austria taking the offensive against Russia to take pressure off Germany in the west. On 31 July 1914, Germany activated the Alliance to demand Austrian support, claiming the threat of Russian mobilisation was forcing her to declare war on Russia. Thus the Alliance condemned Austria to fight a European war in support of Germany, instead of the 'police opera-tion' against Serbia that she had originally contemplated.

1.2 THE TRIPLE ALLIANCE BETWEEN GERMANY, ITALY AND AUSTRIA-HUNGARY (20 MAY 1882)

This secret agreement remained in force until 1915. Its terms were not revealed until after the First World War. Originally it was a defensive alliance engineered by Bismarck, who saw it both as a means of deterring a French war of revenge after her defeat of 1871, and as a lever to force Britain to co-operate with Germany. Austria saw it as protection against Russian aggres-sion, and a means of getting German support for her ambitions in the Balkans. For the Italians, it represented a German guarantee against French attack, and also provided the possibility of German support for her colonial ventures.

Main terms

- If France attacked Italy, Germany and Austria-Hungary would come to her aid.
- If France attacked Germany, Italy would come to her aid.
- If one of the signatories were attacked by a combination of any two Powers, the others would come to her aid.
- If one of the signatories went to war with another Power, the other two would maintain benevolent neutrality.
- In the event of a threat to peace, all three signatories would consult about their military response.
- The Treaty was to be renewed at five-year intervals.

Added in 1891

- Article VI: The status quo in the Ottoman Empire, the Adriatic and the Aegean to be maintained.

- Article VII: If any partner contemplated a change of the status quo in the Balkans, the partners should consult in advance. Partners should be compensated for any changes thus mutually agreed.

Development by 1914

The longevity of the Alliance meant that the interests of the partners and their relationships changed. By 1914, for instance, Germany and Austria-Hungary had become economic competitors in the Balkans. However, it was the relationship between Italy and Austria-Hungary that strained the Alliance to breaking point. Italy wanted to annex land in the Alps and on the Adriatic coast that were part of the Habsburg Empire, and also had her eye on Albania if it should escape from Ottoman rule. Austro-Italian rivalry in the Balkans reached a low point in 1908–9 during the Bosnian Crisis, when Italy's Alliance partners ignored her, and offered no compensation to offset Austria's annexation of Bosnia. For a while Austria-Hungary saw Italy as her most likely enemy, and in 1911, the Austrian Chief of Staff demanded a preventive war against her, and an Austro-Italian naval race began. Despite this the Alliance was renewed in 1907 and 1912, when a Naval Convention was added that caused great consternation in France. However, the July Crisis of July 1914 brought the Italians face to face with their Alliance obligations. Initially, the Italian High Command began preparations for a war against *France*, but after a fierce internal debate, the politicians chose to stay neutral, claiming that Vienna and Berlin had not fulfilled the requirements of Article VII of the Treaty (1891). In the spring of 1915 Italy tore up the Triple Alliance and joined the war on the side of the Entente.

1.3   THE AUSTRO-ROMANIAN ALLIANCE (30 OCTOBER 1883)

This treaty was a response to the Russian occupation, in 1878, of Southern Bessarabia, regarded by Romanians as part of their national territory. It confirmed Romania's desertion of her traditional ally, Russia. As Europe solidified into two competing blocs, friendship with Romania, which controlled the mouth of the Danube and provided a traditional invasion route for Russian armies, became an essential component of Austria's security. A hostile Romania would open a fourth front for the hard-pressed Habsburg army.

Main terms

- If Russia attacked Romania, Austria and Germany would come to her aid.
- If Russia or Serbia attacked the Habsburg Empire, Romania would come to its aid.
- Romania was not obliged to become involved in a Russo-German conflict.

Development by 1914

The alliance comprised a personal commitment to the Austrian Emperor by the King of Romania, King Carol I, who was related to the German Royal Family. It was kept secret from the Romanian public, and revealed only to a select group of ministers. Although the treaty was regularly renewed, the Austrians became increasingly concerned that the Romanians would repudiate it or even switch sides. Austro-German offensive plans against Russia were based on an assumption of Romanian support, or at the least neutrality. In November 1913, an Austrian mission failed to obtain a clear Romanian commitment to the Alliance, and in June 1914 a Russian State visit to Romania caused panic in Vienna on the eve of the Sarajevo Crisis. When war broke out Romania stayed neutral, joining the Entente in 1916.

1.4 THE FRANCO-RUSSIAN ALLIANCE (FINALISED 4 JANUARY 1894)

This agreement (also known as the Dual Alliance) grew out of Germany's decision not to renew her treaty with Russia in 1889. Russia had, in common with France, diplomatic isolation and a colonial rivalry with Britain, but Russia and France had a long history of political conflict and international rivalry. However, timely French loans facilitated a Military Convention, signed in 1892, and a triumphant visit of the Russian fleet to Toulon in October 1893 smoothed the path to a Treaty of Alliance, finally ratified in 1894. The Alliance faced Germany with Bismarck's nightmare of a war on two fronts. Her response was the Schlieffen Plan, which made France a target of German attack, even if the quarrel was between Germany and Russia in Eastern Europe.

Main terms

- The two Powers agreed to consult in case of a war crisis.
- If France was attacked by Germany (or by Italy supported by Germany) Russia would employ all available forces to fight Germany.
- If Russia was attacked by Germany (or by Austria supported by Germany) France would come to her aid.
- If any member of the Triple Alliance mobilised, France and Russia would also mobilise without prior consultation.
- The Convention would last as long as the Triple Alliance (of Germany, Austria-Hungary and Italy) remained in being.
- In 1899, the scope of the Alliance was extended to cover the contingency of a war with Britain and the maintenance of the balance of power in Europe.

Development by 1914

Although the Alliance started as an anti-British combination concerned with imperial issues, its focus shifted to combat German aggression in Europe. During the Fashoda crisis of 1898 and the two Moroccan crises of 1905 and 1911, Russia made it clear that she would not go to war to support French colonial adventures. For her part, France refused to be drawn into Russian adventures in the Balkans and did nothing to help Russia during the Russo-Japanese War. The Alliance fed Germany's fear of encirclement, especially after Britain drew closer to it and military links developed between the partners. By 1914, close liaison between the French and Russian general staffs, the shortening of Russian mobilisation schedules, and Russia's adoption of an offensive war plan in return for French loans for armaments and strategic railway construction, made the German war-planners increasingly nervous. In the July Crisis of 1914 the Alliance had become essential to the survival of both France and Russia. If either party broke their commitment to it, the other would be left hopelessly vulnerable to German attack. France needed to be sure that Russia would fulfil her promises, but at the same time she needed to restrain Russia in order to avoid war. In fact, during the July Crisis of 1914, Russia broke its Treaty obligations to France by failing to keep her informed about its mobilisation. France did not immediately respond to Germany's declaration of war on Russia. In the end it was the logic of the Schlieffen Plan (drawn up in *response* to the Alliance) rather than contractual obligations that dragged France and Russia into the war.

1.5   THE ANGLO-JAPANESE ALLIANCE (30 JANUARY 1902)

The experience of the Boer War brought home to Britain the limitations of 'Splendid Isolation' and her vulnerability if several European states combined against her. In September 1901, realising that the combined Franco-Russian fleet could soon outnumber the British fleet in the Pacific, Britain began negotiations with Japan for mutual naval assistance. Japan, having had her overtures to Russia for the peaceful partition of Korea and Manchuria rebuffed, was contemplating military action to expand its empire, and welcomed an accommodation with Britain.

Main terms

- In the event of either signatory being involved in a war with another Power the other would remain neutral.
- If either signatory became involved in a war with more than one enemy, the other would come to its assistance.
- In 1905, the terms were altered to make attack by only *one* Power activate it.

Development by 1914

The agreement insured Britain against the possibility of a Russo-Japanese combination, and provided her with a counter-balance to the naval power of the Franco-Russian Alliance. For her part, Japan attacked Russia in 1904, secure in the knowledge that her treaty with Britain would deter France from using her navy to assist Russia. The Alliance allowed Britain to reduce the strain of its world-wide naval commitments by relying upon the Japanese fleet in the Pacific. Thus in 1905 the Admiralty was able to transfer five battleships from the Far East to the Channel squadron. The agreement increased the threat of an Anglo-German naval confrontation by concentrating the British and German fleets in European waters, and increasing Germany's reluctance to limit naval construction.

1.6 THE ENTENTE CORDIALE BETWEEN BRITAIN AND FRANCE (8 APRIL 1904)

That colonial rivalry made it impossible for Britain and France to be reconciled was a central assumption of German foreign policy. Bismarck had encouraged France's colonial ambitions because they would inevitably embroil her with England, and indeed Britain's occupation of Egypt in 1882 led to twenty years of Anglo-French rivalry that came to the brink of war at Fashoda in 1898. However, this narrow escape convinced French Foreign Minister Théophile Delcassé that France's interests would best be served by bringing about a détente with Britain. After the Boer War, a chastened Britain was not averse to his advances. Edward VII's visit to Paris in 1903 gave a boost to the negotiations, that were concluded, much to Germany's consternation, in the spring of 1904.

Main terms

- The signatories accepted that Egypt should be in the British sphere of influence and Morocco in the French.
- Siam's independence was confirmed (as a buffer between British Burma and French Indo-China).
- Britain abandoned her claims to Madagascar.
- The New Hebrides was put under joint administration.
- The division of Newfoundland fishing rights was agreed.

Development by 1914

The Entente Cordiale would be more accurately described as a 'détente'. It settled two centuries of colonial rivalry and removed most reasons for conflict, but it was certainly not an 'alliance', although Germany believed that it was. It contained no obligations or military commitments. However, German actions – the 'Naval Race', the two Moroccan crises, the Bosnian Crisis – forced Britain and France together, and an informal military understanding did develop before the war. Secret military conversations began in January 1906 during the Moroccan Crisis, and continued sporadically until 1914, by which time the British Staff had developed a contingency plan for deployment alongside the French army in Flanders. The French understandably believed that constant British affirmations of solidarity, together with the creation of a British Expeditionary Force and the Naval Agreement of 1912, implied that Britain had a military and moral commitment to them. However, Britain refused to turn the Entente into a formal alliance. Even after Germany had declared war on France in 1914 the French Ambassador Paul Cambon was unable to persuade Sir Edward Grey to explicitly say whether Britain would support his country.

1.7   THE ANGLO-RUSSIAN AGREEMENT (31 AUGUST 1907)

Germany assumed that colonial rivalry and political incompatibility made an Anglo-Russian détente 'impossible', but as in the case of Britain and France in 1904, mutual fear of Germany persuaded the two colonial rivals to eliminate areas of potential conflict.

Main terms

- Persian independence was guaranteed, but the country was divided into a Russian sphere in the north, a British sphere in the south, and a neutral central zone.
- Tibet was agreed to be under Chinese sovereignty, and both signatories agreed not to interfere in its affairs.
- Russia accepted that Afghanistan lay within the British sphere of interest, and Britain agreed to refrain from formally annexing the country.

Development by 1914

Like the Entente Cordiale, this was a colonial agreement that did not address European questions. It was unpopular with the British Left, and with many Russian conservatives who favoured friendship with Germany. Unlike the Anglo-French agreement, it was not wholly successful in defusing colonial tensions. Anglo-Russian disputes in Persia, Central Asia and Tibet continued right up to 1914. A detrimental effect of the agreement was to enable Russia to shift her attention to the Balkans, which brought her increasingly into conflict with Austria. The Russians were keen to develop military co-operation with Britain, and in the spring of 1914, Grey reluctantly sanctioned secret naval talks, which were revealed to Berlin by German intelligence just before the Sarajevo assassination. The agreement increased Germany's fears of 'Encirclement' and that the military tide was turning against her, thus strengthening the argument of those German statesmen who advocated a preventive war.

1.8 THE ANGLO-FRENCH NAVAL AGREEMENT (NOVEMBER 1912)

This series of naval agreements was the nearest Britain came to a pre-war military alliance. Her failure in efforts to limit naval competition with Germany and the threat posed by the expansion of the Italian and Austro-Hungarian navies caused Britain to begin discussions with France about naval co-operation. This culminated in an exchange of letters in November 1912 known as the 'Grey Cambon Correspondence'.

Main terms

- The British Mediterranean fleet to be reduced and concentrated in Gibraltar, with only one battle squadron remaining at Malta.
- The British Atlantic fleet to be concentrated in the Channel and North Sea.
- The French Atlantic fleet to be reduced and concentrated in the Mediterranean.
- Both admiralties to make specific agreements on disposition of ships and issues of command.

Development by 1914

The British Cabinet only agreed to endorse the agreement if it was made clear that it did not constitute a commitment to go to war. However, by signing it, Britain assumed a moral obligation to protect the French Channel coast. Churchill believed that she had burdened herself with 'all the obligations of an Alliance and none of the advantages'. The agreement tipped the naval balance in the North Sea further against the German High Seas Fleet, and contributed to the German decision to shift the emphasis of her military spending to land forces. It also meant that German naval action could be used by France as a lever to force Britain to fight for her. Thus, on 1 August 1914, the French Ambassador told Grey that because France had gone ahead and concentrated her fleet in the Mediterranean as agreed in 1912, Britain was obliged to protect her western coast.

1.9 THE GUARANTEE OF BELGIAN NEUTRALITY (1839)

This old and ambiguous 'scrap of paper' led directly to Britain's involvement in the war. By violating Belgian neutrality in 1914, Germany lost the moral high ground in the eyes of neutral opinion in the United States and elsewhere, and made it easier for Britain and France to claim that they were fighting a 'just war'.

Main terms

- Britain, France, Prussia, Russia and Austria guaranteed Belgium's 'perpetual neutrality'.
- Belgium was required to maintain its neutrality in all European conflicts.

The 1839 Treaty was regularly renewed by the signatories, but no one knew how it would operate in practice. Originally, the Treaty was aimed at combating *French* aggression, and in reality Belgium could only be threatened by her geographical neighbours, and these were the very states that had signed the Treaty of Guarantee. It was thus unlikely that the signatories would ever present a common front against a potential aggressor. In the Franco-Prussian War of 1870–1, Britain had been forced to consider her response if either of the belligerents entered Belgian territory. It was fortunate for London that neither of them found it advantageous to do so, for there was no agreement in the British Cabinet about how to interpret the 1839 Treaty, and certainly no popular enthusiasm for going to war to protect Belgium. In 1912, the French Chief of Staff Joffre unsuccessfully asked his government for permission to enter Belgium to pre-empt a German attack. In 1914 the British High Command considered entering Belgium *even if Germany's invasion of France did not entail a violation of Belgian territory*. It was also debatable whether the treaty could come into operation *without the agreement of the Belgians themselves*. If, in August 1914, Belgium had accepted Germany's request to let her army cross a corner of Belgian territory peacefully, it would have been very difficult for Sir Edward Grey to sell the war to the British people as a moral crusade.

1.10 THE TREATY OF LONDON, 1867

This treaty established the neutrality of Luxembourg along similar lines to Belgium, but allowed Germany control of the Duchy's railways.

1.11 ATTEMPTS TO REVERSE THE ALLIANCES

The pre-war arrangements between the power blocs were by no means set in concrete. Various international initiatives and agreements cut across the alliances, raising the possibility that, like other such arrangements in the past, time would dissolve them.

The relationship with Russia was embarrassing to liberals in Britain and France, who resented being yoked to Russian autocracy. Many Russian Conservatives favoured coming to an arrangement with Germany, with whom they had far more in common. Thus at Björko in 1905, Nicholas II came within a whisker of signing an agreement with the Kaiser.

There was always the possibility of an improvement in Anglo-German relations and there had been no history of hostility between the two countries;

contacts between the British and German business community had been excellent. The offspring of the German élite (in contrast to the French) attended the ancient British universities. In 1899, serious negotiations took place for an Anglo-German agreement, and just before the war the two countries were co-operating over the Balkan Wars and agreed over the partitioning of the Portuguese Empire and railway construction in the Ottoman Empire.

Russia and Austria-Hungary had a tradition of conservative co-operation, based on a common interest in curbing revolutionary nationalism, and keeping the lid on the Balkans. Thus in 1897 and 1903 they had signed agreements to co-operate. Neither Britain nor France had any quarrel with Austria-Hungary, while the national ambitions of Italy made the Empire·its natural enemy. In many ways Italy's interests would be better served by siding with the Entente against her Triple Alliance partners.

1.12   THE FRANCO-ITALIAN AGREEMENT (30 JUNE 1902)

Two days after she had put her signature to the renewal of the Triple Alliance, Italy also signed a secret agreement with the French Ambassador Camille Barrère. Eighteen months previously, in December 1900, Barrère and the Italian Foreign Minister Venosta had prepared the way for colonial co-operation by agreeing that France should have predominance in Morocco, and Italy a free hand in Libya.

Main terms

- If either signatory were the object of aggression by a third power, the other would observe strict neutrality.
- The same would also apply if either signatory was 'provoked into taking the initiative in defence of her national security'.

Development by 1914

Although this agreement was in essence defensive, it threw into question Italy's reliability as an ally of Germany and Austria. In 1905 Italy accepted France's forward policy in Morocco, and in 1911, 'cashed the French cheque' when she invaded Libya. Despite all this, the Italian High Command continued to plan for an attack on France right up to the outbreak of war.

1.13   THE RUSSO-ITALIAN RACCOGNIGI AGREEMENT (OCTOBER 1909)

This was a reaction to the resentment of both signatories with Austria's unilateral action in annexing Bosnia in 1908. The Russians were deeply wounded by what they regarded as Austrian duplicity and German bullying, while the Italians believed that they should have been consulted before the annexation and offered compensation after it.

Main terms

- The signatories agreed to preserve the status quo in the Balkans.
- Russia expressed sympathy for Italian ambitions in Libya.
- Italy expressed sympathy for Russia's desire to change the arrangements regarding the Black Sea Straits.

Development by 1914

This agreement marked a further stage in Italy's estrangement from the Triple Alliance, whose members had begun to pursue forward policies in the Balkans that ran counter to Italy's ambitions in the region. It provided support for Italy's invasion of Libya in 1911, which in turn began a chain reaction ending in the expulsion of Turkey from Europe and dangerous instability in the Balkans. For Russia the agreement was part of a diplomatic offensive designed to undermine the influence of the Dual Alliance in the Balkans, following her humiliation in the Bosnian Annexation Crisis.

CRISES AND CONFRONTATIONS

2.1 COLONIAL COMPETITION

Although disputes over colonial issues had died down by 1914, the effect of a century of colonial rivalry was to poison the international atmosphere and generate an environment of chauvinism and militarism. Between 1898 and 1912, a series of crises intensified the division of Europe into two armed camps: Britain and France were forced together and the military bonds between them strengthened. Germany's feelings of exclusion and humiliation were exacerbated by failure to win a colonial empire, and inability to make her will felt on the international stage. Naval competition between Britain and Germany, which was the prime reason for Anglo-German hostility, was a direct result of Germany's determination to assert herself as a colonial power.

Major landmarks in colonial expansion

1823	The Monroe Doctrine: The USA declares its hostility to interference in the American continents.
1830	France starts her occupation of Algeria.
1845–8	The USA seizes California, New Mexico and Texas from Mexico.
1860–70	Russia occupies the Caucasus and Central Asia.
1864–7	Abortive French intervention in Mexico.
1878	The Congress of Berlin: Austria takes Bosnia-Hercegovina.
1880	The Madrid Conference. Twelve states guarantee Moroccan independence and equal access to Morocco.
1881	France occupies Tunis, causing Italian resentment.
1882	Britain establishes de facto rule in Egypt, sparking 20 years of Anglo-French colonial rivalry.
1884	The Berlin Conference on Africa. The European Powers draw up spheres of influence in Africa.
1885	France occupies Indo-China.
1891–1905	The Trans-Siberian Railway opens up the Far East to Russia.
1896	Ethiopia defeats Italy at Adowa and secures its independence.
1898	Victory at Omdurman secures British rule on the Upper Nile.
1898	The Fashoda Crisis: Britain and France on the brink of war, France is forced to back down.
1898	The US–Spanish War: America takes Cuba and the Philippines from Spain.

1899–1900	The Great Powers co-operate to crush the 'Boxer Rebellion' in China.
1899–1902	The South African (Boer) War: Britain struggles to defeat the Boer republics.
1904	The Entente Cordiale: Britain and France settle their colonial disputes.
1904–5	Russia is defeated in the Russo-Japanese War, leaving Japan dominant in the Far East.
1905–6	The First Moroccan Crisis brings the Powers to the brink of war.
1906	The Algeçiras Conference: the Powers guarantee Moroccan independence.
1907	The Anglo-Russian Agreement: Britain and Russia try to settle their colonial disputes.
1909	The Franco-German Agreement on Morocco.
1911	The Second Moroccan (Agadir) Crisis threatens a European war.
1911–12	The Italian-Turkish War: Italy annexes Libya and destabilises the Ottoman Empire.
1914	Britain and Germany amicably discuss the partition of Portugal's colonies.

Colonial Empires in 1913

	Area (sq.km.)	Population
Britain	33,000,000	400,000,000
France	11,500,000	56,000,000
Germany	2,950,000	12,000,000
Belgium	2,400,000	15,500,000
Portugal	2,100,000	7,000,000
Holland	2,000,000	38,000,000
Italy	1,500,000	1,600,000
USA	324,000	10,000,000
Japan	300,000	17,000,000
Spain	250,000	700,000

The First Moroccan Crisis (1905–6)

The two Moroccan crises of 1905–6 and 1911 seriously undermined the international system before the war. Germany felt that her legitimate interests as a Great Power were being ignored, while inept German diplomacy during both crises confirmed Britain and France in their belief that Germany was aggressive, militaristic and unstable. The crisis intensified the naval race between Britain and Germany, and it sowed the seeds of a military relationship between France and Britain.

Background

1856	Britain forces the Sultan of Morocco to open his country to trade.
1860	Spain attempts to occupy northern Morocco, but is thwarted by Britain.
1880	By the Madrid Convention, 12 nations guarantee the integrity of Morocco.
1898	Théophile Delcassé, a convinced imperialist, becomes French Foreign Minister.
1900	Italy allows the French freedom to act in Morocco in return for freedom to interfere in Tripoli.
1900	Abdul Aziz becomes Sultan of Morocco.
1902–3	A series of uprisings in Morocco, prompted by resistance to taxes levied to pay for French loans, and French border incursions.
1903	Col. Louis Lyautey, a convinced imperialist, is appointed to a command in Algeria.
1903–4	French and German businesses begin to exploit Moroccan natural resources. France starts building a military railway from Oran to Bechar.

1904–6

Feb. 1904– Sep. 1905	The Russo-Japanese War prevents Russia giving support to France in the coming confrontation.
8 Apr.	The Entente Cordiale makes Delcassé confident that Britain will support his plan to act in Morocco.
3 Oct.	Delcassé gets Spanish agreement by making vague offers of partition. He believes all interested Powers now agree that France can act in Morocco, but he has not consulted Germany.
29 Jan.	A French mission arrives in Fez to implement a 'reform programme'.
Feb.	Germany warns France that she will not stand idly by while France takes control in Morocco. German leaders believe that the Madrid Convention of 1880 gives them a right to decide the future of Morocco. They also hope to put the recently signed Entente Cordiale to the test, believing that Britain will not support France if war threatens.

31 Mar.	Kaiser Wilhelm II lands in Tangier and speaks in favour of Moroccan independence. A violent anti-German tirade is unleashed in the French and British press, and nationalist politicians in Paris and London demand military action against Germany.
17 May	Britain proposes an international conference to discuss Morocco, but Delcassé believes that France has achieved a *fait accompli* and is reluctant to reopen the question.
27 May	The annihilation of the Russian fleet at Tsushima weakens the French position by eliminating the possibility of Russian military assistance.
28 May	The Sultan of Morocco agrees to an international conference.
1 Jun.	German Chancellor von Bülow offers to negotiate an agenda with the French.
6 Jun.	Théophile Delcassé resigns under intense German pressure and the failure of colleagues to support his stand against German interference. The Kaiser regards this as a great diplomatic triumph and makes von Bülow a Prince. The French PM is pleased with British support, but remarks that 'the British fleet does not run on wheels' and would be little use if Germany attacked France in Europe.
8 Jul.	France agrees to an international conference after the United States offers to resist unreasonable German demands.
20 Jul.	The Björko Agreement leads the Kaiser to imagine that he has destroyed the Franco-Russian Alliance, but the Tsar's ministers convince him that such a sudden realignment agreement is impossible.
28 Sep.	Both France and Germany finally agree to attend a conference at Algeçiras.
5 Dec.	Germany hopes that the newly elected British Liberal government might weaken Britain's support for France, but the hard-line Liberal Imperialists Grey, Asquith and Haldane take key positions in it.
16 Jan.– 7 Apr. 1906	The Algeçiras Conference. Germany's apparently strong bargaining position disintegrates as the Entente and the neutrals range themselves against her. Britain and Russia line up solidly behind France, and reject President Roosevelt's mediation.
5 Apr.	Kaiser Wilhelm II dismisses the hard-liner von Holstein, making it clear that Germany does not intend to resort to military force.
8 Apr.	The Algeçiras Act. The Conference upholds Moroccan independence but gives France and Spain a leading rôle in Morocco, leaving the door open for future French incursions.

Impact and implications

- Germany feels that her attempt to assert her legitimate rights where international law is on her side has been rejected, and that the Powers have ganged up against her.
- Britain and France believe that Germany has behaved with unnecessary aggression and assertiveness. The Anglo-French Entente is strengthened, and the two countries begin military discussions in January 1906.
- Britain's realisation of her vulnerability provokes the reorganisation of the British army (1907) and the creation of an Expeditionary Force for a possible continental commitment.
- The flagging Franco-Russian Alliance is revived by French loans and Staff talks (1906).
- An impetus is provided for an Anglo-Russian détente (1907).
- The crisis is seen both by Britain and Germany as justifying the need for further naval expansion.

The Second Moroccan Crisis (1911) 'Agadir Crisis'

After the Algeçiras Conference, France is still determined to occupy Morocco. The Algeçiras provisions give her scope to extend her interests through economic penetration, railway concessions, loans, and border incursions. Germany is resentful and suspicious of French motives, and despite an agreement in 1909, the new German Foreign Minister, Kiderlen-Wächter, determines to assert Germany's rights. When France sends a military mission to Fez, he orders a German warship to Agadir. The consequent three-month crisis causes a further serious deterioration in the international climate.

1907

Mar.	A French force moves into Morocco, provoking a civil war.
Jul.	Germany's protégé Mulay Hafid stages a revolt in Casablanca.
4 Aug.	The French fleet bombards Casablanca, claiming that French citizens have been molested.

1908

May	France occupies a large part of Morocco.
Aug.	Mulay Hafid proclaims himself Sultan of Morocco.
25 Sep.	The Casablanca Incident. German deserters from the French Foreign Legion are seized from a German consular official.

1909

9 Feb.	The Franco-German Morocco Agreement pledges the two states to develop the country co-operatively.

21

1910

Feb.	German Chancellor Bethmann Hollweg says that Germany will put no difficulties in France's way over Morocco, but objects to the exclusion of foreign firms from mining rights and railway projects.
Jun.	The new German foreign minister, Alfred von Kiderlen-Wächter, brings a new assertiveness to German policy.

1911

6 Apr.	France announces that she may have to 'undertake military measures' to maintain order in Morocco.
19 Apr.	France informs Germany of an impending military expedition to Fez.
28 Apr.	Kiderlen says that if France intervenes in Morocco Germany would regard the Algeçiras Act as void, and would 'resume complete liberty of action'.
7 May	The French politician Joseph Caillaux holds secret conversations with a German embassy official; possibly making unauthorised offers of French concessions.
May	The French expedition arrives in Fez.
8 Jun.	Spain occupies northern Morocco, claiming her rights under the Franco-Spanish agreement of 1904.
16 Jun.	Kiderlen accepts a plan for German intervention in Morocco, bringing about a significant escalation of the crisis.
21 Jun.	The Kissingen Interview. Kiderlen asks the French Ambassador for compensation for Germany, saying 'bring us something back from Paris'.
26 Jun.	The Kaiser approves the dispatch of the gunboat *Panther* to Agadir.
28 Jun.	Joseph Caillaux becomes Prime Minister of France.
1 Jul.	The *Panther* arrives in Agadir, greatly raising the temperature of the crisis.
4 Jul.	Caillaux cancels a proposed Anglo-French naval demonstration off Agadir after Britain accepts the possibility of a German base on the Atlantic.
6 Jul.	Russia warns Germany that she might support France.
7 Jul.	Caillaux holds talks with Berlin behind the back of his Foreign Minister Justin de Selves.
15 Jul.	When Kiderlen demands the whole of French Congo as 'compensation', a violent press campaign against 'extreme German demands' begins in Britain and France.

Throughout July, all the European powers begin military preparations in an atmosphere of insecurity and mutual suspicion.

17 Jul.   Kaiser Wilhelm undermines Kiderlen by saying that he will *not* allow war over Morocco.

21 Jul.   Britain takes a hard line on Germany's claims in the Congo. The German Ambassador is told that Britain must be consulted if the Algeçiras Act is to be altered.

21 Jul.   The Mansion House Speech. The erstwhile British radical, David Lloyd George raises the international temperature, by saying that 'Britain could not be treated as if she was of no account in the Cabinet of nations'.

25 Jul.   Sir Edward Grey warns the Admiralty to be prepared for war.

29 Jul.   The Kaiser meets Kiderlen at Swinemünde, probably instructing him to back down.

1 Aug.   Kiderlen says that French proposals form an acceptable basis for discussion.

1 Aug.–4 Nov.   Franco-German talks proceed under the constant threat of war.

5 Aug.   Caillaux threatens to send a French warship if an agreement is not concluded in a week.

21 Aug.   The British Committee of Imperial Defence discusses military contingency plans; while the Kaiser talks of Germany's 'place in the sun' which her navy will secure for her.

25 Aug.   France accuses Germany of 'sending France an ultimatum'.

31 Aug.   Franco-Russian military talks are held.

17 Sep.   Grey warns the Admiralty to be on the alert, and enquires about Russia's state of war readiness.

18 Oct.   After four days of negotiations, Germany accepts a French compromise. The Crisis is over.

4 Nov.   The Franco-German Convention. Germany recognises a French protectorate over Morocco, in return for a strip of territory in the Congo.

Impact and implications

- The 'war scare' provides a stimulus to armament programmes and new conscription laws.
- The German Reichstag passes Tirpitz's Supplementary Naval Bill in 1912.
- Britain and France sign a Naval Agreement in 1912, tightening their 'alliance'.
- In France, nationalism and hostility to Germany are intensified.
- In Britain the crisis provokes a radical revolt against Grey's 'warlike' policy, giving Germany a false picture of the strength of isolationism in Britain.
- Italy seizes the opportunity to invade Libya, thus destabilising the Ottoman Empire.

The Turkish-Italian War (1911–12)

This often-forgotten conflict profoundly disturbed the pre-war balance of power by hastening the collapse of Turkish power in Europe and encouraging the Balkan states to band together to eject Turkey from Europe. The resultant instability and insecurity made the crisis of 1914 immeasurably more dangerous.

1882	France occupies Tunisia, which Italy regards as part of her former Roman patrimony.
1896	Italy's expansion in Africa is blocked by her defeat at Adowa; simultaneously her ambitions in Albania, which she also regards as her historic territory, are frustrated.
1902	
Mar.	Britain recognises that Italy has a legitimate sphere of interest in Tripoli (Libya).
Jun.	In the secret Prinetti–Barrère Agreement, France also accepts that Libya lies in the French sphere of influence.
1904	The Entente Cordiale blocks Italy's efforts to enlist British help against France.
1905	The Asmara Conference. The delegates express enthusiasm for colonial expansion, and set up an Italian Colonial Institute in Rome. At the Algeçiras Conference Italy gives lukewarm support to her ally.
1908–9	The Bosnian Annexation Crisis. Italy feels that her Triple Alliance partners have failed to consult or compensate her. Thus, she is entitled to compensation elsewhere.
1909	The Raccognigi Agreement. Russia supports Italian claims in Tripoli.
Nov.	Foreign Minister San Giuliano is criticised for failing to protect Italian interests in Libya.
1910	
Dec.	The Nationalist Association in Florence demands action in Tripoli. San Giuliano warns Turkey that public opinion is 'forcing him to take action'.

1911

Celebrations marking the fiftieth anniversary of Italian Unification arouse patriotic and expansionist fervour. French success in securing Morocco increases the pressure for the Italian government to assert its interests in Africa.

17 Jul.	Italy recalls her Ambassador to Constantinople.
28 Jul.	Britain says it does not object to Italian action in Tripoli.

28 Sep.	Italy sends an ultimatum to Turkey demanding that Italian demands in Tripoli are met. An Italian invasion force is already at sea.
29 Sep.	Italy declares war on Turkey. The Italian fleet bombards the Tripoli coast.
Oct.	The Prevesa Incident. When the Italian navy interferes with commercial vessels in the Adriatic Sea, Rome is told by Austria-Hungary to keep the war out of the Adriatic.
5 Nov.	Italy formally annexes Tripoli, but there is strong military resistance, leading her to consider attacking the Straits and extending the war to Syria and the Balkans.
27 Nov.	The Charykov Proposal. Fearing that the closing of the Straits will cripple Russian trade, Russia says it will guarantee the Ottoman Empire if the Straits are opened to Russian warships.

1912

Jan.	The Carthage Incident. The Italian navy stops three French ships, causing a crisis with France.
18 Apr.	Italian warships bombard the Dardanelles. Later Italy occupies Rhodes and the Dodecanese Islands.
Jun.	Peace negotiations begin in Constantinople, but little progress is made, and the war drags on through the summer, exhausting Italian resources.
Jul.	The Italian Chief of Staff proposes an attack upon the Turkish port of Smyrna (Izmir).
8 Oct.	The Balkan Wars begin, making it essential for Turkey to end the war with Italy quickly.
18 Oct.	The Treaty of Lausanne ends the war giving Italy control over Tripoli.

Impact and implications

- Italy's aggression destabilises the Ottoman Empire and encourages the Balkan League to attack it.
- The first war between European states since 1870 increases international anarchy, and enhances the notion that national goals can be achieved by war.
- Italian military losses make it less likely that she will join a future European war.
- The closure of the Straits brings home to Russia her vulnerability should the waterway fall under the control of a hostile Power.

The Anglo-German Naval Race

Germany's decision in the 1890s to develop a great navy brought her into conflict with England, with whom she had no historic conflicts. The effect of this on pre-war international relations was catastrophic: Anglo-German relations were poisoned, attempts at détente undermined, and Britain was pushed into a closer military relationship with France and Russia.

The project attracted the Kaiser because of his rivalry with England, and it was popular with the German middle classes because the Prussian aristocracy dominated the army. Over the next twenty years, naval competition became the main issue that divided Britain and Germany. It was driven by relentless technical innovation that made constant upgrading of fleets essential. Longer-range guns would inevitably sink an enemy ship before it could get in range. Increases in speed, even by only a few knots, meant that faster ships would always overhaul the enemy, even if it took hours to do so. Thus in 1906 the innovative British battleship *Dreadnought* made all existing battleships obsolete and triggered a new round of warship building, which Germany had neither the shipbuilding capacity nor the financial muscle to sustain. Money essential for the success of the Schlieffen Plan was diverted to warship building.

Naval competition was easily sensationalised by the Press. Naval pressure groups kept it constantly before the public eye. It generated a decade of hysteria, Press wars, 'Naval Scares', and fear of espionage, invasion, and pre-emptive strikes.

1889	The British Naval Defence Act establishes the 'two power standard', whereby Britain undertakes to match the world's next two largest navies.
1890	Alfred Mahan's book *The Influence of Sea Power upon History, 1660–1783* claims that British imperial success was based upon its naval supremacy. It has a powerful influence on Kaiser Wilhelm II and German naval planners.
1892	Alfred von Tirpitz is charged with developing German naval tactics. He convinces the Kaiser that Germany should build a large battle fleet to put into practice his naval philosophy – the so-called 'Risk Theory'. Accepting that Germany can never gain naval equality with Britain, he proposes to concentrate the entire German fleet in the North Sea, posing a sufficient threat to the Royal Navy, with its vast world-wide commitments, to force Britain to come to terms with Germany.
1894	Britain, alarmed by Germany's plans, begins a major naval building programme.
1898	The First German Naval Bill. Nineteen battleships to be built by 1905.
1899–1900	Attempts at détente with Britain fail. Chancellor Bülow calls for a stronger German fleet.
1900	The Second German Naval Bill doubles the number of battleships to be built by 1916.
1902	In Britain, Admiral Sir John Fisher inaugurates a programme of naval reforms. In October 1904, he becomes First Sea Lord.

1902 Feb.	Revelations about the scope of German warship construction arouse the British Press.
1902	The Anglo-Japanese Alliance allows Britain to withdraw ships from the Far East to strengthen defence in home waters.
1903	Naval strength of the Powers. Britain has 63 battleships, France 19, and Germany 12.
1904 May	The sinking of the Russian fleet at the Battle of Tsushima demonstrates the potency of modern naval power.
1905 24 Jun.	Fisher orders a study of how a naval war might be fought in alliance with France against Germany.
1905–6	The First Moroccan Crisis strengthens the case for maintaining naval supremacy.
1905	Renewal of the Anglo-Japanese Alliance. Britain is able to transfer five battleships from the Far East to the Channel fleet.
1906 Feb.	Britain launches HMS *Dreadnought*, which makes all other capital ships (including her own) obsolete. The Cawdor Programme plans for four Dreadnoughts each year from 1906 onwards.
1906 5 Jun.	The Third German Naval Bill provides for a German Dreadnought programme.
1907	The Hague Conference fails to halt the naval race; the Liberals reduce the British Dreadnought programme to three a year.
1908	Germany lays down four battleships, Britain only two. Launch of the first British battle-cruiser, *Inflexible*, a new type that is faster than a Dreadnought, has as heavy guns, but much thinner armour-plate.
1908	The London Naval Conference agrees on regulations of naval warfare, but it is never ratified.
1909	'The Naval Scare'. The Admiralty demands that six Dreadnoughts be laid down in 1909 and in the following three years. Social reformers, including Churchill and Lloyd George, want only four. Under Asquith's compromise, four ships will be laid down for 1909–10, and, if necessary, four more for 1910–11. The Press demands 'We want eight and we won't wait'. Eventually all eight ships are built.
1911	
29 Jan.	Austria-Hungary announces a Dreadnought programme.
1 Feb.	The 'Super-Dreadnought' HMS *Thunderer* is launched.
23 Feb.	France orders two Dreadnoughts.

27

13 Jul.	The Anglo-Japanese alliance is renewed for four years.
Jul.–Nov.	The Agadir Crisis raises the international temperature and plays into the hands of the naval lobby in Germany and Britain.

1912

Feb.	The Haldane Mission fails to negotiate an end to the naval race based on the establishment of a fixed ratio of ships. Germany will only agree to limit her programme if Britain gives a pledge of neutrality in a European war. The Kaiser reveals a forthcoming German Naval Bill, causing consternation in London.
Feb.	In a speech at Glasgow, Winston Churchill claims that Germany's fleet is a 'Luxury Fleet' unnecessary for her national interests, whereas for Britain, as a maritime trading nation, her fleet was a legitimate and essential instrument upon which her national survival depends.
18 Mar.	Churchill's Naval Estimates envisage considerable increase in spending for the next year. He abandons the 'two power standard' in favour of maintaining 60% superiority in battleships over Germany. Churchill also proposes a 'Naval Holiday', whereby Britain and Germany would cease all construction for a year, saving themselves vast sums, while maintaining the existing naval balance. Over the next two years, Churchill continues to press this idea, but it is treated with suspicion by both the German and British naval establishments.
22 Mar.	The Supplementary German Naval Bill increases the tempo of German battleship building, and increases the number of trained crews, allowing German ships to be kept at sea for longer periods.
Nov.	The Anglo-French Naval Agreement allows Britain to concentrate her fleet in the North Sea, and France to move ships to the Mediterranean, where her main interests lie.

1913

The end of the Naval Race. In February, Admiral Tirpitz implicitly accepts the 60% ratio laid down by Churchill. Germany realises she cannot sustain a massive military *and* great naval programme. British shipyards can always out-build Germany's. Simultaneously, Anglo-German relations improve as the two countries co-operate in the Balkans. However, the damage had been done: naval competition had built up mutual suspicion between the two countries and generated in Britain strong anti-German feeling that had not existed before.

2.2 THE BALKANS

The obdurate problems of the Balkan peninsular led to a series of crises and eventually provided the spark that led to war. The Ottoman Empire was in turmoil after the Young Turk revolution in 1908, and small Balkan states saw an opportunity to expel it from Europe. They then competed with each other for the spoils. Austria-Hungary, suspicious of Russian designs in the region, and fearing that Serbia was a focus for South Slav discontent within the Empire, adopted a new aggressive posture in the region. Russia feared that Austrian and German ambitions threatened her Slav brethren in the Balkans, and endangered her own vital economic and strategic interests. Other Great Powers, particularly Italy, Germany and France, began to meddle in the region. It is not surprising that all this led to a series of Balkan crises that pushed the competing alliance blocs even further apart.

The Bosnian annexation crisis

1878	The Treaty of Berlin. Austria is allowed to occupy and administer Bosnia and Hercegovina, which remained nominally under Ottoman sovereignty.
1881	The Austro-Serbian Treaty. Serbia under Austrian domination until 1903.
1885–1908	Austro-Russian co-operation. They agree in 1897 to 'put the Balkans on ice', but Austria raises the question of a *future* annexation of Bosnia-Hercegovina.
1903	
Jun.	The assassination of King Alexander of Serbia. His successor, Peter Karageorgevic, is a Russophile and Slav nationalist, and challenges Austrian domination.
1906–11	The 'Pig War'. Austria tries to bring Serbia to heel by closing her borders to Serbian livestock imports.
1906	Aehrenthal and Izvolski, both supporters of an active foreign policy in the Balkans, appointed foreign ministers in Austria and Russia. Aehrenthal believes that it is essential for the Habsburg Empire to settle the status of Bosnia-Hercegovina.
1908	
27 Jan.	Aehrenthal proposes a rail link between Bosnia and the Adriatic crossing the Sanjak of Novi Bazar, which divides Serbia and Montenegro. Serbia regards this as a threat to her national ambitions. Austria also asks Turkey for exclusive economic rights in Macedonia.

2 Jul.	Izvolski's Note hints that Russia might accept an Austrian annexation of Bosnia if Austria supports a revision, to Russia's advantage, of the arrangements governing the Straits.
6 Jul.	The Young Turk Uprising causes Vienna to fear that a regenerated Ottoman Empire will try to reassert its rights in Bosnia-Hercegovina.
10 Sep.	The Prime Ministers of Austria and Hungary consent to the annexation of Bosnia and Hercegovina.
16 Sep.	Izvolski and Aehrenthal meet privately at Buchlau. They emerge with completely different interpretations of what was agreed. Aehrenthal believes that Izvolski has given Russian consent to the annexation of Bosnia. Izvolski believes that Aehrenthal agreed to back Russia over the Straits question in return for support for a Bosnian annexation at some later date. He assumes nothing will happen until he has prepared the ground diplomatically.
6 Oct.	Aehrenthal announces the *immediate* Austrian annexation of Bosnia. Tsar Nicholas II is outraged, and the Russian Press rages at this 'betrayal of the Slav nation'.
9 Oct.	Britain suggests an international conference. Izvolski is told that Britain disapproves of Austria's flouting of the 1878 Treaty, but she will not support Russian ambitions in the Straits.
22 Oct.	Austria rejects a conference unless it agrees to the annexation of Bosnia *in advance.*
Nov.	The Serbian army is mobilised. Serbia is outraged by Austria's seizure of what it regards as its historic territory.

1909

Feb.	Vienna demands immediate Serbian recognition of the annexation.
21 Mar.	Tsar Nicholas II asks Germany to mediate in the dispute, but Germany sends a Note, which amounts to an ultimatum, demanding immediate acceptance of Austrian demands.
22 Mar.	Russia is forced to back down. She is in no condition to fight after the recent war with Japan, and is forced to accept the annexation.
27 Mar.	Austria mobilises her army against Serbia, which still refuses to accept the annexation.
31 Mar.	Serbia is forced to climb down, in the face of an ultimatum, presented in the name of the Great Powers, but reflecting Austrian determination to crush her if she resists.

Impact and implications

- Russo-German relations are shattered. Russia begins to rearm, and organises a Balkan League to check further Austrian expansion.
- Serbia's feud with Austria intensifies. Nationalist groups *Narodna Odbrana* (1909) and *Crna Ruka* (Black Hand) (1911) plan action against her.
- Serbian expansionism is deflected southwards against the remaining Ottoman territories in Europe (Macedonia and Albania).
- The Balkan states begin actively to plan Turkey's expulsion from Europe.
- Italy is outraged that her partners in the Triple Alliance have ignored her. Her commitment to them is further weakened.

The Balkan Wars

The Macedonian and Albanian questions

Balkan states that had gained their independence earlier in the nineteenth century – Serbia, Greece, and Bulgaria – were determined to conquer the lands still ruled by the declining Ottoman Empire, namely Macedonia and Albania. All of them could claim historical precedent for ruling Macedonia and each of them could point to large ethnic, linguistic and religious representation among the Macedonian population. The province was agriculturally rich, strategically important, and contained the great port of Salonika. In the case of Albania, Greece and Italy had a historic claims, but for Serbia, Albania was of central importance because it would provide the outlet to the Aegean Sea which she craved.

1870	Separate Bulgarian Church (Exarchate). This action by the Ottoman Sultan sparks off a competition between the Bulgarian, Greek and Serbian Churches for the allegiance of Macedonian Christians. All three states sponsor secret societies and guerrilla bands to assert their claims to it. The Great Powers believe the strife in Macedonia is a threat to the peace of Europe.
1903	The Mürsteg Agreement. Russia and Austria present a programme of Macedonian reforms to Turkey.
1908	
9 Jun.	The Hardinge–Izvolski Programme. This Anglo-Russian programme of Macedonian reforms infuriates the Turks, and irritates Austria-Hungary and Germany who feel they have been by-passed.

The Formation of the Balkan League

After her setback over Bosnia, Russia encouraged Balkan states to combine to counteract Austrian influence. However, the small Balkan states wanted to expel Turkey from Europe before confronting Austria, and this was the goal of the eventual Balkan League. The Italian-Turkish War made Turkey vulnerable to attack, and her attempts to deter the League were blocked by Russian threats. When the Balkan Wars began in 1912, the Great Powers had little influence on the outcome. They were now prisoners rather than manipulators of Balkan politics.

1908

5 Oct.	Ferdinand of Bulgaria declares his independence from the Ottoman Empire, and begins an aggressive programme of military and diplomatic expansion.
1909 Jul.	Nicholas Hartwig becomes Russian Minister in Belgrade. He supports Serbian nationalists and advocates a Balkan League to block Austrian ambitions.

1910

18 Oct.	Eleptherios Venizelos becomes Prime Minister of Greece. He is the chief exponent of 'The Great Idea' a project to re-establish Greece's former glories. He favours a Balkan alliance to push Turkey out of Europe to regain 'lost' Greek territory.
Sep. 1911– Oct. 1912	The Turkish-Italian War provides an opportunity for the Balkan states.
1912	The Balkan League. Under the Serbo-Bulgarian Treaty (13 March) the partners agree to partition Macedonia, and sign a military convention in April. This is followed by the Greek-Bulgarian Treaty (29 May) and the Montenegrin-Bulgarian Military Convention (September).

The First Balkan War (8 October 1912–30 May 1913)

8 Oct.	Montenegro attacks Turkey.
12 Oct.	Turkey rejects the Macedonian Reforms supported by the Powers.
17 Oct.	Turkey declares war on Serbia and Bulgaria.
18 Oct.	Treaty of Lausanne ends the Italian-Turkish War.
3 Nov.	Turkey asks the Powers to intervene and stop the war.
11 Nov.	Serbian forces reach the Adriatic at Durres.
21Nov.	Turkey rejects the peace terms of the Balkan League.
3 Dec.	Armistice signed.
16 Dec.	The St James's Conference of the belligerent Powers convenes in London.

1913

6. Jan.	First session of the London Ambassadors' Conference. This meets in parallel with the St James Conference and comprises the Ambassadors of the Great Powers resident in London.
3 Feb.	Turkey restarts the war and is again defeated.
31 Mar.	Turkey accepts Great Power recommendations for peace.
16 Apr.	Bulgaria and Turkey agree an armistice.
30 May	Turkey and the Balkan States sign The Treaty of London.

Impact and implications

- The Concert of Europe works effectively to secure peace.
- Germany and Britain work together to diffuse the crisis, leading Sir Edward Grey to believe Germany would act with similar goodwill in future.
- Although the crisis threatens war (see below), it does not end in conflict, fostering the belief that Europe can go to the brink of war and draw back.
- Despite the success of the Balkan League, none of its members is satisfied with the outcome. Their expansionist appetites are whetted.

Austria-Hungary and Russia confront each other (November 1912–March 1913)

While negotiations were going on in London, Austrian and Russian armies confronted each other in an episode that was of great relevance to the July Crisis 18 months later. Serbia's success in the First Balkan War was a great shock to Austria-Hungary, who feared that Serbia might turn her mobilised forces against her. Conrad (the Austrian C-in-C) demanded military action to take advantage of Serbia's involvement in Macedonia, and Russia reacted very strongly to this threat to her Slav protégé. She was now willing and able (unlike in 1909) to back her diplomacy with military force, and mobilised her forces along the Austrian border. For nearly six months mobilised Austrian and Russian armies faced each other in Galicia. A precedent that would have an important bearing on the subsequent Sarajevo crisis.

Nov.	Austria puts Bosnia on a war footing and begins to mobilise on the Russian border (in Galicia). By the end of the year over 80,000 men face Russia.
7 Dec.	Conrad returns as Austrian C-in-C and the 'hawk' Krobatin becomes War Minister (9 December).
11–27 Dec.	Emperor Franz Josef and his heir Franz Ferdinand resist demands for war against Serbia.
Jan.–Feb.	Berlin says that it will not support Austrian military action against Serbia.

| 11 Mar. | The crisis ends. Austria and Russia both pull back their armies from Galicia. |

Impact and implications

- Russia mobilises against Austria-Hungary, and conducts 'armed diplomacy', but war does *not* ensue.
- Berlin chooses to exercise a *moderating* influence on Austria-Hungary.
- The moderates in Vienna are able to restrain those who want a punitive war against Serbia.

The First Albanian Crisis (30 April–6 May 1913)

The decision at the London Ambassador's Conference to establish an independent Albanian State is a triumph for Austrian diplomacy. Austria believes it has blocked the possibility of either Serbia or Russia obtaining a naval base on the Adriatic. However, Montenegro and Serbia refuse to abide by the decision of the Conference, and continue to occupy Albanian territory, leading to another crisis in the Spring of 1913.

1912

1 Nov.	Advancing Serbian forces reach the Adriatic at Durres (Durazzo). Austria warns Serbia that the Triple Alliance will not accept this.
9 Nov.	Russia warns Serbia that it will *not* go to war to support Serbian ambitions in the Adriatic.
20 Dec.	Serbia says it *will* abide by the London Ambassadors' Conference decision for an independent Albanian State, and it agrees to leave the question of Serbian access to the sea in the hands of the Great Powers.

1913

20 Mar.	Austria-Hungary stages a naval demonstration against Montenegro because Serbia and Montenegro are still occupying Albanian territory and besieging Scutari.
5 Apr.	A combined European fleet blockades the Montenegrin coast.
11 Apr.	Serbia again says it will withdraw all of its troops.
23 Apr.	Montenegro defiantly occupies the Albanian town of Scutari.
2 May	Austria orders military preparations and brings in emergency rule in Bosnia.
4 May	After a combined naval demonstration by the Powers Montenegro withdraws (6 May). An international mission arrives (14 May) to assist the building of an Albanian State.

Impact and implications

- Austria successfully intimidates a small Balkan state by military threats.
- Russia *declines* to support Serbian expansionism.
- The Powers show that they are still able and willing to act in concert to defuse a Balkan conflict.

The Second Balkan War (29 June–31 July 1913)

None of the Balkan Powers was satisfied with the outcome of the First Balkan War: Bulgaria had done most of the fighting (losing more men proportionally than Britain in the First World War) but was very dissatisfied with its reward. Greece wanted more territory in Western Thrace. Serbia wanted a larger slice of Macedonia because her Adriatic ambitions had been thwarted. Romania was determined to share the spoils. Turkey was waiting for an opportunity to strike back. Eventually Bulgaria's disastrous decision to make a pre-emptive strike against her erstwhile allies led to her total defeat and the loss of most of her wartime gains.

1913

1 Jun.	Greek-Serbian Alliance for common action against Bulgaria.
26 Jun.	Austro-Bulgarian Treaty for mutual defence.
28 Jun.	Romania warns she will 'not remain neutral' in a future conflict.
29 Jun.	Bulgaria attacks Serbia and Greece, who quickly defeat her. Turkey also attacks Bulgaria, regaining Adrianople.
10 Jul.	Romania declares war on Bulgaria.
31 Jul.	Bulgaria signs an Armistice after her army is overwhelmed.
10 Aug.	The Treaty of Bucharest ends the Second Balkan War.

Impact and implications

- A disaster for Austria-Hungary as Serbia further increases her territory. Austria looks to Bulgaria to provide a counter-weight.
- Bulgaria is determined to get revenge on her erstwhile allies, prefiguring her later alliance with the Central Powers.
- Turkey's appetite for revenge is whetted.

The Second Albanian Crisis (Sep.–Oct. 1913)

1 Oct.	Austria issues a warning to Serbia over her continuing occupation of Albanian territory. During a visit to Vienna (3 Oct.) Serbian PM Pašic refuses to make a clear commitment to withdraw.
1 Oct.	Austria-Hungary demands Serbian evacuation within eight days.

| 18 Oct. | Kaiser Wilhelm II of Germany says he is willing to 'draw the Sword' in support of his ally Austria. |
| 26 Oct. | Serbian forces evacuate Albania in compliance with the Austrian demand. |

Impact and implications

- Serbia, as in 1909 and 1912, *gives way* to an Austrian ultimatum.
- Russia does little to support Serbia, making it more imperative to do so 'next time'.
- This time, Germany chooses to encourage rather than restrain Austria's desire to crush Serbia.

The Liman von Sanders Affair (Nov. 1913–Jan. 1914)

After Turkey's poor performance in the Balkan Wars, a German military mission led by General Otto Liman von Sanders was sent to Turkey at the end of 1913. Liman was given charge of all military training establishments, made a member of the War Council, and given command of the 1st Army in Constantinople. Russia reacted with great hostility to this development, insisting on Liman's removal and demanding that her Entente partners put pressure on Germany to do so.

1913

May	Turkey requests a German military mission.
7 Nov.	Russia warns Germany that she will not accept a German commander in the Straits. Russia is assured that Germany will 'consider her objections' (18 Nov.).
4 Dec.	The appointment of Liman von Sanders is announced.
7 Dec.	Sazonov urges the Entente to seize Turkish ports in retaliation.
13 Dec.	Britain and France protest about the appointment.

1914

13 Jan.	A Russian Special Conference proposes the occupation of Turkish territory in retaliation. Russia warns Britain that if she does not support her, it would endanger the Entente.
14 Jan.	Liman is removed from his 1st Army command, but the German Mission remains, and Liman is promoted and retains his other functions.
2 Feb.	Another Russian Special Conference decides to raise military preparedness, and approves an increase in the Black Sea fleet.
2 Mar.	An anti-Russian article in *Kölnische Zeitung* sparks a Russo-German Press war; *Birshevaia Viedmosti* announces 'Russia desires peace, but is prepared for war'.

Impact and implications

- A further worsening of Russo-German relations.
- Russia's vulnerability to German influence in Turkey is brought home to her.
- The warlike atmosphere helps the passage through the Russian Parliament (Duma) of the 'Great Programme' of military reform in July 1914.
- The military bonds of the Entente are strengthened: Russia goes along with French demands to speed up her strategic railway programme, and actively seeks a naval agreement with Britain.

EUROPE ON THE BRINK

3.1 THE CLIMATE OF OPINION

Generals and politicians could not have taken Europe to war unless the people had supported them. Without 'that great reserve of enthusiasm, patriotism and endurance built up over a century of careful training' writes the distinguished historian Michael Howard, 'the military instruments . . . were as useless as empty suits of armour'. Clearly, there was a predisposition in the pre-war mood that caused millions to obey the call to arms. Turning their backs on the Socialist International, very few working people resisted the war. In Britain, where there was no conscription, over two million young men joined up – an eventuality inconceivable in our times. In every country political truces bound competing classes and factions behind the war. Apart from in Russia, ordinary people continued to support the war until the end, long after the initial euphoria had perished in the mud and misery. Historians have identified various intellectual currents and developments that may have contributed to this extraordinary phenomenon.

- *Mass literacy and a popular Press*: Since the 1870s, compulsory elementary education had created, at least in Western Europe, a populace (brilliantly depicted in the novels of H.G. Wells) that was literate but politically unsophisticated. In all countries, school text-books projected a nationalist and sometimes inflammatory interpretation of national history. At the same time, there sprang into being in the decade before the war a popular Press that was often militaristic, xenophobic and sensationalist.
- *Conscription*: By 1914 millions of young men in continental Europe spent formative years in the barracks. Most states used the period of military service to 'improve' the patriotism and loyalty of conscripts by programmes of education and indoctrination.
- *The surge of nationalism*: On the eve of war national passions burned throughout the multinational Habsburg, Russian and Ottoman Empires. Young men like Gavrilo Princip poured their energies and idealism into the cause of national freedom, while many governments recognising the populist potential of the national message, stirred the flames by mounting crusades for long-lost national territories. The efforts of the Imperial elites to nip separatism in the bud by launching 'Russification' or 'Magyarisation' campaigns only increased the emotional ferment.
- *Racist and elitist ideas*: The pre-war period was remarkable for the popularisation and misuse of the ideas of respectable philosophers by popular writers and the Press. The ideas of Darwin were fashioned by Houston Stewart Chamberlain into the crude theory of 'Social Darwinism' by applying the concept of 'survival of the fittest' to short-term competition between nations and social groups. The sophisticated moral concepts of Nietzsche

became simple justifications of racial purity and dictatorship. The speculations of the Italian political theorists Mosca and Pareto were chewed up and spat out as justifications for vulgar elitism. However distorted, these ideas became deeply etched into the pre-war consciousness.

- *The cult of action and violence*: Politics and culture on the eve of war were permeated with a spirit of activism and energy. Terrorist acts and assassinations were commonplace. Under the influence of Syndicalists like Georges Sorel, workers were choosing violence as the way to achieve their goals. Lenin had convinced his followers that violent revolution was the only route to change. In Britain, the Women's movement had embraced direct action and arson. Even in the concert hall, Schoenberg and Stravinsky were smashing centuries of musical tradition, while in the summer of 1913, the bourgeoisie of London and Paris had been both shocked and exhilarated by the primal force of Diagilev's *Ballet Russe*. In contrast to the resigned and world-weary acceptance of war in 1939, European society in July 1914 seemed to be exploding with vigour, optimism and naïve expectation.
- *Delusions about war*: Western Europeans had not experienced war since 1871. They did not fear war because they had no idea what modern industrial war would be like. Plenty of evidence existed for the murderous impact of modern firepower (the siege of Mukden, the bloody Bulgarian assaults on the Turkish Chatalja Lines) but even generals and admirals closed their eyes and subscribed to comfortable 'over by Christmas' illusions. Those who did predict the truth (Ivan Bloch, Trotsky, Wells) made little dent in the armour of complacency.
- *The pressures of domestic politics*: All the belligerents were in a state of internal crisis on the eve of war, and the link between *Innenpolitik* and decisions to choose war has been much debated. It is undeniable that for both kings and young factory workers, 'a short and glorious war' might have seemed preferable to slow national collapse or the grey poverty of everyday life.

3.2 AUSTRIA-HUNGARY

State structure and decision-making processes

Under the *Ausgleich* (Compromise) of 1867, Austria-Hungary was divided separately but equally between its dominant German and Magyar (Hungarian) races. Eighty-four-year-old Franz Josef I von Habsburg ruled as Emperor of Austria in Vienna and as King of Hungary in the Magyar capital, Budapest. Two parliaments, governments and sets of state institutions separately decided most matters of everyday life. In the Austrian *Reichsrat*, all ethnic groups had attained equal democratic rights by 1906, while in Hungary an undemocratic Magyar parliament dominated the other nationalities and sought to impose the Magyar language and culture upon them. Decisions about foreign affairs, war, and the armed forces were, in practice, decided by the Emperor, his family, and a few appointed Imperial ministers, who usually came from the Empire's various national aristocracies. In reality, war could not be declared without the assent of the Magyar Prime Minister, Istvan Tisza. Decrees for mobilisation and declarations of war had to be signed by the aged Emperor himself, but by 1914 he usually deferred to his advisors. The unpopular heir to the throne, Archduke Franz Ferdinand acted as a counter-balance to an increasingly belligerent and intrusive Army High Command and a hawkish group of foreign office officials. The Archduke's assassination tipped the balance strongly towards those who favoured war to solve the Empire's problems.

The Nationalities of the Habsburg Empire, 1910

	Percentage of Empire's total population
German	23.9
Magyar (Hungarian)	20.2
Czech	12.6
Polish	10.0
Ruthenian (Ukrainian)	7.9
Croat	5.3
Slovak	3.8
Serb	3.8

Population Distribution in the Habsburg Empire

	Land area	
Austria-Hungary	261,179	51,336,000
Austria	115,802	28,568,000
Hungary	125,609	20,886,000
Bosnia-Hercegovina	19,768	1,898,000

Domestic concerns

- *German-Magyar disputes*: These challenged the very basis of the Austro-Hungarian State. In 1903–5, a major confrontation occurred over the Magyar contribution to the Imperial Army. This was only ended when the Emperor threatened to impose universal suffrage on Hungary, but in 1914 there were still fundamental disagreements about the future of the Empire, and the balance of power within it.
- *Magyar misrule*: Attempts by the Magyars to impose their language and culture on other national groups caused increasing tension. For instance, a decree of 1907 required railway-workers in Croatia to speak Magyar, and the Romanians of Transylvania suffered severe legal disabilities.

- *South Slav assertiveness*: In 1908, the victory of the Serbo-Croat Coalition in the Croatian assembly sparked fears of Slav separatism in both capitals. A ham-fisted attempt by the regime to try Slav leaders for treason backfired when the government's main witness, Professor Friedjung, was himself exposed as having used government-supplied forgeries. By 1914, Slav autonomy had become a very disruptive issue for the Empire.
- *Paralysis of the Austrian Reichsrat*: The introduction in 1907 of universal suffrage unleashed parliamentary mayhem between competing national parties. Revolutionary Socialists became the largest party, and the violent tactics of rival Czech and German deputies caused Parliament to be suspended in March 1914.

International concerns

- *Serbian expansionism* was perceived as the greatest threat to the Empire. By annexing Bosnia, and blocking Serbian attempts to gain an outlet to the sea by creating the State of Albania, Austria-Hungary made itself the main target of Serb terrorist groups like the Black Hand. Vienna was shocked by Serbia's success in the Balkan Wars of 1912–13, and 'hawks' in the Austrian Establishment, notably army commander Conrad von Hötzendorf, looked for an opportunity to crush Serbia once and for all and halt the Balkan ambitions of Serbia's protector, Russia.
- *Romanian irredentism*: In 1914, this was the major foreign policy issue for the Magyars. Romanian nationalists like Ionel Bratianu were determined to absorb the ethnic Romanians of Magyar Transylvania. On 14 June 1914 a Russian State visit to Romania raised suspicions that Russia was supporting Romanian irredentism, and called in question Romania's loyalty to her 1883 alliance with the Empire.
- *Competition with Italy in the Balkans*: Austro-Italian relations had reached such a low point on the eve of war that Albania was allowed to advertise in Viennese newspapers for mercenaries to resist Italian encroachment. Italy's loyalty to the Triple Alliance was increasingly called into question in Vienna.
- *A tough stance against the Empire's enemies*: On 24 June, the Matscheko Memorandum called for an aggressive Balkan policy to meet the threat of Serbian and Romanian nationalism. Some Austrian diplomats were worried about Germany squeezing Austria out of her traditional sphere of influence and believed that she must *act* to preserve herself.
- *'Going down fighting'*: The Emperor and others in Court circles often said that if the Empire was dying it should go down honourably, fighting for its survival.

The economy

Austria was a mainly agrarian state. Industrial development was concentrated in Vienna and in the Czech lands, and there was a profitable armaments industry based on the Skoda complex in Bohemia, but it was heavily dependent on Germany for most manufactured goods. Agriculture was labour intensive and inefficient and suffered severe manpower shortages if the army was mobilised. In the summer of 1914, the army was forced to release large numbers of conscripts to assist with the harvest. Railways were restricted to links between the major cities of Prague, Vienna, Trieste and Budapest. For political reasons there was no railway along the Adriatic coast, and the northeast part of the Empire, which would be the site of a conflict with Russia, was very badly served by transport. Efforts had been made to develop Bosnia and Hercegovina, but the expansion of Serbia had interfered with attempts to build a rail-link to the Aegean via Salonika.

Military preparedness

In peacetime, the 395,000 man Austro-Hungarian army was divided into three constituent parts. The Imperial and Royal (*Kaiserlich und Königlich*) Army, owed direct allegiance to the monarch and recruited from throughout the Empire. The *Landwehr* was the home defence force of the Austrian half of the Empire, and the *Honved* served the same rôle for the Magyar half. Because the Hungarian Parliament consistently obstructed attempts to carry out army reform, the army's size did not reflect the Empire's population. The 2.25 million men mobilised in August 1914 (compared to France's 4 million) were completely inadequate for the task. Although 80% of its officers were German, the army was a multinational force, whose loyalty would be severely strained by defeat. It was reasonably well equipped for a *short* campaign, and although its quick-firing 90-mm field gun was an excellent weapon, field artillery and machine guns were in short supply. Heavy artillery, apart from the giant Schlanke Emma howitzer, was mainly obsolete, or employed in outmoded fortresses.

The actions of the Austro-Hungarian Navy in 1914 depended upon what Italy would do. In combination with Italy, Austria could mount a credible naval challenge with its six modern battleships and magnificent bases at Pola and Kotor. But if Italy stayed neutral, or joined the Entente, the Austrian fleet would be bottled up in the Adriatic by superior forces.

Plans for war

The Austrian Commander in Chief, General Franz Conrad von Hötzendorf faced massive problems in the event of war. Austria-Hungary had four potential enemies: Russia, Serbia, Italy and Romania. Her army was far too small to respond even if only two of these enemies attacked her simultaneously. Under Austria's treaty obligations to Germany, Austria was obliged to come to Germany's aid in the event of a Russo-German war. Conrad had committed himself in conversations with the German commander Moltke to undertake an immediate offensive in the north against the Russians if war broke out. However, Conrad's chief ambition was to crush Serbia, far to the south. These contradictory goals posed an intractable dilemma about where he should position his forces. In addition, Conrad could not be sure whether a war against Serbia would also involve Russia, and he also had to guard against the contingency of an attack by his ostensible allies, Italy and Romania.

Conrad's solution was to draw up 'flexible' plans that would in practice make it impossible to carry out *any* of his objectives effectively. Austria's 50 divisions were divided into three parts.

1. *A Staffel*, the largest section, would face Russia, but it would consist of at the most 30 divisions, and would be deployed in defensive positions 100 miles back from the point necessary for an invasion of Russian Poland.
2. *Minimalgruppe Balkan* made up of 20 divisions, would be deployed in the south, poised for an invasion of Serbia.
3. *B Staffel*, a flexible reserve of 12 divisions, would be stationed midway between the two, ready to move north or south according to the circumstances that presented themselves.

Conrad's elaborate plan was based more upon his hatred of Serbia than on rational strategic and logistical appraisal. He was determined to attack Serbia despite his commitment to Germany. He grossly underestimated the task of subduing Serbia, and the number of troops that this would require. He closed his mind to the probability of a simultaneous Russian attack, and plainly did not intend to mount the immediate offensive required by Germany. He landed his railway planners with the logistical nightmare of moving thousands of troops from front to front on totally inadequate railways.

The first weeks of war exposed the fantasies upon which the Austrian war plans were based. Conrad, sleep-walking towards his long-awaited Serbian invasion, ordered *B Staffel* to move south, only to find Russian armies poised to sweep into Austrian Galicia. Unable to turn *B Staffel* round in mid-journey, Conrad's railway planners were forced to let them continue hundreds of miles to the south, and *then* turn round and head north again to the Galician Front. Consequently, the invasion of Serbia failed, and the Austrian armies in the north were too few and too exhausted to resist the Russian onslaught.

3.3 FRANCE

State structure and decision-making processes

The French Third Republic was founded in 1870 in the midst of defeat, national humiliation, and German invasion. It was a democratic and constitutional regime, with a National Assembly comprising a Chamber of Deputies elected by universal male suffrage, and an indirectly elected Senate. The President was not directly elected by the people, but by both houses of the National Assembly voting in joint session every seven years. Decisions relating to the armed forces, diplomacy and war were subject to the democratic control of the National Assembly. Although the President was nominal commander of the armed forces of the Republic, day-to-day administration was vested in the War Minister (often an army officer) and the Superior War Council, which was a committee of serving officers. In time of crisis, as in all countries, politicians found themselves in the hands of experts, the army commander General Joffre, and the General Staff (*Grand Quartier General*). Nonetheless, no French decision to go to war could be taken without the assent of the National Assembly.

Domestic concerns

Instability and corruption: In July 1914 all France was obsessed by the forthcoming trial of the wife of the leading Radical Joseph Caillaux, who on 1 March had shot the editor of the newspaper *Le Figaro*. Although Mme Caillaux had acted for personal reasons, many politicians expected scandal in high places to be revealed at the trial. Some feared for their reputations, others hoped for ammunition to use against their enemies.

Nationalist revival: The election of President Raymond Poincaré in 1913 heralded a revival of revanchism and patriotism, exacerbated in November 1913 by revelations of German high-handedness at Zabern in occupied Alsace. The patriotic atmosphere was fuelled by a revival of the cult of Joan of Arc, and celebration of the anniversary of the famous French victory over the Germans at Bouvines. The Three Year Law and an Income Tax Bill passed to fund it pointed to a revived willingness to redress old grievances.

Internationalism and anti-militarism: In April Radicals and Socialists won a majority in the parliamentary elections, and the Radical–Socialist government formed on 13 June opposed military spending and challenged the Three Year Law. So opposed were many trade unionists and socialists to war, that the authorities had compiled a list of potential wartime internees (Carnet B). The prestigious French politician Jean Jaurès was a leading light in the International, and was due to speak at its August anniversary meeting in Vienna.

International concerns

Fear of Germany: Determination to reverse the defeat by Germany in 1871 and regain Alsace-Lorraine underpinned the foreign policy of every French government since 1871. Few French people regarded the regaining of the lost provinces as an immediate prospect in 1914, but most accepted that it would lead to conflict with Germany at some point.

Tightening links with Russia: In 1914 French politicians were striving to improve Russian military effectiveness and stiffen Russia's diplomatic resolve. The Franco-Russian Alliance was regarded as essential to deter German aggression and help France to redress the wrong Germany had done her.

Persuading Britain to commit herself: On the eve of war the French Ambassador, Jules Cambon was telling the *Quai d'Orsay* he feared Britain would leave France to fight Germany alone. Despite the Entente Cordiale and the Naval Agreement of 1912, the lack of a formal alliance with Britain caused great insecurity in Paris.

Imperial expansion: Having made Germany accept French predominance in North Africa, French ambitions had turned by 1914 towards the Middle East and the Balkans. A 500 million franc loan to Greece was rewarded with a Military Mission, contracts for railway construction and a new harbour for Salonika. Turkey had been given a similar loan, and Serbia persuaded to buy French arms.

The economy

France in 1914 was still a predominantly agricultural country. Her turbulent history and relative lack of raw materials meant that industrialisation was slow. Apart from a profitable arms industry and certain innovative engineering enterprises, production was backward and inefficient. Development had suffered from a static population, and a peasantry that was reluctant to leave the land. Rich iron-ore deposits were lost to Germany in 1871, and most of her coal-mines were close to the Belgian border. Industry was also concentrated in the strategically vulnerable north and east. France had an excellent transport network and was virtually self-sufficient in foodstuffs. Her financial strength, built on colonial trade and the savings of her hard-working peasantry, was an effective tool of foreign policy, and would prove a great asset in wartime.

Military preparedness

The standing French army in peacetime consisted of 777,000 French and 46,000 colonial troops, divided into five armies made up of 47 infantry and five cavalry divisions. Germany was the only likely enemy, and French armies were to be deployed along France's eastern frontier. In a war crisis, France could mobilise a trained conscript army of about 3 million men. In 1905, the high number of exemptions had been eliminated, bringing French manpower levels close to that of Germany, which had 25 million more people. The Three Year Law of 1913 would greatly increase peacetime strength by 1916, but its immediate effect was to weaken the French army by increasing the proportion of untrained conscripts. Although the 1913 law doubled expenditure on equipment, Senator Charles Humbert revealed serious deficiencies in the Senate on 13 July 1914. Equipment reflected fast-moving tactics envisaged in Plan 17, deploying large numbers of the superb '75 (*Soixante-quinze*) in small mobile batteries in support of rapidly advancing infantry. Heavy artillery had been neglected, and the army had only about 2000 machine guns. In 1914 the French navy was concentrated in the Mediterranean confronting the

Italian and Austro-Hungarian fleets and poised to escort French reinforcements from North Africa. This arrangement had been made possible by the 1912 naval agreement with Britain. Large sums had been authorised to expand the fleet after 1909, but on the eve of war only two of the projected 14 Dreadnoughts were in service. The navy was still dependant upon older vessels that were quite adequate for its limited rôle.

In air power France led the world in 1914, both in aircraft design and in numbers deployed. When war broke out the *Aéronautique Militaire* had 21 squadrons (132 aircraft) in service, and hundreds more about to be delivered.

Plans for war

French military planning was distorted by two obsessions: the longing of nationalist politicians and military planners to regain the 'lost provinces' of Alsace and Lorraine, and the fixation of French strategists with the tactic of all out offence. Influential military thinkers, like Foch and De Grandmaison, believed that past French victories were based on the inherent vitality, élan and initiative of the French soldier. They ignored abundant evidence of the potency of modern firepower, and placed their faith in an all out attack by infantry supported by highly mobile quick-firing artillery. The final French war-plan, Plan 17, approved by the High Command in May 1913, reflected both these preconceptions. Although French intelligence knew that the Schlieffen Plan was based on a massive attack through Belgium, the bulk of the French army was deployed far to the south, ready to launch its long-awaited invasion of Germany. All available forces, including reserves would be deployed to retake Alsace and Lorraine and then sweep across the Rhine into central Germany. Joffre welcomed evidence that Germany was weakening the forces in the way of his great advance by shifting resources to the north. He underestimated the number of men available to Germany, and refused to believe that the German army would commit its reserves straight away to its advance through Belgium. As an expert on the French army remarks, 'Had Moltke walked into the French War Ministry and dropped the Schlieffen Plan on Joffre's desk, it would have made little difference (Porch, 1997). Intelligence in French war planning was simply irrelevant'.

3.4 GERMANY

State structure and decision-making processes

The German Empire founded in 1871 consisted of a federation of 25 historic Kingdoms, Principalities and Free Cities. Economically, socially, and politically the Empire was dominated by its largest State, Prussia, which comprised some 64% of the country's land area. Wilhelm II, Emperor of Germany and King of Prussia, had ruled since 1888. Under the Imperial

Constitution, foreign policy, the armed forces and diplomacy were placed under his personal control, as was the right to appoint and dismiss ministers and officials, including the Imperial Chancellor. The Imperial Parliament or *Reichstag* was elected by universal suffrage, but by 1914 no longer represented the social composition of the country because electoral boundaries had never been redrawn. The power of the *Reichstag* to influence Germany's foreign relations and military policy was limited to its right to give its assent periodically to government spending programmes. The *Landtag* (State government) had great power over the everyday life of citizens, but very little over Imperial foreign relations. The Federal Parliament (*Bundesrat*) was no more than a rubber stamp for the Emperor's policies, in which Prussia, as the largest State, had an absolute veto over decisions. The army, which comprised a virtual 'state within a state' with direct personal allegiance to the Emperor, made an important input into the formation of foreign policy. In times of crisis, foreign policy decisions lay in reality in the hands of the Emperor and his close circle of advisors, experts and ministers, whose dependence on the Emperor's patronage placed severe limits on their autonomy. Nonetheless, Germany could only go to war if the *Reichstag* voted for war credits, making it essential for the ruling clique to present their decisions as in the national interest.

Domestic concerns

Fear of revolution: The majority won by the SPD in the elections of 1912 had been a blow for the Kaiser and his allies in the German military industrial complex and the landed aristocracy. They were now convinced that violent revolution was only a matter of time. The spread of socialism to the southern states meant that it would now be difficult to use armed force to crush the Left, a solution often advocated by the Kaiser.

Political stalemate: In 1914 those who wanted constitutional monarchy, responsible government and the end of the undemocratic franchise in Prussia were deeply divided: Liberals feared social revolution and supported many of the goals of the Empire while Socialists wanted fundamental change. There seemed no peaceful way out of this impasse, and reactionaries could defy a divided opposition.

Militarism and patriotic euphoria: Many observers comment on how Prussianism and militarism seemed to have so deeply permeated German society before the war. Uniforms were everywhere. Military officers were treated with obsequious deference. 1913 had been a year of double celebration: ceremonies marking the anniversaries of Germany's triumph over France at the Battle of Leipzig and Wilhelm II's Coronation, spilled over into orgies of military spectacle and jingoism. Many Germans seemed to welcome the prospect of a 'just war' as an escape from intractable internal and international problems.

Impending tax battles: The funding of military expansion sanctioned in the Army Law of 1913 had yet to be agreed, and on the eve of war the *Reichstag* was preparing to do battle over Chancellor Bethmann Hollweg's tax proposals to fund the increased military spending.

International concerns

- *The failure of Weltpolitik*: By 1914, most Germans realised that the drive to obtain a colonial empire that had so upset the international balance had clearly failed.
- *Détente with England*: Between 1912 and 1914 Germany sought to improve relations with England in the hope of securing British neutrality; negotiating a share of Portugal's colonies should she collapse and joint participation in economic projects in Africa and the Near East.
- *Fears for the future of Austria-Hungary*: The disastrous impact of the Balkan war on Germany's only ally, made many Germans think that unless drastic action was taken soon, the Habsburg Empire would collapse, leaving Germany completely isolated.
- *'Encirclement' and pre-emptive war*: Austria-Hungary's decline, the recent French and Russian rearmament programmes, and Britain's apparent drift towards the Dual Alliance was leading to calls for an immediate war to remove the threat while Germany was still relatively strong.
- *Revival of 'Mittleeuropa'*: Failure to obtain colonies revived the idea of a Central European bloc dominated by Berlin. Possibly this could be fused with Germany's Balkan and Ottoman projects to create a German dominated zone stretching from Berlin to the Persian Gulf.
- *War as an alternative to reform*: The Kaiser and his circle were contemplating the possibility of crushing the 'revolutionaries' at home by waging a war to unify the nation and justify authoritarian rule.

The economy

Germany's economic growth was the highest in the world between 1880 and 1914. After unification in 1871, and after 10 years of standardisation and integration, the country had all the requisites of an industrial superpower: there were rich natural resources and excellent river and railway communications. Germany was a world leader in scientific research, and had a large and highly educated workforce. Based on the mineral wealth of the Ruhr region, Germany's industrial development was the fastest in the world, with virtually every index of production showing remarkable growth. Since 1880, steel output had grown tenfold, coal output four times, and Germany had become a world leader in the new chemical and electrical industries. Foreign trade had grown fourfold, although Germans were convinced that lack of colonial markets was putting a break on their country's future.

However, while Germany might have been poised to dominate the world, it was not particularly well suited to sustaining a long war of attrition. Even before the war lack of finance-capital had proved an embarrassment. Agriculture was still labour intensive, and vulnerable to mass military conscription. Germany was heavily dependent on imports ranging from Russian grain to West Indian sugar. More ominously, German industry including the arms industry, relied on imported oil, rubber, nitrates and cotton.

The Growth of German Trade

	Exports	Imports
1860	70,000,000	54,750,000
1872	124,600,000	173,250,000
1880	148,850,000	142,200,000
1890	170,500,000	213,650,000
1900	237,650,000	302,150,000
1910	373,735,000	446,705,000
1913	504,825,000	538,515,000

Military preparedness

The peacetime Imperial German army consisted of 700,000 men in 25 Corps divided into two Divisions with supporting cavalry and other services. Each corps was responsible to a particular region. In time of war, matching reserve formations would mobilise simultaneously, ensuring 3.8 million men were ready for action within a week of the mobilisation order. A large cadre of professional officers and long-serving NCOs ensured the highest quality of training, and all young men were liable to short-term military service, followed by a longer period in reserve. A General Staff headed by the army Chief of Staff controlled all aspects of contingency planning and strategic control, although this was theoretically subject to the Emperor. The army had a very high level of equipment and a meticulously prepared system of logistics and commissariat. Although heavy artillery grenades, mortars, and engineering tools were plentiful, there were only 24 machine guns per division, and ammunition stockpiles and other logistical necessities were only adequate for a *short* campaign.

The German navy was the second largest in the world. In the Spring of 1914, the widening of the Kiel Canal enabled the largest warships of the High Seas Fleet to pass between its main bases at Wilhelmshaven in the North Sea and Kiel in the Baltic. Apart from commerce raiding, the only function of the German fleet was to challenge the British navy in the North Sea. Its ships were designed to operate at short range and did not have the capacity for a world-wide rôle. Since the realisation in 1912 that Germany had no hope of matching the size of the British fleet, Tirpitz had concentrated on breaking a possible British blockade by conducting short-range sorties. To this end, it had many light cruisers, destroyers and torpedo boats, but the potential of the submarine had yet to be realised. Germany had only

10 seaworthy U-boats. Likewise, the possibilities of air power were barely realised in 1914. German field armies had aircraft units attached, but these were usually unarmed and intended for reconnaissance and artillery spotting. Although Germany had been a pioneer in lighter than air flight, only seven Zeppelins were in military service in August 1917.

Plans for war

After the signing of the Franco-Russian Alliance, the German Army faced a war on two fronts against a numerically superior enemy. Its answer was the Schlieffen–Moltke Plan, conceived by Count Alfred von Schlieffen, Chief of Staff from 1891–1906, and modified by his successor Helmuth von Moltke. At the core of the plan was the assumption that Russia would take so long to mobilise that Germany had time to knock France out of the war before switching her forces eastwards to deal with the Russians. Ninety per cent of the German army would be used in a massive offensive in the west, leaving only a thin defensive screen to protect Germany's eastern frontier. Schlieffen calculated that the western offensive must be over within 42 days. German armies would by-pass the hilly and fortress-studded frontier of eastern France, sweeping in a great arc across the plains of neutral Belgium and Holland, and crossing the Seine to the west of Paris. Then they would turn east, to envelop and destroy the French armies busy with their doomed assault on impregnable defences along the Franco-German border. Schlieffen's intention was not to capture French territory, but to destroy the fighting capacity of the French army in a definitive 'battle of annihilation'. He believed that the key to success would be the speed and the strength of his *right wing*. 'The right sleeve of the rightmost German infantryman must brush the English Channel'. He would commit his *reserves* from the outset, and exploit the labour and material of the territories he occupied to lessen his dependency on cumbersome supply lines.

After 1906, Moltke made certain important modifications to the plan. In 1913, he cancelled contingency planning for an eastern offensive, making an attack upon Belgium and France Germany's *only* military option in the event of war. He abandoned the idea of crossing the 'Maastricht Appendix' of Holland, so that when the Germans invaded Belgium they would be forced to advance on a very narrow front. Demands on the German rail network would be colossal. The task of destroying the Belgian fortresses blocking the line of advance would be paramount. Any delay would result in an enormous logistical pile-up and disrupt fatally the German invasion timetable. Thus, the plan must be implemented decisively and diplomatic discussion limited. This explains the panic of the German High Command in July 1914. They suspected that while the statesmen talked, their enemies were stealing a march on them.

The basic weaknesses of the German plan have often been pointed out. It gambled all on the assumption that the war could be won quickly, and made impossible demands on the German army. Although initial mobilisation and concentration made full use of railways, once detrained, German soldiers were expected to march for 400 miles, fighting all the way. It did not take into consideration the devastating effect of modern firepower. No previous general had been asked to control such vast numbers of men in battle, and no living German commander had experienced war at first-hand.

The German army did not have enough men to reduce stubborn points of resistance, garrison captured towns, protect lines of communications, or besiege the fortified city of Paris (which in 1870 the German army had taken three months to subdue). It assumed that France would capitulate once Paris fell, but in 1870 a much smaller French army had resisted for 6 months.

The Schlieffen Plan was the single most important reason that the July Crisis became a European war. Unlike the war plans of the other Great Powers, the Schlieffen Plan dictated an immediate advance into enemy territory. Germany could not hold her army in readiness while the statesmen talked. It gave German political leaders very little time to negotiate a peaceful outcome. The plan's tight schedule meant that even the initial order for Preliminary Preparations for War would trigger an irrevocable sequence: full mobilisation, concentration at the frontier, seizure of the Luxembourg and Belgian railway systems, rapid destruction of the Belgian fortresses. Such was the complexity of the plan that any check to this sequence would lead to logistical chaos. The German army could not allow other Powers to gain a head start. No other German war plan existed. Germany was compelled to attack France and Belgium, *even if her quarrel lay with Russia*, thus almost certainly bringing Britain into the war.

3.5 GREAT BRITAIN

State structure and decision-making processes

Great Britain was a constitutional monarchy in which a Parliament elected by a very wide franchise held ultimate control over foreign policy. The government was responsible to Parliament, and was drawn from the largest party in the lower House of Commons. The unelected House of Lords had no formal power to change foreign policy, and the monarch (George V, since 1910) implicitly accepted the rule of Parliament. On a day to day basis, foreign policy was determined by permanent officials drawn from the higher reaches of the diplomatic corps and ambassadors, whose expertise and long service allowed them to frame British foreign policy according to their strongly held views. The Foreign Secretary in 1914, Sir Edward Grey, had been in office for nine years and had been allowed great freedom by Cabinet colleagues, who were largely uninterested in foreign affairs.

Domestic concerns

- *Consciousness of decline*: After a century of world mastery, British public opinion was concerned that British predominance was on the wane.

National confidence had been shaken by American and German economic competition, Germany's naval challenge, and a plethora of invasion and spy scares.

- *The Irish question*: On the eve of war many commentators warned that the impasse over Irish Home Rule threatened to develop into civil war. On 24 July 1914, the Buckingham Palace Conference had broken up without progress, while in March Unionist army officers at the Curragh camp had threatened to disobey orders if the Liberal government pressed ahead with the project. Leading Ulster politicians were preparing to defy attempts to include the Province in an autonomous Ireland.

- *Industrial strife*: By 4 June over two million building workers, railwaymen and miners were striking in Britain, and leading trade unions were planning a General Strike. The period preceding the war was one of unprecedented industrial unrest.

- *Militancy and violence*: Willingness to use violence to achieve political ends characterised the last month of peace. The Women's Suffrage Movement in particular had adopted direct action, arson, vandalism and attacks upon politicians to press its demands. In June suffragists had burned down a church and disrupted numerous services in the latest of a series of direct actions.

International concerns

- *Relations with Germany*: The perceived economic and naval threat posed by the German Empire had been by far the most important foreign policy issue for Britain during the previous 20 years. However, by 1914 relations were better than they had been for a long time. By 1913, Britain seemed to have won the naval race. The two countries had co-operated to stop the spread of the Balkan Wars. On 15 June they had agreed to settle their differences over the Baghdad railway. They were negotiating over the division of Portugal's colonies in Africa. In June, the British fleet was even visiting Kiel on a goodwill visit. However, Britain was about to sign a secret anti-German naval agreement with Russia, and both diplomats and public still regarded the German fleet as the greatest threat to national security.

- *Relations with France*: Since 1904, Britain had drawn ever closer to France. The unspoken assumptions of politicians, informal military planning, the creation of the BEF, and above all the Naval Agreement of 1912 had inexorably tightened the links. However, a major concern of Grey and his officials in 1914 was to fight off French demands for a more *formal* commitment that would be unacceptable to parliament and might encourage French revanchism.

- *Friction with Russia*: In the summer of 1914 Russian activities in Persia and Afghanistan were still regarded as a major threat to the British Empire, despite the Anglo-Russian détente of 1907.

- *The Near East*: By 1914, the increasing use of oil to power warships had made the security of oil supplies almost as important as control of the Suez

Canal to the security of the British Empire. Thus, Germany's attempts to infiltrate the Ottoman Empire through trade, railway building, and military missions had become a major concern of the British foreign office on the eve of war.

The economy

By 1914, the dominance of the First Industrial Nation was being eroded by countries with larger populations, greater natural resources and more recent infrastructure. In recent industrial developments, such as chemical and electrical engineering, vehicle production, and machine tools, she had already been overtaken by the USA, Germany, and in some areas even by France. However, in 1914 Britain remained a formidable economic power, far better suited than Germany to wage a long war of attrition. Her industrial base and skills pool was still huge. She had an excellent railway network, plentiful supplies of coal, a large arms industry, and the world's largest shipbuilding capacity. Above all, her naval strength and her huge merchant marine would allow her to continue to import raw materials, food, and industrial products, and her immense financial resources and realisable overseas assets would enable her to pay for them.

Germany's Rise and Britain's Decline

| | Production (millions of tons) | |
	Germany	Britain
	Coal and lignite	
1880	59,000,000	149,000,000
1890	89,000,000	184,000,000
1900	150,000,000	228,000,000
1913	279,000,000	292,000,000
	Steel	
1880	1,500,000	980,000
1900	6,260,000	4,900,000
1913	18,700,000	6,000,000
	Pig iron	
1880	2,890,000	8,295,000
1900	7,925,000	8,778,000
1913	14,800,000	9,790,000

Military preparedness

Britain differed from other European countries in 1914 by not having any compulsory military service. The professional standing army was thus the only strength at her immediate disposal in August 1914. It comprised 247,432 regulars, consisting of 120,000 in the British Expeditionary Force (BEF) and the rest overseas. In addition, there were 224,223 reservists and 268,777 Territorials.

By 1914 the British Expeditionary Force was organised in six infantry and one cavalry divisions for deployment to continental Europe. It was backed by 14 volunteer Territorial divisions. The deficiencies revealed by the South African War had led to major reforms. Administrative functions had been concentrated in the War Ministry and a new Army Council, and a Chief of Imperial General Staff created to liaise between military and political authorities. The equipment of the British army reflected its experience in mobile colonial wars. There was a shortage of artillery, machine guns, mortars, and a continuing belief in the utility of cavalry. The British army was extremely well organised and well trained. It had outstanding small arms skills, but it was too small to have much initial influence on the massive collision of conscript armies that would shortly be unleashed on the plains of northern France. The British navy, in contrast, was the most powerful force that the world had yet seen, but 'it did not run on wheels'. In the short term, its only influence upon events would be to transport the six divisions of the BEF safely across the Channel to take their place alongside the 82 French ones. Its war-winning rôle as protector of the Allied lifelines and strangler of the German war effort would only come into play if the Schlieffen Plan failed.

Plans for war

In 1914, Britain was completely unprepared to fight a continental land war. It would be 1916 before she was able to make a contribution that reflected her wealth and size of population. This situation was brought about by two particular aspects of her history: first, the overwhelming bulk of her military spending had been concentrated on her massive navy. Second, she had never, even during long conflicts like the Napoleonic Wars, introduced compulsory military service. As a result, with a population of 45 million, Britain was able to commit to the continent an initial force only equivalent to that of Belgium – about 150,000 men, or six divisions.

From 1907, by forming a BEF and a trained reserve of Territorials, Britain had tacitly accepted that she might become involved, for the first time since 1815, in a continental war. However, her jealously guarded freedom from binding commitments, maintained right up to the outbreak of war in 1914, precluded any detailed plans to co-ordinate the BEF with the French army. Informal 'conversations' had begun in the wake of the First Moroccan Crisis, but it was not until 1910 that the new British Director of Military Operations, Sir Henry Wilson, began detailed planning for the movement of the BEF to France. Meticulously detailed timetables and exhaustive plans for the concentration, logistics and supply had been drawn up by 1914. However, it had not been decided exactly where the BEF would be sent or how it would co-ordinate its efforts with the French when it got there. Indeed it had not been decided whether to send it at all. The nearest thing to a plan of deployment was Sir Henry Wilson's bicycle trips around northern France during his vacations, in which he reconnoitred possible areas where the BEF might be deployed. It was not until a week after Britain's declaration of war on Germany that the politicians finally agreed to dispatch the BEF. The navy, charged with the vital task of guarding the vulnerable troopships, was not brought into the planning process at all.

3.6   THE RUSSIAN EMPIRE

State structure and decision-making processes

In Russia, matters of international relations, the armed forces and war were decided by the Tsar, Nicholas II. Since 1906, Russia had had a Parliament, the Duma, but the Tsar could and did dissolve it at any time if it displeased him. The Foreign Minister, Sazonov, and senior military commanders, could be dismissed at the whim of the monarch, and were not responsible to the Duma. In reality, the Tsar's power to act autocratically in time of crisis was limited: Nicholas II was not an able man, and could be influenced by powerful personalities and expert opinion. Russian representatives abroad, whose powerful connections often made them feel superior to humble foreign office officials, often pursued maverick agendas. In reality, it would be suicidal to start a war without winning the support of the Duma and public opinion. However, by 1914 many influential statesmen had been eliminated. Stolypin had been assassinated in 1911, and in February 1914, the Tsar had casually replaced the able and forceful Prime Minister Kokovtsov with the aged courtier, Goremykin. These men would be badly missed in the heat of the July Crisis.

Domestic concerns

- *Strikes and the revolutionary threat*: On 16 July 1914 thousands of workers in St Petersburg struck, often becoming involved in violent confrontation with the authorities. Since the massacre in 1912 of hundreds of striking miners at the Lena goldfields, industrial unrest in Russia had been escalating to revolutionary levels. In the first half of 1914, almost half of the workforce was involved.
- *The national question*: The discontent of Russia's Polish, Finnish and Baltic peoples was increasing on the eve of war. The State's imposition of Russian language and culture and growing anti-Semitism was further enflaming ethnic relations and creating demands for regional autonomy.
- *Paralysis and corruption*: For educated Russians in 1914, there seemed to be no way forward under the existing system to achieve a civil society and full political rights. The Tsar resisted and obstructed all change with a pig-headed belief in his divine right to rule, while the Empress Alexandra was becoming a centre for reactionary and corrupt elements.

- *Imperialism and pan-Slavism*: In 1914 Russia's new middle class was turning increasingly outwards towards Russia's Slav brethren in the Balkans and a revival of Russia's historic 'mission' as the 'Third Rome'. For the bourgeoisie, supporting the regime's foreign adventures might carry the reward of political concessions, while for the regime, foreign success might deflect attention from reform.

International concerns

- *Defeat and rearmament*: On 7 July 1914 the Duma passed the 'Great Pro-gramme' of military expenditure to ensure that by 1917 Russia would never have to kow-tow to the Triple Alliance again. Her 1905 defeat by Japan had not only unleashed revolution but revealed such weaknesses in Russia's armed forces that she had been virtually disqualified from behaving as a Great Power during the Balkan crises of 1908–9 and 1912–13. Her reaction had been to draw closer to her ally France, mend fences with her colonial rival England, and rebuild her armed forces.
- *The German threat to Russia's lifeline*: Russia's economy was completely dependent on freedom to pass through the Turkish Straits. The Liman von Sanders Affair had revealed the extent of Germany's penetration of the Ottoman Empire, and by 1914 many Russians were convinced that she must establish direct control of the waterway.
- *Serbia and the Balkans*: For the previous 10 years, Russian weakness had stopped her playing her historic rôle as protector of the Slav peoples in the Balkans. Twice, in 1909 and in 1913, she had been forced to stand by while her Balkan protégés, Serbia and Montenegro were bullied by Austria-Hungary and Germany. In 1914, pan-Slavs and nationalists were determined that this would not happen again.

The economy

Since the 1890s, the Russian economy had been one of the world's fastest growing. It was a country of colossal potential, with huge resources of minerals and agricultural land. Russia had become the world's largest food exporter before 1914. Foreign capital poured in, particularly from France, in the decade before the war. The huge programme of strategic railway building and rearmament had created runaway growth. On the other hand, Russia was still largely an undeveloped country. Land reform had hardly begun. The workforce was uneducated and largely illiterate, and there was a serious skill shortage. The construction of a modern communications network had barely begun. Industrialisation had created huge social problems, and the autocratic system left workers with violent revolution as their only remedy for change. Development was very unbalanced, with both industry and agri-culture concentrated in the west, vulnerable to Russia's likely enemies. The lack of warm-water ports put Russia's trade at the mercy of whoever control-led the Turkish Straits.

Military preparedness

The 'Great Programme' approved by the Duma in May and June 1914 would give Russia overwhelming military superiority against the Dual Alliance by 1916–17. The peacetime army would increase by 39.2% and the officer corps by 28.2%. Lavish new equipment would be provided for every arm, including artillery and military aviation. However, all this was in the future: although Russia had 25 million men of combat age in 1914, most of them were illiterate and untrained. The 37 corps that the army could put into the field immediately were spread over the 12 Military Districts, linked by a railway system that was still completely inadequate to supply a protracted campaign. There was a shortage of competent officers and NCOs, and a catalogue of failings in equipment. Heavy artillery was diluted by the determination of the High Command to maintain a chain of huge fortresses in the west that had little relevance to modern conditions.

Nonetheless, great strides had been made since the defeat of 1905. With French help many of the multi-track strategic railways envisaged in the Franco-Russian agreement of August 1913 had been built, and mobilisation and deployment was already much quicker than German planners bargained for. The Russian navy also benefited from huge spending increases. Between 1909 and 1912, naval spending doubled, after 1911 overtaking that of the army. Russian naval spending was second only to that of Britain, although none of the Dreadnoughts of the 1912 Programme was yet at sea, and Turkey's entry into the war would imprison the Black Sea fleet for the duration. Despite this, the Russian navy posed a real threat to Germany in the Baltic, intensified by the projected naval agreement with Britain. Russia was a pioneer of military air-power, although the 360 aircraft deployed in 1914 would be lost in the vast sweep of the Eastern Front.

Plans for war

The Russian Empire faced a particular set of constraints and dilemmas in mobilising its huge resources: vast size, poor communications, thinly dispersed population, and the distance to be covered before engaging the enemy. Historically, Russia had prepared for two eventualities: Plan A, for a war against Austria-Hungary alone, in which Germany would either remain neutral, or merely defend her frontier; Plan G, for a war against Germany and Austria-Hungary together. However, given the terms of the Austro-German and Franco-Russian alliances, there was no realistic prospect that Russia would have the luxury of fighting Austria-Hungary alone.

In 1912, a Russian military conference concluded that a Russian offensive in Galicia would be essential to prevent Serbia from being overwhelmed if Austria attacked her. In August 1913, both Russia and France had committed themselves to immediate and simultaneous offensives. Russia would attack on day 15 of mobilisation with 7–8 million men, and France would attack on day 11, with 1.3 million men. Thus, Russia was obliged to invade Germany before her Russian army was fully mobilised. Under Plan 20, approved by the Russian High Command in October 1913, simultaneous offensives were envisaged against Austria and Germany. Thus, Plan A was only available as a means of putting *diplomatic* pressure on Vienna. But to mobilise only the military districts facing Austria would raise huge logistical problems if Germany subsequently attacked her as well.

When they debated their options on 24–25 July 1914, the Tsar and his advisors did not seem to understand the military and logistical implications of their decisions. They saw no reason why their armies should not be put in a state of readiness while diplomatic discussions continued. They believed that for Russia, mobilisation did not *automatically* lead to military action. Russia had conducted 'armed diplomacy' during the Balkan Crisis of 1912–13, which had *not* led to war. Above all, they did not grasp that Germany could not afford to allow Russia any head start in military preparations because of the way the Schlieffen Plan operated. Even the initial Russian 'Period Preparatory to War' caused German planners to suspect (with some justification) that a 'secret' or 'creeping' mobilisation was under way, and pushed the Kaiser to order German mobilisation immediately.

3.7 SERBIA

State structure and decision-making processes

Serbia was a monarchy that had been ruled, since a military–nationalist coup in 1903, by King Peter Karageorgevic. There was a Parliament, the Skuptshina, elected on a fairly wide franchise, and a government appointed by the King but responsible to Parliament. Theoretically, foreign policy decisions were made by King Peter and his Cabinet, but in the extremely volatile atmosphere preceding the war, various nationalist pressure groups like *Narodna Odbrana*, and shadowy terrorist organisations *Ujedinjenje ili Smrt* ('The Black Hand') sought to by-pass the official processes. The head of intelligence Colonel Dimitrijevic, and the Russian Ambassador Nicholas Hartwig both sought to propel the country along paths that would suit their disparate ends.

Domestic concerns

The Balkan Wars had left Serbia exhausted and vulnerable, wracked by deep internal divisions. Moreover, the conquest of large parts of Macedonia and Kosovo in the Balkan Wars had provoked major political disagreements about how they should be administered and the status of their large non-Serb populations. Serbia was certainly in no condition to fight another war. Only four days before the Sarajevo Assassination the King had stepped down in favour of the Regency of his second son Alexander. A potentially divisive election campaign was in the offing.

International concerns

- *The south Slav question*: Most Serbs supported the goal of liberating south Slavs within the Habsburg Empire, but there was no consensus on how or when this should be achieved. Some believed in a federal Slav state, others argued that Serbia had earned the right to be the dominant force.
- *Bulgarian revanchism*: Land taken at the expense of Bulgaria in the Second Balkan War generated concern about Bulgarian links with Austria prior to a war of revenge.
- *Links with France and Russia*: The hostility of Bulgaria and Austria-Hungary made it essential to obtain foreign support. France was already supplying money and arms. Serbian diplomats, with the support of the Russian Ambassador, were striving to obtain firm guarantees from St Petersburg.
- *An outlet to the sea*: Serbia was determined to press for the outlet to the Adriatic it had failed to secure in 1912 and 1913. This was believed to be essential to her economic progress.

The economy

The Serbian economy was extremely undeveloped and depended almost entirely upon agricultural exports. There was a small arms industry at Kragujevac, but other manufacturing capacity was located in Belgrade, which was very vulnerable to Austrian bombardment and occupation. Transport was very poor, making it difficult for Serbia's allies to supply her. On the other hand, underdevelopment made for self-sufficiency and made the country less vulnerable to an enemy and rendered more easy a reversion to self-sufficient guerrilla warfare.

Military preparedness

In July 1914 the Serbian Army was able, because of the doubling of the country during the Balkan Wars, to mobilise nearly 360,000 men. All males between 21 and 46 were liable for compulsory military service, and were liable to serve for ten years or be available on active reserve. Recruits spent ten years either in uniform or on the active reserve list, and another eight in the territorial militia. Quality of equipment varied greatly and the army had not had time to provide for its greatly expanded numbers. The infantry was plentifully provided with modern Mauser rifles, but artillery ranged from modern Schneider and Krupp quick-firing weapons to ancient pieces that had seen service in the war of 1885. Much of the army was still involved in pacifying the newly conquered territories. The Balkan Wars had left it experienced but exhausted and in need of urgent re-equipment and refurbishment.

Plans for war

Although the Serb army was a formidable force for such a small and poor country, the task it faced was huge. It could expect a three-pronged Austro-

Hungarian invasion from the fanatically anti-Serb Austrian commander Conrad von Hötzendorf: from across the Danube, from the Hungarians in the north-east, and out of Austrian-occupied Bosnia-Hercegovina to the west. In addition, the eastern frontier had to be guarded against an attack from the Bulgarians who were smarting from their treatment by Serbia in the Second Balkan War. The Serbian Commander Putnik was obliged to keep approximately a quarter of his forces on the Bulgarian border. The remainder was divided between a defensive screen in the north and a force enthusiastically poised to invade Bosnia and overturn the injustices of 1878 and 1909. Putnik realised it would be difficult to defend the capital Belgrade, which lay close to the frontier, and had contingency plans for a fighting retreat into the interior.

Land Area and Population of Main Belligerent States

	Land area (square miles)	Approximate population
Austria-Hungary	261,179	51,336,000
Austria	115,802	28,568,000
Hungary	125,609	20,886,000
Bosnia-Hercegovina	19,768	1,898,000
Belgium	11,373	7,424,784
Bulgaria	43,305	5,500,000
France	210,075	39,666,000
German Empire	208,781	64,926,000
Great Britain	121,432	45,370,530
Greece	41,933	4,800,000
Italy	110,632	35,597,784
Portugal	35,490	5,960,000
Romania	53,671	7,510,000
Russian Empire	8,247,642	158,942,000
Serbia	33,728	4,500,000
Ottoman Empire	710,194	23,000,000
USA	3,574,659	91,972,226

Military Potential of the European States in 1914

	Population (million)	Peace-time army	Mobilised army*	Infantry divisions	Cavalry divisions
Austria	49.8	480,000	2,000,000	49	11
Germany	65	782,344	4,500,000	82	11
Russia	167	1,300,000	4,500,000	114	29
Britain	46.4	192,590	713,514	6	1
France	39.6	700,000	3,781,000	72	10
Belgium	7.5	48,000	217,000	6	
Serbia	5	300,000	459,500	12	1

*Including reservists.

The Navies of the European States in 1914

	Britain*	France	Russia	Germany	Italy†	Austria-Hungary
Dreadnoughts	24*	6	6	13	5	3
Pre-Dreadnoughts	39	20	8	22	8	3
Battle Cruisers	8	0	3	5	0	12
'Old' Cruisers	63	19	6	7	18	5
Light Cruisers	35	7	8	33	3	2
Destroyers	180	80	100	163	35	18
Submarines	44	75	35	38	25	5

* This includes three very modern ships being built for the Chilean and Turkish navies requisitioned (with compensation) for the Royal Navy in August–September 1914.
† The Italian navy also had 85 torpedo boats that were unsuitable for long-range actions, but proved very effective in the Adriatic when Italy 'changed sides' in 1915.

Non-European Naval Powers

	USA	Japan
Dreadnoughts	8	3
Pre-Dreadnoughts	22	13
Battle Cruisers	0	2
Cruisers	15	13
Light Cruisers	14	16
Destroyers	48	64
Submarines	36	14

Leading Mercantile Fleets (tonnage)

	1870	1900	1910–12
Britain	5,601,000	9,304,000	11,700,000
Germany	982,000	1,942,000	3,000,000
United States	1,517,000	827,000	928,000

THE JULY CRISIS

CALENDAR OF THE CRISIS

	Sun	Mon	Tue	Wed	Thu	Fri	Sat
June	28	29	30				
July				1	2	3	4
	5	6	7	8	9	10	11
	12	13	14	15	16	17	18
	19	20	21	22	23	24	25
	26	27	28	29	30	31	
August							1
	2	3	4	5	6	7	8
	9	10	11	12	13	14	15

KEY STAGES ON THE ROAD TO WAR

28 Jun.	Archduke Franz Ferdinand, heir to the Habsburg throne, is assassinated at Sarajevo, by a Bosnian Serb.
5–6 Jul.	Germany issues the 'Blank Cheque', giving Austria-Hungary a free hand to punish Serbia.
14 Jul.	The leaders of Austria-Hungary agree to send an 'unacceptable' ultimatum to Serbia, and to use force if it is rejected.
23 Jul.	Austria issues her ultimatum to Serbia.
25 Jul.	Austria rejects Serbia's conciliatory reply.
25 Jul.	Russia decides on military measures to support Serbia.
27 Jul.	Austria-Hungary rejects Sir Edward Grey's peace proposals.
28 Jul.	Austria-Hungary declares war on Serbia and bombards her capital, Belgrade.
30 Jul.	Russia orders the general mobilisation of her army.
	Britain refuses a German request to pledge neutrality.
31 Jul.	Austria-Hungary rejects all offers of mediation.
	Germany issues an ultimatum to Russia to cease all military preparations.

1 Aug.	France refuses a German demand to pledge neutrality.
	Germany declares war on Russia.
	The British Cabinet decides to support France.
	German military leaders refuse to abandon the Schlieffen Plan.
3 Aug.	Germany declares war on France.
	Belgium refuses to allow German troops free passage.
4 Aug.	Germany invades Luxembourg and Belgium.
6 Aug.	Britain decides to send land forces to the continent.

4.1 SERBIA

On 28 June 1914 the heir to the Austro-Hungarian throne was assassinated by a 19-year-old Bosnian Serb militant, giving Austria the opportunity to crush Serbia for which she had been waiting. The fact that the Black Hand terrorist organisation was behind the outrage, and the head of the organisation was a highly placed army officer, Colonel Dragutin Dimitrijevic, made it clear that sections of the Serbian armed forces were out of control. This made it difficult for Prime Minister Pašic to distance his government from inevitable Austrian accusations of complicity. In the month while they awaited Austrian demands for retribution, the Serbs got little support from their allies Russia and France, who had no wish to be dragged into war by her. In their reply to the Austrian ultimatum, the Serbs went as far as they could to appease Austria. But Austria's uncompromising refusal to accept anything less than total Serb surrender pushed Russia into mobilising her army. This stiffened Serbia's resolve to resist any concession (such as the Kaiser's 'Halt in Belgrade' proposal) which might have given Europe a way out of the crisis.

Leading participants

Dimitrijevic, Col. Dragutin	Serbian army officer. Head of Black Hand organisation
Gieslingen, Baron Giesl von	Austro-Hungarian Minister
Hartwig, Nikolai	Russian Minister, 1909–14
Karageorgevic, Peter,	King of Serbia (stepped down temporarily on 24 July)
Karageorgevic, Alexander	Crown Prince of Serbia. Regent, 24 July
Pašic, Nicholas	Prime Minister of Serbia
Potiorek, General Oskar	Austrian Governor of Bosnia
Princip, Gavrilo	Assassin of Archduke Franz Ferdinand

Timetable of events

| 28 Jun. | The assassination at Sarajevo takes place on Vivdovan, the most important Serbian national festival. |

29 Jun.	The nationalist Press hails the assassin Princip as a martyr, hampering attempts by Pašic to calm the situation, and inflaming anti-Serbian feeling in Austria and Germany.
29 Jun.	The Serbian Minister in St Petersburg asserts that Vienna had been warned in advance about a possible assassination attempt. He attacks Austrian rule in Bosnia.
8 Jul.	Kaiser Wilhelm II dismisses the claim by Pašic that Serbia is already acting against extremists.
14 Jul.	The State Funeral in Belgrade of the Russian Minister Hartwig, who died in July. The funeral turns into a massive demonstration of nationalist and anti-Austrian feeling.
19 Jul.	In a message to all European Foreign Ministers Pašic denies Serbian involvement in the assassination. He warns, while Serbia will co-operate with reasonable requests for an investigation, she will resist 'unacceptable demands' from Austria. Over the next fortnight foreign governments urge Serbia to co-operate, but there are few concrete promises of support.
19 Jul.	The Serbian Cabinet rejects demands to dissolve the nationalist societies and to conduct an internal investigation on the grounds that this would provoke a popular revolution.
20 Jul.	Pašic leaves Belgrade on an electioneering campaign.
23 Jul. 18.00	The Austrian ultimatum is presented to Pašic's deputy. The Regent Alexander and his ministers unanimously reject it. They request support from Tsar Nicholas II, and begin military preparations.
24 Jul.	In St Petersburg, the Council of Ministers agrees to resist Austrian demands on Serbia. Ambassador Spalajkovic reports Russia's commitment to Serbian independence, thus strengthening Belgrade's determination to resist extreme Austrian demands.
25 Jul.	Sazonov recommends the Serbs not to resist Austria but to evacuate Belgrade, withdraw their army southwards, and appeal to the Great Powers for justice. (Both the Serbs and the Russians expect an immediate Austrian attack.)
16.00	The Serbian army is mobilised.
18.00	Pašic delivers Serbia's reply to the Austrian Ambassador. He instantly declares it unacceptable, and breaks off diplomatic relations. Within half an hour, he has left Belgrade. Expecting an immediate Austrian attack, the Serbian Court and government leave for Niš.
26 Jul.	After a minor Austro-Serbian exchange at Temes Kubin, Austria announces that hostilities 'have already begun'.

27 Jul.	Crown Prince Alexander is told by the Tsar that 'Russia will in no case disinterest herself in the fate of Serbia' – the nearest that Russia comes to giving support to Serbia.
Night of 28–29	Austrian gun-boats shell Belgrade from the River Danube.
29 Jul.	The Regent Alexander issues a War Manifesto.
30 Jul.	The speech from the throne becomes a patriotic call to arms. Austria's slowness to attack allows Serbia to mobilise without interference. It is now unthinkable that she will accept the occupation of her territory envisaged by the Kaiser's 'Halt in Belgrade' proposal.

4.2 AUSTRIA-HUNGARY

For foreign policy 'hawks' like Army Commander Franz Conrad von Hötzendorf, the Sarajevo assassination provided an opportunity to save the Empire by eliminating the Serbian threat. Cheated of the opportunity to settle with Serbia in 1909 and 1912, Austria-Hungary was determined on this occasion to act. It resisted international conferences or neutral mediation, obstructing attempts by Britain (and eventually by Germany) to defuse the crisis, and undertaking provocative military actions to thwart a diplomatic solution. Having obtained 'the Blank Cheque' from her German ally, Vienna believed it could proceed with a *local* action against Serbia in the knowledge that it was 'covered' by Germany against Russian intervention. Russia would probably be deterred by the German threat (as in 1909) and if not, Germany would come to Austria's aid. Having won over the reluctant Magyar Prime Minister Tisza, Vienna prepared an unacceptable ultimatum to Serbia as a prelude to military action.

If her strategy was to work, Austria needed to crush Serbia quickly. The international community would probably have accepted a swift punitive action against Serbia, and Russia, faced with a *fait accompli*, would have found it difficult to act. But it was not easy for Austria-Hungary to act quickly. Her mobilisation procedures were slow and complex, and many soldiers were absent on 'harvest-leave'. She needed to obtain the consent of the Hungarians for her action, and her decision-making processes were complex and cumbersome. Also, Vienna was reluctant to act until the French State visit to Russia ended on 23 July. Historians disagree about the extent to which Vienna concealed her intentions from her German ally, and whether Germany was secretly urging Vienna to take a hard line. Certainly Austrian decision-makers did not grasp that their limited 'police action' against Serbia would trigger a series of military responses all over Europe. They underestimated Serbia's will to resist. They did not grasp the pressure the Russians were under to uphold their national pride and to help the Serbs on this occasion after letting them down so often in the recent past. They forgot their military obligations to Germany, failed to pursue direct negotiations with St Petersburg, dragged their feet over Wilhelm II's 'Halt in Belgrade' proposals, and declared war prematurely in order to forestall international mediation.

Leading participants

Berchtold, Count Leopold von	Minister for Foreign Affairs
Bunsen, Sir Maurice de	British Ambassador in Vienna
Conrad von Hötzendorf, Franz	Chief of General Staff
Dumaine, Alfred	French Ambassador in Vienna
Frenz Ferdinand, Archduke	Nephew of the Emperor and heir to the Habsburg throne
Franz Josef I	Emperor of Austria and King of Hungary
Giesl von Gieslingen, Baron	Austrian Minister in Belgrade
Hoyos, Count Alexander	Chief Secretary at the Foreign Ministry
Krobatin, General Alexander von	Minister of War
Szápáry von Szápár, Count Friedrich	Austrian Ambassador in St Petersburg
Szögyény-Marich, Count Ladislaus	Austrian Ambassador in Berlin
Tisza, Count Stephan	Prime Minister of Hungary
Tschirschky, Count Heinrich Leopold von	German Ambassador in Vienna

Timetable of events

28 Jun.	The heir to the throne, Franz Ferdinand and his wife are assassinated during a state visit to Sarajevo, capital of the Austrian province of Bosnia-Hercegovina. The assassin is a 19-year-old Bosnian Serb, Gavrilo Princip, a member of The Black Hand, a terrorist organisation secretly backed by members of the Serbian army.
29 Jun.	The Russian Ambassador reports that the Stock Market and business confidence are unaffected.
I Jul.	Magyar Prime Minister Istvan Tisza says only diplomatic action should be taken against Serbia.
2 Jul.	An Austrian police investigation identifies seven Serb conspirators.
4 Jul.	The funeral of Franz Ferdinand and his wife is conducted in very low key. The German Emperor does not attend.
5–6 Jul.	In Berlin, Count Hoyos is given German support for Austrian action against Serbia (The 'Blank Cheque').
7 Jul.	The Imperial Council meets: most ministers agree to make demands on Serbia that 'will prepare the way for a radical solution based on military force'. Only Tisza expresses reservations.
12 Jul.	Berchtold tells Conrad that an ultimatum will be sent to Serbia on 23 July. Austrian mobilisation will follow on 28 July.

12 Jul.	Bulgarian neutrality is secured with the promise of a German loan.
13 Jul.	The Austrian Wiesner investigation fails to produce evidence of official Serbian involvement in the assassination.
19 Jul.	The ultimatum is finalised, and transmitted to the Austrian minister in Belgrade, on 20 July.
23 Jul.	King Carol of Romania promises to remain neutral, after Vienna informs him that Austria has no territorial ambitions in the Balkans.
25 Jul.	18.00 The ultimatum is handed to the Serbs. 19.00 News arrives that the Serbs have not fully complied with it, and that diplomatic relations have been severed.
25 Jul.	Franz Josef signs partial mobilisation order for an invasion of Serbia (implemented on 28 July; conscripts to report on 29 July). Conrad says that he must know by 1 August whether to prepare for Russian intervention as well.
26 Jul.	Demonstrations in Vienna urging war. Reports come in of a Russian military build-up. Berchtold tells Conrad that it was essential to act *quickly* against Serbia. Conrad replies that the army will not be ready until 12 August. He *must* know, by 4 August, whether the army will also have to face Russia.
27 Jul.	Berchtold and Hoyos press the Emperor for an immediate declaration of war against Serbia. Conrad admits that the army is in no condition to fight Russia as well as Serbia, and asks Berchtold to seek German help in deterring Russian intervention.
27 Jul., 23.50	Berchtold rejects Grey's proposal for Four Power mediation. He tells Tschirschky that Austria will quickly issue a declaration of war to 'frustrate any attempt at intervention'.

Tuesday 28 July

11.00	Austria declares war on Serbia.
28 Jul. 22.15	The 'Halt in Belgrade' compromise (proposed by Kaiser Wilhelm at 10 am that morning) is at last transmitted to Vienna. It arrives too late to influence the Austrian declaration of war.
Night of 28–29	Austrian gun-boats bombard Belgrade from the Danube.

Wednesday 29 July

Overnight	A series of telegrams arrives from Berlin urging moderation.
Evening	News arrives that Russia has begun military preparations.

Thursday 30 July

17.00   The Emperor agrees to allow the invasion of Serbia and to General Mobilisation, which will be announced on 1 August. Reservists will be called up on 4 August, and report on 5 August.

Berchtold tells the Russian Ambassador that he does not regard a Russian partial mobilisation as meaning war. Austria and Russia could face each other in Galicia *without* fighting (as in 1912–13).

Friday 31 July

Morning   Conflicting messages arrive from Berlin: Chancellor Bethmann Hollweg urges negotiations with Russia, but German C-in-C Moltke demands immediate Austrian mobilisation against Russia and an end to further diplomacy. The Austrian Common Ministerial Council rejects an international conference, and endorses preparations to attack Serbia.

Wilhelm II tells Franz Josef that he is preparing to go to war with Russia and France. Austria must concentrate her forces against Russia. 'Serbia plays a quite subordinate rôle' he says. News arrives of Russia's general mobilisation, throwing Conrad into confusion because he has already ordered his reserves to the Serbian Front.

5 Aug.   Austria-Hungary declares war on Russia.

10 Aug.   France declares war on Austria-Hungary.

12 Aug.   Britain declares war on Austria-Hungary.

4.3 THE AUSTRIAN ULTIMATUM TO SERBIA 23 JULY 1914

1. To suppress all publications inciting hatred of Austria-Hungary and directed against her territorial integrity.
2. To dissolve forthwith the Narodna Odbrana, and 'to confiscate all its means of propaganda'; to treat similarly all societies engaged in propaganda against Austria-Hungary, and to prevent their revival in some other form.
3. To eliminate from the Serbian educational system anything which might forment such propaganda.
4. To dismiss all officers or officials guilty of such propaganda, whose names might be subsequently communicated to Vienna.
5. To accept 'the collaboration in Serbia' of Austro-Hungarian officials in suppressing 'this subversive movement against the Monarchy's territorial integrity'.
6. To open a judicial enquiry against those implicated in the murder, and to allow delegates of Austria-Hungary to take part in this.

7. To arrest without delay Tankosic and Ciganovic, who had been implicated by the Austrian investigation into the assassination.
8. To prevent the illicit traffic in arms, and to punish the officials who helped the conspirators cross the frontier.
9. To explain the 'unjustifiable language' used by Serbian officials after the murder.
10. To notify Vienna without delay of the execution of these measures.

All the demands were fully accepted in the Serbian Reply of 25 July, but in the case of Point 6, Belgrade said that it was willing to conduct an enquiry, and would keep Vienna fully informed, but that the participation of foreign officials would violate the Serbian Constitution.

4.4 GERMANY

According to Professor Fritz Fischer and his followers, Berlin had already laid plans in December 1912 to unleash a war in the summer of 1914. If one accepts this, the events of June to 4 August 1914 become almost irrelevant. Germany simply used the assassination to justify a pre-ordained plan to strike down her enemies before their rearmament programmes put Germany at a hopeless disadvantage, and to heal domestic wounds by unleashing a unifying national struggle. The subsequent actions of the Kaiser, diplomats, and generals were nothing more than a smokescreen to confuse Germany's enemies. However, the events of July still raise a host of questions. When the German decision-makers backed Vienna unconditionally on 5 July did they believe they were sanctioning a small regional war, or did they accept, or even welcome, the near certainty of a European war? Why did Germany fail to control Austria-Hungary, as she had done so often before? Did the Kaiser and his ministers understand the rigid mechanisms of the Schlieffen Plan? Did they understand that the generals had *no other plan* but to attack France and invade Belgium? Were they aware that the invasion of Belgium would inevitably follow once any military preparations were ordered? Why did the Kaiser and Bethmann not order the High Command to improvise plans for an attack on Russia alone? A few weeks later Moltke found no difficulty in switching large forces to the east to deal Russia a devastating blow.

Leading participants

Bethmann Hollweg, Theobald von	Imperial German Chancellor
Cambon, Paul	French Ambassador in Berlin
Falkenhayn, General Erich von	Prussian War Minister
Goschen, Sir William	British Ambassador in Berlin
Henry, Prince of Prussia	Kaiser Wilhelm II's brother
Jagow, Gottlieb von	State Secretary for Foreign Affairs
Moltke, General Helmuth von	Chief of the Great General Staff
Pourtalès, Count Friedrich von	German Ambassador in St Petersburg

Riezler, Kurt	Advisor to Chancellor Bethmann Hollweg
Schoen, Freiherr Wilhelm von	German Ambassador in Paris
Sverbejev, Sergei Nikolaievich	Russian Ambassador in Berlin
Szögyény-Marich, Count Ladislaus	Austro-Hungarian Ambassador in Berlin
Tirpitz, Admiral Alfred von	Minister for the German Imperial Navy
Tschirschky, Count Heinrich von	German Ambassador in Vienna
Wilhelm II	Imperial Kaiser and King of Prussia
Zimmermann, Arthur	Under-secretary of State for Foreign Affairs

Timetable of events

3 Jul.	The Kaiser stays away from the funeral of the assassinated Archduke Franz Ferdinand.
5–6 Jul.	The Mission of the Austrian official Count Hoyos. The Kaiser issues the 'Blank Cheque' to Vienna, offering to support Austria's plan to punish Serbia. Falkenhayn assures him Germany is prepared for war, and is told not to make any special military arrangements. Chancellor Bethmann Hollweg sends an official statement of German support to Vienna.
7 Jul.	The Kaiser departs for his annual Baltic cruise (returning 27 July). All the leading German military and political leaders are encouraged to leave Berlin and proceed with their annual holidays.
Saturday, 25 Jun.	Kaiser Wilhelm sees the text of the Austrian ultimatum to Serbia for the first time. Jagow agrees to convey to Vienna Britain's request to give Serbia more time to reply, but his wire to Vienna is delayed and arrives too late.

Sunday 26 July

Morning	Moltke arrives back in Berlin and drafts a German ultimatum to Belgium.
Evening	Jagow agrees to convey British mediation proposals to Vienna, but he tells the Austrian Ambassador that he is 'not in the slightest degree' in favour of them.

Monday 27 July

14.35	St Petersburg: The German military attaché reports that Russia has made only preparatory military measures. Nonetheless, he has warned the Russians of the consequences of these.
15.25	St Petersburg: Pourtalès warns Jagow that Russian mobilisation is already under way.
Noon	Berlin: The text of the Serbian reply arrives.

13.00	Berlin: Bethmann rejects Grey's proposal (submitted and endorsed by Lichnowsky earlier that morning) for a Four Power Conference.
15.00	The Kaiser arrives back in Potsdam.
16.37	Tschirschky in Vienna reports that Austria is about to declare war on Serbia, but the message is not passed on to the Kaiser.
21.30	Bethmann sends the text of the Serbian reply to Potsdam, but the Kaiser has gone to bed.

Tuesday 28 July

07.30	The Kaiser at last reads the Serbian reply: 'A brilliant achievement. All reason for war disappears' he concludes.
10.00	The Kaiser proposes a 'Halt in Belgrade', under which Austria would occupy the Serbian capital until her demands were met.
11.00	Austria declares war on Serbia.
Afternoon	Sazonov informs Germany that Russia has begun a partial mobilisation in the southern military districts only. But German Intelligence is reporting military activity in the Warsaw, Vilna and St Petersburg districts bordering Germany.
22.15	Bethmann at last transmits the Kaiser's 'Halt in Belgrade' proposal to Vienna (telegram 174) 'If Austria continues to maintain its previous aloofness in the face of such proposals, it will incur the odium of having been responsible for a world war, even, finally, among the German people themselves'. (The cable arrives in Vienna at 4.30 next morning, but the Austrians do not respond to it.)

Wednesday 29 July

Early hours	Arrival of a wire appealing for peace from Tsar Nicholas II to the Kaiser.
Morning	Moltke explains in a Memorandum to Bethmann that *any* Russian mobilisation is unacceptable because it will allow Russia to steal a march on Germany. Bethmann tells Ambassador Pourtalès to warn Russia about the implications of mobilisation. The Socialist leader Südekum ends five days of anti-war demonstrations, telling Bethmann that his Party would not oppose a war caused by Russian aggression.
16.40	The Kaiser meets Bethmann, Moltke and Falkenhayn to discuss the military situation.
17.00	Jagow is told that Russia will begin mobilisation next day.

18.10	The Kaiser's brother, Crown Prince Henry, reports that on the 26 July King George V of Great Britain assured him that Britain would remain neutral.
22.30	Bethmann makes a proposal to British Ambassador Goschen: Germany would refrain from annexing French territory in return for British neutrality. He does not include French colonies, nor guarantee Belgian neutrality. This proposal makes it clear to Goschen that Germany *intends* to attack France and violate Belgian neutrality. The German proposal is later rejected by Grey.
23.00	Bethmann receives Lichnowsky's telegram from London conveying a warning from Grey that Britain cannot remain neutral in a Franco-German war.

Thursday 30 July

00.20–03.00	During the night Bethmann sends a series of telegrams to Ambassador Tchirschky in Vienna telling him to urge Austria to open direct talks with Russia. He warns that unless Austria does this Germany would be 'drawn into a world conflagration' by Vienna.
11.55	Arrival of a warning from Pourtalès saying that the Russian military build-up is more extensive than previously reported.
13.00	Moltke claims that 14 Russian army corps are mobilising.
14.00	The newspaper *Lokal Anzeiger* runs story saying that the Kaiser has ordered mobilisation.
15.00	Ambassador Goschen receives Grey's cable rejecting Bethmann's 'neutrality offer' of the previous evening.
15.30	The Kaiser cables the Tsar complaining that Russia's military build-up has weakened his personal attempts to defuse the crisis.
Afternoon	Hearing that Conrad is concentrating his forces against Serbia, Moltke demands that Austria mobilise immediately and exclusively against Russia. He also recommends Vienna to reject British mediation proposals.
21.00	Bethmann resists calls from Moltke and Falkenhayn for immediate mobilisation, but promises to decide whether to proceed by 13.00 next day.
21.00	Bethmann cables Tchirschky to 'urgently' advise Vienna to accept Grey's mediation proposal.
23.00	A cable arrives from George V, conveying Grey's latest peace formula.
23.20	Having been told that Russia has ordered general mobilisation, Bethmann cables Vienna cancelling his instructions to encourage Vienna to accept mediation.

Friday 31 July

12.00	Germany issues the order for 'The State of Imminent War'. From now onwards, it becomes very difficult to reverse Germany's unfolding mobilisation schedules. In the afternoon, the Kaiser addresses cheering Berliners from the palace balcony.
Evening	Jagow tells Ambassador Goschen that that he cannot promise that Germany will respect Belgian neutrality. Ambassador Schoen in Paris is instructed to demand a French pledge of neutrality.
22.00	(Berlin time) A German ultimatum is delivered to Russia demanding that Russian military preparations cease. A reply must be given by noon next day.

Saturday 1 August

Noon	The German deadline passes with no response from St Petersburg.
13.00	A draft Declaration of War is cabled to Pourtalès.
17.00	In St Petersburg: Pourtalès announces Germany's declaration of war on Russia.
18.10	From Paris, Schoen reports that France has refused to pledge neutrality.
19.00	The order for general mobilisation is sent out. Shortly afterwards cables arrive from Lichnowsky in London suggesting that England might remain neutral. Wilhelm proposes that the invasion of France is cancelled and the army moved east to concentrate on attacking Russia. Moltke explains that this is impossible, given the imperatives of the Schlieffen Plan. It is decided to concentrate the army in the west but delay the invasion. Cables are sent to London accepting the British 'offer'. But Britain must remain neutral until Germany judges the war to be over.
21.00	News arrives that France has ordered general mobilisation.
23.00	Moltke orders the invasion of Luxembourg to begin next morning (reversing a previous decision of the Kaiser to delay it).

Sunday 2 August

19.00	Belgium receives a German ultimatum demanding free passage for German armies.

Monday 3 August

10.55	Belgium rejects Germany's ultimatum.
17.30	(Berlin time) In Paris, Ambassador Schoen delivers the German declaration of war on France.
Tuesday 4 Aug.	Great Britain declares war on Germany.

4.5   THE RUSSIAN EMPIRE

Although Russia had no treaty obligation to Serbia, she had strong racial and religious ties to the Serbs. It was felt that Russia had let Serbia down badly in 1909 and 1913, and the Tsar's advisors believed that his popularity would be dangerously weakened if he did not take a hard line in defending Russia's Great Power status. Russia's military reconstruction was three years from completion, but Austria's actions – her 'unacceptable ultimatum' to Serbia, her unnecessarily swift declaration of war, her provocative bombardment of Belgrade – forced St Petersburg to choose between capitulation or defiance. By a strange historical coincidence, President Poincaré of France and his Foreign Minister René Viviani were paying a State visit to St Petersburg at the height of the crisis. They probably encouraged Russia to take a firm line with Austria, but not to go to war over the issue. However, by the time news of the Austrian ultimatum reached St Petersburg, the French delegation was already at sea, unable to exert a moderating influence as the crisis worsened.

At first the Tsar decided to put his armed forces on standby: this was a sensible precautionary measure, in line with the traditional 'armed diplomacy' of 1912 which had not resulted in war. Russian diplomats believed they could again pressurise Austria by mobilising the Imperial Army against the Austrian frontier without posing a threat to Germany. The Russian generals were unhappy with this, saying it would make the country very vulnerable if Germany decided to attack her anyway, but soon the tortuous debate about whether to call up some or all of Russia's armies became irrelevant. For the German generals, *any* Russian preparations posed an unacceptable threat to the Schlieffen Plan. Military necessity would compel them to unleash Germany's full might against the Dual Alliance in response to any move that would give Russia a head-start in the mobilisation race. Given Austria's determination to crush Serbia, and Germany's willingness to support her, the only way Russia could have avoided war was to do nothing, and accept the national humiliation of abandoning once more the Serbs to their fate.

Leading participants

Buchanan, Sir George	British Ambassador in St Petersburg
Danilov, Gen. Juri Nikiforovich	Army Quartermaster General
Eggeling, Major Bernard von	Military Attaché at the German Embassy
Izvolski, Alexander	Russian Ambassador in Paris
Krivoshein, Alexander	Russian Minister of Agriculture
Nicholas II	Tsar of Russia
Palèologue, Maurice	French Ambassador in St Petersburg
Pourtalès, Count Friedrich von	German Ambassador in St Petersburg
Sazonov, Sergei Dmitrievich	Russian Foreign Minister
Schebeko, Nikolai Nikolaievich	Russian Ambassador in Vienna
Yanushkevich, Gen. Nikolai	Chief of the General Staff

Timetable of events

1914

28 Jun.	The assassination. The Tsar is shocked by an attack on another royal family, and asks for his local representatives to find out the facts. The Serbian Ambassador is given re-assurances of Russian support, but no specific commitments are made.
20–22 Jul.	The State visit by French President Poincaré and Foreign Minister Viviani.
23 Jul.	News of the Austrian ultimatum to Serbia arrives after the French party has left. Russia does not expect Austria to attack Serbia immediately, and there is plenty of time for diplomatic manoeuvring.

Friday 24 July

Morning	French Ambassador Paléologue pledges full support, but British Ambassador Buchanan warns that British public opinion would not support a war over Serbia.
15.00	Council of Ministers Meeting to decide Russia's response to the Austrian ultimatum. Agriculture Minister Krivoshein's argument that Russia must stand up to Vienna and Berlin carries the day: it is agreed that Austria should be asked to give the Serbs more time to reply to the ultimatum; that the 'Period Preparatory to War' Order be issued, and mobilisation of the military districts adjoining Austria (Kiev, Odessa, Moscow and Kazan) put under way. It is stressed that these measures are not intended to threaten Germany.
19.00	Sazonov warns Germany that Russia will fight Austria if she attempted to take territory from Serbia.

Saturday 25 July

11.00	Meeting of Crown Council. The Tsar agrees to the preliminary military measures agreed by the Council of Ministers, and puts the Black Sea and Baltic fleets on alert.

Sunday 26 July

	The State Duma votes to 'stand up in defence of the country, its honour and its possessions'. Only 13 left wing deputies vote against the motion.
13.00	Orders for the 'Period Preparatory to War' sent out. These measures apply to the whole of European Russia, including those areas adjoining Germany. The Russians regard these moves as precautionary, but in Berlin they are seen as

a 'creeping mobilisation' that would give Russia a head-start and threaten the timetable of the Schlieffen Plan.

Afternoon   The German Attaché Eggeling is reassured that Russia is only taking preparatory measures. Four military districts will be mobilised only if Austria crosses the Serbian frontier. Eggeling warns of the consequences of any form of mobilisation.

Evening   Sazonov assures Ambassador Pourtalès that the Russian army is not mobilising, but Pourtalès warns him of the serious consequences of military preparations. Sazonov proposes that Serbia appeal to the Great Powers, allowing Russia to stand aside and accept the mediation of Britain, Germany, France and Italy.

Monday 27 July

The nationalist Press demands that Russia defend Serbia. Cheering crowds surround the Serbian legation. Janush-kevitch tells the General Staff that Russia will only mobilise if Serbia's borders are crossed. In Paris, the Russian Attaché is told that 'France is prepared to fulfil her obligations', but reminded that Russia is committed to support France with an offensive in East Prussia (which will require full rather than partial mobilisation).

Tuesday 28 July

News arrives that Austria has declared war on Serbia. The Russian Ambassador in Vienna reports that Austria has re-jected direct talks with Russia. Paléologue tells Sazonov that France is 'ready to fulfil her Alliance obligations' – a stronger message than Paris has authorised.

Afternoon   Sazonov tells Berlin that partial mobilisation in the Southern Districts will begin the next day, but this was neither a threat to Germany nor a preparation for war.

Wednesday 29 July

01.00   The Tsar ('Nicky') cables his cousin Wilhelm II ('Willy') 'I will be soon overwhelmed by the pressure brought upon me'. He asks the Kaiser to 'stop your allies going too far'. The message is crossed by a wire from Wilhelm asking for help to defuse the crisis, and saying that he is doing his best to get the Austrians to 'deal straightly' (sic), with him.

Yanushkevitch obtains draft orders from the Tsar for both partial and general mobilisation. Further authorisation from the Tsar will be required before their implementation. However, the generals go ahead anyway and issue informal instructions to prepare for general mobilisation.

19.00	Pourtalès passes on to Berlin Russia's reassurance that her preparations are not aimed at Germany (given to the German Military Attaché by Yanushkevich at 15.00).
Afternoon	During a meeting with the Austrian Ambassador, Sazonov is informed that the Austrians have bombarded Belgrade. The meeting breaks up in recrimination. Sazonov telegraphs Izvolski that Russia had no alternative but to prepare for war.
19.00	Ambassador Pourtalès warns Sazonov that Germany will react to any military build-up (including the 'Period Preparatory to War').
20.00	The Tsar signs the order for general mobilisation, after Sazonov conveys to him the army's view that further delay will compromise Russian security.
22.00	The Tsar changes his mind and cancels general mobilisation after receiving a telegram from Wilhelm II (21.40) warning that further Russian military activity would weaken his efforts to restrain Vienna.

Thursday 30 July

Morning	The Tsar refuses to order general mobilisation, despite the requests of Sazonov, Sukhomlinov and Yanushkevich, who are convinced that Austrian and German military preparations are well under way.
16.00	Sazonov at last persuades the Tsar to authorise general mobilisation. He believes that this can be done in secret and will not lead to war.
19.00	The order is sent out to all military districts.

Friday 31 July

Early morning	Red mobilisation placards are put up in all public places in Russia.
Midnight	Pourtalès delivers the German ultimatum: by 12.00 next day Russia must confirm that her mobilisation has been called off. (Sazonov and the Tsar do not grasp the fact that rejection will not just lead to German mobilisation, but to an automatic German invasion of France.)

Saturday 1 August

Noon	The deadline for a Russian reply passes.
17.00	Germany declares war on Russia. (Diplomatic relations between Russia and Austria remain open.)
5 Aug.	Austria-Hungary declares war on Russia.

4.6 FRANCE

Few historians believe that France wanted war in 1914. Aggressive French colonial policy had helped to poison international relations before the war, and Raymond Poincaré's election to the presidency in 1912 pointed to a revival of French appetite for 'revenge' for her defeat by Germany in 1871. Nonetheless, in the parliamentary elections of April 1914 the French people elected a majority of radicals and socialists who wanted peace and opposed the recent increase in military service. However, under the terms of the Franco-Russian Alliance, if war broke out in the east France would be dragged in whether the majority of French people desired peace or not. France's only hope was to stop Russia taking military measures in response to the Austrian threat to Serbia. She had restrained Russia in the past, and as the 'senior partner' in the alliance she had the financial and military muscle to do so again. However, French political leaders had to maintain a difficult balancing act: to avoid being dragged into a war by Russia, they needed to hold their ally back. On the other hand, if it did come to war, Russian military support would be essential to French survival, so the Russians needed to feel confident of French solidarity. Likewise, to avoid being caught cold by a German onslaught, France needed to begin military preparations in good time. However, it was also vital for her to maintain the moral high ground in order to demonstrate that she was the *victim* of German aggression. Thus national unity would be preserved, anti-war activists undermined, and the possibility of British backing kept alive. This balancing act was made more precarious by the absence of President Poincaré and Prime Minister Viviani on a State visit to Russia during the height of the Crisis. While at sea, their communications with the inexperienced ministers who had been left in charge of foreign policy were jammed by German Intelligence. If this were not enough, the French and Russian Ambassadors in Paris and St Petersburg were both anti-German hawks. French diplomacy was hamstrung by the knowledge that Germany had broken the French diplomatic codes, necessitating a time-consuming re-routing of cables. It is not known what advice the French leaders gave to the Russians while in St Petersburg, but it seems likely that they encouraged Russia to take a firm line, without carrying it to the point of war. However, the Austrian ultimatum was timed to arrive after the French leaders had left, and by the time they got back to Paris on 29 July, Russia was already on the brink of full mobilisation. Last-minute efforts to hold Russia back were hampered by the failure of Ambassadors Izvolski and Palèologue to keep the French informed, despite the terms of the Franco-Russian military agreement. The strategy of allowing Germany to make the first military move was undermined by army commander Joffre's demands for rapid mobilisation. But when the moment came, there was little popular resistance to the call-up, and French restraint was not an important consideration in Britain's decision to fight. Above all, the brutal logic of the German Schlieffen Plan dictated that German armies would roll westwards, however peaceful the intentions of French leaders, Parliament and people might be.

Leading participants

Poincaré, Raymond	President of the Republic, 1912–1920
Viviani, René	Prime Minister and Foreign Minister
Bienvenu-Martin, Jean-Baptiste	Acting Foreign Minister (15–29 July)
Messimy, Adolphe	War Minister
Joffre, General Joseph	Chief of the General Staff
Jaurès, Jean	Socialist deputy. Leading figure in the Second International
Palèologue, Maurice	French Ambassador in St Petersburg
Dumaine, Alfred	French Ambassador in Vienna
Cambon, Jules	French Ambassador in Berlin
Cambon, Paul	French Ambassador in London
Bertie, Sir Francis	British Ambassador in Paris
von Schoen, Wilhelm	German Ambassador in Paris

Timetable of events

Apr.	Radicals and Socialists win a majority in parliamentary elections.
13 Jun.	Formation of a Radical-Socialist government hostile to military spending and nationalist assertiveness. René Viviani combines the rôle of PM and Foreign Minister, although he has no experience of foreign affairs.
15 Jul.	Poincaré and Viviani leave for their State visit to Russia and Scandinavia. Foreign policy is left in the hands of inexperienced ministers.
20 Jul.	The Trial of Madame Caillaux begins. Ministers are distracted by the fear of revelations. The Press is obsessed with it, to the exclusion of the unfolding Balkan crisis.
20–23 Jul.	Poincaré and Viviani are in St Petersburg. Poincaré recommends that Russia respond firmly but moderately to Austria's threat to Serbia. The Serbian Ambassador, Spalajkovic, is offered only moral support.
23 Jul.	Paris. Intelligence that Germany has begun preparations for mobilisation is not forwarded to the War Ministry for five days.
24 Jul.	Ambassador Palèologue fails to warn Paris that Russia has decided to begin military preparations.
25 Jul.	The Russian Attaché Ignatiev is told by French C-in-C Joffre that 'France is prepared to fulfil her obligations', and reminded that Russia has promised an offensive in East Prussia, requiring *full* Russian mobilisation. Joffre's admonition runs counter to parallel French efforts to stop Russia taking military action.

Belgrade	Jules Boppe takes up the post of French Minister. (France has had no effective diplomatic representation in Serbia for several weeks due to the mental breakdown of the previous incumbent.)

Tuesday 28 July

The trial of Madame Caillaux ends. For the first time, the Press turns its attention to the Balkan crisis. A dispatch from Berlin warning of covert German military preparations (received five days earlier) is, at last, passed on to the Foreign Office.

Wednesday 29 July

08.00 Poincaré and Viviani arrive back from Russia and resume control of foreign policy. They learn for the first time that Austria has declared war on Serbia, and that Russia has ordered a *partial* mobilisation. They do not regard this as a threat to peace.

18.00 The German Ambassador Schoen warns that Germany will be forced to take military measures in response to Russian mobilisation.

23.45 Belated arrival of Palèologue's Telegram 116, informing Paris that Russia has decided to mobilise, but not making clear whether a partial or general mobilisation has been ordered.

Thursday 30 July

In the early hours, a cable from Sazonov asking for French support implies by its wording that Palèologue has been encouraging Russia to think that Paris *supports* Russian mobilisation.

02.00 Ignatiev wakes Messimy to tell him that Russia has begun to mobilise. He asks for an assurance of French support.

07.00 Responding to Russia's request for support, Viviani urges her 'not to take any step which may offer to Germany a pretext for the mobilisation of her forces'. It arrives too late to affect Russia's decision.

09.30 The start of a day-long cabinet meeting in which ministers (who are unaware of the advanced stage of Russia's mobilisation) decide not to ask the Russians to stop their preparations, but to make them as unobtrusive as possible. Joffre's demand for immediate French mobilisation is rejected.

17.00 Covering units protecting the French frontier are ordered to withdraw 10 kilometres, to avoid giving the Germans any excuse to attack.

Friday 31 July

08.30	Public mobilisation orders having been posted all over Russia, Palèologue belatedly cables Paris that Russia has ordered a general mobilisation, but the message is not given to ministers until 20.30 that evening.
Afternoon	Joffre warns the government that each 24 hour delay in mobilising the French army will result in the loss of 15–20 kilometres of French territory.
17.40	Covering troops are ordered forward to the frontier, but no order for the calling up of reserves is issued.
	Fearing that Britain will not come to France's aid, Poincaré sends a direct appeal to King George V asking for support.
19.00	The German Ambassador warns Viviani that unless all military preparations are suspended by Russia, Germany will mobilise against her. In an oblique demand for French neutrality, he asks 'what France's response' to this will be. Viviani tells him that he will receive a reply next day at 13.00.
20.30	Arrival of Palèologue's wire confirming Russian general mobilisation (sent on morning of 30 July) Russia has still not officially informed France of her actions, as she is required to do under the Treaty of Alliance.
21.00	The Cabinet is told that the great socialist Jean Jaurès has been assassinated. Despite the fears of ministers that this will spark revolution, Paris remains calm.
	Later Messimy reassures Ambassador Izvolski of France's firm resolve, but he warns Russia to concentrate her attack upon Germany rather than Austria.

Saturday 1 August

Morning	The socialist Press responds to the assassination of Jaurès by rallying round the flag '*National Defence above all! They have assassinated Jaurès! We will not assassinate France!*' is the headline of *La Guerre Socialist.*
12.00 Noon	German Ambassador Schoen arrives (an hour early) to receive the reply to Germany's demand for French neutrality. Viviani replies that France would 'act in accordance with her interests'.
16.00	The order for general mobilisation is sent out, to take effect at 12.01 am on 2 August. The cabinet decision is swayed by Joffre's threat to resign if there is further delay. (In Berlin German mobilisation begins.)
17.30	Viviani again refuses to give Schoen a pledge of French neutrality.

| 23.30 | Ambassador Izvolski informs Poincaré that Germany has declared war on Russia. Although this automatically triggers the provisions of the Franco-Russian Alliance, Izvolski is told that France will not respond immediately. |

Sunday 2 August

Midnight– 03.00	Ministers decide to delay a declaration of war on Germany, because of the need to maintain popular consensus and win British support. The Russians are told that France will fulfil its alliance obligations, but will not be ready to act for 10 days, when Parliament will be summoned to debate the issue.
14.00	Joffre given 'full liberty of action' to protect the frontier. A State of Emergency is declared.
17.30	The French armies are ordered to move up to the frontier.

Monday 3 August

| 18.30 | Germany declares war on France, claiming that French planes have bombed Nuremberg. |

4.7 GREAT BRITAIN

Britain, unlike the other Great Powers, had no formal alliance that would automatically involve her in the war, but she had obligations to France by the Naval Agreement of 1912, and the creation of the British Expeditionary Force after 1907 implied that she accepted the possibility of fighting on the continent. Sir Edward Grey realised that the Sarajevo assassination could lead to a European war, but believed that the crisis could be resolved by diplomacy. He was encouraged by the moderate stance of German Ambassador Lichnowski, and hoped to build on the success of Anglo-German co-operation during the Balkan Wars, which seemed to herald an Anglo-German rapprochement. Unfortunately for Grey, German priorities had changed in the ensuing eighteen months. Far from restraining Vienna, as she had done in 1912–13, Germany had given the Austrians a 'blank cheque' to proceed vigorously against Serbia. All Grey's efforts to solve the conflict through an international conference foundered on the determination of the hawks in Berlin and Vienna to settle accounts with Serbia this time round. Hitherto, Grey had been conscious that overt support for France and Russia might encourage the hard-liners in Paris and St Petersburg to go to war, and destroy any possibility of co-operation with Germany. On the other hand, he and his advisors also believed it would be disastrous for Britain to stand by while Germany defeated France and dominated Europe. Once Grey became convinced that war was inevitable, his task became one of persuading Cabinet and Parliament that it was in Britain's vital interests to go to war alongside France and Russia. Unfortunately for him, a majority in the Cabinet and the

Liberal Party would not fight merely to preserve the balance of power. This made it impossible for him to make a clear statement of Britain's intentions, either to his allies or to Berlin. Grey's critics say that he should have warned Berlin at an early stage that Britain would stand by France. This would have forced Germany to give up her dream of a quick victory in the west, and caused her to compel Austria to withdraw her threat to Serbia, thus removing the pressure on Russia to take military action. However, Grey's colleagues would not have supported such a statement. Moreover the German High Command hoped to win the war long before Britain could mobilise an army of significant size to influence events. Germany's threat to Belgian neutrality was a godsend to Grey, enabling him to unite most Liberals behind a war of moral principle rather than one of national self-interest or obligations to France. A decade of anti-German Press rhetoric eased the task of mobilising public opinion, while politicians and people continued to delude themselves that the war would be a relatively bloodless naval conflict. Indeed, it was not until 6 August that the Cabinet reluctantly concluded that the BEF must be sent to France.

Leading participants

Asquith, Herbert Henry	British Prime Minister, 1908–16
Benckendorff, Count Alexander	Russian Ambassador in London
Bertie, Sir Francis	British Ambassador in Paris
de Bunsen, Sir Maurice	British Ambassador in Vienna
Cambon, Paul	French Ambassador in London
Churchill, Winston S.	First Lord of the Admiralty
Crowe, Sir Eyre	Assistant Under-secretary at the Foreign Office
George V	King of Great Britain, Emperor of India
Goschen, Sir William	British Ambassador in Berlin
Grey, Sir Edward	Foreign Secretary, 1905–16
Haldane, Richard Burdon	Secretary of State for War
Lichnowsky, Prince Karl Max	German Ambassador in London
Lloyd George, David	Chancellor of the Exchequer. Long-term opponent of war
Mensdorff, Count Albert von	Austro-Hungarian Ambassador in London
Nicolson, Sir Arthur	Permanent Under-secretary of State at the FO
Tyrrell, Sir William	Private secretary to Sir Edward Grey

Timetable of events

28 Jun.	The Sarajevo assassination.
6 Jul.	Lichnowsky tells Grey that the Austrians intend to take strong measures against Serbia.
9 Jul.	Grey tells Lichnowsky that he intends to follow the same policy of mediation as in 1912 (when he and Bethmann Hollweg worked together to defuse the crisis).

21–24 Jul.	The Buckingham Palace Conference on the Irish problem absorbs the attention of politicians and Press.
23 Jul. Morning	Grey is informed that Austria will present a 'Note' to Serbia later that day. A reply will be expected within 48 hours. In St Petersburg, Ambassador Buchanan proposes bilateral talks between Austria and Russia.
24 Jul.	The terms of the Austrian ultimatum to Serbia become known in London. Grey suggests that the four 'neutral' Powers (GB, France, Germany and Italy) should mediate, and calls for an extension of the time limit of the ultimatum.
Evening	Grey raises the Balkan Crisis for the first time in Cabinet, where foreign policy has not been discussed for a month. There is a clear majority against involvement in a continental war. Grey and many other ministers leave London for the weekend. Grey is told that an unsatisfactory answer by Serbia will not lead to war.
25 Jul.	Churchill orders the fleet to remain concentrated after the Spithead Naval Review.
Sunday, 26 Jul.	In Grey's absence, Sir Arthur Nicolson proposes to Lichnowsky a Four Power Mediation such as had defused the Balkan Crisis of 1912–13. Grey telegraphs his assent to this idea.
Monday 27 Jul.	During a full Cabinet meeting, several members threaten to resign if Britain goes to war to support France. The *Manchester Guardian* says 'if Russia and France . . . went to war, we should not be in it'. Germany rejects Grey's proposal for a Four Power Conference.
29–31 Jul.	Liberal anti-war groups fail to agree a coherent strategy to check the drift to intervention.

Wednesday 29 July

Morning	The Cabinet again rejects Grey's proposal to support France. The majority argues that the 1839 Guarantee of Belgian neutrality is a *collective* responsibility of the Powers, and asks what would happen if Belgium allowed free passage to German troops. British involvement is thus a decision of 'policy rather than legal obligation'. Grey and Asquith again hint that they will resign if their views are rejected.

After the meeting, Asquith supports Churchill's decision to prepare the fleet. Government departments are told to implement precautions set out in the 'War Book'.

Grey tells Ambassador Cambon that Britain is 'free from engagements', and will act according to British interests. But later he tells Ambassador Lichnowsky that Britain 'could not stand aside' in a Franco-German war. (Bethmann receives this warning at about 22.00 Berlin time, after he has made his abortive neutrality proposal to Ambassador Goschen.)

Thursday 30 July

Conservative leaders offer to postpone the second reading of the Irish Home Rule Bill in the interest of national unity. The Parliamentary Labour Party declares that Britain should stay out of the war.

15.30   Grey instructs Goschen to tell Bethmann that although his neutrality proposal is unacceptable, if this crisis is resolved, the Entente will not pursue an aggressive policy towards Germany. (This would constitute a great diplomatic victory for Germany.)

Later, Grey is again unable to answer when Ambassador Cambon asks him what Britain will do if Germany attacks France.

Friday 31 July

Morning   The Cabinet majority again refuses to support France.

18.40   Arrival of Ambassador Buchanan's wire telling London that Russia has ordered a general mobilisation (24 hours after it has been proclaimed).

Saturday 1 August

Over the weekend   The Labour Party sponsors large 'Stop the War' demonstrations in provincial cities.

13.00   Ambassador Bertie in Paris cables Viviani's assurance that France will respect Belgian neutrality.

15.30   King George V sends a cable to the Tsar, drafted by Asquith and other leaders, calling for Russian restraint.

Afternoon   Cambon reminds Grey of Britain's 1912 naval commitment to France, but is again fobbed off.

Overnight   Churchill orders full mobilisation of the fleet.

Sunday 2 August

Ambassador Cambon informs Grey that German troops have entered Luxembourg. He is told that Luxembourg's neutrality is the collective responsibility of the Powers. Later Cambon says that 'honour should be struck out of the English vocabulary'.

11.00–14.00   Cabinet Meeting. Asquith presents a letter of support from the Conservative Opposition, implying that a pro-war coalition is waiting in the wings if the anti-war ministers choose to resign. Grey argues that Britain has a 'moral obligation' to defend the coast of France under the 1912 Naval Agreement.

Resistance to intervention gradually crumbles, and eventually it is agreed to warn Germany that Britain will not tolerate naval action against the French coast, and that a 'substantial' violation of Belgian neutrality would compel British action. The meeting refuses to sanction the sending of the BEF to France. Only two members of the Cabinet (Burns and Morley) resign. Later, Grey is able to tell Cambon that the Cabinet has agreed to intervene if the German fleet attacks France.

13.25   Grey is told that Belgium will not request assistance, but will rely on its own armed forces.

Late evening   News of the German ultimatum to Belgium arrives in London.

Monday 3 August

09.31   Belgium informs London that it has received the German ultimatum, and says that it will be rejected. Later, King Albert I requests diplomatic (but not military) support from King George V.

Morning   Cabinet Meeting approves the mobilisation of fleet and army.

15.00   Grey's Speech in the House of Commons. After emphasising Britain's freedom of action, and saying that Britain's actions will be in her own interests, he reveals that under the 1912 Naval Agreement, 'the Northern and Western Coasts of France are now completely undefended'. He then spells out Britain's treaty obligations to Belgium, and reads King Albert's appeal for support. He contends that Britain must uphold these 'obligations of honour'. He implies that only the navy would be involved.

The Commons authorises the navy to protect the French coast, and agrees that Germany should be warned that Britain would act if she invaded Belgium.

Tuesday 4 August

Morning   The Cabinet is told that German troops have entered Belgium. Grey is authorised to send an ultimatum requiring Germany to withdraw by 12.00 midnight.

18.00   In Berlin, Goschen delivers the British ultimatum. Jagow tells him that Germany's invasion of Belgium is dictated by 'military necessity' and 'impossible to reverse'. Later, Bethmann tells Goschen that Britain's actions are 'like striking a man from behind while he was fighting for his life against two assailants'. And all for 'a scrap of paper'.

23.00   In Berlin, the time-limit for the British ultimatum expires.

The Cabinet finally agrees to send the BEF to France on 6 Aug.

4.8 BELGIUM

Since 1839, Belgian neutrality has been protected by international treaty. During the Franco-Prussian War of 1870–1 the belligerents scrupulously refrained from violating it. The Belgians seem to have been completely unaware of the implications of the German Schlieffen Plan. King Albert I was determined to prevent either side from entering Belgian territory, even when it became obvious that Germany was about to cross the frontier.

1913

Mar.	The political director of the Foreign Ministry recommends that if German troops only cross a small piece of southern Belgium, the country should remain neutral.

1914

27 Jul.	The army is put on the alert.
28 Jul.	The Belgian minister in Paris reports that Germany is prepared to enter into any arrangement to preserve peace.
29 Jul.	The French minister in Brussels reports that he is unsure whether Belgium will resist a German invasion.
29 Jul.	Partial mobilisation ordered, followed by general mobilisation on 31 July.
2 Aug. 06.00	News arrives of massive German troop movements towards the Belgian border. The German minister in Brussels is only now told by Berlin that an attack on the Liège forts was an essential part of German plans.
2 Aug. 19.00	The German Ambassador delivers an ultimatum (in German) drafted by von Moltke: it demands free passage for the German army, and promises compensation for damage and a financial indemnity.
21.00–04.00	A Council of Ministers meeting followed by a Crown Council unanimously decides to reject the German demands.
3 Aug. 07.00	The German Ambassador is handed the Belgian document of rejection. When these events become public, there is an outburst of patriotic demonstrations. The impact of the ultimatum is to unify the nation even before German troops cross the border.
4 Aug. 08.00	German troops cross the Belgian frontier. A meeting of Parliament unanimously endorses the decision by the King and his ministers to resist. An appeal is sent to Britain requesting military co-operation.

BATTLE FRONTS

5.1 THE WESTERN FRONT

1914: The failure of the Schlieffen Plan

4 Aug.	German troops enter Belgium. Under the Schlieffen Plan, the German army has forty two days to defeat France before troops must be transferred to the Eastern Front.
6–24 Aug.	The Battles of the Frontiers. South of the German line of advance, the French armies advance according to the principles of all-out attack embodied in Plan 17. The offensive fails with huge losses.
9–16 Aug.	The British Expeditionary Force (BEF) lands in France.
16 Aug.	The Liège forts are captured, freeing the way for a German advance into Belgium.
20 Aug.	Brussels falls to the Germans. The Belgian army retreats into the fortified port of Antwerp.
23–4 Aug.	The battle of Mons. The BEF briefly delays the German advance.
25 Aug.	The Germans capture the Belgian fortress of Namur, clearing the way for an advance into the plains of northern France. Tacitly acknowledging the failure of Plan 17, General Joffre orders a general retreat, and transfers divisions northwards. A Belgian sortie from Antwerp, which might have seriously threatened the German flank, peters out through lack of co-ordinated support.
26 Aug.	Moltke breaks faith with the Schlieffen Plan by ordering the transfer of troops to East Prussia. French and British commanders confer at St Quentin, but fail to agree a co-ordinated strategy.
28 Aug.	The Kaiser orders the advance on Paris to begin.
29 Aug.	The Battle of Guise. The French slow the German advance with a successful counter-attack.
30 Aug.	'Kluck's Turn'. General Kluck, believing that he has a chance to envelop and destroy the retreating Allies, begins to wheel his army eastwards (i.e. to the north of Paris rather than enveloping it from the west, as envisaged by Schlieffen).
1 Sep.	Kitchener meets Sir John French at the British Embassy in Paris, and orders him to co-operate with the French and give

up his plans to withdraw the BEF from combat and evacuate it from France. French has been shocked by the losses incurred by the BEF. He is very aware that he is entrusted with the only army available to defend Britain's shores. He is afraid that the BEF will be wiped out in the service of misguided French strategies.

2 Sep.

The French government leaves Paris for Bordeaux. The Germans have reached the River Marne, and German cavalry patrols enter the outskirts of Paris.

4–10 Sep.

The Battles of the Marne. Joffre, alerted by Gallieni to the vulnerability of the German flank strung out north of Paris, orders a counter-attack.

9–14 Sep.

The Great Retreat. Moltke's envoy, Lt Col. Hentsch, orders a pull-back to a defensive line along the River Aisne. With no prospect of the swift victory remaining, Moltke cracks under the strain of battle, and is replaced by Erich von Falkenhayn.

**12 Sep.–
24 Oct.**

The First Battle of the Aisne and the 'Race to the Sea'. Having failed to break the German line on the Aisne, the Allies try to by-pass it to the west, leading to a series of outflanking movements by both sides that only stop when they run out of space at Nieuport on the Belgian coast. The BEF escapes being cut off from its bases on the Channel coast, but Germany captures Ostend and Zeebrugge (15 Nov.), which become important U-boat bases.

**26 Sep.–
10 Oct.**

The Germans take Antwerp. Despite the belated arrival of Churchill and a small British naval force, the allies fail to do enough to support Belgian efforts. This vital strategic port is lost.

24 Oct.

The Belgian army floods the low-lying coastal plain to make German advance impossible.

**18 Oct.–
12 Nov.**

The First Battle of Ypres. The Germans mount a fierce offensive to salvage their campaign by cutting the British off from their Channel bases. Thousands of young student volunteers are recklessly sent to their deaths (the *Kindermord*) but the Allies hold out, at the cost of the virtual destruction of the original BEF.

16 Nov.

The trench system. As heavy rain starts to fall in Flanders, defensive weaponry is in the ascendant. The belligerents have suffered 3.5 million casualties, and fought each other to a standstill along a front stretching four-hundred miles from Switzerland to the North Sea.

Germany has failed to win the swift victory in the west upon which her strategy was based. France has recovered from the disastrous strategies of Plan 17 to stage a heroic recovery. Great Britain, unimportant in the context of the Schlieffen gamble, will become a formidable enemy now that a long war has become inevitable. On the other hand, Germany is in possession of Belgium and some of France's richest provinces. She could afford to stand on the defensive and exploit her conquests.

1915: Germany stands on the defensive

The strategy of the German High Command for 1915 was to stand on the defensive in the west and stake all on an onslaught in the east to knock Russia out of the war. In contrast, General Joffre was determined to liberate French territory by mounting offensives against vulnerable points in the German line. His British allies matched his confidence that a breakthrough could be achieved.

10–13 Mar.	An attempted British advance at Neuve Chapelle makes little progress.
17 Mar.	Joffre suspends the Champagne Offensive, which began on 10 December. Flooded trenches and knee-deep mud render operations impossible. Criticism from Joffre's military rivals and politicians grows.
1 Apr.	The French army uses trench mortars for the first time. All combatants have found that traditional artillery (particularly weapons like the vaunted French 75s) do not fit the needs of the new warfare.
22 Apr.	The Germans use poison gas for the first time as the Second Battle of Ypres begins. Despite an outcry in the Allied Press, both Britain and France hasten to develop their own gas weapons. Gas does not prove to be the 'breakthrough weapon' that all sides are seeking.
1 May	British troops are issued with the Mills Bomb hand-grenade.
4 May	The German High Command moves from Luxemburg to Pless in Silesia, emphasising German pre-occupation with the Eastern Front.
9 May	Beginning of the Allied Spring Offensive in Artois. British efforts are hampered by shortage and poor quality of shells, compounded by the need to send munitions to Gallipoli.

25 May	The Second Battle of Ypres ends. The BEF has suffered three times as many casualties as the Germans, who are standing on the defensive.
24 Jun.	Joffre and French agree at Chantilly that the war will be won on the Western Front. They plan summer offensives to achieve this.
11 Jul.	Joffre announces that the French army will mount an autumn offensive in Champagne.
30 Jul.	The German army uses flame-throwers against the BEF.
5 Aug.	France decides to strip its fortresses of heavy artillery for use at the front. Verdun suffers particular depredations.
16 Aug.	Kitchener and Joffre agree they need to act to take pressure off the Russians. On 23 August French reluctantly agrees to commit the BEF to the projected offensive.
21 Sep.– 6 Nov.	Combined Allied offensives in Champagne, Artois and Loos. After six weeks of fighting, neither army has made any significant gains.
21 Oct.	King George V visits the BEF, where he is subjected to backstairs criticism of Sir John French's ability to command.
31 Oct.	Steel helmets are issued to British troops.
1 Dec.	Colonel Driant, a Deputy and serving officer, tells the French Chamber that the defences of Verdun have been neglected.
6 Dec.	An Anglo-French Summit at Chantilly resolves to persist with the Salonika Expedition, but to mount a co-ordinated and war-winning offensive in the summer of 1916.
18 Dec.	After months of intrigue, Douglas Haig replaces Sir John French as British C-in-C. King George and leading Conservative politicians favour Haig.
19 Dec.	The German army uses phosgene gas for the first time.
20 Dec.	The Falkenhayn Memorandum. Falkenhayn proposes an attack upon the historic fortress of Verdun that would 'bleed the French white' in a war of attrition. Verdun's historical associations oblige the French army to defend the fortress at all costs and in defiance of military logic. Four days later preparations are put in hand to prepare the manpower and infrastructure for a massive February offensive.
21 Dec.	Sir William Robertson, a proponent of total concentration on the Western Front, is appointed Chief of Imperial General Staff (CIGS).
29 Dec.	Joffre and Haig agree on an all out co-ordinated offensive for the summer of 1916.

1916: Attrition

1 Feb.	The BEF, swelled by Kitchener's volunteers, is now over one million strong.
14 Feb.	The French and British High Commands agree to a Somme offensive for 1 July.
22 Feb.	The German assault on Verdun begins.
24 Feb.	General Henri-Philippe Pétain takes command of French forces.
25 Feb.	The Germans capture the key strongpoint of Fort Douaumont.
1 Mar.	President Poincaré urges the beleaguered fortress to hold out at all costs.
1 Apr.	French casualties at Verdun stand at 89,000, but German losses are not much less. The French have accumulated nearly 1300 guns, and are building strategic railways to supplement the vast stores of supplies and men reaching the fortress along *La Voie Sacrée* (the 'Sacred Way'). Pétain's decision to rotate the garrison means that almost the entire French army experiences the horrors of the siege.
9 Apr.	A renewed German assault makes little progress.
19 Apr.	French High Command orders the recapture of Fort Douaumont.
1 May	General Robert Nivelle takes over command from Pétain.
29 May	The Germans take the strongpoint of Mort Homme.
30 May	French heavy artillery production greatly increased.
31 May	Poincaré warns that Verdun is in danger of falling, necessitating immediate relieving attacks on the Somme.
7 Jun.	The Germans capture Fort Vaux.
20 Jun.	An intensive barrage precedes a massive new German assault, prompting Nivelle's Order *'On ne passe pas!'*
24 Jun.–18 Nov.	**The Anglo-French offensive on the Somme.**
24 Jun.	The British open an unprecedentedly heavy week-long artillery barrage. Nearly 2 million shells are fired, but many German machine-gunners survive in deep bunkers.
1 Jul.	Thousands of Kitchener's volunteers move forward to 'occupy' German lines that have been theoretically devastated by the artillery. Enormous casualties are suffered and very little progress made.
2 Jul.	Verdun. All German attacks are halted because of the Somme offensive.

19 Jul.	Germans reorganise their defences on the Somme.
21 Jul.	Falkenhayn admits that German manpower resources are near breaking point.
23 Jul.	Start of the second phase of the Somme battle (Pozières).
29 Jul.	Robertson warns Haig that London is becoming uneasy about casualties (already 150,000 on the Somme since 1 July). But the campaign continues throughout August with little ground gained.
29 Aug.	Falkenhayn is dismissed, largely because of the failure of the Verdun campaign.
8 Sep.	The new German commanders Hindenburg and Ludendorff decide to reorganise German armies on the Western Front according to the doctrine of 'defence in depth'. German Headquarters returns to Pless, emphasising the switch away from Falkenhayn's offensive philosophy.
13 Sep.	President Poincaré bestows a symbolic Legion of Honour on the heroic fortress of Verdun.
15 Sep.	Britain uses tanks for the first time at Flers-Courcelette on the Somme. A potential war-winner is wasted by employing it before it has been technically perfected, and not providing sufficient infantry to exploit the openings created by it. The element of surprise is lost, but the initial failure of tanks discourages the Germans from developing them. Haig demands 1000 tanks.
23 Sep.	Construction of the Hindenburg Line begins. Germany has now assembled 120 divisions in the west.
6 Oct.	Haig confirms his determination to continue the Somme campaign until the winter. He tells the French the enemy 'must not be given a moment's peace'.
24 Oct.	Verdun. France retakes the symbolically important ruins of Fort Douaumont, and a week later recaptures Fort Vaux.
15 Nov.	The Chantilly Conference decides on simultaneous allied offensives for 1917.
19 Nov.	Deteriorating weather brings the Somme offensive to a halt.
6 Dec.	David Lloyd George, a critic of attrition tactics, becomes British PM, but Haig and Robertson retain support in high places.
12 Dec.	General Robert Nivelle replaces Joffre as French commander on the Western Front. He convinces British and French politicians that he knows how to make a breakthrough in 1917.

1917: Disaster for the Allies

15 Jan.	Nivelle explains his plan to an impressed British Cabinet.
22 Jan.	France and Switzerland discuss the possibility of a German invasion of Switzerland.
3 Feb.	A Portuguese Expeditionary Force joins the Allies.
6 Feb.–16 Mar.	The German army undertakes Operation Alberich, a planned withdrawal to the meticulously prepared Hindenburg Line. By shortening their line by 25 miles, the Germans save manpower. The scorched earth zone they create as they pull back is a killing ground for advancing infantry.
20 Feb.	Nivelle postpones his offensive from 15 March to 10 April, giving the Germans more time to prepare.
27 Feb.	Haig reluctantly agrees to support Nivelle's plan.
6 Apr.	Despite knowing that the Germans have captured details of his campaign plan, Nivelle threatens to resign if his offensive is cancelled. He offers to halt the offensive after two days if success is not achieved.
9 Apr.–16 May	British and Canadian troops take part in the battles of Arras and Vimy Ridge, designed to complement the French offensives further south.
16 Apr.–9 May	The Nivelle Offensive. The French attack founders along the Chemin des Dames against German defences that have been waiting for it for weeks. The French suffer 100,000 initial casualties (compared with the 15,000 predicted by Nivelle). Progress is measured in hundreds of yards. Great damage is done to French army morale.
17 Apr.–10 Jun.	Sparked by the failure of the Offensive, mutinies spread through the French army. The soldiers claim to be 'strikers'. They object to bad food, low pay and poor leave arrangements rather than the war itself. They remain determined to hold the front line, but are unwilling to undertake fresh offensives. The Germans never find out the turmoil in their opponents' line.
4 May	Haig decides to continue with a limited offensive to relieve pressure on the French and to assist the forthcoming Russian (Brusilov) offensive.
10 May	General John Pershing is appointed commander of the American Expeditionary Force (AEF) in France, but it will be a year before US troops begin to cross the Atlantic in significant numbers.

15 May	Nivelle is replaced by Pétain as C-in-C in the field, with General Ferdinand Foch taking a co-ordinating rôle.
17 May	Pétain's Directive Number One accepts that the French army must stand on the defensive for the moment ('wait for tanks and the Americans').
26 May	The first US troops land in France.
2 Jun.	Pétain tells Haig that because of the mutinies, he can only offer minimal support during the forthcoming British offensive.
7–14 Jun.	A 500 ton mine is detonated under the German positions before the successful British attack at Messines Ridge.
30 Jun.	Ludendorff learns for the first time of the French mutinies.
6 Jul.	General Pershing calls for a million US soldiers by May 1918.
12 Jul.	The Germans use mustard gas for the first time.
20 Jul.	The British Cabinet approves Haig's forthcoming offensive, after he undertakes to stop it if no progress is made.
31 Jul.–18 Nov.	The Third Battle of Ypres (Passchendaele). With the British army at its peak of over two million men, Haig plans to break the German line in Flanders and isolate the German U-boat bases of Zeebrugge and Ostende.
28 Aug.	Verdun. The French get back to the line they held before the titanic German onslaught of 1916.
2 Sep.	Lloyd George fails to secure the transfer of troops to the Italian Front. He accepts the continuation of the Flanders offensive, despite its cost, because of the vulnerable state of the French army.
9 Sep.	The Étaples mutiny is provoked among British troops by conditions in the base camp.
25 Sep.	The Boulogne Conference decides to transfer heavy equipment to the Italian front. The British accept the need to take over more of the line.
7 Oct.	Haig rejects requests by senior commanders to stop his Flanders offensive. He maintains that Britain is capable of sustaining the war with minimal French and Russian assistance.
12 Oct.	First Battle of Passchendaele. Unusually wet weather and the destruction of the drainage system by preliminary bombardment turns the northern part of the battlefield into an impassable swamp. There is little advance, but the pressure forces the Germans to retain 12 divisions bound for Italy.
23 Oct.	German High Command concludes that the key to victory still lies in the west.

24 Oct.– 30 Dec.	Collapse of the Italian Front ('Caporetto').
26 Oct.– 10 Nov.	The Second Battle of Passchendaele.
5 Nov.	At the Allied Rapallo Conference to meet the emergency on the Italian Front (QV), the Allies agree to establish a Supreme War Council to co-ordinate their efforts.
11 Nov.	German Staff Conference at Mons. Ludendorff believes that the imminent end of war in the east has given him the chance to win the war. Before the American build-up redresses the balance, he will bring the best units of the German army to bear on the Western Front against a numerically inferior enemy. He wins support for a Great Spring Offensive in 1918.
20 Nov.– 3 Dec.	The Battle of Cambrai. The British use massed tanks for the first time, opening up a six mile breach in the German line. But sufficient reserves have again not been assembled to exploit the breakthrough. By 12 December, the Germans have regained all their lost ground in a surprise attack.
29 Nov.– 3 Dec.	The Allied Paris Conference. The Allied Maritime Transport Council and the Allied Council on War Purchases and Finance are set up with American representatives to centralise war purchases and allocate shipping. The Supreme War Council meets for the first time at Versailles, but fails to agree on an overall commander for the Western Front.
17 Dec.	Armistice on the Eastern Front. Germany has already begun to transfer 46 divisions (half a million men) to the west, despite promising the Bolsheviks not to do so.

1918: Germany fails to break through: the Central Powers collapse

21 Jan.	Ludendorff decides that his March offensive will strike at the point where British and French lines join. This sector is held by the British 5th Army, an exhausted force that has recently been sent to this apparently quiet part of the line, and has not yet had time to prepare it.
26 Jan.	A German paper on 'position warfare' sets out the innovative tactics to be employed in the coming offensive, based on the 'blitzkrieg' tactics used successfully at Riga and Caporetto. Preceded by a short but intense bombardment, German élite forces will move rapidly forward, outflanking centres of stubborn resistance to 'punch a hole' in the Allied line to cause maximum disruption.
3 Mar.	The Treaty of Brest-Litovsk. German manpower in the west increases by 30%, although vast numbers of German troops are tied up garrisoning the newly occupied territories.

10 Mar.	Hindenburg issues final orders for the offensive. German High Command moves forward to Avesnes to direct the break-through.
21 Mar.– 5 Apr.	Ludendorff's 'Kaiserschlacht' Offensive. After a short but ferocious barrage by 6000 guns using vast quantities of gas, the German advance breaks the British line, pushing it back 40 miles. However, the German advance soon runs out of steam and Ludendorff calls a halt, realising that the offensive's objectives of Amiens and Arras are 'beyond our powers'. His exhausted troops, fast outrunning their supply lines, have sustained 250,000 casualties. The Kaiser still honours Hindenburg with a decoration last bestowed on Blucher, the conqueror of Napoleon.
23 Mar.	Bombardment of Paris from a range of 75 miles.
26 Mar.	The Doullens Conference. Haig, who has lost all faith in Pétain because of his refusal to commit reserves to prevent the separation of the Allied armies, at last accepts the authority of Foch as allied co-ordinator, with the key rôle of allocating reserves.
9–29 Apr.	Ludendorff's second offensive (The Battle of Lys) against the British in Flanders, aimed at breaking through to the Channel ports. Its initial success prompts Haig's exhortation 'Every position must be held to the last man', but again the British hold on, and the German offensive is called off. Although the German spring onslaughts have created the worst crisis for the Allies since 1914, none of Ludendorff's primary objectives have been gained. Germany has sustained 440,000 casualties.
14 Apr.	Foch becomes Allied 'Generalissimo' in the west.
27 May– 5 Jun.	Ludendorff's third offensive (The Third Battle of the Aisne). He intends to use the salient captured in March as the springboard for an advance down the valley of the Oise to threaten Paris. Using his habitual tactics he reaches the Marne, and pushes the French back to within 56 miles of the capital, but again the attack slows the further it gets from its supply lines.
28 May	American troops undertake their first offensive of the war at Catigny. On 4 June, American Marines counter-attack against the faltering Germans, who have already been ordered to halt the offensive.
9–14 Jun.	Battle of the River Matz (Gneisenau Offensive). French and American troops halt a German attempt to widen the front.

30 Jun.	Six fresh American divisions (of 28,000 men each) land in France, bringing the American total to over a million. In contrast, Germany has lost nearly 900,000 men since 21 March.
15 Jul.	Second Battle of the Marne. Ludendorff again attacks with his remaining 52 divisions in a desperate attempt to gain the essential breakthrough. Little progress is made, and there are now too few conscripts to make good his monthly losses, now compounded by the influenza pandemic.
22 Jul.	Ludendorff orders a retreat from much of the territory captured since March. He abandons his projected *Hagen* offensive in Flanders, and admits to the Kaiser that his spring offensives have failed.
24 Jul.	Allied commanders decide on a series of counter-offensives.
8 Aug.	Fresh Canadian and Australian divisions mount a massive offensive north of Amiens spearheaded by 600 tanks. The German 2nd Army is crippled and the Hindenburg Line threatened. Ludendorff calls it 'the Black Day of the German Army in this war'.
11 Aug.	Ludendorff's offer of resignation is refused by the Kaiser, but he says the war must be ended.
21–29 Aug.	Allied Albert and Scarpe offensives.
31 Aug.	The Canadians capture Peronne – 'the finest single feat of the whole war'.
12–16 Sep.	The first independent American action of the war drives the Germans out of the St Miheil Salient.
26 Sep.	Foch launches 126 Allied divisions against the German line: Americans and French advance on the Meuse, and through the Argonne forest. British, Australians and Canadians breach the Hindenburg Line along the Canal du Nord.
28 Sep.	Hindenburg and Ludendorff say that Germany must seek an immediate armistice.
29 Sep.	Allied forces cross the St Quentin Canal.
9 Oct.	Canadian troops breach the Hindenburg Line and take Cambrai.
12 Oct.	Hindenburg urges German soldiers to resist strongly to obtain the best armistice terms.
14–24 Oct.	The Allied Courtrai and Selle offensives.
26 Oct.	Ludendorff resigns and is replaced by Gröner.
2–11 Nov.	The Allied Sambre offensive.
5 Nov.	Allied Supreme War Council accepts German armistice terms.
8 Nov.	Foch receives German armistice delegates.
11 Nov. 11.00	All fighting stops on the Western Front.

5.2 THE EASTERN FRONTS

1914: Russia invades East Prussia and the Central Powers hit back (Aug.–Dec. 1914)

8 Aug.	In response to French requests for an offensive to take pressure off them, Stavka (Russian High Command) decides to strike directly towards Berlin from Central Poland. Troops are withdrawn from the Russian 1st and 2nd Armies poised for the invasion of East Prussia.
15 Aug.	On the 16th day of mobilisation, a two-pronged Russian invasion of East Prussia begins, with Rennenkampf's 1st Army in the north, and Samsonov's 2nd Army in the south. Although this region is the heartland of the Prussian military caste, the Schlieffen Plan dictates that only a light defensive screen is deployed by the Germans. They are surprised that the Russian offensive has begun so soon.
17 Aug.	The Battle of Stallupönen. General Rennenkampf's 1st Army, comprising the northern wing of the Russian forces advancing on either side of the Marsurian Lakes, thwarts a German counter-attack.
20 Aug.	The Battle of Gumbinnen. Another victory by Rennenkampf, who stops, expecting a German retreat. The German commander Prittwitz is convinced that he is about to be enveloped by vastly superior Russian forces. He plans to withdraw to the Vistula River.
22 Aug.	Leading elements of Samsonov's 2nd Army make contact with the Germans. For the next six days they unwittingly advance into a trap prepared by German High Command.
23 Aug.	Prittwitz and his chief of Staff von Waldersee are replaced by retired General Paul von Hindenburg, and Major-General Erich Ludendorff, who adopt an aggressive plan of attack (already prepared by Col. Hoffman) to destroy Samsonov's 2nd Army.
24–5 Aug.	The Germans pick up two uncoded Russian wireless messages revealing Russian dispositions, and making it clear that Samsonov will receive no support from Rennenkampf's 1st Army to the north.
26–30 Aug.	**The Battle Of Tannenberg.**
26 Aug.	The Battle of Bishofsberg. Mackensen routs the left wing of Samsonov's army, leaving his centre still advancing and dangerously exposed.

26 Aug.	Despite the strengthening of the German army with rein-forcements from the Western Front, Russian northern com-mander Zhilinski does not order Rennenkampf to move south to support Samsonov, but *north* towards Königsberg.
27 Aug.	General François breaks through the Russian lines after a devastating artillery barrage.
28 Aug.	The encircling German armies of François and Mackensen meet at Willenberg. Samsonov belatedly realises the danger and orders a retreat, which turns into a chaotic rout. Next day Samsonov shoots himself in the forest as his army dis-integrates around him.
7–14 Sep.	The First Battle of the Masurian Lakes. Although the Germans are too exhausted to exploit their victory, only 10,000 men of the Russian 2nd Army survive of its original 150,000. Tannenberg is a spectacular German victory. It creates the myth of Ludendorff's military genius and feeds German expectations that the war can be won in the east, but its impact on Russia's potential strength is trivial. It does not remove the Russian threat to East Prussia.
4 Oct.–13 Dec.	**The Austro-German invasion of Russian Poland.**
12–20 Oct.	German forces besiege Warsaw, but by 26 October are forced to pull back from their exposed position.
1 Nov.	Hindenburg appointed German Commander in Chief on Eastern Front.
6 Nov.	The Germans force the Russians to evacuate Lodz, but are unable to make further progress.
13 Dec.	Austro-German offensives in Poland are suspended. In the Northern Sector Russia has suffered enormous casualties and revealed major deficiencies in logistics, co-ordination and military security. But with her colossal manpower reserves and great industrial potential she still poses a formidable threat to Germany. Russia's sacrifices in East Prussia have forced Germany to withdraw troops from the Western Front, contributing to the failure of the Schlieffen Plan, and she has won great victories against the Austrians in the Southern Sector.

5.3 THE GALICIAN AND CARPATHIAN CAMPAIGNS (AUG.–DEC. 1914)

5 Aug.	Austria-Hungary declares war on Russia. Both sides are eager to join battle, but both High Commands misread each other's dispositions. Conrad believes the main Russian threat comes

from the north rather than the east. The Russian High Command (Stavka) thinks that Austria will strike eastwards rather than push northwards into Poland. Consequently, the initial campaigns become a 'revolving door' with both sides pushing their left flank forward against the enemy's weakest side.

9 Aug.

Moltke tells Conrad he can spare no troops for the joint Austro-German operation in the north upon which Conrad has been counting.

10 Aug.–
1 Sep.

The Austrian invasion of Russian Poland. Austrian cavalry penetrates deep into Russian territory, without contacting the enemy. Superior Austrian forces advance upon Lublin, threatening to encircle the Russian 5th Army, but stiffening Russian resistance forces a withdrawal.

18 Aug.–
9 Oct.

Russian invasion of Eastern Galicia. The Russian 3rd and 8th Armies enter Austrian Galicia from the east and make rapid progress. They capture Lemburg (Lvov) (3 Sep.), lay siege to the great fortress of Przemysl (24 Sep.–10 Oct.), and threaten the Carpathian Passes leading to the plains of Hungary.

11 Sep.

In the face of the Russian advance, Conrad orders a general withdrawal from Galicia.

28 Sep.

The newly formed German 9th Army relieves the Austrians by attacking from north-west of Krakow.

10 Nov.–
22 Mar.

1915   The Second Russian Siege of Przmysl.

1–17 Dec.

The Battles of Limanowa. A turning point in the war in the East. The Austrian 4th Army rallies to save Krakow and prevent a Russian breakthrough towards Vienna.

25 Dec.

Austro-German armies have established a defensive line from the Vistula to Tarnow and the line of the Carpathians. But the Russian army is intact and still besieging Przemysl.

1915: The year of Russian defeat

8 Jan.

The German Südarmee formed to support the Austrians.

23 Jan.

The Austrians fail to relieve Przemysl in sub-zero temperatures.

31 Jan.

Germany uses poison gas for the first time at Bolimow in Poland.

7–21 Feb.

The Second Battle of the Masurian Lakes. German fears for the survival of Austria-Hungary (because Italy and Romania may enter the war) prompts a major effort to defeat Russia quickly or force her to sign a separate peace. The offensive is planned to coincide with an Austrian attempt to relieve Przemysl (spearheaded by the Südarmee). Although the

German offensive in Masuria kills many Russians, it gains little territory. In the south, Austro-German forces also fail to make progress.

22 Mar.   Przemysl falls to the Russians. Its garrison of 150,000 and vast stores of guns and equipment are captured.

2–13 May   The Gorlice–Tarnow Offensive is spearheaded by Mackensen's new 11th Army, using shock tactics based on massive artillery preparation and innovative infantry tactics. The Russians are driven back 80 miles to the River San, and their hold on the Carpathian Passes is loosened. But a counter-attack by the Russian 9th Army drives the Austrians out of Bukovina.

23 May   Italy enters the war further stretching Austria's resources, although she already has many divisions tied up on the Italian border.

3 Jun.   The Central Powers retake Przemysl.

20 Jun.   Russia undertakes the complete evacuation of Austrian Galicia. She leaves behind 250,000 POWs, abandoning the capital, Lemburg (Lvov) on 22 June.
           Russian losses since the start of the war now stand at 3.8 million.

The Triple Offensive and the 'Great Retreat' from Poland.

2 Jul.   The Kaiser agrees to Hindenburg's and Ludendorff's plan to envelop the Russian army in the Polish salient with simultaneous attacks from north and south. Their goal is not to occupy Russian territory, but to envelop and utterly destroy the Russian army before it can escape to its vast hinterland. They will then turn their attention to the west.

13–15 Jul. Three simultaneous offensives by the Central Powers.
           • The Narev Offensive. German 12th Army (Gallwitz) attacks towards Warsaw pushing the Russians back on a 25 mile front.
           • The Northern Offensive. The German Niemen Army advances along the Baltic coast towards the Russian port of Riga.
           • The Bug Offensive. Mackensen attacks the Russian 3rd Army.

22 Jul.   Stavka sanctions 'The Great Retreat'; over the next two months all the military, administrative and economic centres of western Russia fall to the enemy: Warsaw (4 Aug.), Kovno (17 Aug.), Novogeorgievsk (19 Aug.), Brest-Litovsk (25 Aug.), Grodno (2 Sep.), and Vilnius (18 Sep.).

2 Sep.   'The greatest victory of the war so far' Ludendorff claims, as he halts the Austro-German offensives. Russia has suffered

over a million casualties and been pushed out of the richest industrial and food-producing area of the Empire. But her decision to abandon Poland was based upon an historic and proven military strategy. Plant and war materials were systematically dismantled and transported to safe areas. A breathing space is created to enable a re-organisation of the Russian war economy that will eventually provide munitions and equipment in abundance. Ludendorff's primary objective of destroying Russia's military capacity had failed, and this would shortly be shown by Russia's continuing ability to mount threatening offensives.

27 Aug.– 12 Sep.	The Austrian Black Yellow Offensive. In an effort to sustain an independent rôle, Conrad launches an Austrian attack into the Ukraine. Its main result, at the cost of 300,000 casualties, is the total subordination of the Austrian army to the German High Command.
5 Sep.	Tsar Nicholas II takes over as Russian C-in-C. He orders a return to strict army discipline. By the end of the year, a series of small victories on all fronts has contained the Austro-German advance.
20 Oct.	German HQ is moved eastwards to Kovno.
6 Nov.	In a joint operation, the Russian army and Baltic fleet checks the German advance on the Baltic coast. Hindenburg threatens to resign if the Kaiser continues to demand resources for the Baltic theatre.
27 Dec.–19 Jan. 1917	The Russians fail to advance on a 90 mile front between the rivers Pruth and Dneister.

1916: Mixed fortunes

22 Feb.	The Tsar appoints 68-year-old General Alexei Kuropatkin as C-in-C Northern Front. He is renowned for loyalty rather than ability.
2 Mar.	Joffre asks Russia to launch an offensive to relieve France, which is reeling under the German assault on Verdun.
18 Mar.– 14 Apr.	The Russian Lake Naroch Offensive. Heavy casualties are incurred for no reward against strong German defences.
4 Apr.	General Alexei Brusilov appointed C-in-C Southern Front. The most able Russian general of the war, Brusilov orders his command to prepare for a May offensive based on his analysis of the tactics for breaching prepared defences.
20 May	Italy appeals to Russia for a diversionary offensive.
26 May	Brusilov tells Stavka that he can attack at a week's notice.

110

4 Jun.– 17 Oct.	The Brusilov Offensive. Brusilov's four armies only slightly out-number the defenders, but he orders all of them to advance simultaneously on a wide front, with minimum artillery preparation. The suddenness and breadth of the attack make it impossible for the Austrians to concentrate their reserves to seal up Russian breakthroughs. Within a month, Brusilov's armies penetrate 60 miles and capture 350,000 prisoners and 400 guns. The Austrian army is dealt a blow from which it never recovers.
6 Jun.	The Russians capture Lutsk.
10–16 Jun.	The Central Powers withdraw four divisions from the Verdun and Italian Fronts.
17 Jun.	The Russians take Czernowitz, capital of Bukovina.
24 Jun.–6 Jul.	The Battle of Kolomea. The Austrian 7th Army is driven out of Bukovina with the loss of 100,000 men. This success tempts Romania to join the Allies.
4 Jul.	The Ukraine Offensive. The Russian 3rd Army fails to take the important rail junction of Kovel, and encounters stiffening resistance from German reinforcements.
14 Jul.	The Battle of Baronovic. An attempt to extend the Russian front northwards is abandoned with the loss of 100,000 men.
28 Jul.	Brusilov resumes the offensive, capturing Brody. Although surprise has been lost, he is determined to fight on.
30 Jul.	Hindenburg and Ludendorff assume overall command of Austro-German forces as far south as Lemburg, despite Conrad's protests.
8 Aug.	The élite Russian Guards again fail to capture the Kovel rail junction. Russian Southern Command has become obsessed with capturing this objective to disrupt Austro-German supply lines. Huge casualties are sustained in persistent assaults though marshland that deadens Russian artillery and provides a suicidal barrier for attacking infantry.

Although Russian offensives continue into October, the Central Powers are able to stabilise the front, amassing reinforcements by using their superior rail network. The Russians are hampered by poor communications and by their commanders' stubborn refusal to apply Brusilov's tactical lessons. The impact of the Brusilov Offensive is to cripple both the Austrian and Russian armies. Austria ceases to play an independent rôle in the east, but Brusilov's victories have been won at the cost of a million Russian soldiers. Incompetent leadership, brutal discipline, starvation, and loss of faith in the regime have destroyed the survivors' will to fight on. However,

	Austria can be propped up by Germany, while Russia's allies have no direct means to sustain her.
29 Aug.	Hindenburg becomes German Chief of Staff with Ludendorff as his deputy. The new Command is determined to smash Russia and undertake major annexations of its territory.

The defeat of Romania

27 Aug.	Romania declares war. She immediately launches an invasion of Hungarian Transylvania. The Central Powers are taken by surprise, Kaiser Wilhelm II believing 'the war is lost'. But Romania is under the illusion that Russia will support her, and is unaware that the Brusilov offensive is already on the wane. Romania is vulnerable on all sides to attack by the Central Powers, and there is little the other Allies can do to assist her.
3 Sep.	Mackensen's Danube Army, made up of German, Bulgarian and Turkish contingents, invades Romanian Dobrudja in the south. Romania has failed to consider a Bulgarian attack. Russia only sends three divisions to assist.
6 Sep.	Falkenhayn's 9th Army is organised to halt the Romanian advance into Transylvania, where they have failed to press forward quickly enough to consolidate their positions.
15 Sep.	The Romanians are forced to transfer half of their forces in Transylvania southwards to stop Mackensen's advance.
19 Sep.	Falkenhayn's 9th Army advances into Transylvania re-taking Hermannstadt (Sibiu) (26 Sep.) and Kronstadt (Kluj) (8 Oct.). Romania requests French military assistance.
13 Oct.	Romanian forces abandon Transylvania.
19 Oct.	Mackensen breaks though in the south, taking the important oil and grain port of Constanza (22 October).
21 Nov.	Falkenhayn captures Craiova, opening the way to the Romanian capital Bucharest.
23 Nov.	In the south, Mackensen crosses the Danube.
5 Dec.	A British mission blows up the Romanian oil installations at Ploesti, to prevent them falling into German hands.
6 Dec.	The Fall of Bucharest. Mackensen enters the city on a white charger on his 67th birthday.
9 Dec.	Romania agrees to a temporary armistice. The Romanian government and army (having lost nearly half its strength) retreats to Jassy in the extreme north of the country, where, by January 1917, winter curtails further advances by the Central Powers.

The defeat of Romania is a godsend to the Central Powers and disaster for the Allies, who have been miserly in their military assistance. The Russians failed to commit enough troops, and the Salonika command was incapable of mounting a relief offensive to deflect the Bulgarians. At little military cost, the Central Powers have gained a million tons of oil and 2 million tons of grain, fuelling their war effort for 1918, and making a nonsense of the Allied blockade.

1917: Collapse of the Eastern Front

1 Mar.	Ars von Straussenberg appointed Austrian C-in-C to replace Conrad.
Mar.–Jul.	The February Revolution in Russia undermines the will of the Russian army. The Central Powers refrain from actions that might stimulate Russian patriotic defence, and begin a campaign of propaganda and fraternisation at the front.
16 May	Alexander Kerensky is appointed Russian War Minister. Convinced that the survival of the revolution depends on preventing defeat and occupation, he advocates a successful offensive to restore Russian morale, appoints Brusilov as C-in-C, and tours the front exhorting the soldiers to fight on.
1–18 Jul.	The Kerensky (Second Brusilov) Offensive. Russian armies attack on a 50 mile front towards Lemburg, winning early successes against the equally demoralised Austrian 2nd and 3rd Armies.
19 Jul.	A German counter-offensive using divisions withdrawn from the Western Front, smashes the Russian 11th Army, which flees in disarray, yielding thousands of prisoners.
23 Jul.	The Russians retreat on a 150 mile front. Only exhaustion of men and ammunition shortages curtails German pursuit.
22 Jul.–11 Sep.	Battles of Marasesti and Focsani. An Austro-German offensive attacks the remnants of the Romanian army. It pushes them and their Russian allies into a corner but fails to destroy them.
1–5 Sep.	The Capture of Riga. The Germans employ tactics devised by General Oskar von Hutier to mount a lightning assault on this important strategic port. The customary laborious preliminary bombardment that alerted the defenders to an impending attack is passed up in favour of a very short but intensive bombardment that used gas and smoke shells to confuse the enemy. There followed an assault by lightly armed and highly mobile infantry units, driving deep into and

beyond the enemy's front line, by-passing his strong points and wreaking chaos to supply and communications in the rear. The success of 'Hutier Tactics' leads to their adoption at Caporetto and the German Spring Offensives of 1918.

8 Dec.   All fighting on the Eastern Front is suspended following the October Revolution. The Romanians sign a cease-fire on 6 December.

5.4   THE ITALIAN FRONT

1915

26 Apr.   The Treaty of London commits Italy to a speedy offensive against Austria-Hungary, but her army is understrength, ill-equipped, and still exhausted from the war against Turkey. The Commander-in-Chief, Cadorna had been keen to fight France in August 1914, but the politicians keep him in the dark about the terms of the Treaty of London until a late stage. Mobilisation proceeds at a snail's pace, with considerable resistance from conscripts, who favoured neutrality.

23 May   Italy declares war on Austria-Hungary. Italy's mountainous frontier with Austria dictates that the only place for an Italian offensive is to the northeast of Venice along the line of the River Isonzo. An offensive here would assist Serbia, and also provide Italy with the opportunity to 'take back' territory long claimed by Italian nationalists.

27 May   General Boroevic, in command of the new Austrian 5th Army, begins to construct a strong defensive position along the River Isonzo.

23 Jun.–8 Jul.   The First Battle of the Isonzo. Proceeded by a week-long artillery bombardment, 200,000 Italians fling themselves against very strong defensive positions, making few gains.

18 Jul.–
8 Aug.   The Second Battle of the Isonzo replicates the first, setting the pattern for nine more Isonzo Offensives over the next three years against the 50 mile entrenched front that the Austrians have now built. Hundreds of thousands of Italian soldiers will die in repetitive assaults against virtually impregnable Austrian positions.

20 Aug.   Italy declares war on Turkey, and Bulgaria (10 Oct.).

21 Oct.–
3 Dec.   The Third and Fourth Battles of the Isonzo. The fully mobilised Italian army now outnumbers the defenders two to one, but once more, the Austrian line holds.

Nov.–Dec.   The defeat of Serbia eliminates one of the chief goals of Italian strategy – linking up with the Serbian army.

1916

12–29 Mar.	The Fifth Isonzo Offensive, fulfilling commitments to the Allies to relieve pressure on Verdun, bogs down in terrible weather conditions.
14 May– 10 Jun.	The Austrian Trentino Offensive. Bolstered by apparent Austro-German successes on the Eastern Front and the failure of the Italian March offensive, Conrad masses 400,000 troops for his first offensive of the war against Italy. His intention is to break though into the Italian plain north of Lake Garda, isolate the bulk of the Italian army facing the Isonzo, and knock Italy out of the war at a stroke. The plan is undermined by Germany's refusal to commit any troops to it.
14 May	The Austrian bombardment begins against Italian defenders who are outnumbered 4:1. By 29 May the Italians have been pushed back 8 miles to the plains beyond Asiago.
4 Jun.	Austrian disasters in the east (the Brusilov Offensive) prevent Conrad from reinforcing the Trentino attackers, and supply problems are causing them to run out of steam.
12 Jun.	The Italian government resigns after enemy troops invade Italian soil for the first time.
17 Jun.	Conrad calls off the Trentino Offensive after successful Italian counter-attacks and the need to send troops to the east.
6–17 Aug.	The Sixth Isonzo Offensive. Recovering from his fright at Trentino with great organisational skill and energy, Cadorna unleashes the most successful of his Isonzo campaigns, capturing Gorizia and advancing several miles against the demoralised Austrians.
28 Aug.	Italy declares war on Germany. In an ill-timed attempt to synchronise the Romanian declaration of war and the Russian Brusilov Offensive, Italy calls down upon herself the German military machine.
14 Sep.– 11 Nov.	The Seventh, Eighth and Ninth Isonzo Offensives. Cadorna fails to repeat his successes at Gorizia. By September 1917 he has only pushed the Italian line forward by 5 miles.

1917

14 May– 12 Sep.	The Tenth and Eleventh Isonzo Offensives. Negligible ground gained at great cost. However, the continuous Italian attacks have so drained Austrian manpower and morale that Ludendorff fears an eventual Italian breakthrough that would undermine the Central Powers.
24 Oct.– 12 Dec.	The Austro-German Caporetto Offensive. For the first time German troops are deployed on the Italian Front. Hutier's

115

	six divisions join Von Belew's 14th Army, employing again the tactics that brought him such success at Riga.
24 Oct.	The German assault takes the Italian centre completely by surprise and forces it back 15 miles, cutting off the bulk of the Italian army.
27 Oct.– 10 Nov.	The Italians retreat to the River Piave, 80 miles behind their original position, and only 20 miles north of Venice. As 600,000 men are lost, it is clear that Italian soldiers, having stoically endured two years of shortages and uncaring leadership, have reached the end of their tether.
30 Oct.	Vittorio Orlando the new Italian PM, announces an immediate programme to transform the conduct of the war, the economy and Italy's relationships with the Allies.
5–11 Nov.	The emergency Allied summit at Rapallo agrees to send French and British troops and equipment to prop up the Italian Front.
9 Nov.	Cadorna is dismissed as Italian Chief-of-Staff, to be replaced by General Armando Diaz.
11 Nov.– 30 Dec.	The Battles of the Piave. The Austro-German offensive is halted by stiffening Italian resistance, Austro-German supply problems, and growing Anglo-French reinforcements.

1918

23 Oct.– 4 Nov.	The Vittorio Veneto Offensive. After months of stalemate on the Piave, Diaz unleashes 57 divisions against the crumbling and retreating Austro-German armies with a view to strengthening Italy's negotiating position at the Peace Conference. 300,000 prisoners are taken and some of the territory lost in 1917 regained.

5.5 THE SERBIAN FRONT

1914: Austria-Hungary fails to subdue Serbia

28 Jul.	Austria declares war on Serbia and Austrian gun-boats bombard Belgrade from the River Danube.
11 Aug.	450,000 Austro-Hungarian troops invade northwest Serbia.
21 Aug.	The Serbs defeat the Austrians at the Jadar River, and drive them out of Serbian territory (25 Aug).
3 Sep.	Austria's defeat by Russia in Galicia eases pressure on the Serbs.

7 Sep.	A second Austrian invasion makes little headway. The Serbs invade Bosnia and attack Sarajevo.
15 Sep.	Serbian victory on the River Drina.
8 Nov.– 15 Dec.	The Austrians invade for a third time along an 80 mile front. Faced with superior Austrian numbers, the Serbian army conducts a planned withdrawal.
2 Dec.	The capture of Belgrade is hailed as a great victory in Vienna.
3–6 Dec.	Great Serbian victory at Kolubara River. The Austrians are forced back across the Drina.
15 Dec.	The Serbian army re-captures Belgrade and King Peter enters the city.

Austria's military plans were based on the assumption that Serbia could be crushed quickly and easily. Failure to achieve this was a crushing blow to Austrian morale. By the end of the year, the sacked Austrian General Potiorek had lost over 225,000 men without gaining an inch of Serbian territory. However, Serbia had also suffered 175,000 casualties and massive losses of equipment. For the next nine months, the Entente failed to use the breathing space won by Serbia's defiance to sustain its only ally in the Balkans. Serbia lay across the vital supply route from Berlin to Constantinople, and a further assault by the Central Powers was only a matter of time.

Serbia overwhelmed, The 'Great Retreat'

Aug.	Falkenhayn and Conrad agree to mount a joint attack upon Serbia.
6 Sep.	Bulgaria signs the Pless Convention committing her to join an attack on Serbia, for which Falkenhayn had already transferred troops from the Eastern Front. The Convention was a disaster for Britain and France, who had held back from aiding Serbia in order to appease Bulgaria.
23 Sep.	The Greek army mobilises. Greece was committed by the treaty of 1913 to aid Bulgaria with 150,000 men, but only if the Entente committed an equal number of troops.
5 Oct.	French troops land at Salonika, but they are 450 kilometres from Belgrade, and can do little to help the Serbs.
6 Oct.	300,000 German and Austrian troops invade Serbia. General Mackensen's battle-hardened veterans sweep away the Serbian army, which is ravaged by typhus and short of equipment.
9 Oct.	General Kovess captures Belgrade.
12 Oct.	Bulgaria invades Serbia from the east, cutting off Serbian forces from Salonika.

12 Oct.	The Entente calls upon Greece to aid Serbia under the Treaty of Bucharest, but Greece claims that the Entente has not committed enough troops to fulfil its conditions.
5 Nov.	The Germans capture Niš.
11 Nov.	45,000 French troops advance north from Salonika, but they make little progress against the Bulgarians, and fail to relieve pressure on the Serbs.
23 Nov.	The Serbian army begins 'The Great Retreat': 150,000 exhausted troops and civilians, led by the octogenarian General Putnik in a sedan-chair, retreat into the Montenegrin and Albanian mountains in appalling winter conditions.
Jan. 1916	Serbian survivors, ravaged by cold and disease, and rebuffed by the Italians in northern Albania, are evacuated to Corfu, which has been annexed by the French army for their reception. Henceforth the island became the headquarters of the Serbian government in exile.
	The Austrians occupy Montenegro.

5.6 THE MACEDONIAN (SALONIKA) FRONT

1915

23 Jan.	The Greek Prime Minister, Venizelos proposes an Allied landing in Greece to help Serbia. The French are very keen, but no decision is made.
9 Feb.	Britain provisionally agrees to commit one division to Salonika, which has a direct rail-link with Belgrade and would form a bridgehead to support Serbia.
19 Feb.	The Allies postpone a landing in Greece in favour of the Gallipoli expedition.
6 Sep.	Bulgaria agrees under the Pless Convention to join in an attack on Serbia.
24 Sep.	Britain and France agree to land troops at Salonika.
28 Sep.	Four French divisions under General Sarrail are ordered to the Aegean. Bulgaria has joined the Central Powers and a concerted attack on Serbia is imminent.
5 Oct.	Allied troops land at Salonika in defiance of the wishes of King Constantine of Greece, and begin to establish a vast fortified base.
6 Oct.	The Central Powers mount a concerted invasion of Serbia.
11 Nov.	An offensive by the Salonika garrison fails to save the Serbs, whose defeat makes the Salonika force strategically irrelevant. However, its size steadily increased to 600,000 by the end of

the war. The Central Powers do not attempt to dislodge it, believing it to be an 'Internment Camp' tying up allied troops that would otherwise be used elsewhere.

1916

11 Jan.	The French set up a refuge on Corfu to replenish the defeated Serbian army, but when it is ready for action, Greece refuses to allow it to cross overland to Salonika.
Mar.	80,000 Serbian troops arrive in Salonika from Corfu. They prove effective when attempting to regain national territory, but reluctant to fight elsewhere.
Apr.	The fortified zone surrounding the Allied enclave is completed.
26 May	Greece surrenders Fort Ruppel, the most important strongpoint of Eastern Macedonia.
3 Jun.	A 'State of Siege' proclaimed in Salonika. General Sarrail finds himself increasingly in dispute with the Greek Royal government and embroiled in Greek politics.
10–18 Aug.	The Battle of Florina. A planned allied offensive is pre-empted by the Central Powers, who force the Serbs to relinquish their recaptured Ostrovo enclave. This failure proves a disaster for the Romanians, who are about to join the war and need a relieving offensive to distract the Bulgarians.
25 Aug.	The Bulgarians take Seres.
13 Sep.–15 Dec.	The Monastir Offensive. The allies advance on a wide front in an attempt to regain territory lost a month earlier, but French, British and Serb efforts are uncoordinated. Little progress is made, apart from the recapture of Monastir (19 Nov.) Bad weather eventually forces the return of stalemate.
14 Sep.	The Greek garrison surrenders Kavalla to the Bulgarians and Germans. This is the last straw for the Allies, who decide to disarm the Greek Royalist forces (see, pp. 190–4).

1917

Jan.	General Sarrail given overall control of Allied forces in Salonika.
11–22 Mar.	The Lake Prespa Offensive. Prompted by the need to relieve pressure on the Western Front, the Allies again attempt a northward advance. No ground is gained. There are 14,000 Allied casualties, and the Allies almost lose Monastir.
May	Mutinies in the Russian contingent at Salonika, prompted by the February Revolution. These spread to French units. The resultant lowering of morale in the Allied camp precludes further offensive action until the autumn of 1918.

119

| 29 Jun. | Greece declares war on the Central Powers. |
| 13 Dec. | General Marie Guillaumat replaces Sarrail at Salonika, marking an improvement in inter-allied relations. |

1918

8 Jun.	Guillaumat is replaced by Franchet d'Esperey, who energetically pushes forward with plans for an offensive against the Bulgarians, who are demoralised by the withdrawal of German troops from their territory.
Jul.	Nine Greek divisions (250,000 men) join the Allied armies in northern Greece.
15 Sep.–4 Nov.	The Allied Vardar Offensive.
18 Sep.	Anglo-Greek forces take positions around Lake Doiran, and advance northwards in conjunction with the Serbian army.
25 Sep.	Franchet d'Esperey refuses a Bulgarian cease-fire offer.
26 Sep.	Strumica falls to General Milne.
29 Sep.	The French enter Skopje.
30 Sep.	Bulgaria surrenders.
1 Nov.	Serbian troops re-occupy Belgrade.
4 Nov.	Allied troops reach the Danube, as Austria-Hungary capitulates.

5.7 THE GALLIPOLI CAMPAIGN

The Gallipoli Campaign of 1915 was a response to the ruinous blow of Turkey's entry into the war on the side of the Central Powers. It was the brainchild of the 'Easterners', those Allied politicians and strategists who thought the stalemate in the west could be broken by opening up another front against weaker members of the Central Powers. Until Britain had gathered enough strength to play her full part on the Western Front, she should use her strongest asset – sea power – to force the narrow Straits linking the Black Sea to the Mediterranean. The rewards for success would be enormous. Turkey would collapse. Supply routes would be reopened to prop up the faltering war effort of Imperial Russia. Such a blow would be dealt to the prestige of the Central Powers that the small Balkan states would be convinced that their future lay with the Entente.

1914

| 20 Aug. | Greece offers 60,000 troops for a joint invasion of Turkey, but Britain still hopes that Turkey will stay neutral, and does not wish to alienate Turkey or the other Balkan neutral, Bulgaria. |

2 Nov.	On Churchill's orders Admiral Carden's squadron bombards the Turkish outer-fortresses in the Straits. The largely fortuitous success of this action makes Churchill believe that the Straits can be forced by naval action alone.
5 Nov.	Turkey joins the war on the side of the Central Powers.

1915

Jan.	Russia warns that it is about to collapse in the Caucasus, and appeals to the Entente for a relieving operation. (These claims are subsequently seen to be alarmist, and designed to strengthen Russia's bargaining position in her diplomatic offensive to gain Constantinople.)
13 Jan.	Churchill wins Cabinet approval for an offensive against Turkey, after putting an optimistic gloss on Admiral Carden's luke-warm endorsement of the effectiveness of naval action in the Straits.
28 Jan.	The War Council formally authorises an action to begin on 19 February.
16 Feb.	A British infantry division is put on standby for the eastern Mediterranean, and Australian and New Zealand Forces in Egypt are also put on alert.
19 Feb.– 23 Mar.	**The failure of the naval bombardment.**
19 Feb.	French and British battleships begin a systematic bombardment of Turkish fortifications. After initial success, they find that Turkish minefields and mobile howitzers make it impossible to come close enough in-shore to be effective.
25 Feb.	A second bombardment of the Dardanelles forts.
5 Mar.	The British Dreadnought *Queen Elizabeth* is pulled out of range of Turkish shore batteries, because the navy is not prepared to put their most modern battleship at risk. It is later revealed that her guns had done serious damage to the fortifications, and the Turks were having serious ammunition shortages.
8 Mar.	The Turks lay a drifting minefield that remains undetected by Allied vessels.
10 Mar.	British minesweepers are again unable to clear the way for large warships to get near enough to their targets.
10 Mar.	France commits 18,000 colonial troops to support the naval operation.
18 Mar.	The most significant Allied attempt to force the Straits ends in disaster. The French battleships *Gaulois* and *Bouvet* and the British warship *Ocean* are sunk by mines, and the *Irresistible*

121

and *Inflexible* seriously damaged. The bombardment is halted and the fleet withdrawn out of range.

23 Mar. Churchill tells the Cabinet that the naval commander, Admiral de Robeck, believes it is too dangerous to risk capital ships in the Straits, and that the attempt to force the Straits by naval action alone has failed. The need for ground troops is now recognised.

The Gallipoli Landings

23 Feb. General Liman von Sanders warns Enver Pasha, who has drawn up plans to withdraw from the Gallipoli Peninsular, of the disasters that would follow an unopposed Allied landing. Liman is subsequently given responsibility to strengthen Turkish defences.

12 Mar. General Sir Ian Hamilton is given a British Mediterranean Expeditionary Force of 75,000, initially comprising mainly Australian and New Zealand troops. Hamilton is surprised by his appointment, and takes up his post with no clear plan of action.

25 Mar. Liman von Sanders, takes formal control of the Gallipoli defences. Allied indecision and delay has given him several weeks to build up his forces.

27 Mar. Hamilton and de Robeck decide to land troops on the Gallipoli Peninsula.

25 Apr. The Allies land at Helles on the southern tip of the Gallipoli Peninsular and Gaba Tepe on the Aegean coast (Anzac Cove). Inappropriate equipment, uncoordinated planning, lack of initiative by commanders, and unexpectedly fierce resistance by the Turks stops them from advancing inland. They never succeed in expanding their precarious and vulnerable beachheads.

28 Apr. The Allies fail to take Krithia in the first of a series of assaults designed to drive the Turks off the high ground and take the commanding hill of Achi Baba.

6–8 May A second attack on Krithia fails with heavy casualties.

18–25 May A Turkish counter-attack fails to dislodge the Allies from Anzac Cove. The British government for the first time debates the possibility of evacuation.

4 Jun. A third British attack on Krithia fails.

7 Jun. The Dardanelles Committee meets for the first time in London. Churchill persuades Kitchener, hitherto sceptical about the campaign, to commit three new British divisions, which are sent to Gallipoli to prepare for a major offensive.

28 Jun.–5 Jul.	A major Allied assault on Achi Baba fails. It is renewed without success from 12 Jul.
6–10 Aug.	The Suvla Bay Offensive fails to make progress.
21 Aug.	Renewed British attacks against Scimitar Hill are foiled by Mustafa Kemal. Kitchener supports General Sarrail's plan for joint landings on the Asiatic shore, but Joffre refuses to divert troops from the Western Front.
11 Oct.	Kitchener tells Hamilton that the British government is considering evacuation.
14 Oct.	Hamilton is sacked after making a defeatist report to the Dardanelles Committee.
28 Oct.	Hamilton's replacement, General Monro, recommends withdrawal.
3 Nov.	Kitchener, now determined to continue the expedition, goes to Gallipoli intending to sanction a renewed naval attack. Having seeing for himself the Allies' hopeless strategic position, he recommends evacuation (15 Nov.).
7 Dec.	The British government orders the evacuation of all three beachheads.
10 Dec.	A gradual and surreptitious withdrawal from Anzac Cove and Suvla Bay gets under way, under the noses of 100,000 Turkish troops.
19–20 Dec.	The last 20,000 men are successfully taken off the beaches.

1916

8–9 Jan.	A brilliant night-time final evacuation from Helles is completed. Despite rough seas, there are again extraordinarily light casualties.

This imaginative and possibly war-winning idea had proved to be a disaster for the Allied cause. 480,000 troops had been taken from the Western Front and had achieved nothing. Vast stores of equipment had fallen into the hands of the enemy. Far from breaking and demoralising the Turks, their great victory at Gallipoli (despite at least 250,000 casualties) restored national pride after the humiliation of the Balkan Wars, and stiffened Turkish will to resist. Conversely the campaign was a blow for the prestige of the British army, and left a legacy of resentment in the ANZAC contingent, which had suffered nearly 34,000 casualties, that damaged the unity of the Empire. The Allied failure helped convince Bulgaria to join the Central Powers, and stiffened the resolve of the pro-German Greek Royal Family to resist the advances of the Entente.

5.8 THE WAR AT SEA

1914

3 Aug.	The German *Mittelmeerdivsion* bombards the French North African ports of Bône and Philippeville. Depite this, French reinforcements from North Africa are transported to the continent without loss, as is the British Expeditionary Force.
Aug.	The Declaration of London. Britain declares it will abide by the London Naval Conference of 1909, which exempted from confiscation the property, apart from contraband, of a belligerent state. Nonetheless Britain puts into operation the 'Distant Blockade' which cuts off all direct imports to Germany.
5 Aug.	Britain severs the marine telegraph cable linking Germany and the US.
10 Aug.	The German battleships *Goeben* and *Breslau* arrive in Constantinople, having eluded the allied fleets.
26 Aug.	Britain obtains Code Books that the Russians have captured from a German ship, enabling Britain to break the German naval codes and initiate the activities of 'Room 40'.
28 Aug.	The Battle of Heligoland Bight. After three German ships are sunk by the Royal Navy. The Kaiser orders his fleet commanders to ask his permission before engaging in future combat.
7 Sep.	German Commerce Raiders. The German cruiser *Emden* sinks nine ships in the Sumatra Channel. Later in the month, *Königsberg* attacks Zanzibar, *Emden* bombards Madras, and *Karlsruhe* and *Dresden* sink many British merchant ships off the coast of Brazil. In October *Emden* sinks the Russian cruiser *Zhemchug* off Penang.
22 Sep.	The torpedoeing of three British warships forces Admiral Jellicoe to withdraw the British fleet to the west coast of Scotland and the north of Ireland until its bases are better protected.
1 Oct.	Turkey closes the Black Sea Straits to Allied ships.
29 Oct.	*Goeben* bombards Russian Black Sea ports.
1 Nov.	The Battle of Coronel. Admiral Spee sinks the outgunned British cruisers *Monmouth* and *Good Hope*.
7 Nov.	The German naval base of Tsingtao surrenders to the Japanese.
9 Nov.	*Emden* is sunk by the cruiser *Sydney* off the Cocos Islands.
8–9 Dec.	The Battle of Falkland Islands. Admiral Sturdee sinks the *Scharnhorst, Gneisenau, Leipzig*, and *Nürnberg*; effectively ending the threat of German surface vessels to Allied shipping.

21 Dec.	The French battleship *Jean Bart* is torpedoed by an Austrian submarine in the Adriatic.

1915

24 Jan.	The Battle of Dogger Bank. Britain sinks the German cruiser *Blücher* forcing the German High Seas Fleet to remain in port for the rest of the year.
4 Feb.	Unrestricted submarine warfare (USW). Germany declares the waters around Great Britain to be a 'War Zone' and begins to sink merchant ships without warning. On 18 February the US warns Germany that she will be accountable for loss of American lives and property.
11 Mar.	The Reprisals Order. Britain responds to the German submarine campaign with an attempt to destroy German trade completely. All neutrals, including the United States, are banned from trading with Germany. Neutral harbours are blockaded and neutral shipping intercepted and taken to British ports.
18 Mar.	Bombarding the Dardanelles. The loss of Allied warships to Turkish mines causes the Allies to abandon the idea of defeating Turkey by sea-power alone.
28 Mar.	An American citizen dies on the torpedoed British liner *Falaba*.
7 May	A German submarine sinks the liner *Lusitania*. 1201 people are killed, including 124 Americans.
19 Aug.	The British liner *Arabic* is sunk, with the loss of more American lives.
Sep.	The Otranto Barrage. A line of linked block-ships and mine-fields is designed to seal the Austrian and German vessels in the Adriatic. However, submarines from the bases at Pola and Kotor have little difficulty getting through.
1 Sep.	The *Arabic* Pledges. In response to American protests, Germany agrees to follow 'cruiser rules' – warning passenger vessels before sinking them. All U-boat action in the Channel and the Western Approaches is suspended. On 6 October the German Ambassador in the US renounces the sinkings and offers an indemnity.
Dec.	Falkenhayn's Christmas Memorial. The German C-in-C argues in favour of a new submarine offensive.

1916

Jan.	Reinhard Scheer takes over the German High Seas Fleet. He is in favour of more aggressive naval action above and below the oceans.

29 Feb.	The Ministry of Blockade in Britain issues a blacklist of firms with whom transactions are forbidden. The Ministry's task is to prevent neutral ships from trading with the enemy, to ration imports into neutral countries, and to prevent them being passed on to the enemy.
3 Mar.	The Kaiser decides not to order the resumption of USW.
23 Mar.	Sinking of the Channel ferry *Sussex* with great loss of life.
25 Apr.	German ships bombard Lowestoft on the east coast of England.
4 May	The '*Sussex* Pledge'. Germany promises the United States to apply 'cruiser rules' to merchantmen as well as liners, but says she may resume unrestricted sinking in the future.
31 May–1 Jun.	The Battle of Jutland. A limited engagement between the main British and German battle-fleets in the North Sea. Britain loses more ships, but the German fleet never attempts to engage again.
7 Jul.	Britain cancels its commitment to the 1914 Declaration of London.
29 Aug.	The new German Third Supreme Command believes that USW must be resumed. Chancellor Bethmann Hollweg knows that this will bring the US into the war. He wins the argument at Pless on 31 August but for the rest of 1916 he fights a losing battle to stop the High Command getting its way.

1917

9 Jan.	German High Command and the Kaiser, persuaded by The Holzendorff Memorandum (22 Dec. 1916) decide to resume unrestricted submarine warfare. The German Chief of Naval Staff argues that if Germany launched a USW campaign without warning, U-boats could starve Britain within five months, before America had time to make an impact on the war.
1 Feb.	The final German USW campaign begins.
Apr.	U-boats sink 881,000 tons of Allied shipping (compared with 386,000 tons in January 1917).
6 Apr.	USA declares war on Germany, hugely enhancing Allied naval power.
10 May	Britain introduces the 'convoy system', which causes a dramatic drop in Allied ship losses.
15 May	The Battle of the Otranto Straits. In the largest wartime naval engagement in the Mediterranean Austro-Hungarian warships fail to break the Otranto Barrage.

1918

22 Apr.	Failure of British attempt to block Zeebrugge and Ostend. On 10 May a second attack on Ostend fails.
22–25 Apr.	The last sortie of the High Seas Fleet. Admiral Scheer sails into the North Sea to attack British convoys and to try to cut off elements of the British fleet, but as at Jutland, the main fleets miss each other.
Jul.–Oct.	The Northern Barrage is built from the Orkneys to the coast of Norway. 69,000 mines are laid, many of them recently invented American magnetic ones, but it is easily evaded by U-boats.
Jul.	Failure of German attempts to prevent the transport of US troopships. Not a single American soldier dies at sea, and Allied counter-measures make U-boats extremely vulnerable.
25 Oct.	Admiral Scheer recalls the U-boats to port.
30 Oct.	Scheer's plan for a 'last heroic attack' is thwarted by mutinies in the High Seas Fleet.
22 Nov.	The German High Seas Fleet sails out to be interned at Scapa Flow, where it is later scuttled.

HOME FRONTS

6.1 AUSTRIA-HUNGARY

1914

Mar.

The Austrian *Reichsrat* is suspended because of the violent behaviour of German, Czech and Socialist deputies. It does not meet again until 1917.

28 Jul.

Austria declares war on Serbia.

30 Jul.

The traditional ban on Sunday working revoked.

Jul.–Aug.

The War Production Law (of 25 July 1912) is put immediately into force. Alone of all the belligerent states, Austria-Hungry has in place from the outset legislation enabling organisation for total war. However, the prior existence of the legal apparatus is offset by the extraordinary complexity of the Imperial structure, the limitations of government, and traditional Habsburg *Schlamperei* (easy-going sloppiness):

- Factories important to the war effort placed under military law, and workforces paid a tiny military wage.
- Railways are taken over by the state, and civilian travel banned.
- All production requisitioned at fixed prices.
- All men under the age of 50 declared unfit for military duty are liable for war production.
- Workers under 50 forbidden to quit their employment, and liable to be directed into employment at the government's discretion.
- Industrial action liable to fines, imprisonment, transfer to the front, or to the *Landsturm* list on reduced pay.
- Factories where workers demanded change were 'militarised' (i.e. placed under army discipline). The army, convinced the war will be short, strips the factories of essential workers, devastating industrial production. The Austrian Kroner falls 240% on the Viennese Exchange.

5 Aug.

Austria declares war on Russia. Reservists must report to their units. Mobilisation of the 15 different nationalities comprising the Austro-Hungarian army proceeds with surprising efficiency. Observers like Sigmund Freud report a wave of loyalty to the Emperor, and a feeling that the cause is just.

Aug.–Dec.

The war goes badly. Russia occupies a third of all arable land in the Austrian half of the Empire, drastically cutting supplies of grains and oil. The drain of farm labour to the

	armed forces dramatically reduces agricultural production, although most of the 1914 harvest has been gathered in.
Oct.	10,000 horses butchered to alleviate the food shortage caused by the call-up of farm labourers and the loss of the grain-producing province of Galicia.
	Repeal of a 1911 law banning women from night work. Throughout the war, the government urges industry to employ women. By 1916, 42.5% of labourers in heavy industry in Vienna will be female, in contrast to 17.5% in 1913.
Dec.	It is decreed that wheat flour must be mixed with barley, rye, corn and potato meal.

1915

Jan.–Feb.	The military situation improves.
13 Jan.	Istvan Burian replaces Berchtold as foreign minister.
Apr.	Ration cards for the 'war bread' are introduced in Vienna and other towns. Cards and vouchers for coffee, fat, milk and sugar follow shortly, and two 'meatless days' a week are ordered.
Apr.	The Prague Infantry Battalion deserts to the Russians, and the pro-Russian opposition leader Karel Kramar is arrested. The loyalty of the army's 15 nationalities begins to loosen under the stress of war.
15 Apr.	The age limit for recruits is raised to 50, but many able-bodied men continue to avoid the draft. Government never solves the problem of balancing scarce manpower between the army and war production.
Easter	Manifesto of the Austrian–German Parties (apart from the Social Democrats) calling for Austria to become a unitary German state. Non-German regions of Dalmatia and Galicia should be given to the Poles and the Italians.
30 Apr.	The formation of a Yugoslav Committee sparks little response from Slavs within the Empire.
2 May–25 Jun.	Austria recaptures the important Galician oilfields during the Gorlice–Tarnow offensive. Although the retreating Russians burn 75% of their facilities, production is restored in June. However, Germany requisitions most of Austria's production, and there are shortages of oil and other raw materials for the rest of the war.
11 May	Women loot food stores in Vienna.
23 May	Italy's declaration of war confronts the Empire with a new enemy committed to breaking it up and to exploiting the grievances of its minorities.

May	War State Bonds worth 2.2 billion are issued, but loans do not begin to cover war costs, and the Empire is dependent upon German subsidies of 100 million marks a month.
Jun.	The Army War Supervisory Office brings back an 1803 law giving the State the right to seize the property of deserters and dissidents. Military interference in civilian life increases.
27 Aug.– 25 Sep.	The 'Black-Yellow' Offensive in Galicia fails.
Sep.	Relations between Austria and Hungary deteriorate. Istvan Tisza (Magyar PM since 1913) suspends the Austro-Hungarian customs union, and refuses to export Hungarian grain. He demands the call up of 384,598 men from the Austrian half of the Empire, saying that Hungary is bearing a disproportionate war burden.
Oct.	Women protesting against shortages and profiteers attack government buildings in Linz.
6 Oct.– 21 Nov.	Austria helps to conquer Serbia. But Germany expropriates two-thirds of Serbian production.
Nov.	On the Italian Front, officers demand that German be used as the language of command to prevent fraternisation, but the government deems this politically unacceptable.
10 Nov.	Conrad demands the removal of 'foreigners' and potentially subversive civilians from a 15 mile military zone along the borders of Serbia.
Dec.	The war has cost 20 to 22 billion. In New York, the Kroner has fallen to 40% of its pre-war value.

Austro-Hungarian casualties by the end of 1915

	Killed	Wounded	Sick	Missing*	Total
Officers	10,238	22,503	30,372	11,642	74,755
Men	377,022	978,423	853,379	906,379	3,115,203

*Mainly taken prisoner

1916

1 Jan.	The government raises the price of bread and flour, but food riots force it to back down.
May–Jul.	Military disasters. Conrad's Trentino Offensive fails. The Russian Brusilov Offensive shatters the Austrian army in Galicia.
May	Desperate for manpower, the army calls up the class of 1898 ahead of schedule, and hurries convalescent soldiers back into combat. One and a half million men are recruited, but

	there are still a million men of military age in war industries, and 13 million in the inefficient agricultural sector.
May	Daylight saving time introduced to save fuel.
Aug.	The emergence of the German Third Supreme Command increases German dominance over Austria-Hungary.
	The 1916 harvest is very poor. Hungary holds back corn from the Austrian half of the Empire. Peasants and local bodies hoard produce and refuse to sell at the government's fixed prices. Steam-powered harvesters run out of coal. Flour rations are cut to 120 grams per week, and potatoes to 118 (493 grams in 1914). Wage Commissions are brought in to peg wages to the cost of living.
Sep.	The German Ambassador reports to Berlin that the Dual Monarchy is bankrupt, demoralised, and divided. He doubts its ability to continue the war.
4 Oct.	Romania is defeated by the Central Powers, but the collapse of the rail network prevents Austria-Hungary getting her share of the spoils of victory (as had been the case after the conquest of Poland, Romania, Serbia and Albania). By 1916, the Empire has received only 37% of the anticipated spoils of conquest.
Oct.	Oil production is put under limited state control, but refineries left in private hands.
21 Oct.	The son of the Socialist leader Victor Adler assassinates Count Carl Stürgkh, the Austrian Prime Minister. The trial becomes an indictment of the regime.
29 Oct.	Ernst von Körber is appointed Austrian Premier.
5 Nov.	A new Kingdom of Poland is set up by the Central Powers ending Austrian dreams of incorporating Poland into the Empire. Germany dominates the new state.
21 Nov.	The Emperor Franz Josef dies. The loyalty of many 'minority' citizens dissolves with the end of his 68-year reign.
2 Dec.	The new Emperor Karl (grand nephew of Franz Josef) is committed to liberal reform, with more autonomy for minority nations. Despite his lack of military experience or organisational talent, Karl takes personal control of the army, sacks many officers, and attempts to curb army's interference in the economy and civilian life.
Dec.	Karl replaces Körber with the more reform-minded Clam Martinic.

1917

4 Jan.	Karl moves army headquarters to the resort of Baden, close to Vienna, but far from the fighting.

27 Feb.	Conrad von Hötzendorf is replaced as Chief of the General Staff by Arz Von Straussenberg, who is more in tune with the Emperor's desire for change. Karl limits the use of poison gas and the bombing of civilian targets. He relaxes the army's harsh disciplinary codes, further undermining the cohesion of the army at a time of increasing nationalist agitation in the ranks.
27 Feb.	A Joint Food Committee is appointed for the whole Empire, but Hungary continues to sell grain to the army, while civilians in the Austrian half of the Empire starve.
Mar.	Wages and Complaints Commissions appointed to regulate industrial relations. They prove to be toothless bodies dominated by the army. Workers are still forbidden to hold meetings in strategically important industries.
16 Mar.	Foreign minister Czernin tells Bethmann that Austria-Hungary was 'at the end of her strength', desperately short of food, manpower and raw materials. The Central Powers must agree on the terms of an acceptable general peace immediately.
1 May	The Council of State calls for an independent Poland.
23 May	The Emperor dismisses conservative Hungarian Prime Minister Istvan Tisza after meeting radical Magyar leaders, but fails to secure a wider franchise in Hungary or more rights to the Slavs. A last opportunity to reconcile the Slav population is lost.
24 May	Nearly 50,000 workers strike in the Vienna arsenal, the Skoda arms factory, and other war-production factories. Many strikers call for an end to the war, but are forced back to work at gunpoint.
31 May	The Austrian *Reichsrat* convenes for the first time since 1914. There is criticism of the war effort, but few calls for the end of the Empire. South Slav *Reichstag* deputies of the Yugoslav Club call for South Slav independence under the Habsburgs.
2 Jul.	The *Reichsrat* is outraged when Karl amnesties Czech nationalists, including leaders Karel Kramar, Alois Rasin and Vaclav Klofac, but strong momentum is given to Czech separatism.
2 Jul.–15 Aug.	Failure of the last major Russian offensives on the Eastern Front.
8 Jul.	Strategically important factories put under military law, with their workforces conscripted in to the *Landsturm*. The working week set at 52.2 hours.
20 Jul.	The Corfu Declaration proclaims the unity of Serb, Croat and Slovene peoples.

Aug.	A ministerial memorandum entitled *Possibilities of Our Lasting Through the Winter of 1917/18* paints a pessimistic picture of the Empire's chances. Tisza's successor, Esterhazy is sacked.
8 Sep.	Italy says that it is committed to the principle of Yugoslav independence, striking a blow at prospects for the Empire's survival.
21 Sep.	Vienna welcomes the Papal peace plan, proposing freedom of the seas, disarmament and arbitration.
Oct.–Dec.	The successful Caporetto Offensive on the Italian Front.
Nov.	War production is to be doubled with huge investments and German loans. This comes too late to save the Empire. Lack of steel has reduced rail freight by 50% from the previous year, and the city of Vienna is getting only 10% the 300 food wagons a day it needs to avoid starvation.
7 Dec.	The United States declares war on Austria.
10 Dec.	The battleship *Wien* is sunk by the Italians, demoralising the civilian population.

1918

Jan.	President Wilson and David Lloyd George back autonomy within Empire rather than its dissolution.
13 Jan.	A cut in the flour ration leads to widespread food riots. Arms production falls below 1914 levels.
15–16 Jan.	General strikes in favour of peace in Vienna, Prague and Budapest.
22 Jan.	Peace with the Ukraine raises hopes of obtaining Ukrainian grain, but Germany monopolises supplies.
1–3 Feb.	Naval mutiny at Cattaro (Kotor) in the Adriatic. The sailors publish a manifesto demanding an end to the war, but give in when German U-boats threaten to sink any Austrian war-ship that attempts to put to sea.
3 Mar.	The Brest-Litovsk Treaty ends the war with Russia. Austro-Hungarian prisoners begin return home imbued with Bol-shevik ideas, but enthusiasm for national independence outweighs socialist fervour. Food for the army is so short that soldiers in their early fifties are sent home.
30 Apr.	Austrian troops seize barges on the Danube conveying Roma-nian grain to Germany. The ensuing diplomatic row ends with Germany being given exclusive right to Ukrainian wheat.
May	Riots and mutinies spread through the Imperial Army, par-ticularly in non-German units.

12 May	Emperor Karl is forced to go to the German headquarters at Spa to apologise for his peace approaches to the Allies the previous year. In his weakness he is browbeaten into accepting complete German military and economic superiority, and commits himself to mobilising the entire Empire for total war in the image of the Hindenburg Plan.
May–Aug.	Factories producing steel for of the key Prague Iron Industry Society are shut down because of coal shortage.
10–22 Jun.	Failure of the final Austro-Hungarian offensive against Italy on the River Piave.
24 Jul.	New Prime Minister Max von Hussarek is ordered to draw up a federal structure for the Empire.
15 Aug.	Foreign Minister Czernin is dismissed when his peace overtures of 1917 are exposed by French PM Clemenceau. Burian replaces him.
4 Oct.	Germany and Austria-Hungary ask President Wilson to mediate a peace settlement.
16 Oct.	The Emperor's Manifesto proposing a federal reorganisation of the Empire. This falls short of nationalist aspirations, and the architect of the plan, Prime Minister Hussarek resigns on 28 October.
18 Oct.	Hungary proclaims its independence.
20 Oct.	President Wilson again declares his support for independent nations within the Monarchy.
28 Oct.	A provisional German–Austrian government is set up in Vienna under Karl Renner.
28 Oct.	Czechoslovakia proclaims its independence from Vienna.
29 Oct.	The Croatian Diet proclaims independence.
30 Oct.	The Austrian army withdraws from Italian territory.
1 Nov.	The Italians sink the Austro-Hungarian battleship *Viribus Unitis*.
3 Nov.	Austria-Hungary signs an Armistice with the Allies.
12 Nov.	Karl I abdicates in Austria and, next day, in Hungary.
1 Dec.	The Kingdom of Serbs, Croats and Slovenes proclaimed, comprising former Habsburg territory in Slovenia, Croatia, Hungary and Bosnia.

6.2 GERMANY

1914

4 Aug.	Addressing the German Parliament (*Reichstag*), Kaiser Wilhelm II declares 'Germany goes to war with a clear conscience. I know no parties any more, only Germans.'

137

All interests declare a *Burgfriede* (Fortress Peace). Buoyed by the 'spirit of 1914', the Socialists vote for war credits. Trade unions renounce strikes for the duration of the war.

Under a special enabling act, the *Reichstag* delegates its legislative powers to the *Bundesrat* (the Constitutional Upper House). None of the 800 emergency decrees promulgated by this un-elected body during the next four years was rejected by *Reichstag* deputies, who met to rubber-stamp war funding every six months.

Under the Prussian Law of Siege (incorporated into the Imperial Constitution of 1871), executive power passes into the hands of the Deputy Commanding Generals of the country's twenty-four Military Districts. Responsible directly to the Emperor, these officers wield dictatorial powers over recruitment, training, supply, and requisitioning, and over civilian matters such as transport, public order, and the Press. Civilian officials are legally subordinated to the Commanding Generals. The overlapping boundaries of civilian and military rule provided a recipe for administrative chaos and economic dislocation.

8 Aug. KRA, The Department of War Raw Materials (*Kriegsrohstoffarbteilung*) is set up by the War Ministry under Walther Rathenau, director of the giant industrial cartel, AEG. Like other belligerents, Germany is completely unprepared for a long war. Although Rathenau improves arms production, private vested interests obstruct KRA efforts to modify the free market. Neither Rathenau nor the War Ministry has the power to coerce big business or the army.

9 Sep. The September Programme. Believing that victory is in sight, Chancellor Bethmann Hollweg sets out the demands that Germany will make upon her defeated neighbours. War aims will become a divisive issue in German politics (see p. 210).

1915

4 Feb. Germany sets up a 'war zone' around the British Isles within which merchant vessels, including neutrals, will be sunk without warning.

May The sinking of the liner *Lusitania* outrages public opinion in the United States.

23 Jun. The SDP Manifesto demands a negotiated peace.

12 Jul. The coal industry is put under state regulation.

19 Aug. Bethmann tells the *Reichstag* that Germany will never restore Poland to Russia. Divisions over German war aims are beginning to threaten the political consensus.

8 Sep.	Germany gives an undertaking that her submarines will cease attacking merchant shipping.
Dec.	The Centre Party leader Peter Spahn, demands territorial acquisitions to safeguard Germany's future security. All the non-Socialist parties concur with his declaration.

1916

Jan.	Bethmann persuades the Emperor to promise reform of the Prussian Constitution in order to bolster the *Burgfrieden* and conciliate the Socialists.
Feb.–Jun.	Germany suffers half a million casualties in the Verdun offensives.
Feb.	The bread ration is cut from 8 to 7 ounces.
Mar.	Eighteen deputies who had voted against war credits form a breakaway parliamentary group.
20 Apr.	A U-boat sinks the passenger liner *Sussex*, causing America to threaten the breaking of diplomatic relations. Bethmann reacts by ordering unrestricted submarine warfare to be suspended, prompting a crisis with the Conservatives.
Jul.–Oct.	The Battle of the Somme. Germany holds the line, but suffers huge casualties.
27 Aug.	Romania enters the war, posing a grave threat to the survival of Austria-Hungary. Falkenhayn's failure to predict this combined with the failure of his futile Verdun campaign and the carnage on the Somme decides Falkenhayn's enemies to move against him.
29 Aug.	The 'Third Supreme Command'. The Kaiser replaces Falkenhayn as Chief of General Staff by the popular Paul von Hindenburg with Erich Ludendorff as Chief Quartermaster-General. The Conservatives believe that Hindenburg will prosecute the war more ruthlessly and effectively, while Bethmann supports Hindenburg believing that Hindenburg's appointment will soften right wing opposition to peace negotiations.

The Hindenburg programme

Military setbacks have exposed the failure of the the 25 departments (KRA) which purport to control every aspect of the economic war. In fact, the KRA has become a tool of the industrialist themselves, who use its powers to maximise their profits and create inefficient cartels that fail to match the productive achievement of Germany's enemies.

In August, the High Command announces ambitious plans to mobilise Germany for total war. An able technocrat, General Wilhelm Groener is put

139

in charge of a Supreme War Office (*Kriegsamt*), charged with implementing the programme. The new War Minister Hermann von Stein, is at last given powers to control the Deputy Commanding Generals of the Military Districts.

- All 'non-essential' industries will be shut down by the spring of 1917.
- Stockpiles of munitions will be doubled, and production of artillery and machine guns tripled.
- 300,000 more workers will be drafted into munitions production.

This ruthless and unrealistic programmer will destroy the *Bürgfrieden*, and bring the High Command into conflict with organised labour and the Socialist parties.

Nov.	The age of conscription is lowered to 18. Clothing is rationed.
13 Nov.	Cardinal Mercier of Belgium protests against the deportation of Belgian workers as forced labour for German factories. By the end of the war, there will be more than 100,000 Belgians, and 600,000 Poles working in German factories and farms.
21 Nov.	Arthur Zimmermann appointed Foreign Minister.
4 Dec.	The Auxiliary Service Law (submitted to the *Reichstag* in November) is finally passed after a bitter struggle:

- Compulsory labour service for all sixteen- to sixty-year-olds.
- Powers to enable labour to be directed into the armaments industry.
- Women are excluded from its provisions (in contrast to the French *Levee en Masse* of 1793, upon which it was loosely based).
- No attempt is made to control employers' profits, or to control rising wages.
- Workers and labour organisations are given power unprecedented in German industry, after a savage debate about the rights of employees under the new laws.
- Trade unions are allowed in war industries; and collective bargaining agreements given the force of law (for the first time in German history).
- Workers' representatives will sit on the committees for directing labour, and adjudicating exemptions and requests to change jobs.
- In firms of more than 50 workers, Factory Arbitration Committees, comprising both labour and management, will referee disputes about wages and conditions of employment.

12 Dec.	Bethmann Hollweg's Peace Note to the Allies outrages Hindenburg and Ludendorff and widens the rift between the Chancellor and the High Command.

140

1917

The 'Turnip Winter' (1916–17)	Very cold weather ruins the potato crop, causing widespread starvation. By November 1918, there will be over 700,000 civilian deaths from malnutrition. The Allied blockade is biting deep. Bethmann realises the need for constitutional and political reform to avoid social unrest, particularly after the outbreak of the Russian revolution.
Jan.	Karl Liebknecht and Rosa Luxemburg, of the *Gruppe Internationale*, start to publish the subversive 'Spartacus Letters', highly critical of the government and the war.
Feb.	Ludendorff ends the transportation of Belgian workers to Germany as forced labour. This has caused an international outcry and provided rich propaganda for the Allies.
1 Feb.	Germany resumes unrestricted submarine warfare.
15 Mar.	The February Revolution in Russia encourages revolutionary Socialists in Germany.
17 Mar.	In the Prussian Landtag, Bethmann's proposals for constitutional change are swept away by Socialist demands for universal suffrage, parliamentary rule and social reform.
Apr.	The food crisis worsens. The railway system is increasingly unable to cope with both military and civilian needs. The bread ration is cut by half, and there are numerous strikes, with 200,000 workers out in Berlin alone.
6 Apr.	The United States declares war sparking a surge of pessimism and stimulating fresh debate about war aims. A concurrent wave of strikes often takes on an anti-war complexion.
11 Apr.	Foundation of the USDP (*Unabhängige Sozialdemokratische Partei Deutchlands*), Independent Social Democratic Party of Germany. It pledges to end the war and bring about social revolution.
Apr.	The Kaiser's Easter Message promises constitutional reform in Prussia, but only *after* the war. Conservatives blame Bethmann for the Kaiser's 'weakness'.
6 Jul.	Matthias Erzberger of the Centre Party, who has hitherto supported the war, attacks unrestricted submarine warfare and calls for a negotiated peace. This prompts Social Democrats, Progressives, Centrists and National Liberals to form a 'Peace Resolution Majority'.
12 Jul.	Bethmann Hollweg resigns after a campaign against him by the High Command, which is outraged by his approval of the Peace Resolution. Georg Michaelis, a Prussian civil servant favoured by the High Command replaces him.

19 Jul.	The *Reichstag* 'Peace Resolution'. Passed by 212 votes to 126, it calls for a 'peace of understanding and a permanent reconciliation of peoples, and declares that forced territorial acquisitions and political, economic or financial oppressions are irreconcilable with such a peace'. However it does not call for an end to the war and leaves open the possibility of German economic domination of her neighbours and the creation of nominally independent buffer states. Thus, the USDP votes against it, while Ludendorff and Hindenburg threaten to resign if it is accepted.
20 Jul.	Despite his apparent liberalism, Erzberger writes to the new Chancellor, Michaelis, proposing that Lithuania should be an independent Duchy with the Kaiser as its Duke, bound in customs union with Germany. Alsace-Lorraine should get autonomy, but stay under German sovereignty, and Longwy Briey could be used as a bargaining counter.
19 Jul.–2 Aug.	Unrest in the High Seas Fleet. Sailors serving on the battleship *Koenig Albert* sign a Peace Proclamation (31 Jul.).
Aug.	Food riots in many German towns.
1 Aug.	Richard von Kühlmann is appointed Foreign Minister.
Aug.	William Groener, head of the *Kriegampt* is sacked by the High Command. Groener's attempts to administer manpower allocation and profit levels have infuriated employers who claim that he is biased towards labour. Vested interests have constantly challenged his attempts to close down 'non-essential' industries. Groener's sacking highlights the failure of the Hindenburg Programme. There is simply not enough manpower to fight the war and increase production. The new agencies have merely added to the web of administrative confusion in Germany.
3 Sep.	The German Fatherland Party, DVP (*Deutsche Vaterlandspartei*) is founded at Königsberg by Admiral Tirpitz and Wolfang Kapp. It pledges to resist peace overtures, pursue the war to victory, and impose a peace based upon German territorial aggrandisement. The party forms a prototype for the right wing movements of the inter-war years. By July 1918, it has a million and a half members.
11 Sep.	Chancellor Michaelis suggests that Germany renounce its annexationist aims in the west to enable peace negotiations to take place.
1 Nov.	Michaelis is sacked and replaced by Count Georg von Hertling, a Bavarian aristocrat of conservative views. However, he commits himself to reforming the Prussian franchise and

pursuing the 'just peace' demanded by the Peace Resolution of 19 July.

5 Dec.   Fighting stops on the Eastern Front.

1918

Jan.   Half a million workers on strike in Berlin, and over a million in the rest of the country. Industrial unrest is now endemic in Germany: there will be 499 strikes before the war ends. The government responds with repression and the arrest of the SDP leader, Ebert.

3 Mar.   The Treaty of Brest-Litovsk ends the war in the east and fulfils the ambition of the German Right to dominate eastern Europe. Only the Independent Socialists vote against the annexationist Treaty. Large resources are needed to hold down the newly occupied territories. The overstretched German railway cannot handle the transfer of potentially war-winning raw materials from the east.

Mar.–Jun.   Successful German offensives on the Western Front break the Allied line.

1 Jul.   At a meeting at Spa, Ludendorff and Hindenburg attack Foreign Minister Richard von Kühlmann's attempts to control the policy of the High Command, and force Chancellor Hertling to repudiate him.

8 Jul.   Wilhelm II is obliged by the High Command, which he is now powerless to resist, to dismiss Kühlmann, despite the fact that he shares the Foreign Minister's views.

18 Jul.   Allied counter-attacks begin on the Western Front. Germany's last chance of victory has gone, and for the rest of the war, her armies are on the defensive.

3 Aug.   The Supplementary Treaty with Russia gives Germany control of vast Russian resources and raw materials.

8 Aug.   The German army breaks under fresh Allied offensives. On 11 September, the Hindenburg line is breached. On 28 September Ludendorff accepts that the war is lost.

14 Aug.   Crown Council at Spa. The process of peace negotiation begins (see Section 8) but despite the obvious failings of the Third Supreme Command, the Kaiser does not attempt to remove it.

29 Sep.   The Kaiser agrees that Chancellor Hertling should be replaced and a government that includes Social Democrats be formed, to which the High Command would be responsible. This marks the end of the dictatorship of the High Command that has lasted since 1917.

3 Oct.	Ludendorff and the Supreme Command transfer executive power to the *Reichstag*. Prince Max of Baden is formally sworn in as Chancellor. He forms a government containing two Social Democrats.
14 Oct.	Wilson's Second Note demands guarantees of 'constitutional change', implying that peace depends on the removal of the Kaiser. The High Command and the Kaiser reject this and suggest that Germany can fight on.
21 Oct.	Disturbances in the High Seas Fleet at Wilhelmshaven.
23 Oct.	Wilson's Third Note says that he will only deal with the 'veritable representatives of the German people'.
24 Oct.	The High Command defies constitutional procedures by sending a telegram to the troops demanding continued resistance.
26 Oct.	Ludendorff resigns.
28 Oct.	Adoption of a Constitutional Monarchy, with a Chancellor responsible to Parliament, and military appointments subject to the War Ministry (The 'October Reforms').
2 Nov.	Philipp Scheidemann, vice-chairman of the SPD, demands the Kaiser's abdication.
3 Nov.	The German Revolution begins with the Kiel Mutiny. Sailors refuse to put to sea, elect a Soviet and take over the port.
7 Nov.	In Berlin the majority Socialist Party threatens to oppose the government unless the Emperor abdicates. In Munich, Kurt Eisner proclaims a Bavarian Socialist Republic. Throughout Germany, workers and soldiers' soviets spring up, but usually concern themselves with immediate grievances rather than overthrowing the State.
9 Nov.	In Berlin revolutionary strikes break out. Wilhelm II flees to Holland, and Prince Max announces the Kaiser's abdication, before handing over to the SDP leader Ebert. After Scheidemann impulsively proclaims a Republic from the *Reichstag* balcony, Ebert forms a Socialist government.
10 Nov.	The Ebert–Groener Pact. The Prime Minister agrees to exclude the extreme left, in return for army support for his government.
11 Nov.	German representatives sign the Armistice at Compiègne.

Aftermath

12 Nov.	German Austria demands to join the Reich.
15 Nov.	Manufacturers and trade unions sign the Central Working Association Agreement, whereby employers recognise unions and agree to improve working conditions, and unions agree to resolve disputes by conciliation. The agreement by-passes the unofficial 'soviets' and factory committees and demonstrates

the determination of both sides of the industrial establishment to avoid Soviet-style revolution.

22 Nov.   The parties agree a transitional government while a new Constitution is drawn up.

1919

The continuation of the Allied blockade causes terrible hardship to German civilians.

1 Jan.   Foundation of the German Communist Party (KPD).

5–11 Jan. The Spartacist Revolt in Berlin, is brutally suppressed. On 15 January Rosa Luxemburg and Karl Liebknecht are murdered.

18 Jan.   The Peace Conference opens at Versailles with representatives of the German republic excluded.

19 Jan.   National Assembly elections.

6 Feb.   The National Assembly meets at Weimar.

11 Feb.   Friedrich Ebert elected President (succeeded by Hindenburg in 1925).

7 May   The terms of the Versailles Treaty are communicated to German delegates. Their unexpected harshness causes consternation in Germany.

16 Jun.   Allied ultimatum to Germany to force her to sign the Treaty.

28 Jun.   Germany signs the Treaty.

11 Aug.   The Weimar Constitution comes into force, initiating the Weimar Republic, which will be overthrown by Hitler in 1933.

Germany' war expenditure

The black segment represents the total expenditure of the Imperial German government in last year of peace

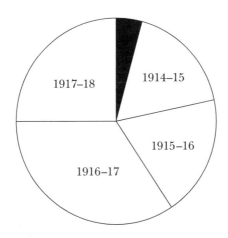

6.3 FRANCE

1914

13 Jun.	René Viviani forms a government.
16 Jun.	The international socialist Jean Jaurès challenges the Three Year Law on military conscription in the Chamber.
14 Jul.	At the instigation of Jean Jaurès, a motion is passed by the Unified Socialist Party in Paris for a co-ordinated strike against mobilisation.
31 Jul.	The Socialist Minister of the Interior, Jean-Louis Malvy decides not to round up agitators on 'Carnet B' (a list of suspected anti-war activists). This later held against him as evidence of his dubious patriotism.
	The assassination of Jean Jaurès eliminates another major figure of the French Left.
1 Aug.	General Mobilisation gets underway with virtually no resistance. Warlike fervour is confined to mainly Paris. Elsewhere, the war is received with resignation rather than enthusiasm.
2 Aug.	Paris Socialists, meeting in the Salle Wagram, unanimously support the war. An Appeal to French Workers issued by the CGT (*Confédération Générale du Travail*) demands support for the nation in its hour of need.
3 Aug.	Germany declares war on France.
4 Aug.	Jean Jaurès's funeral becomes a focus of national patriotism. The government-sponsored eulogy helps to reconcile the French Left to the national cause. The trade union leader Leon Jouhaux asks workers to rally to the defence of the nation, and pledges the support of the leadership of the CGT.
In the afternoon	President Poincaré addresses both houses of parliament, speaking of the 'sacred union' (*union sacrée*) of all Frenchmen. This phrase becomes synonymous with the political truce observed by most French parties for the next two years. The Chamber unanimously passes 18 emergency proposals, giving the executive exceptional powers over the economy, the press and national defence. Rents are frozen at 1914 levels (which will have a permanent impact on French property prices). A 'Zone of the Armies' is created, ruled by C-in-C Joffre from his headquarters at Chantilly, and outside civilian control. The Chamber and Senate then adjourn indefinitely.
5 Aug.	The Censorship Law bans criticism of the government or the war-effort. 'Provided', said *Le Figaro*, 'that one does not write about the authorities, the government, politics, constitutional

bodies, banks, the wounded, German atrocities and the postal service, one can print freely.' On 14 August private owner-ship of radio receivers is banned.

8 Aug.   Soldiers' families are given 1.25 francs a day subsistence allowance, with an additional 50 sous for every child under 16. Many poor families find themselves better off than ever before.

26 Aug.   The Government of Sacred Union. Without consulting parliament, Viviani announces a coalition ministry. Aristide Briand is Vice-president of the Council and Ribot Minister of Finance. It comprises right-wingers Delcassé (Foreign Affairs), Millerrand (War); 'old fashioned' Radicals Leon Bourgeois and Émile Combes; Radical Socialists Malvy (Interior), Sarraut (Public Education), Doumergue (Colonies) and Bienvenue Martin (Labour); and unusually, two Socialists – Guesde and Sembat.

2–3 Sep.   As the German armies approach Paris, government and parliament leave for Bordeaux, accompanied by nearly 40% of the capital's inhabitants.

8 Sep.   'State of War' regulations are extended to the whole country, giving even more arbitrary power to the central authorities.

20 Sep.   At the Arms Conference in Bordeaux, large companies form consortia to improve war production. Believing that the war will be short, the government is content to leave arms pro-duction to market forces and traditional suppliers. Inevit-ably, industrial monopolies take advantage of the situation to maximise prices.

25 Sep.   National Defence Bonds are launched. 217 million francs are raised in 24 days.

20 Dec.   Parliament returns to Paris and three days later votes to hand over even more power to the High Command. Within the 'Zone of Armies' Joffre reigns supreme. Politicians are forbidden even to visit the front line.

The occupied territories. At the end of the year 10 Departments are under enemy occupation, and will remain so until the war's end. German rule is extremely harsh, and there is virtually no resistance to it. The impact on the French economy is devastating: millions of acres of rich agricultural land producing 20% of France's wheat and over half her sugar beet are lost. The occupied lands contain 10% of the French population, 14% of her industrial workforce, 75% of her iron and steel capacity, and 40% of her coal mines. Production lost due to enemy occupation was as follows: coal 49%, pig iron 64.5%, steel 58%. In addition to the land lost, much of the fighting took place in France's industrial heartland.

1915

Jan. André Citroen contracts to produce more then a million shells, with the government undertaking to fund a new factory and pay him in advance.

5 Feb. The last in a series of inter-Allied financial agreements allowing France to borrow to meet the ever-rising cost of war imports.

4 Apr. A decree forbids any business relationship with enemy enterprises.

1 May Adolphe Merrheim, a close friend of Leon Trotsky, and the head of the Metalworker's Union, attacks 'the ignoble war in which French soldiers commit as many atrocities as the Germans' who 'merit the first place in the world because of their social qualities, both economic and hygienic'. At the CGT Conference Merrheim's anti-war motion is defeated, but cracks have begun to appear in left wing support for the war.

18 May The socialist Albert Thomas is appointed Under-secretary for Artillery and Military Equipment. He brings an enormous energy to the task, organising the release of skilled workers from the army, and diverting mobilised men to the factories. But the policy of using market forces as the basis of war production persists. By the end of 1915, private companies (compared with 25% in August 1914) employ 75% of workers in armaments. By 1917, around 518,000 soldiers have been released from the army to return to war industries and 300,000 to work on the land. (Out of 1,400,000 men killed in the war, over 900,000 were peasants, who, although they constituted only 40% of France's population, bore 64% of her casualties.)

24 Jun. War Minister Millerrand, questioned on the lack of accountability of the High Command, says there should be 'absolutely no confusion between parliamentary power and military authority'.

2 Jul. The public are asked to hand in their gold coins for paper money, bringing in 2.5 billion francs worth of gold by the end of the year. But the balance of payments deficit for 1915 will be 200 billion francs (1914, 5.7 billion, 1916, 300 billion) and an American Loan of 7.5 billion francs is required.

10 Jul. A minimum rate of pay is applied to women home-workers, who had previously been paid extremely low rates for war work.

14 Jul. In a patriotic ceremony at *Les Invalides*, the remains of Rouget de Lisle, composer of the Marseillaise, are re-interred.

Jul. At the Congress of the Socialist Party a minority group led by Marx's grandson, Jean Longuet, declares its opposition to the

	war. However, the Congress votes to continue the war until the victory and the ruin of 'German militarist imperialism'.
4 Aug.	The High Command agrees to 'temporary Parliamentary missions' to the front, enabling a limited reassertion of parliamentary supervision over the army.
13 Aug.	The Dalbiez Law attempts to regulate discrepancies between the contracts and living conditions of mobilised workers and civilians working alongside them.
5–8 Sep.	The Socialist Zimmerwald Conference is attended by Adolphe Merrheim and other French opponents of the war. They accept the conference call for 'an unconditional peace, free from annexations and indemnities'.
Sep.	A Contracts Commission directly responsible to Albert Thomas' department is set up to monitor prices and increase the number of companies tendering for war work.
29 Oct.	The Ministry of Aristide Briand replaces that of the exhausted Viviani. Briand confirms his commitment to the politics of national unity by retaining the Socialists Sembat and Guesde and bringing in the rightist Catholic, Denys Cochin. General Gallieni becomes War Minister, replacing Millerand, whose pronouncements ('There are no more workers' rights, no more social laws. There is nothing now but war') made him a *bête noire* to the Left, with Albert Thomas given control over munitions production, and another technocrat, Étienne Clémentel, becoming Minister of Trade and Industry.
Oct.	A Wall Street syndicate agrees to lend France $193 million (out of a $500 million loan to the Entente).
Nov.	The government issues the first of a series of short-term 5% bonds to pay for the war. Failure to introduce income tax means that nearly 30% of government war spending is funded by the sale of these high interest stocks, which are very expensive for the State to repay.
12 Nov.	The Mistral–Voilin proposal aims to establish strict State control over the war industries in order to curb profiteering and exploitation of labour. In return, munitions workers would be expected to accept direction of labour and military discipline off-site, but would be entitled to civilian wages. Industrialists would be submitted to strict accounting procedures, and their profits limited. The proposal meets stiff resistance from vested interests and makes no progress.

1916

Jan.	Production of metals has returned to its pre-war level, and chemicals to 93%.

149

29 Jan.	Paris suffers a Zeppelin raid which causes disproportionate panic in a population that has so far been insulated from many of the discomforts of the war.
21 Feb.	The German attacks on Verdun begin, lending fuel to criticisms of the High Command.
16 Mar.	Briand caves in to Joffre's demands and removes War Minister Gallieni, replacing him with Joffre's protégé General Roques.
24 Apr.	French socialists attend the Kienthal Conference, whose the anti-war resolutions strike a chord with French workers who are becoming dissatisfied with low wages, employers' profiteering, and the goals for which the war is being fought.
May	The *Comité des Forges* obtains a monopoly for importing iron and steel from Britain. Before the end of the war, all French iron and steel is distributed through the *Comité*.
16–22 Jun.	The Chamber meets in secret session for the first time. Deputies attack lack of political control over the army. Briand replies: 'The government is *running* the war, the command is *executing* it, under the *supervision* of the government – *responsible* to you.'
20 Jul.	The Armaments Minister forbids the employment of drafted male workers on work that can be done by women. By the end of the war over a million women are employed in national defence, armaments and aeronautics.
28 Jul.	The Senate unanimously adopts a Rent Control Law.
29 Jul.	The price of wheat is fixed by law.
Aug.	Over one-third of the delegates at the Congress of the Socialist Party vote against the war, showing that cracks are appearing in the Union Sacrée.
16 Sep.	Leon Trotsky is expelled from France, but the government refrains from repressive measures against the French Left.
5–25 Oct.	The government issues a Second National Defence Loan.
21 Nov.	The Chamber secretly discusses conscripting younger men.
12 Dec.	Briand reshuffles his government, making General Lyautey Minister of War, and promoting Albert Thomas to manage war production. He creates a War Committee (Briand, Ribot, Lyautey, Lacaze, Thomas) on the model of Lloyd George's War Cabinet. Parliament grants the Executive limited powers to rule by decree, but its powers still fall far short is what is required to wage total war.
17 Dec.	In response to sustained parliamentary criticism of Joffre's tactics and the lack of civilian control over the Army, Joffre

is replaced by General Robert Nivelle who persuades many politicians that his offensive strategy can win the war.

1917

28 Feb.	Nivelle complains that anti-war propaganda is undermining the morale of his troops.
14 Mar.	War Minister Lyautey resigns in protest at Nivelle's planned offensive, which he believes to be irresponsible and potentially disastrous.
15 Mar.	The February Revolution in Russia excites the French Left and stimulates an upsurge of pacifist and socialist publications.
20 Mar.	*The Ministry of Alexandre Ribot.* The octogenarian Ribot forms a government after the collapse of the Briand Ministry on 17 March.
16–18 Apr.	The Nivelle Offensive fails utterly, with huge loss of life, shattering the morale of the army.
29 Apr.–10 Jun.	Mutinies spread throughout the French armies on the Western Front. The mutineers claim the issue is not the war itself, but about leave, pay, rations and persistence with futile and costly offensives.
May–Jun.	The largest outbreak of strikes since the start of the war. Pacifist and revolutionary slogans are as common as economic demands. Government surveys show very low civilian morale.
16 May	Nivelle is replaced as C-in-C by General Philippe Pètain, who ends the mutinies with firmness but restraint, and addresses the soldiers grievances.
19 May	Pétain's Directive No 1 states that bloody offensives are a thing of the past.
27–29 May	A meeting of a special National Council of the SFIO accepts an invitation to the proposed socialist Stockholm Peace Conference. A delegation asks Ribot to annul the Secret Treaties.
2 Jun.	The Ribot government refuses to grant passports to delegates to the Stockholm Peace Conference, causing great resentment in socialist and trade union circles. Industrial strife, the army mutinies, and resistance to Ribot's announcement of 'annexationist' war aims, generate an atmosphere of social crisis. As well as working class disenchantment with the war, a growing pacifist movement among Radical–Socialist deputies is gathering around Joseph Caillaux.
12 Jul.	The *Suritée Genèrale* reveals that pacifist and 'Caillautiste' newspapers have been receiving mysterious subsidies. The Minister

	of the Interior, Malvy, suspends the newspaper *Le Bonnet Rouge*, the most outspoken anti-war journal, and orders the arrest of the editor, Almeyreda.
22 Jul.	Clemenceau mounts an attack on Malvy. Referring to a long list of incidents dating back to his failure to arrest the suspects on *Carnet B* in 1914, Clemenceau says Malvy has betrayed France by failing to deal with pacifists and traitors. He reveals that Malvy's private secretary has returned to Almeyreda a German cheque that had been confiscated by the police.
31 Jul.	Income Tax is finally adopted. The revenues will arrive too late to have much impact on war finance.
	Throughout the summer, the Ribot Ministry faces a series of scandals that destroy public confidence and provoke demands for purges and strong government.
18 Aug.	Almeyreda is found hanged in his cell.
31 Aug.	Malvy resigns from the government.
12 Sep.	Ribot steps down when his entire cabinet resigns over the Almeyreda affair.
13 Sep.	*The Ministry of Paul Painlevé and the end of the Union Sacrée.* Because of disagreements over war aims and the Stockholm Conference, the SFIO refuses to participate.
23 Sep.	Arrest of 'Bolo Pasha', an adventurer whom American sources have revealed to be in the pay of Berlin.
7 Oct.	Arrest of Turmel, a Radical Socialist deputy accused of taking money from Berlin for giving information about secret parliamentary sessions.
16 Oct.	At a secret session the Painlevé government is pilloried for the abortive peace negotiations conducted by Briand with the German governor of Belgium, Count Lancken. The exchanges further embitter hatred between 'bitter-enders' and those who seek a way out of the war. Painlevé has to replace his Foreign Minister, Ribot.
13 Nov.	Arrest of Charles Humbert, a distinguished senator accused of receiving money from 'Bolo Pasha'.
13 Nov.	Painlevé loses a vote of confidence, becoming the first leader to be voted out of power since 1914.
17 Nov.	*The Ministry of Georges Clemenceau.* Clemenceau announces he will end scandal, political feuding and class rivalries in a single-minded drive to win the war. He excludes all the political figures of the past from his government, acting as his own War Minister and maintaining an independent private secretariat.

20 Nov.	Parliament votes 418 to 65 to back the Clemenceau administration, but the Socialists abstain.
18 Dec.	Clemenceau proclaims 'No more pacifist campaigns, no more German intrigues. Neither treason, nor demi-treason. War: Nothing but war . . . The country shall know that it is defended.'
24 Dec.	The Chamber votes to postpone all elections until the end of the war.

1918

14 Jan.	Joseph Caillaux is arrested (and will be tried after the war). The Senate investigates Malvy, who, in August, is sentenced to five years' banishment for 'abuse of authority'. In February, 'Bolo Pasha' is sentenced to death for 'secret dealings with the enemy'.
10 Feb.	Clemenceau is given sweeping powers to regulate the production, retail, and supply of foodstuffs. Parliament is willing to let the executive run the war, and to give Clemenceau virtual *carte blanche* to do as he sees fit.
8 Mar.	The Socialists attack Clemenceau in Parliament, as a wave of strikes sweep the country. He wins a vote of confidence by 374 to 41, telling the assembled deputies 'Domestic policy? I wage war. Foreign policy? I wage war. I continue to wage war.'
21 Mar.– 7 Jul.	Germany launches five great offensives in the west, pushing the Allied armies back to the Marne. On 23 March Paris comes within range of German long-range cannon. On 6 June it is declared to be once more within the Zone of the Armies.
Jul.	The government establishes consortia in industries essential to the war effort. Raw material and factory prices are strictly regulated. As the war ends the state is at last beginning to establish control over the economy.
18 Jul.– 4 Aug.	The second Battle of the Marne marks the beginning of the Allies' victorious offensive.
28 Jul.	Longuet's 'Centrist' faction wins a majority in the Socialist Party for refusing military credits and opposing intervention in Russia.
6–9 Oct.	At the Socialist Party Congress in Paris, 'minority' members sympathetic to Lenin win the day.
17 Oct.	The advancing Allied armies recapture Lille and Douai. The retreating Germans follow a 'scorched earth' policy, blowing up mines and factories, destroying orchards and crops, carrying off rolling-stock and industrial plant. This devastates some of the richest industrial and agricultural areas of France, and poisons Franco-German relations for a generation.

7 Nov.	The Senate formally acclaims Clemenceau and Foch for their heroic victory.
11 Nov.	The Armistice ends all fighting on French soil.

Production of Essential Commodities in France, 1914–18

	% Home produced	% Imported
	Pig iron	
1913	5.2	0
1914	2.7	0
1915	0.6	0.2
1916	1.5	0.6
1917	1.7	0.7
1918	1.3	0.4
	Coal	
1913	40.8	23.9
1914	27.5	17.2
1915	19.5	19.6
1916	21.3	20.3
1917	28.9	17.3
1918	26.3	15.0
	Steel	
1913	4.7	−0.4
1914	2.7	−0.2
1915	1.1	1.0
1916	2.0	2.6
1917	2.2	2.6
1918	1.8	1.8

Workers in Arms Manufacturing in France

	In state-owned factories	In privately owned factories	Total
August 1914	38,000	12,000	50,000
May 1915	71,000	242,000	313,000
1918	295,000	1,280,000	1,675,000

Movement of Wages and Prices in France during the War

	General wages	Munitions workers	Cost of living (Paris)	Cost of living (Provinces)
1913–14	100	100	100	100
1916	125	125	134	138
1917	130	150	160	173
1918	175	240	211	235

Wartime employment of women in France

In August 1914 there were 7,000,000 women in a total working population of 21 million, but most were employed in family enterprises, and very few in manufacturing industry.

Women in Manufacturing in France 1914–18

Aug. 1914	80,000
Jul. 1915	350,000
Jul. 1916	500,000
Nov. 1918	1,240,000

Women also replaced conscripted men as teachers, postal workers, and clerks. On the north–south Paris Metro line, for instance 3,000 of the 4,000 employees were women by the end of the war, compared with 124 in 1914.

6.4 GREAT BRITAIN

1914

4 Aug. Britain declares war on Germany.

Chancellor of the Exchequer David Lloyd George announces 'business as usual' claiming that the war will not seriously affect the lives of ordinary people or the working of the economy. However, over the next few weeks, Parliament sanctions a series of measures that run counter to the traditional Liberal principles of Free Trade, laissez-faire, and individual rights. Most MPs assume that the war will be over in a few months, making these emergency measures purely temporary.

The Defence of the Realm Act (DORA) (8 August). Parliament gives the government virtually open-ended powers to legislate by decree. Over the next four years, DORA will enable the State to expand its power over the economy and everyday life in response to the pressure of war.

Trade: The government bans trading with the enemy (8 August) and restricts export of goods useful to the war-effort. Under the Unreasonable Withholding of Foodstuffs Act (8 August) the Board of Trade takes powers to act against 'hoarders and profiteers' by confiscating goods held back from the market.

Import substitution: The Cabinet Committee on Food Supplies issues orders to replace goods previously purchased from Germany.

Insurance: The Huth–Jackson Scheme (3 August) subsidises cover for ship-owners who would otherwise find their insurance voided by hostilities.

Finance: The War Loan Act relaxes pre-war the restrictions on Treasury powers to raise loans. The Currency and Bank Notes (Amendment) Act allows the Bank of England to issue paper money not backed by gold reserves. Unnerved by this unprecedented State interference in the economy, the Stock Market closes on 31 August to control panic selling. In November, the Finance (Session 2) Act almost doubles income tax and super tax, and raises duties on beer and tea. But the Treasury completely underestimates the likely deficit caused by the war, which it proposes to cover by an offer of 3.5% War Loan worth £350 million.

Social provision: Local authorities are obliged to provide school meals during vacations as well as term time. Injured workers in the war industries are granted pensions and allowances.

Restraint of foreigners: The Aliens Restriction Act places strict controls on the entry and exit of foreign nationals, and monitors their movement and place of residence. The British Nationality and Status of Aliens Act adopts a narrow definition of British nationality, makes naturalisation subject to stringent conditions, and limits the right of aliens to own property. Many 'aliens' are deported, and during August, there are numerous attacks on German residents and people believed to be German. On 19 November there is a riot by German and Austrian internees on the Isle of Man.

Start of the mass recruiting campaign: General Herbert Kitchener is appointed Secretary of State for War on 5 August, with responsibility for strategy, recruitment, and munitions. He shocks the Cabinet by stating that the war will last for three years, which will require Britain to recruit and equip a mass army for the first time in her history. On 5 August, the Labour Party chairman Ramsey MacDonald resigns because of his opposition to the war. However, his successor, Arthur Henderson, reflects the Party's commitment to national defence.

7 Aug.	Kitchener makes a public appeal for the first 100,000 volunteers. By the end of the year, a million men have joined up.
15 Sep.	The Irish Home Rule and Welsh Church Bills are suspended for the duration of the war.
29 Oct.	Sir John Fisher appointed First Sea Lord, in place of Prince Louis Battenberg (whose crime is to have a German name).
30 Nov.	British casualties already exceed the strength of the original BEF that left for France in August.

1915

1 Jan.	Final meeting of the Shells Committee, which had been holding ineffectual discussions since October to try to resolve the army's chronic shortage of ammunition. Trench warfare has created an unforeseen demand for high explosive shells. By October 1914, the army had already ordered ten times more

artillery pieces than in the previous ten years. A Munitions Committee set up in March fails to resolve the problem.

4 Jan.   The Stock Exchange reopens for trading.

19 Jan.   Several towns on the east coast are bombed by a German airship. There is little loss of life but great moral indignation at this novel targeting of civilians.

Feb.   Engineers on Clydeside, led by an unofficial committee of shop stewards, strike in defiance of their union. This coincides with a serious rent strike in Glasgow, reflecting the housing shortage caused by the cessation of domestic building. The government is forced to pass the Increase of Rent and Mortgage Interest Act, under which rents of cheaper property are fixed at pre-war levels, mortgage rates are frozen, and foreclosure for non-payment is suspended.

18 Feb.   The German submarine blockade begins, with little impact at first on the civilian population.

19 Feb.   The Dardanelles Campaign opens.

24 Feb.   A thousand former suffragettes arrive in France to do voluntary war work. In March, Lloyd George promises Sylvia Pankhurst that women will receive equal pay for war work. A women's army battalion is set up.

19 Mar.   The Treasury Agreement. Lloyd George persuades unions in the munitions industries to accept the suspension of traditional trade practices, to allow the employment of women and untrained labour ('dilution') and to observe an 'industrial truce' while the war lasts. The main points of the deal had already been agreed in the 'Shells and Fuses Agreement' earlier in the month.

29 Apr.   The Commons accepts Lloyd George's call for deterrent increases in duties on alcohol. King George has declared that he will abstain from alcohol for the duration of the war as an example (30 March).

14 May   The Shell Scandal exposes the Asquith government to criticism and public pressure. *The Times* newspaper (secretly briefed by General Sir John French) claims that British military reverses have been caused by lack of ammunition and equipment.

15 May   Resignation of the First Sea Lord, Admiral Sir John Fisher, over fundamental disagreement with Winston Churchill over the Dardanelles expedition. His departure worsens the crisis faced by Asquith's government.

25 May   **The Asquith Coalition.** Battered by the Shells Scandal, military reversals, Cabinet bickering and resignations, Asquith

157

broadens his government to include eight Conservatives. The Labour leader Arthur Henderson joins the Cabinet as President of the Board of Education, and advisor on labour matters. Lloyd George heads a new Ministry of Munitions to organise and co-ordinate war production in conjunction with major industrialists. Reginald McKenna becomes Chancellor of the Exchequer.

31 May/ 1 Jun.	London suffers its first Zeppelin raid, as, later in the month, does Hull. Small by later standards, the raids re-ignite anti-German feeling.
19 Jun.	The 'Treasury Agreement' is reinforced by the Munitions of War Act, under which designated 'controlled establishments' (enterprises producing war materials) are placed under strict regulations. These include compulsory arbitration in industrial disputes, leaving certificates giving employers' permission for workers to change jobs, and a formal commitment to accept 'dilution' by the unions.
21 Jun.	The War Loan Act authorises a £587 million flotation at 4.5% (unusually high interest for the times). This greatly profits those rich enough to subscribe to it. In July, the government says that the war is costing £3 million a day.
14 Jul.	National Registration Act (Derby Scheme). Army demands for more manpower cause Asquith to set up a voluntary register of all men and women between the ages of 15 and 65. Married men are assured they will not be called up while there are single men available for service. When the register opens in August, there is a very poor response.
17 Jul.	In London, 40,000 women led by Mrs Pankhurst demand the right of women to participate in the war effort. Despite the Treasury Agreement, employers and unions are dragging their feet over allowing women into the workplace.
31 Aug.	Settlement of the South Wales coal dispute: 200,000 miners have been striking for two months for more pay. Although their action is declared illegal, they win most of their demands.
Sep.	Unprecedented taxes levied to finance the war. The starting point for income tax is lowered to £130. A 50% Excess Profits Duty (EPD) is introduced. Imported luxuries are taxed at 33.3% (the 'McKenna Duties'). Other indirect taxes are increased by 100%. Although the new taxes enrage many Liberals, they fall far short of what is needed to finance the war, which is now costing £2.1 million a day.
7 Sep.	The Trades Union Congress votes against conscription.

29 Sep.	The US agrees to lend Britain and France up to $500m.
29 Oct.	Ten thousand people attend memorial service at St Paul's Cathedral for Nurse Edith Cavell (executed in Brussels by the Germans on 11 October). Her execution is a propaganda disaster for Germany.
Nov.	The Naval and Military War Pensions Act provides a minimal living for the families of casualties.
13 Nov.	Winston Churchill resigns from Cabinet, and later takes a command on the Western Front.
16 Dec.	Douglas Haig succeeds John French as C-in-C France and Flanders. On 21 December, Sir William Robertson is appointed Chief of the Imperial General Staff (CIGS).
28 Dec.	The Cabinet agrees to the principle of compulsory military service. By the end of the year, 2,466,719 have volunteered for military service, and almost 1.2 million are working in 'controlled' establishments. Two million additional women have joined the workforce. Munitions production, traditionally monopolised by a few large firms, has expanded to include 70 new companies (200 by the end of the war). Two thousand small businesses have been co-opted into the war effort.

1916

4 Jan.	Home Secretary Sir John Simon resigns in protest at the imminent introduction of conscription. The Labour Party and most unions have made plain their hostility to it.
27 Jan.	Munitions of War (Amendment) Act extends the 1915 Act to a wider range of businesses.
Feb.	War Savings Certificates introduced to encourage small savers.
9 Feb.	The Military Service Act comes into force. All single men between the ages of 18 and 41 are liable for military service. Local tribunals will examine the claims of essential war-workers and conscientious objectors.
17 Mar.–4 Apr.	Clydeside munitions workers strike.
3 Apr.	Execution of Sir Roger Casement for plotting to smuggle arms into Ireland.
24 Apr.– 1 Mar.	The Easter Rebellion in Dublin. The British government's over-reaction alienates moderate Irish opinion: 794 civilians, and 521 members of the police and army are killed or wounded. Great destruction is caused to public buildings in the centre of Dublin.
2 May	Military Service (No. 2) Act. All males between 18 and 41 are called up. A second Act later in the month conscripts married men and remaining widowers between the ages of

18 and 41. The provisions will not be enforced in Ireland. Compulsory military service had no effect in increasing the size of the armed forces, as the figures below demonstrate. There were a finite number of men capable of fighting. Essential services still needed to be manned. Expectations of compulsion caused people who may have volunteered to wait for their call-up papers.

Yearly Recruitment in Great Britain during the War

	Total joining the armed forces	Size of army on 1 Oct. each year
1914	1,186,357	1,327,372
1915	1,280,000	2,475,764
1916	1,190,000	3,343,797
1917	820,646	3,883,017
1918	493,562	3,838,265

20 May	Britain will supply France with coal to replace French coal lost because of German occupation.
21 May	British Summer Time. Clocks are put forward one hour to assist production through 'daylight saving'.
1 Jul.	Start of the Somme Offensive.
6 Jul.	Lloyd George becomes Secretary of War, in place of Lord Kitchener, drowned when HMS *Hampshire* sinks in the North Sea.
19 Aug.	The east coast is bombarded by German warships.
10 Oct.	The Irish Nationalists resolve unanimously to resist conscription.
10 Oct.	The government announces plans to control wheat supplies.
28 Nov.	The US Federal Reserve Board advises against the purchase of foreign bills and warns investors about overseas investments. This forces Britain to transfer vast quantities of gold to the US to support her exchange rate.
29 Nov.	Troops occupy the south Wales coal-field under the Defence of Realm Act.
29 Nov.	The government announces it will take control of vacant agricultural land for food production.

The fall of Asquith's government

1 Dec.	Lloyd George proposes a three-man War Council, to be chaired by himself.
3 Dec.	Asquith accepts Lloyd George's proposal.

4 Dec.	An article in *The Times* criticises Asquith and praises Lloyd George.
4 Dec.	Under pressure from Liberal colleagues, Asquith goes back on his agreement with Lloyd George.
5 Dec.	Lloyd George resigns.
6 Dec.	Asquith resigns.
7 Dec.	The Lloyd George Coalition Government is formed with the support of the Conservative and Labour parties, and around one-third of Liberal MPs. The remaining Liberals form an opposition headed by the sulking Asquith.
	Lloyd George appoints a five-man War Cabinet to organise the country for total war. It comprises the Conservative leader, Bonar Law (Chancellor of the Exchequer) and the party's former leader, Arthur Balfour (Foreign Office). Two other Conservatives, Curzon and Sir Alfred Milner, both chosen for their administrative energy, are given roving commissions divorced from formal departmental duties, as is the Labour leader Arthur Henderson.
	Five new ministries are created: Pensions, Labour, Food, Shipping, and Air, and a Food Controller (Lord Devonport, soon to be replaced by Lord Rhondda).
19 Dec.	The government takes powers to regulate coal supplies and shipping freight. They join rail transport, munitions, farm output, food retailing, iron, and wool production under the ever-growing umbrella of government bureaucracy.
Dec.	The War Loan Act authorises the raising of a £966 million loan at 5%, which critics claim will burden future generations with the cost of the war.

1917

2 Feb.	The Corn Production Act guarantees farmers minimum prices for wheat and oats, and sets up a Board to supervise a minimum wage for farm workers. The Board of Agriculture is empowered to ensure that all land is fully cultivated, bringing an additional 3 million acres into production by the end of the war.
20 Mar.	First meeting of the Imperial War Cabinet agreed at an Imperial Conference earlier in the month. Commonwealth leaders are integrated more closely into war planning. The South African, Jan Smuts, emerges as one of Lloyd George's most effective trouble-shooters.
Apr.	The worst month of the war for shipping losses following the start of Germany's USW campaign in February. U-boats sink

	881,000 tons of Allied shipping, bringing Britain to the brink of defeat. Food reserves are down to 6 weeks supply.
23 Apr.	The First War Loan Act passed by the US Congress authorises $3 billion for the Allies. This comes at a timely moment for Great Britain, which is on the point of bankruptcy having lent vast sums to finance her Entente partners over the previous three years.
10 May	The first convoy leaves Gibraltar, following Lloyd George's imposition of the convoy system on the Admiralty on 30 April.
10 May	A 'secret session' of Parliament discusses rationing and direction of labour.
26 May	76 civilians are killed in German bombing raids along the south-east coast of England.
10 Jun.	Nationalist Riots in Dublin.
15 Jun.	An Amnesty is announced for Irishmen arrested in the Easter Rising.
19 Jun.	The Royal Family renounce their German family name 'Saxe-Coburg-Gotha', and adopt the name 'Windsor' (Battenberg is transformed into Mountbatten).
11 Jul.	British representatives are invited to attend the Stockholm Peace Conference. At first only anti-war left-wingers like Ramsey MacDonald accept.
17 Jul.	Winston Churchill is promoted to Minister of Munitions. (He returned to Government on 7 June as Chairman of the Air Board.)
24 Jul.	The Commons is told that the war is now costing Britain £7 million a day.
25 Jul.	The War Cabinet supports Haig in his forthcoming Flanders offensive (popularly known as Passchendaele). This drags on from 31 July to 10 November, provoking widespread questioning about the desirability of continuing the war.
10 Aug.	A special Labour Party Conference agrees to accept an invitation to the Stockholm Conference. Without consulting his War Cabinet colleagues, Arthur Henderson, the labour leader, has recommended this. Meanwhile the government has refused to issue passports to go to Sweden.
Aug.	The Finance Act increases indirect taxes and raises EPD from 60% to 80%.
Aug.	Arthur Henderson resigns from the Cabinet because of his enthusiasm for the planned Socialist Stockholm Conference to end the war. Labour stays in the government, with George Barnes taking Henderson's place.

29 Sep.	German aircraft bomb London on successive nights, leading to calls for a British bombing campaign of German cities.
Dec.	The TUC and the Labour Party agree to make a joint statement of war aims.

1918

5 Jan.	Lloyd George sets out Britain's war aims at a conference of trade union leaders (see p. 215).
21 Jan.	Sir Edward Carson resigns from the War Cabinet.
Feb.	The Ministry of Information set up under Beaverbrook.
18 Feb.	Lloyd George provokes a political crisis by forcing the resignation of Sir William Robertson, Chief of the Imperial General Staff.
25 Feb.	Meat and dairy products are rationed in the southeast, and in April all over the country. Ration books are issued in July. Until now, the government had been reluctant to go beyond exhortation to control consumption. During 1917 limited controls were put on beer, confectionery and other basic commodities (Jun/Aug) and coal (Nov).
21 Mar.	The start of a series of massive German offensives that break though the British lines threatening defeat.
23 Mar.	Lloyd George takes personal charge of the War Office.
14 Apr.	The War Cabinet accepts the appointment of the General Ferdinand Foch as C-in-C of Allied armies, with 'strategic direction of military forces' (as agreed at the 3 April Beauvais Conference).
18 Apr.	Military Service (No. 2) Act. Men aged 41–50 are called up. The potential age limit is raised to 56. Conscription is extended to Ireland, leading Sinn Fein to call a one-day general strike (23 April). In practice, no attempt is made by the government to apply the Act to Ireland.
19 Apr.	Lord Milner becomes Secretary of War.
6/7? May	*The Times* publishes the Maurice Letter demanding an enquiry into Lloyd George's alleged misleading statements about British manpower on the Western Front.
9 May	The Maurice Debate. The Opposition mounts a futile challenge to Lloyd George's leadership in the House of Commons. This causes a split in the Liberal Party, from which it never recovers.
10 Jun.	The Representation of the People Act (passed by the Commons in June 1917 and by the House of Lords in February 1918) gives the vote to all men over 21 and married women

	over 30. The electorate grows from 7.5 million (1910) to nearly 21 million, with over 90% of the population now enfranchised.
21 Jun.	The government abandons its attempts to introduce conscription in Ireland, and postpones Irish Home Rule.

The Labour Party Conference votes for a new constitution drawn up by Arthur Henderson and Sidney Webb: people are allowed to join the party as individuals. Twenty-two 'socialist aims' are adopted, including public ownership of the 'commanding heights of the economy'. The pamphlet *Labour and the New Social Order* spells out the party's new direction.

Mid-Jun.	First instances in Britain of the world-wide influenza epidemic. By the end of the year, it will kill 200,000 Britons.
Jul.	Ration books issued for all meat and dairy products.
Jul.	The Finance Act increases income tax, super tax, and many indirect taxes.
Aug.	Police and prison officers in London strike to secure the right of trade union representation. The strikers go back after Lloyd George grants a pay increase, and hints that their union will be recognised after the war.
8 Aug.	A massive British offensive begins on the Western Front.
8 Aug.	H.A.L. Fisher introduces his Education Act for England and Wales. This paves the way for a national system of education for all. The school-leaving age is raised to 14, and local authorities told to draw up plans for the progressive development of the system. The 'Fisher Act' embodies the widespread hope that the end of the war will mark the beginning of a fairer society in Britain.
19 Sep.	A dispute between the rail companies and women workers over equal pay is settled.
23 Oct.	Parliament votes 274 to 25 in favour of admitting women MPs.
5 Nov.	King George V agrees to dissolve parliament prior to a general election.
14 Nov.	The Labour Party decides to leave the coalition.
22 Nov.	Lloyd George and Bonar Law issue a joint Election Manifesto.
14 Dec.	The 'Khaki' or 'Coupon' Election. The Lloyd George Coalition wins an overwhelming majority with 262 MPs, made up mainly of Conservatives. Sinn Fein (including the first woman MP, Countess Markiewicz) refuses to take its seats, making Labour (57 seats) the main opposition party. Many leading Labour figures, including MacDonald and Henderson, fail to win seats.

6.5 THE RUSSIAN EMPIRE

This chronology uses the Russian Orthodox Calendar, which was thirteen days behind the Western Calendar until 14 February 1918. When events in Russia are significant in a wider context, both the Old Style (OS) and Western (NS) dates are given.

1914

15 Jun. (28, NS)	The Sarajevo assassination.
13 Jul.	The Duma (Parliament) enthusiastically supports measures to defend the national interest. Most of the parties adhere to this pact until 1917.
16 Jul.	Decree giving commanders of military zones complete supremacy over the civilian authorities. This soon becomes a recipe for administrative confusion and civilian resentment.
19 Jul. (1 Aug., NS)	Germany declares war on Russia. The Tsar's brother, Grand Duke Nikolai Nikolaevich is appointed Commander in Chief.
20 Jul. (2 Aug.)	At a ceremony in the Winter Palace, Tsar Nicholas II repeats the vow made by Suvarov in 1812, 'not to make peace so long as one of the enemy is on the soil of the fatherland'. Throughout Russia, there are demonstrations of patriotism and loyalty. Millions of peasants report to their units with enthusiasm. In the factories strikes cease immediately.
26 Jul.	In the Duma, the Menshevik deputy Khaustov reads a statement against the war. Menshevik and Bolshevik deputies leave the Chamber to avoid voting for war credits. In the Russian Parliament (alone of all the belligerents, apart from Serbia) there is substantial opposition to the war.
1–5 (14–18) Aug.	The army suffers huge casualties at the battle of Tannenberg, but civilian morale holds.
3 Aug.	The Tsar agrees to an All-Russian Union of Cities, comprising the Mayors of 45 leading towns of the Empire.
9 Aug.	The Duma sets up a Provisional Committee under its president, Rodzianko. Its ostensible function is to deal with war victims, but in reality, it helps to keep Parliament in touch when the Duma is not sitting (as is usually the case).
11 Aug. (24 Aug.)	A telegram from the International Socialist Bureau in Brussels calling for Russian workers to support the war effort of the Entente is published in the Press and circulated in factories.
12 Aug.	Formation of an All-Russian Union of Zemstvos for the Relief of the Sick and Wounded under the chairmanship of Prince Lvov. All but one of the 36 Zemstvos (municipal

assemblies) join the organisation, showing the eagerness of the middle classes to become involved in the war effort. However, the Union is prohibited from operating in the military zones that cover much of the country – the first of many frustrations for civilian patriots.

11–18 Aug. (24–31 Aug.)	Russia is forced out of East Prussia after the Battle of the Masurian Lakes.
18 Aug.	St Petersburg is given its traditional wartime name 'Petrograd'.
20 Oct. (2 Nov.)	The closure of the Black Sea Straits by Turkey is a catastrophe for the Russian economy: her foreign trade is crippled, her allies can no longer supply her war effort, and additional resources are needed for the new Turkish Fronts. However, previously exported grain is now available for home consumption.
5 Nov.	Arrest of five Bolshevik Duma deputies for anti-war agitation. However, most Social Democrats, including some Bolsheviks, support a patriotic war. Despite the loss of about a million men in the first few months of the war, and the revelation of gigantic deficiencies in logistics and leadership, army and civilian morale remain high.

1915

3 Feb.	A law confiscating the assets of enemy nationals resident in Russia is used against German settlers who have lived in Russia for centuries. Already, large numbers of German peasants and Galician Jews have been deported during the Russian occupation of Austrian Galicia.
9 Feb.	The Duma re-convenes, but only for 2 days.
10–13 Feb.	Trial of the Bolshevik anti-war deputies, who are sentenced to perpetual exile in Siberia.
10 Apr.	The Straits Agreement. Concessions by Britain and France over Constantinople and the Black Sea Straits reinforces support for the war among the nationalist and liberal middle classes.
2–13 May	The Gorlice–Tarnow Offensive: Russia is forced out of Galicia. Vast numbers of refugees move eastwards, leading to outbursts of popular xenophobia and anti-Semitism in Russia. The Russian army carries out a scorched earth policy during its retreat, brutally deporting thousands of Jews from their homes. Mobs rampage in Moscow, attacking the property of 'foreigners'.

6 Jun.	The Kadet Party Conference demands a government responsible to the Duma. The Tsar responds by sacking the unpopular War Minister, Sukhomlinov.
28 Jun.	Zemstvo and City Unions amalgamate in ZEMGOR ('Committee of the All-Russian Unions of Zemstvos and Cities for the Supply of the Army').
1 Jul.	The Central War Industries Committee is set up under Guchkov, representing over 200 local committees. Its task is to co-ordinate war production and adapt industry to munitions production. The Provision for worker representatives on the Committee sparks off a long dispute on the Left as to whether labour should co-operate with this.
Jul.–Aug.	The 'Great Retreat' Russia is forced to abandon vital industrial and mining areas in Poland, Belorussia, and the Baltic lands. This has a crippling impact on the Russian war economy, and ushers in a period of great political and economic turmoil.
1–16 Aug.	The Duma reconvenes. Politicians stress their loyalty to the Tsar and their commitment to the war, but demand wider involvement in the war effort.
8 Aug.	A group of leading ministers ask the Tsar to allow the Duma to nominate a cabinet to run the war effectively.
9 Aug.	The six main parties in the Duma set up the Progressive Bloc. They demand to be allowed to contribute to the war effort, and aspire to a 'Government of Public Confidence' as visualised by Paul Miliukov, leader of the Kadets. Tsar Nicholas II spurns the opportunity to work with these loyal and patriotic monarchists for the national interest.
17 Aug.	The Tsar approves creation of four Special Councils for Defence, Fuel, Food and Transport to plan war production and balance civil and military needs. Both the War Industries Committees and ZEMGOR are represented on the Councils.
20 Aug.	Eight ministers sign a letter begging the Tsar not to take over from his brother Grand Duke Nikolai Nikolaevich as Supreme Commander of the Army.
23 Aug. (6 Sep.)	Nicholas II leaves for Mogilev to take personal command of the army.
23–26 Aug. (5–8 Sep.)	The socialist Zimmerwald Conference intensifies the debate within the Russian Left. Lenin's formula to 'transform the imperialist war into civil war' is rejected by the Conference, but it demands 'an immediate peace without annexations or indemnities and the right of the peoples to self-determination'.
8 Sep.	The Nine Point Programme of the Progressive Bloc includes:

- A responsible government, to which the military would be accountable.
- An amnesty for political prisoners.
- Concessions to national minorities, and an end to religious persecution.
- The ending of government interference in the affairs of trade unions and other representative bodies.

16 Sep.   The Tsar dissolves the Duma.

Oct.   The Tsar dismisses his able Agriculture Minister, Alexandr Krivoshein and, during the next few months, he removes all the ministers who have shown support for responsible government.

1916

20 Jan.   The Tsar makes Boris Stürmer Chairman of Council of Ministers. He is loathed by the public, a protégé of Rasputin and the Tsarina, with a German name and a (false) reputation as a German spy.

8 Feb.   Tsar opens the Duma session in person.

11–17 Apr.   The second International Socialist Conference at Kienthal. Lenin and his supporters again fail to win support for their 'defeatist' line.

25 Jun.   Foreign minister Sergei Sazonov is sacked – another victim of Palace intrigue.

Oct.   Attempts to control the grain trade. The cities, swollen by an influx of refuges and war workers, are beginning to experience severe food shortages. By the end of 1915, the area under cultivation has fallen by half. The enemy had overrun many of the most efficiently farmed private estates. Commercial food production had fallen because of shortage of fertilisers, machinery and labour. By autumn 1916, peasant food production has also collapsed. Peasants, finding little to buy with money earned by selling food to the towns, restrict production to their family needs.

17 Oct.   Petrograd is hit by a wave of strikes: factory inspectors classified industrial disputes during the war as 'economic' – protesting over wages and conditions, or 'political' – protesting at government actions at home or abroad, or intended to destabilise the regime.

22–24 Oct.   The Kadet Party Conference decides to confront the Tsar in the next Duma session.

1 Nov.   The Duma reconvenes. The Tsar expects it to rubber-stamp war credits, but Miliukov denounces treason in high places,

	and demands that more liberal and effective men run the war.
10 Nov.	The Tsar appeases the Duma by replacing Stürmer with the relatively moderate Trepov, whom he charges with securing the Duma's dissolution once it has voted for war credits.
17 Dec.	The Duma adjourns peacefully having yielded to Trepov's appeal for co-operation, despite the Tsar's refusal to dismiss the hated interior minister, Protpopov.
Night of 17–18 Dec.	Rasputin is murdered by a group of aristocrats led by Prince Yusupov.
27 Dec.	The Tsar defies all political parties, arbitrarily replacing Trepov with the ineffectual Prince N.D. Golytsin.

1917

27 Jan.	Arrest of Worker Representatives belonging to the Workers' Group of the War Industries Committee.
31 Jan.	Discontent about food shortages and rising fuel prices among industrial workers in Petrograd.
7 Feb.	Grain is rationed in Moscow, leading to panic buying and hoarding.
14 Feb.	The Workers' Group calls out 90,000 workers to support its arrested leaders.
18 Feb.	The Tsar orders General Khabalov to maintain order in the capital. On the same day, a strike begins in the enormous Putilov factory. When the management locks out 27,000 workers, the action spreads to many other factories.
21 Feb.	Rodzianko, President of the Duma, explains to the Tsar the need for a new government enjoying public confidence. His advice is treated with contempt.
22 Feb.	The Tsar leaves Petrograd for military headquarters at Mogilev.
23 Feb.	A demonstration to mark International Women's Day is joined by striking Putilov workers.
25 Feb.	The Tsar orders street demonstrations to be suppressed by force. Troops fire on the crowds.
26 Feb.	Deputies refuse to accept the Tsar's decree dissolving the Duma. A unit of the of Volynskii Regiment fires into a crowd of demonstrators. In protest, a company of the Pavlovskii Regiment mutinies.
Night of 26–27 Feb.	The Pavlovskii Regiment votes to disobey orders to fire on civilians.

27 Feb.	Most of Petrograd is now in the hands of the mutinous garrison. Order has broken down and government buildings are set alight. The Tsar sends General Ivanov to Petrograd to quell the disorder.
27 Feb.	A Provisional Committee of the Duma is set up, chaired by its president Rodzianko. Simultaneously, at the Tauride Palace, the Petrograd Soviet of Workers' Deputies calls for Soviets (councils) to be elected throughout the country.
28 Feb.	In the morning, the Tsar sets out to return to Petrograd. The first formal session of the Petrograd Soviet takes place, and the first edition of its newspaper, *Izvestia*, is published. Factories and garrison troops begin to elect local soviets.
Night of 28 Feb.– 1 Mar.	The train carrying the Tsar is halted by mutinous troops and diverted to Pskov. The Tsar agrees to form a government drawn from the Duma, and cancels General Ivanov's orders to crush the revolution in Petrograd.
1 Mar.	*Izvestia* publishes the Petrograd Soviet's 'Order Number 1'. Although intended to pre-empt a counter-revolution by Tsarist officers, the Order is interpreted by ordinary soldiers as the transfer of military authority to their elected representatives. Unpopular officers are attacked, and grass roots committees begin to debate and challenge military instructions.

Main provisions of Order No 1 of the Petrograd Soviet:

- Committees to be elected immediately from the rank and file of military units at all levels.
- Representatives are to report to the State Duma building at 10 am on 2 March.
- In all political actions, troop units are subordinate to the Soviet of Workers' and Soldiers' Deputies, and its committees.
- The orders of the Military Commission of the State Duma are to be obeyed, except when they contradict the orders and decrees of the Soviet of Workers' and Soldiers' Deputies.
- All arms must be put under the control of company and battalion committees, and not be issued to officers, even upon demand.
- When on duty, soldiers must observe the strictest military discipline, but off duty, they enjoy fully the same rights as all citizens. In particular, standing at attention and compulsory saluting when off duty are abolished.
- Addressing officers by honorary titles (Your Excellency, Your honour) etc. is abolished, and is replaced by the following forms of address: Mr General, Mr Colonel etc.

	• Addressing soldiers rudely by anyone of higher rank is prohibited, and any breaches of this must be reported to the Company Committees.
1 Mar.	The Moscow Soviet is convened as Soviets emerge all over the Empire.
Night of 1–2 Mar.	Duma and Soviet representatives hammer out an Eight Point Programme to allow both institutions to co-exist in a situation of 'Dual Power'. It includes the eight hour day, confiscation of royal and monastic lands, the abolition of the death penalty, increased taxation for the rich, and equal rights for women.
2 Mar.	A Provisional Government is announced headed by Prince G.E.Lvov.
2 Mar. (15 NS)	Tsar Nicholas II abdicates.
8 Mar.	The Royal Family is arrested and held under guard in the palace of *Tsarskoe Selo*. Britain makes an initial offer of asylum for the Imperial family, but withdraws it later in the month.
9 Mar.	The US recognises the new Russian government; followed by France, Great Britain and Italy.
22 Mar.	The Miliukov Note defines Russian war aims identical to those of the Tsar, provoking a split between the Left and the Liberals.
25 Mar.	A State monopoly of grain distribution is announced.
3 Apr.	Lenin arrives at the Finland Station in Petrograd.
4 Apr.	Lenin reads his 'April Theses' to the Petrograd Soviet (see p. 201).
20 Apr.	Miliukov resigns after demonstrations in Petrograd against his note of 22 March. Prince Lvov's government is fatally weakened. He concedes, on 26 April, that he is unable to maintain public order.
28 Apr.	A Red Guard militia is set up by the Bolsheviks.
Night of 4–5 May	Formation of a new Coalition Government which includes six Socialists. Its dominant figure is the Socialist Minister of War Alexander Kerensky.
4 May	Leon Trotsky arrives in Russia from New York.
25 May– 4 Jun.	Socialist Revolutionary Party Congress. The agrarian SR Party is by far the largest Russian political grouping, supported by millions of land-hungry peasants. The Left Socialist Revolutionaries (LSR) leave and associates themselves with the Bolsheviks.
3–24 Jun.	The First All-Russian Congress of Soviets of Workers and Soldiers Deputies, comprising elected representatives of local

	Soviets all over the country. The overwhelming majority are Socialist Revolutionaries and Mensheviks.
10 Jun.	The Petrograd Soviet persuades the Bolsheviks to give up the idea of staging an armed uprising to overthrow the Provisional Government.
19 Jun. (1 Jul., NS)	The 'Kerensky Offensive' provokes demonstrations in Petrograd, in which Bolshevik slogans predominate for the first time.
1 Jul.	The Provisional Government orders the arrest of leading Bolsheviks including Trotsky. Lenin flees over the border to Finland (29 June).
2 Jul.	Trotsky's group (the *Mezhraiontsy*) merges with the Bolsheviks, strengthening the anti-war forces.
4 Jul.	An attempted Bolshevik seizure of power fails, and the party is damaged by government accusations about Lenin's dealings with the German government.
5 Jul.	Lenin goes into hiding again.
11 Jul.	Alexander Kerensky appointed Prime Minister.
	The failure of the 'Kerensky Offensive' causes the desertion of millions of demoralised peasant soldiers, who are sick of the war and fearful of missing out on the promised land distribution. The influence of Bolshevik agitators in the Soldiers' Soviets increases, undermining the authority of officers and the will of soldiers to carry on fighting. (Russia has suffered some 5,400,000 casualties since 1914.)
18 Jul.	General Lavr Kornilov appointed Commander in Chief of the Army.
9 Aug.	The Provisional Government announces that on 12 November elections will begin for a Constituent Assembly, which will convene on 28 November.
22–30 Aug.	The Kornilov Affair. The army commander challenges the authority of the government. He issues a virtual ultimatum to Kerensky, who is granted dictatorial powers to crush the rebellion. Kornilov's march on Petrograd is thwarted by railway workers and loyal troops. The part played by the Bolsheviks in rallying the anti-Kornilov forces leads to an upsurge of popular support for them and the release of their leaders.
12 Sep.	Lenin tells the Bolshevik Central Committee (CC) that the time is now ripe to take power.
10 Oct.	Lenin comes out of hiding to attend a meeting of the Bolshevik Central Committee. As the Bolsheviks now have a majority in both the Petrograd and Moscow Soviets (but not in the Soviets as a whole), the CC decides to organise an armed uprising against the Provisional Government.

11 Oct.	Zinoviev and Kamenev openly debate the Bolshevik plan to seize power in the newspaper *Novaya Zhizn*, and state their opposition to it.
16 Oct.	The Petrograd Soviet sets up a Military-Revolutionary Committee (Milrevkom) headed by Trotsky, 'to defend the capital'. Commissars are dispatched to win over the Petrograd garrison.
24 Oct.	Street fighting erupts when the government tries to close down Bolshevik newspapers.

The October Revolution

Night of 24–25 Oct. (5–6 Nov., NS)	Bolshevik Red Guards and sailors from the Kronstadt naval base occupy key buildings in the capital. Lenin, in disguise, appears at the Smolnii Institute where the Second Congress of Soviets is due to meet next day.
25 Oct.	In the morning, Lenin declares the Provisional Government deposed. Power now resides in the Soviets. However, the Provisional Government is still besieged in the Winter Palace. In the afternoon, Lenin tells an Extraordinary Session of the Petrograd Soviet 'We shall now proceed to build, on the space cleared of historical rubbish, the towering edifice of a socialist society'. Trotsky consigns the other socialist parties (including the Socialist Revolutionaries, who are about to win a majority in the Constituent Assembly elections) to the 'rubbish tip of history'.
Night of 25–26 Oct.	The Winter Palace is captured, and the remaining representatives of the Provisional Government arrested.

Lenin's revolutionary Decrees

- The Decree on Peace: The government proposes an 'immediate democratic peace for all nations'.
- The Decree on Land: Private ownership of land is abolished. Land passes to Peasants' Soviets and Land Committees for eventual redistribution. This causes even more peasant soldiers to desert so as not to miss the promised share-out.
- The Press Decree: The opposition Press is outlawed.
- The Decree on Workers' Control: Employees are granted the right to 'supervise' production and the administration of companies, and to make their decisions binding upon employers.

(For the Russian negotiations to leave the War: see Section 7.)
(For Russian attempts to seek international peace: see Section 8.)

30 Oct.	Bolshevik forces easily beat off an attempt by Cossacks to dislodge them from the capital.
2 Nov.	After several days of fighting, the Soviet wins control of Moscow.

1–2 Nov.	Kamenev and four other Commissars resign in protest at Lenin's refusal to broaden the Cabinet to include representatives of other left wing parties.
8 Nov.	Leon Trotsky appointed Commissar for Foreign Affairs.
12 Nov.	Elections to the Constituent Assembly.

Results of Elections to the Russian Constituent Assembly

Party	Seats
Socialist Revolutionaries	370
Bolsheviks	175
Left Socialist Revolutionaries	40
Kadets	17
Mensheviks	16

15 Nov.	First meeting of Sovnarkom (The Council of People's Commissars) Russia's new government.
17 Nov.	Bolshevik troops break into the State Bank after officials refuse to co-operate with the new regime.
22 Nov.	Revolutionary Tribunals set up to replace Tsarist courts. Lawyers are done away with.
22–23 Nov.	The Union for the Defence of the Constituent Assembly is set up, representing those who feel the Bolsheviks and their allies have usurped the Assembly's power.
26 Nov.	A Peasants' Congress is broken up by Bolshevik and Left SR militants.
28 Nov.	Leading members of the Kadet Party are arrested.
Dec.	The Supreme Council of the National Economy (Vesenkha) set up to manage the transition from capitalism to state socialism.
7 Dec.	First meeting of the Cheka (the forerunner of the NKVD and KGB).
14 Dec.	Nationalisation of Banks.
Late Dec.	Generals Alekseev and Kornilov found the Volunteer Army in South Russia to resist the Bolsheviks.

1918

5 Jan.	The Constituent Assembly convenes in Petrograd. The next day it is dispersed by Red Guards, and several pro-Assembly demonstrators are killed.
15 Jan.	The Red Army is founded.
19 Jan.	Decree on Socialisation of Land. The first move towards the collectivisation of agriculture.
21 Jan.	Cancelling of foreign and domestic debts.

3 Mar.	Under the Treaty of Brest-Litovsk Russia loses 89% of its coal, 73% of its iron ore, 32% of its most productive agricultural land, and 55 million people (32% of its former population).
20 Apr.	Purchase and leasing of industrial and commercial enterprises is banned. All securities and bonds are to be registered with government.
1 May	All rights of inheritance abolished.
13 May	The Commissar of Supply is given extraordinary powers to wage war on 'peasant bourgeoisie'.
20 May	Decree establishing 'Food Detachments' which are empowered to requisition peasant produce.
28 Jun.	Nationalisation of a range of industrial enterprises.
10 Jul.	The Constitution of the Russian Soviet Federated Socialist Republic is ratified.
27 Aug.	The Supplementary Treaty. Germany forces the Bolsheviks to give up Livonia and Estonia, recognise Georgian independence, give Germany 25% of Baku oil, and pay a large war indemnity.
11 Nov.	Russia repudiates the Treaty of Brest-Litovsk and the Supplementary Treat of August 1918.

Wartime Strikes in Russia

	Political strikers	Economic strikers		Political strikers	Economic strikers
1914			**1916**		
Jul.	16,099	11,504	Jan.	61,447	16,418
Aug.			Feb.	3,200	53,723
Sep.	1,400	905	Mar.	77,877	11,811
Oct.		160	Apr.	14,152	25,112
Nov.	3,150	785	May	8,932	26,756
Dec.		1,020	Jun.	3,452	15,603
1915			Jul.	5,333	20,326
Feb.	340	120	Sep.	2,800	24,918
Mar.		461	Oct.	174,592	15,184
Apr.		4,064	Nov.	22,950	18,592
May	1,259	2,571	Dec.	1,000	8,798
Jun.		1,141	**1917**		
Jul.		17,934	Jan.	151,886	24,869
Aug.	23,178	11,640	Feb.	123,953	19,809
Sep.	82,728	7,470			
Oct.	11,268	13,350			
Nov.	11,020	6,838			
Dec.	8,985	13,284			

DIPLOMATIC WARFARE

INTRODUCTION

Throughout the war, both sides tried to break the stalemate through diplomatic offensives that were another means of waging war, rather than attempts to negotiate an end to the conflict. The wartime diplomacy of the belligerents was waged on two fronts: endeavours to persuade neutral states to join them, and efforts to prise their more vulnerable enemies away from their alliances. Both sides achieved great success in seducing neutrals, but in practice, Austria-Hungary and Russia were the only realistic targets for a separate peace.

7.1 THE QUEST FOR ALLIES

The obsession with manpower, and a growing realisation that the war would drag on led all the belligerents to try to persuade neutral states to join them by offering territorial inducements. These they often had no power to make good, or did not intend to make good. They were often contradictory, and made at the expense of their allies, and they would eventually make peace negotiations far more difficult and poison the atmosphere of the post-war world.

The war faced neutral states with agonising decisions. The United States could debate the question of intervention in an atmosphere of Olympian detachment, and in the knowledge that with every month of delay America's world economic dominance grew greater, but for Turkey, Italy, Bulgaria, Romania and Greece, the question presented excruciating dilemmas. All of them had territorial goals that made them susceptible to inducements from the belligerents, but these rewards could only be delivered in the future, and only if one's patron was victorious. Joining the war presented a rare opportunity to achieve national objectives or to avenge recent setbacks, but none of the neutrals was in any condition to fight. The question of which side to join was made difficult by the ebb and flow of battle which made it difficult to judge at any time which side was winning. Delay might mean forfeiture of territory to reward rivals who *had* taken the plunge. Joining the wrong side might lead to national extinction. The debate over intervention led to bitter and divisive debates in all the neutral countries, with advocates of neutrality being pilloried for lack of patriotism, cowardice and treason.

The Ottoman Empire (Turkey)

In retrospect, it is extraordinary how the Entente ignored Turkey's ability to cripple the Russian war effort by closing the Black Sea Straits. It was certainly no foregone conclusion that Turkey would join the Central Powers, and

179

before the war Turkish approaches were regularly rebuffed by both sides. The Young Turks were equally divided in their sympathies for the competing alliances, and it was not until the last few days of peace that they made the fateful decision to ally with Germany. The decision was as much the fault of the short-sightedness of the Entente as the machinations of German diplomacy.

Obligations at the outbreak of war. Allied to Germany under the secret Treaty of 2 August 1914.

Leading participants

Javid, Mehmed (Cavid Bey)	Minister of Finance
Talat, Mehmed (Talaat Pasha)	Minister of the Interior
Jemal, Ahmed (Cemal Bey)	Minister of Marine
Enver, Mehmed (Enver Pasha)	Minister of War
Wangenheim, Konrad, Freiherr von	German Ambassador
Lowther, Sir Gerrard	British Ambassador
Limpus, Sir Arthur	Commander of British Naval Mission
Liman von Sanders, General Otto	Inspector General of the Ottoman Army
Souchon, Admiral	Commander of German Naval Squadron

Oct. 1911	Turkey approaches Britain with a view to an alliance, but is rebuffed.
1912–13	Turkey defeated in Balkan Wars. Losing most of European Turkey.
1913	The Young Turks (Committee of Unity and Progress) take power in Istanbul with the goal of modernising Turkey. They believe the country needs the security of a foreign alliance, but there is no consensus about whether to approach the Entente or the Triple Alliance. Some leading figures have been educated in Germany, while others have strong pro-Entente inclinations.
Sep. 1913	Britain completes a battleship for the Turkish navy, and wields strong influence through the British Naval Mission commanded by Admiral Limpus.
13 Dec.–Jan. 1914	The Mission of Liman von Sanders causes tension with Russia. But Liman was specifically instructed by the Kaiser to keep out of politics, and he played no rôle in Turkey's decision to enter the war.
1914	
13 Feb.	A ruling in favour of Greece over disputed Aegean Islands outrages Turkish nationalists.

180

May	Turkey signs the Convention of Livadia with Russia, signalling an improvement in Russo-Turkish relations. Turkey wanted a closer arrangement, or even an alliance.
18 Jul.	Jemal returns from France, having had his offers of an alliance and requests for a loan rebuffed.
22 Jul.	Enver Pasha sounds out the German Ambassador for an anti-Russian alliance. The Kaiser orders negotiations to proceed.
1 Aug.	Winston Churchill orders the requisitioning of two Turkish battleships *Rehsadiye* and *Sultan Osman*, that are nearing completion on Tyneside. The delivery of these ships, financed partly by public conscription, has been eagerly awaited as a means of establishing naval supremacy over Greece. The episode has a disastrous impact on Anglo-Turkish relations, greatly strengthening the war party in Istanbul.
2 Aug.	The German-Turkish Treaty. Turkey will remain neutral if Austria-Hungary attacks Serbia, and intervene on Germany's side if Russia attacked Germany. Germany will defend Turkey in the case of a Russian attack, and place her military mission at Turkey's disposal. The Treaty will remain secret. Although the terms of the Treaty have *already* been activated, it is not certain that Turkey will join the war.
10 Aug.	The German battleships *Goeben* and *Breslau* arrive in Constantinople, having escaped from a British fleet in the Mediterranean. They are promptly 'sold' to the Turkish government, posing an immediate threat to the Russian fleet and providing a powerful lever for German diplomacy.
1 Oct.	Turkey closes the Straits to Allied ships and unilaterally ends the historic privileges of foreigners (the Capitulations).
29 Oct.	The *Goeben* bombards the Russian Black Sea ports of Odessa and Novorosisk.
2 Nov.	Russia declares war on Turkey.
5 Nov.	Turkey declares war on the Entente. Later in the month the Sultan in his capacity of *Caliph*, calls for a Holy War against the British and French Empires.

Italy

Obligations at the outbreak of war. Allied to Austria-Hungary and Germany under the Triple Alliance of 1882.

Leading participants

Albertini, Luigi	Editor of pro-interventionist *Corriere della Sera*
Barrère, Camille	French Ambassador
Bülow, Bernhard von	German Ambassador, December 1914
Cadorna, General Luigi	Army Chief of Staff, July 1914
Giolitti, Giovanni	Main advocate of Italian neutrality
Pollio, General Alberto	Army Chief of Staff until 1 July 1914
Rodd, Sir James Rennell	British Ambassador
Mussolini, Benito	Editor of pro-interventionist *Populo d'Italia*
Salandra, Antonio	Prime Minister, March 1914
San Giuliano, Antonio di	Foreign Minister until 16 October 1914
Sonnino, Sidney	Foreign Minister, November 1914
Victor Emmauel III	King of Italy

1914

7–12 Jun.	'Red Week' a series of serious strikes and disturbances, centred on the Romagna, but extending throughout the country. The government comes close to losing control, and decision-making over the next few months is coloured by the threat of revolutionary disorder.
14 Jul.	San Giuliano asks the Foreign Ministry to examine whether Italy is obliged to fight under the terms of the Triple Alliance.
21 Jul.	Austria refuses to promise Italy that she will not annex Serb territory.
3 Aug.	Italy formally declares herself neutral, on the grounds that her allies have not fulfilled their obligations. They have not kept her informed, particularly about the ultimatum to Serbia, and have refused to offer her compensation under Article VII of the revised Treaty. San Giuliano believes that Italy's territorial claims against Austria are best served by neutrality, or eventually by joining the Entente. However, he keeps the door open to his Triple Alliance partners, hinting that Italy might eventually fulfil her obligations.
7–11 Aug.	Russia makes territorial offers to Italy to induce her to join the Entente, but San Giuliano makes claims at the expense of the South Slavs that Russia cannot accept.
8 Sep.	The German defeat on the Marne causes Italy to doubt eventual German victory.
23 Sep.	Italy and Romania agree to give each other eight days warning if they intend to join the war.
16 Oct.	Death of San Giuliano. He is replaced in November by Antonio Salandra, a strong advocate of regaining Italy's 'lost territories'. Salandra naively describes Italian policy as

Sacro Egoismo (Sacred Self-Interest). His Foreign Minister, Sidney Sonnino, is less qualified to sustain Italy's diplomatic balancing act.

7 Nov.	Sonnino speaks favourably to the British Ambassador about joining the Entente.
15 Nov.	Benito Mussolini's newspaper *Il Populo d'Italia* starts a campaign in favour of intervention (to fulfil 'Italy's national destiny').
17 Dec.	Bernhard von Bülow, ex-Chancellor of Germany, becomes German Ambassador, with the brief of keeping Italy neutral. However he can only make offers at the expense of his ally, Austria-Hungary, and Emperor Franz Josef refuses to be 'peeled like an artichoke'.
Dec.	Formation of the *Banca Italiana di Sconto*, by Salandra's business associates who favour the Entente. But most of the business community, and most Italians, oppose war.
Dec.	Giovanni Giolitti attacks Salandra and the interventionists in Parliament.

1915

3 Jan.	The British Ambassador warns London that Germany will succeed in mobilising Italian opponents of the war if the Entente does not come up with strong inducements to Italy.
13 Jan.	Count Stephan Burian, utterly opposed to concessions to Italy, becomes Austrian Foreign Minister.
Feb.	Giolitti's letter suggesting Italy could gain 'quite a lot' (*parecchio*) by doing a deal with Austria is published in the Press, outraging the interventionists lobby.
19 Feb.	The Dardanelles Campaign raises the prospect of the Entente partitioning the Ottoman Empire while Italy stands on the sidelines.
23 Feb.	The German Catholic politician Matthias Erzberger asks Pope Benedict XV to persuade Austria to concede territory to Italy to keep her neutral.
3 Mar.	The Italian Ambassador in London, Imperiali, warns Rome that Constantinople might fall to the Entente within days.
4 Mar.	Imperiali presents a list of Italian demands to Sir Edward Grey in return for joining the Entente at the beginning of April (see p. 217).
8 Mar.	The Austrian Crown Council reluctantly agrees to offer Trentino to Italy.

11 Mar.	Russia is told of Italy's demands, and is offered Constantinople and the Straits to persuade her to agree to Italy receiving Slav territory.
24 Mar.	The British Cabinet accepts Italy's demands in full. The French also agree, but it takes Russia several weeks to come round to the loss of 600,000 Slavs to Italy.
25 Apr.	British and French landings in the Dardanelles convince the Italians that they must act quickly.
26 Apr.	Italy, Britain, France and Russia sign the secret Pact of London, based upon the Italian demands of 4 March. Italy agrees to declare war against all of the Central Powers within one month. The agreement is so secret that Army commander General Luigi Cadorna is not told about it. The King, Salandra and Sonnino have pledged to fight, but would parliament and people accept their decision? Italy's 69 Prefects report overwhelming hostility to joining the war.
3 May	The Austro-German breakthrough in Galicia (Gorlice Tarnow) throws doubt upon whether Italy is joining the winning side.
4 May	The Italian Cabinet renounces the Triple Alliance.
6 May	An interventionist speech by Gabrielle d'Annunzio sparks anti-German riots in Turin and Milan.
7 May	The Cabinet is told for the first time that the King and Salandra have agreed to join the war.
9 May	Giovanni Giolitti returns to Rome for meetings with his anti-interventionist political allies.
12 May	Germany and Austria make a final offer of territory to Italy. This adds to Allied military setbacks in casting doubt on the wisdom of Italy joining the war.
13 May	Salandra and Sonnino resign after Giolitti publicly questions whether Italy will benefit from the Pact of London. The King sits on their resignations several days, but ensures that military preparations for war with Austria proceed.

'Radiant May'

The decision for war or peace becomes entangled with Italy's internal power struggle. Most people are still apathetic or hostile, but Benito Mussolini and the poet Gabriele D'Annunzio ally themselves with noisy pro-war demonstrations by intellectuals and students.

14 May	D'Annunzio whips up anti-German fever over the sinking of the *Lusitania.*
16 May	The Salandra government is re-instated, and Giolitti retires to his estates, acknowledging that he must accept the *fait accompli.*

20 May	Parliament reconvenes amidst patriotic euphoria, and votes overwhelmingly for emergency powers.
22 May	The official decree of mobilisation is issued.
24 May	Italy declares war on Austria-Hungary, but not (as agreed) on Germany.

Bulgaria

Obligations at the outbreak of war. None.

Leading participants

Tsar Ferdinand	Ruler since 1887
Radoslavov, Vasil	Leader of the Liberal Coalition
Stamboliiski, Alexander	Leader of the Agrarian Party. Supporter of the Entente
Savinski, A.A.	Russian Ambassador
Bax-Ironside, Sir Henry	British Ambassador until 1915
O'Beirne, Hugh	British Ambassador, July–October 1915

1913

29 Jun.– 31 Jul.	The Second Balkan War. Bulgaria is defeated by her erstwhile allies Greece and Serbia, and Romania attacks her from the north.
Jul.	Vasil Radoslavov appointed prime minister in the wake of defeat. He shares the King's preference for Germany and Austria.
10 Aug.	The Treaty of Bucharest. Despite doing most of the fighting, Bulgaria is stripped of most of her gains. She is determined to regain the lost territory, and bitter that her traditional protector, Russia, has failed to support her.
29 Sep.	The Treaty of Constantinople. Bulgaria and Turkey, two losers of the Balkan Wars, agree on a territorial settlement.

1914

| Mar. | Election victory for Radoslavov, who intends to move Bulgaria away from her traditional protector, Russia. |
| Jun. | Rejecting a French loan that would have bound Bulgaria to the Entente, Radoslavov agrees to large loans from Germany and Austria. The terms (loss of control of Bulgaria's mines and railways) provoke a riot in Parliament, during which Radoslavov threatens deputies with a revolver. Bulgaria is now economically tied to the Dual Alliance, which also provides 55% of her imports. |

185

24 Jun.	The Austrian diplomat Matscheko suggests that Austria-Hungary should draw Bulgaria into an alliance against Serbia.
Aug.	Bulgaria declares her neutrality. For the next year both sides court her. If she joins the war Serbia will be doomed, and she is a vital link in Germany's dream of extending her influence from Berlin to Baghdad. Tsar Ferdinand and Radoslavov believe that neutrality is Bulgaria's best policy. Until it is clear who is winning the war, they are content to evaluate the territorial offers of the competing power blocs.
6 Aug.	Bulgaria and Turkey sign a secret treaty of co-operation.
1 Sep.	Serbia reluctantly agrees to cede part of Macedonia to Bulgaria if she joins the Entente (but only in return for concessions elsewhere).
6 Sep.	Bulgaria signs a treaty with Austria-Hungary to join the war if the latter is attacked by Romania. Bulgaria allows German supplies to Turkey to cross her territory, and rejects a Russian request for the use of Bulgarian ports and territory.
17 Nov.	Britain proposes that Bulgaria be offered the whole of Macedonia, with Serbia compensated elsewhere. Russia objects to this.

1915

Feb.	The Central Powers offer Bulgaria 'all the territory she is able to win by force of arms'.
Spring and early Summer	The bargaining position of the Entente is undermined by the failing Gallipoli expedition and Russian reverses on the Eastern Front. Bulgar–Serb relations deteriorate because of the activities of Bulgarian guerrillas in 'Serb occupied' Macedonia.
29 May	The Entente offers Bulgaria (after the war) the portion of Macedonia that the Serbs occupied in 1913, which the Bulgarians believe to be theirs (the 'uncontested zone') but only if Serbia gets compensation elsewhere. They promise to persuade Greece and Romania to give Bulgaria Kavalla and Southern Dobrudja.
15 Jun.	Sir Henry Bax-Ironside, British Minister in Sofia, resigns because of Britain's treatment of its fighting ally, Serbia. This highlights the dilemma of the Entente negotiators: they can only offer Bulgaria inducements at the expense of Serbia or another potential ally, Greece.
Jun.	The Russians set up a secret fund to buy influence in the Bulgarian Press, but Germany and Austrian have already won the propaganda war.

17 Jul.	The new British Ambassador Hugh O'Beirne, adds to the Entente offer of May, but the Serbs steadfastly refuse to give up territory to their hated Balkan rival.
Jul.–Aug.	Major gains for the Central Powers on the Eastern Front. The tide of war seems to be running against the Entente.
25 Aug.	A consortium of Entente bankers starts to buy up surplus Bulgarian wheat to prop up the economy and win support, but the scheme gets underway too late, and is too incompetently run, to influence events.
6 Sep.	Bulgarian representatives sign the Pless Convention and two other treaties with the Central Powers. Bulgaria agrees to be ready to invade Serbia within a month, and to fight Greece and Romania if either of them attacks Germany. In return, Bulgaria will get most of Macedonia, Serbian territory east of the Morava river, and more territory at the expense of Greece and Romania if *they* join the Entente. Germany also persuades Turkey to hand over a strip of territory that will give Bulgaria a rail link to her otherwise useless Aegean port of Dedeagach. Germany will attack Serbia with six divisions in thirty days, and Bulgaria will support the attack with four divisions in thirty-five days.
21 Sep.	The Bulgarian army begins to mobilise.
4 Oct.	Russia delivers an ultimatum demanding the dismissal of all German military 'advisors' and demobilisation of the army. This is rejected, and the Entente representatives leave the country immediately.
11 Oct.	Bulgarian forces join the Austro-German invasion of Serbia which started on 6 October. Within two months, all Serbian territory is in the hands of the Central Powers, which now control a contiguous mass of territory stretching from Hamburg to Baghdad.

Romania

Obligations. Romania is bound by a secret alliance with Austria signed in 1883 by King Carol I. Only the King and a few of his immediate confidants know its exact terms.

Leading participants

Carol I of Hohenzollern	King of Romania, 1881–1914
Ferdinand I of Hohenzollern	King of Romania, October 1914 to 1927
Czernin, Ottokar	Austrian Minister in Bucharest 1913–16
Bratianu, Ionel	Prime Minister 1914–18. Champion of 'Greater Romania'

1913

Jul.	Romania renews the 1883 secret alliance with Austria-Hungary and Germany.
10 Jul.	Romania declares war on Bulgaria, which has attacked its fellow victors in the First Balkan War (29 June). Romanian troops easily occupy the northern Bulgarian territory of Dobrudja while the Bulgarian army is fighting the Serbs and Greeks.
10 Aug.	The Treaty of Bucharest. Bulgaria is forced to give up a slice of Dobrudja to Romania.
Nov.	Count Ottokar Czernin, sent by Vienna to ascertain Romania's loyalty, is unable to say whether Romania will honour the Treaty. The German Kaiser remains confidant that Romania will fight.

1914

4 Jan.	King Carol appoints the agrarian reformer and consummate politician Ion Bratianu as Chief Minister. Both men are admirers of Germany, but Magyar misrule in Transylvania has weakened their support for the Habsburg Empire.
27 Mar.	An official visit to Russia by Crown Prince Ferdinand, the heir to the Romanian throne, reveals an about-turn in Russo-Romanian relations, which have been soured since 1878 by Russia's annexation of 'Romanian' Bessarabia. Prince William sounds out Russian support for Bucharest's designs on the Hungarian ruled Habsburg territory of Transylvania.
14 Jun.	Russian State visit to Romania. The two countries agree to co-operate against foreign threats to the freedom of the Black Sea Straits. Russian Foreign Minister Sazonov infuriates the Austrians by provocatively crossing the border to meet Romanian residents of Transylvania.
24 Jun.	In Vienna, the Matscheko Memorandum recommends that Austria actively cultivate Bulgaria as a counterweight to Serbia in the Balkans.
30–31 Jul.	At the height of the July Crisis Romania is offered Transylvania by Russia, in return for her neutrality, and Bessarabia by Germany, in return for her involvement.
3 Aug.	The Crown Council gives virtually unanimous support for neutrality. Ministers reject the idea of fighting alongside the 'odious Magyar regime', and Bratianu says that 'the question of the Romanians of Transylvania dominates the whole situation'. The Central Powers assume that Romania is merely putting off meeting her obligations.

Aug.–Sep.	Russian armies push the Habsburg forces back towards the Romanian frontier, leading interventionists to demand that Romania join in to deliver the 'death blow'. But Austria resists urgent German request to offer Romania concessions.
23 Sep.	Romania signs an agreement with Italy by which the two countries agree to co-ordinate their diplomacy.
2 Oct.	A Russian–Romanian neutrality agreement is signed.
10 Oct.	King Carol dies, and is succeeded by his nephew Ferdinand, who is much more favourably inclined to the Entente and open to their territorial inducements. His wife Queen Marie is a granddaughter of Queen Victoria. The King's weak character and lack of experience allow Bratianu to dominate diplomatic negotiations.

1915

25 Jan.	The Entente offers Transylvania to Bucharest if it joins the war immediately. Bratianu declines, believing that Romania must make sure it is joining the winning side.
6 Feb.	The Romanians and Italians sign a mutual assistance pact in case of an attack by Austria-Hungary.
3 May	Influenced by Italy's imminent entry into the war and the Gallipoli expedition, Romania presents a list of territorial demands to the Entente via St Petersburg. They include, as well as Transylvania, the Bukovina and the Banat regions of Austria-Hungary. The Allies reject them as excessive.
23 May	Military reverses force the Allies to climb down and accept Romania's demands. But by this time Allied defeats in Galicia and Gallipoli cause Bratianu and the King to change their minds.
Aug.	Months of negotiation between Romania and the Entente break down in failure, due to Bratianu's uncompromising negotiating stance and his lack of confidence in the ability of the Allies to win the war.

1916

7 Apr.	The pile-up of massive grain surpluses and economic stagnation force Bratianu to give up Romania's economic neutrality and sell large quantities of grain and oil to the Central Powers.
Jun.	Violent demonstrations and strikes, that are motivated by economic grievances rather than the issue of intervention.
4 Jul.	Following Brusilov's spectacular breakthrough, and telegrams from the French and Russian High Command, Bratianu announces that he is ready to sign a military convention if

five conditions are met: formal acceptance of Romania's territorial claims; the continuation of Allied offensives; security against Bulgarian attack; continued Russian pressure in Bukovina and Galicia; guaranteed arms supplies from the Allies. Although the Allies meet most of these requirement, Bratianu's obstinate adherence to the letter of his demands, and his claim for equal status at the eventual peace conference mean that the negotiations drag on while Brusilov's offensive runs out of steam.

23 Jul.   The Romanian military attaché in Paris signs the Chantilly Convention, by which a Romanian army of 150,000 troops, supported by the Russians, would attack Bulgaria a week after the Allies had launched an offensive from Salonika.

5 Aug.   Bratianu orders the suspension of mobilisation, after major disagreements emerge in the interpretation of the agreement.

17 Aug.   Romania signs a secret treaty with Great Britain, France, Russia, and Italy: Romania is guaranteed Transylvania as far as the River Tisza, the Banat, and Bukovina as far as the River Pruth. (Some of the key issues are glossed over and will later lead to recrimination at the Peace Conference.)

26 Aug.   Romania declares war on Austria-Hungary and invades Transylvania.

30 Aug.   Germany declares war on Romania.

1 Sep.   Bulgaria and Turkey declare war on Romania, which is is attacked on three fronts by German, Austrian and Bulgarian armies.

3 Dec.   The King and members of the government flee Bucharest for Jassi, the capital of Moldavia. Three days later the Central Powers occupy Bucharest.

Greece

Obligations. Under the Treaty of Bucharest, 1913 Greece was committed to assist Serbia if she was attacked. Britain and France claim that Greece is obliged, under the 19th-century treaties setting up the Kingdom, to accept their intervention at times of international crisis.

Leading participants

Alexander	King of the Hellenes, 1917–20
Constantine	King of the Hellenes, 1913–17, 1920–2
Venizelos, Elepherios	Prime Minister since 1910
Ziamis, Alexander	Pro-German politician
Gounaris, Demitrios	Pro-German politician
Metaxas, Ioannis	Pro-German deputy commander of army

1913

18 Mar.	King George of the Hellenes is assassinated in Salonika. His successor, Constantine I, brother-in-law to Kaiser Wilhelm II, has strong pro-German inclinations, but favours Greek neutrality and 'a small but honourable Greece'. However, his Prime Minister, Elepherios Venizelos, believes that Greek interests are best served in alliance with Britain and France. In 1913, he discusses terms for joining the Entente with Lloyd George and Churchill in London.
10 Aug.	The Second Balkan War ends. In less than a year Greece has achieved, at the expense of Turkey and Bulgaria, most of the territorial ambitions that she has nurtured since independence. Thessaly, Macedonia, including the great port of Salonika (Thessaloniki), Western Thrace, Crete, and numerous smaller islands are incorporated into the motherland. Only the conquest of Constantinople and Western Anatolia remains to complete the national project (*Megali Idea*). In the short term Greece needs to hang on to her gains in the face of Bulgarian and Turkish revanchism.

1914

25 Jul.	During the July Crisis, Venizelos assures Serbia that Greece would 'oppose' a Bulgarian attack on Serbia.
Aug.	King Constantine rejects Germany's appeal for Greece to join the Central Powers, but Venizelos rejects an Entente proposal to cede Kavalla to the Bulgarians. Instead, he proposes (12 August) a complex and statesmanlike re-drawing of the Balkan frontiers, which would satisfy *all* potential Balkan Entente adherents.
18 Aug.	A proposal by Venizelos for Greece to enter the war is rejected: Britain fears that this would cause Turkey to join the Central Powers. Russia sees Greece as a rival to her ambitions in the Straits.
7 Sep.	Venizelos resigns because of disagreements with the King over the issue of Greek neutrality.
5 Nov.	Britain's annexation of Cyprus following Turkey's entry into the war enrages Greek public opinion.
9 Nov.	The Entente offers Bulgaria parts of Greek Thrace and a portion of Macedonia as an inducement for her to join the war.
6 Dec.	The Romanian leader, Bratianu, refuses the request of the Entente to guarantee Greece against Bulgarian aggression.
25 Dec.	The Italians occupy Southern Albania, which the Greeks regard as part of their historic territory.

1915

23 Jan.	Venizelos proposes an Allied landing in Greece to assist Serbia. The French are very keen, but discussions drag on because Romania refuses to join in, and the Russians are suspicious of Greek ambitions.
24 Jan.	Sir Edward Grey offers Cyprus to Greece, and 'important concessions' in Asia if Greece will cede the Kavalla area to Bulgaria and join a Balkan bloc to help Serbia. Constantine is against the offer and Venizelos rejects it because it gives no guarantee against Bulgarian attack, or assurance that Romania will join in.
19 Feb.	The Allies postpone a landing in Greece in favour of the Gallipoli expedition.
6 Mar.	Venizelos resigns when Constantine refuses to back his plan to send Greek troops to the Dardanelles. His successor, Demitrios Gounaris, is an opponent of the Entente. Greece is now deeply split over the merits of intervention ('The National Schism').
12 Apr.	Gounaris rejects another Allied offer of territory in Asia Minor because Greece is still not being guaranteed against Bulgarian aggression.
Jun.	Elections: Venizelos wins a clear majority, which he regards as a mandate to join the Entente, but the King delays his return to office until 22 August.
6 Sep.	The Central Powers promise Bulgaria Greek territory in return for joining them (the Pless Convention). Bulgaria begins preparations for war.
21 Sep.	Serbia calls upon Greece to intervene under the terms of the agreement of May 1913. Venizelos mobilises the Greek army (23 September) but insists that the Allies also commit 150,000 men to assist Serbia.
24 Sep.	Britain and France agree to send troops to Greece, and Venizelos secures the King's secret approval for this. However, the King refuses to agree to an Allied landing at Salonika.
3 Oct.	Allied troops begin to land at Salonika despite the King's wishes. King Constantine abrogates his agreement with Venizelos, and refuses to declare war.
5 Oct.	Venizelos resigns again, to be replaced by Alexander Zaimis, who opposes intervention.
16 Oct.	Britain offers Cyprus to Greece as an inducement, but the offer is rejected on 20 October.
8 Nov.	Greece reaffirms her neutrality, pledging not to actively aid either side.

Dec.	Venizelos boycotts elections, leaving Parliament dominated by anti-interventionists.

1916

11 Jan.	In defiance of the King's wishes, the French occupy Corfu as a refuge for the defeated Serbian army, which begins to land there on 15 January. Greece refuses to allow the re-equipped Serbian army to cross Greek territory to reach Salonika.
26 May	The Greek army surrenders Fort Ruppel, the most important strongpoint of Eastern Macedonia. The Allies are convinced that Constantine is secretly collaborating with the Central Powers.
21 Jun.	Having enforced a 'pacific blockade' of Greece, the allies demand the demobilisation of the Greek army, and a change of government.
23 Jun.	The King accepts the Entente's demands, standing down his army, and bringing back Zaimis as PM.
30 Aug.	Greek officers loyal to Venizelos set up a pro-Entente National Defence regime in Salonika, supported by the Allies.
18 Sep.	The Greek army surrenders Kavalla to German forces without firing a shot.
29 Sep.	Venizelos leaves for his native Crete, with the aid of French Intelligence. Having denounced the King's pro-German policy, he proclaims a Greek Provisional Government.
9 Oct.	Venizelos moves to Salonika to lead the Provisional Government. Greece is now split in two: in Athens the 'neutral' regime of King Constantine; in the north the pro-Entente Venizelist regime, which by November is fighting the Bulgarians alongside general Sarrail's army.
11 Oct.	King Constantine yields to an Allied ultimatum to surrender the Greek fleet to the Allies.
19 Nov.	The Allies demand the surrender of all materials of war, and the removal of representatives of the Central Powers.
1 Dec.	Allied marines suffer casualties at the hands of the Royalist army. They have landed at Piraeus after the Greek government rejects the Allied demands of 19 November. France is now determined to get rid of King Constantine.
8 Dec.	The Allies begin a naval blockade of Greece.
15 Dec.	Constantine accepts an Allied ultimatum to withdraw his forces from northern Greece.
19 Dec.	The Allies recognise the Venizelist government in Salonika.

193

1917

12 Jun.	Yielding to French pressure, Constantine abdicates in favour of his second son, Alexander, who is favoured by the Entente. Allied troops occupy northern Greece and the Isthmus of Corinth.
25 Jun.	Venizelos reconvenes the parliament elected in 1915 (the 'Lazarus Parliament') and returns as Prime Minister of a united Greece.
29 Jun.	Greece declares war on the Central Powers and deploys nine divisions on the Macedonian Front.

The United States

Obligations. None.

Leading participants

Bernstorff, Johann Heinrich von	German Ambassador, 1908–17
Bryan, William Jennings	Secretary of State, 1913–15
House, Colonel Edward	President Wilson's special representative
Lansing, Robert	Secretary of State, 1915–20
Spring Rice, Sir Cecil	British Ambassador
Wilson, Thomas Woodrow	President, 1912–16, 1916–20
Zimmermann, Arthur	German Foreign Minister, 1916–17

1914

20 May– 2 Jul.	The Niagara Falls Conference discusses the American occupation of Veracruz in Mexico. American public opinion is diverted from events in Europe by the crisis in US–Mexican relations, which will continue to preoccupy American foreign policy for the next three years.
31 Jul.	Closure of the New York Stock Exchange, because of the collapse in confidence brought about by the July Crisis. President Wilson appeals to Congress to allow foreign ships to sail under the American flag, which greatly assists the war effort of the Entente.
4 Aug.	Britain declares war on Germany. During the July Crisis President Wilson's half-hearted offers of mediation are not taken up.
5 Aug.	Britain cuts the marine cable linking Germany with the United States. Berlin can only send secure communications to its embassy in Washington via Liberia and Brazil (taking 80 hours to send a message and get a reply).
15 Aug.	The Department of Commerce bans loans to all belligerents in the European war.

18 Aug.	Wilson officially declares US neutral.
20 Nov.	Britain's declares a maritime blockade of the Central Powers: this will lead to serious friction between Britain and the US, but it locks the US economy into the Allied war effort by cutting off American exports to the Central Powers and diverting them to Britain and France.
8 Dec.	Wilson's Annual Message reaffirms his commitment to neutrality.

1915

4 Feb.	The first German submarine campaign begins.
18 Feb.	United States warns Germany that she will be held accountable for the loss of American lives and property in the naval war zone declared on 4 February.
11 Mar.	Britain bans all neutrals, including the United States, from trading with Germany.
7 May	A disastrous day for Germany's supporters in America: 128 Americans die when the British liner *Lusitania* is sunk, and the Bryce Report publicises German atrocities in occupied Belgium.
4 Apr.	Germany complains that the US is favouring the Entente in its trading policies.
15 Jul.	The British Ambassador warns London of the need to conciliate powerful American business interests who are becoming hostile to Britain's blockade policy.
1 Sep.	Germany agrees to warn passenger vessels before sinking them, after American protests over two Americans deaths on the torpedoed liner *Arabic*.
4 Nov.	Wilson announces, to the fury of the neutralist lobby, an expanded military and naval programme.
Dec.	The American Rights Committee is founded in New York to work for the US to join the Entente. It reveals German subversive activities in Mexico and United States.

1916

Since the beginning of the war American trade with the Allies has grown 400% while with the Central Powers it is 1% of the pre-war figure.

24 Apr.	The harsh British response to The Easter Rising in Dublin alienates many Irish Americans.
4 May	Germany announces that its navy will abide by internationally agreed rules of stop and search, following the sinking of the cross-channel ferry *Sussex* with 80 casualties, on 24 March,

	and Wilson's demands (18 April) that Germany stop sinking unarmed passenger ships.
13 May	The US army is doubled to over 200,000. The National Guard is reorganised, and arms production increased. These measures increased American 'Preparedness', but do little to create a convincing military force should she choose to enter the war.
10 Jun.	Charles Evans Hughes, a strong supporter of the Entente, is adopted as Republican Presidential candidate.
16 Jun.	In his re-nomination speech in St Louis, Wilson calls for a League of Nations and a new international order based on collective security, but it is plain that the delegates support him because of his neutralist stance ('He kept us out of war').
19 Jul.	Britain publishes a blacklist of US firms alleged to be trading with the enemy.
2 Nov.	Wilson tells Colonel House 'I do not believe the American people would wish to go to war no matter how many Americans were killed at sea.'
7 Nov.	Re-election of Woodrow Wilson with a narrow majority based on neutralism and progressive reform.
18 Dec.	Wilson's Note asking the belligerents to state their war aims meets with a tepid response from both sides.

1917

3 Jan.	German Chancellor Bethmann Hollweg agrees to accept a secret American offer of mediation.
19 Jan.	Ambassador Bernstorff tells Colonel House that although America might be part of a post-war peace conference, discussions on ending the war must take place only between belligerents.
26 Jan.	Great Britain tells Wilson it is prepared to accept American mediation.
1 Feb.	Germany resumes unrestricted submarine warfare.
3 Feb.	Wilson tells Congress that he is breaking off diplomatic relations with Germany.
8 Feb.	Wilson and Lansing say that private shipping lines might put guns on their own merchant ships, but the US navy would not become involved.
11 Feb.	Germany says it will not relax the submarine blockade out of concern for American opinion.
13 Feb.	Wilson tells his Cabinet that he will not go to Congress for authority to arm merchant vessels until Germany had forced

	his hand. He would do nothing to give the Germans the impression that he wanted war.
22 Feb.	Wilson prepares a message proposing the arming of merchant vessels, to be delivered to Congress on 26 February. Most American shipping lines cancel sailings to European waters after 1 February, causing mountains of goods to pile up at the docks.
25 Feb.	The British secret service gives Washington a telegram from German Foreign Minister Arthur Zimmermann to the German minister in Mexico urging Mexico to attack United States in alliance with Germany.
26 Feb.	Wilson asks Congress for permission to arm US merchant ships and to use any other means of protecting US vessels and people.
1 Mar.	The Zimmermann Telegram is released to the Press, causing popular outrage. Congress approves the Armed Ship Bill by 403 votes to 13.
15 Mar.	The 'February Revolution' in Russia undermines the resistance of Americans reluctant to fight alongside the Tsarist autocracy. Many politicians now believe that the survival of Russian freedom depends on the defeat of Germany.
18 Mar.	A German submarine sinks three American merchant vessels without warning.
2 Apr.	Wilson asks joint session of Congress to support his formal declaration of war on Germany.
6 Apr.	Congress approves Wilson's declaration of war by 434 votes to 1.

7.2 ATTEMPTS TO DIVIDE THE ENEMY

Both military strategists and diplomats realised that a sure way to victory would be to destroy the unity of the opposing alliance by ether forcing or persuading one of its members to sign a separate peace. Diplomatically this might be achieved either when a country's situation became so desperate that it was forced to desert its allies and sue for peace, or if it could be made an offer that was too tempting to refuse. The only belligerents that did leave the war unilaterally were Russia and Romania, although technically, Bulgaria, Turkey and Austria-Hungary abandoned Germany in the last days of the war. In the case of the Entente, by The Pact of London of 5 September 1914, they had pledged not to negotiate separately with the enemy or to make peace unilaterally. Until November 1917 this commitment held remarkably firm.

Britain and France

There was never any real prospect of prising the two Entente partners apart unless Germany offered to evacuate Belgium and return Alsace-Lorraine, or if either of them was so crippled, by military defeat or submarine blockade, to sue for a Carthaginian peace. None of these eventualities ever materialised, and neither government was prepared to negotiate with Germany, even at their lowest military ebb. Although unofficial voices, like Lord Lansdowne and Joseph Caillaux called for compromise, they stopped short of advocating that their countries should unilaterally leave the war. Both Britain and France dutifully informed each other when tentative German advances were occasionally made.

Romania

On 9 December 1917, the collapse of Russian resistance forced Romania to sign the Armistice of Foçsani with the Central Powers. She did not intend at this time to sign a separate peace, but the Brest-Litovsk Treaty, the inability of her erstwhile allies to help her, and relentless pressure from Germany forced her on 7 May 1918 to sign the Treaty of Bucharest. She lost (for a few months) considerable territory to Hungary and Bulgaria, and was mercilessly stripped of raw materials by her German occupiers, but re-rejoined the Allies the day before the Armistice on the Western Front.

Austria-Hungary

Austria-Hungary was by far the weakest link in the Central Power axis, and from 1916 onwards her economic plight and military collapse made her a tempting target for Allied diplomatic advances. The peace feelers of Emperor Karl and Ottokar Czernin in 1917 (see pp. 220–1) were presented as efforts to find a general peace, but they were conducted behind Germany's back and seemed at times to seek a way out for Austria alone. All Allied efforts were checkmated by the Treaty of London of 1915 which committed them to give Habsburg territory to Italy, which resisted all efforts (such as at St Jean de Maurienne in 1917) to ease her demands.

In the Armand–Revertera Conversations of August 1917, Armand offered Silesia, Bavaria and a reunited '1792 Poland' to Austria in return for a separate peace. Unfortunately, he went far beyond his brief, and was repudiated by Lloyd George and Ribot. In December 1917 during the Smuts–Mensdorff Conversations, Britain held out the prospect of an Austrian-controlled Poland, but Austria was again unwilling to do a deal. In any case, Germany would never allow Austria to have these rewards, or let her leave the war.

Russia

Russia's allies were always unsure about her willingness and capacity to remain in the war. They were haunted by the possibility that Russia would sign a separate peace, aware that many Russian Conservatives felt a historical affinity to Germany and Austria, and that a section of the Russian Left opposed the war or even hoped for Russia's defeat. Russian statesmen played upon these fears to negotiate Allied promises of territory, while the Central Powers continued to hope that Russia could be split from the Entente, and plotted to make use of the Bolsheviks to undermine the Russian war effort.

1914

5 Nov.	Arrest of five Bolshevik Duma deputies for distributing Lenin's *Theses on the War* saying that a Russian defeat would be 'the lesser evil', and calling for the 'imperialist war' to be transformed into a 'civil war' to further the cause of social revolution. However, most Russian Social Democrats, including some Bolsheviks, still support the defence of the fatherland.
1 Dec.	The Andersen–Ballin negotiations. Albert Ballin the German ship-owner and Hans-Nils Andersen, a Danish industrialist, try to draw up a programme to win over Russian Conservatives to a separate peace. Thus begins a diplomatic offensive by Germany that lasted (with nothing to show for it) until 1916.

1915

Mar.	The Hohenlöhe Letter. An approach to the Tsar from Austria-Hungary offers such paltry concessions that Russia dismisses the possibility of a separate peace with Austria.
11 Mar.	The wealthy revolutionary Alexander Helphand persuades Berlin to provide 2m gold marks for revolutionary propaganda in Russia. He has has convinced Berlin that the best way to get Russia out of the war is to support the Bolsheviks and anti-war exiles.
10 Apr.	The Straits Agreement. Britain and France accept that Russia should have Constantinople and the Straits after the war. The offer is designed to calm Russia's fears about the Gallipoli expedition, and to compensate her for agreeing to give up Slav territory to Italy. Appeasing Russia is regarded as a way of keeping her in the war.
May	Lenin rejects Helphand's offer of German money.
5–8 Sep.	Lenin tries to persuade the socialist conference at Zimmerwald to adopt his slogan 'Transform the Imperialist War into Civil War!' but the majority supports the more moderate formula 'An immediate peace without annexations or indemnities and the right of the peoples to self-determination'.

1916

Mar.–May   The Stinnes–Uchida Conversations. The German industrialist holds abortive discussion with Japanese representatives in Stockholm on the possibility of getting Russia out of the war via a Russian–German–Japanese agreement.

24 Apr.   At the second Socialist Conference at Kienthal, Lenin and his supporters again fail to get agreement to 'defeatist' resolutions.

13 Oct.   Writing in a Swiss socialist newspaper, Lenin says that if the Tsar is overthrown, there should be no co-operation with a regime that takes over and persists with the war.

1917

The February Revolution. The Allies welcome the overthrow of the Tsar, believing that Russia's fighting capacity will improve under the new democratic and modernising regime. The Provisional Government assures them Russia will continue to fight, and affirms it still supports Tsarist war aims. On 22 March, the US recognises the new Russian government, followed by France, Great Britain and Italy.

Germany refuses to make concessions to the Provisional Government

29 Mar.   Bethmann makes it clear that Germany will persist with its territorial demands against Russia.

Mar.–Apr.   The Erzberger–Kolyschko Conversations. The German politician and the Russian official meet in Stockholm. Erzberger makes minor concessions but both envoys are repudiated by their governments.

29 Apr.   German Armistice terms are rejected by the Provisional Government.

14 May   Germany again proposes harsh terms to General Dragomirow, but Kerensky rejects them out of hand.

Jun.   The Grimm–Hoffmann Conversations. Discussions between the Swiss socialist and Foreign Minister lead nowhere. It is now clear that Germany is not prepared to make sufficient concessions to tempt Russia into separate peace, and the Russian Provisional Government is not prepared to desert its allies.

The Soviet and the Bolsheviks move towards peace

14 Mar.   Order Number 1 of the Petrograd Soviet (see p. 170) undermines the morale of the Russian army, allowing the Central Powers to put the Eastern Front on ice for several months.

27 Mar.   The Petrograd Soviet's 'Manifesto to the Peoples of the World' calls for peace without annexations or indemnities.

31 Mar.	The Soviet newspaper *Izvestia* denounces secret diplomacy and calls for a new revolutionary foreign policy.
4 Apr.	Lenin's *Letters from Afar* call for the repudiation of Russia's treaties, an immediate peace initiative, the publication of diplomatic documents, and the liberation of colonies.
16 Apr.	Lenin arrives in Russia having cynically taken advantage of German travel assistance.
17 Apr.	Lenin's April theses.

- Despite the overthrow of the Tsar 'the war unquestionably remains a predatory imperialist war' owing to the capitalist nature of the new government.
- Russia can only carry on fighting on condition that 'the power of government passes to the proletariat', 'all annexations renounced in deed as well as in words'; and 'a complete and real break be made with all capitalist interests'.
- The Russian people genuinely believe they must defend their country, but 'the indissoluble connection between capital and the imperialist war' and the reality that the war 'can only be ended by overthrowing the existing order' must be brought home to the fighting soldiers through propaganda.

13 Apr.	The former French minister Albert Thomas arrives in St Petersburg to sound out the new regime.
11–17 Apr.	The Conference of Soviets meeting in Petrograd calls for a negotiated peace.
1 May	Prince Lvov's Declaration to the Allies. Lvov states that Russia has no expansionist aims, and wishes to conclude peace based on self-determination. However, Miliukov's Note, which accompanies it, stresses the need for 'decisive victory' and 'Russia's obligations' to her allies.
2 May	Russian C-in-C Alexeev tells the government that 'the army is on the very brink of ruin' with a breakdown of discipline and over two million desertions since March.
18 May	Tereschenko, Foreign Minister of the new Coalition Government, accepts the Soviet policy of seeking a negotiated settlement with 'no annexations and indemnities'.
16 May	Trotsky arrives in Russia determined to end the war as a means of kindling international revolution.
2 Jun.	The Petrograd Soviet issues an invitation to European Socialists to attend a peace conference in Stockholm.
16 Jun.	Lenin demands immediate peace at the First All-Russian Congress of Soviets of Workers and Soldiers Deputies, but the

conference decides to continue the war to defend the country from invasion and to protect the gains of the revolution.

1–19 Jul.	The 'Kerensky Offensive' fails and the Russian army begins to disintegrate.
12 Oct.	The German advance threatens Petrograd.
5 Nov.	The October Revolution. Until February 1918, the Bolsheviks try to secure a General Negotiated Peace, which they hope will spark mass revolution in the belligerent states (see pp. 222–4). But by antagonising the Allies, overestimating the revolutionary fervour of the European working class, and underestimating the ruthlessness of the German High Command, they are relentlessly propelled towards a *separate* peace.
9 Nov.	Britain and France reject Lenin's call for an armistice, reminding him of Russia's obligation under the Pact of London.
15 Dec.	All fighting stops on the Eastern Front. The Bolsheviks demand that no German troops be transferred to the west.

1918

8 Jan.	Trotsky takes over the peace negotiations at Brest-Litovsk, using them as a propaganda platform for 'World Revolution' rather than a forum for practical negotiations. The Bolsheviks distance themselves from the Entente. The Third Congress of Soviets passes the 'Declaration of the Rights of the Toiling and Exploited Masses' which the Allies regard as an attempt to encourage uprisings in their colonies. *Repudiation of Foreign Debts.* On 21 January, the Russian Republic writes off the vast sums invested by the west in Tsarist Russia, driving another wedge between the Allies and the Bolshevik regime.
18 Jan.	Frustrated by Trotsky's delaying tactics, Germany presents an ultimatum to the Soviet delegation, Trotsky returns to Petrograd to consult with his colleagues.
21 Jan.	At a meeting of the Bolshevik Central Committee Lenin argues that Russia can no longer depend on 'World Revolution'. Their situation is so precarious that a peace treaty must be signed on any terms. Trotsky proposes the formula 'Neither War nor Peace' by which Russia would stop fighting but refuse to sign a peace treaty, but the Central Committee votes to continue the war as a 'Revolutionary War'.
24 Jan.	Trotsky narrowly wins the consent of the Central Committee for his 'Neither War nor Peace' formula.
9 Feb.	The Central Powers sign a separate peace with the Ukraine.

10 Feb.	Trotsky walks out of the negotiations with the words 'We are leaving the war, but we find it necessary to forego the signing of a peace treaty'.
13 Feb.	Germany decides to break the Armistice. At a Crown Council meeting at Bad Homburg, Kühlmann argues in favour of a pragmatic peace preventing German forces from being tied up in the east. The Kaiser and Ludendorff favour a massive attack to take Petrograd and sweep away the Bolsheviks. They compromise with a limited offensive to force the Bolsheviks to sign the treaty.
18 Feb.	The Austro-German armies advance along the length of the Eastern front. Within days Petrograd itself is under threat, causing the Bolsheviks to transfer the government to Moscow.
23 Feb.	The Germans present the Russian government with a new list of stringent terms. They give it two days to start negotiating, and three more to sign a treaty.
1 Mar.	The Russian delegation returns to Brest.
3 Mar.	Russia signs the Treaty of Brest-Litovsk (see pp. 212–13).

Russia Mar.– Nov. 1918: Intervention and Civil War

Although Russia officially left the war in March 1918, her fate remained of supreme importance to both sides until the signing of the Armistice in November. The German High Command was determined to seize as much Russian territory and resources as possible, while keeping the Bolsheviks in power as 'the lesser evil'. The Allies were desperate to keep some sort of Eastern Front in being, and were prepared to support any group in the unfolding Russian Civil War that would fight the Central Powers. The objective of Lenin and Trotsky was survival. They loathed both sides equally and were prepared to make concession, promise reconciliation, or resort to arms against either of them to keep the revolution alive in Russia.

1. Continuing German encroachment

Apr.–May 1918	German troops intervene in Finland to defeat the Finish Reds and set up a puppet State. In The Ukraine, Germany removes the elected Rada and installs its protégé Skoropadsky. In the Crimea Germany invades and sets up an 'independent' government.
27 Aug.	The Supplementary Treaty. Germany forces the Bolsheviks to concede sovereignty over Livonia and Estonia to Germany, recognise Georgian independence, give Germany 25% of Baku oil, and pay a large war indemnity. Lenin is told to expel the Allies from the Arctic.

2. Russia and the Allies

23 Dec. 1917   After the Bolsheviks' unilateral Armistice with the Central Powers, Britain and France divide Russia into 'spheres of influence' to protect Allied supplies and encourage forces that might continue to resist with loans and advisors. The Allies tell Lenin they have no wish interfere in Russian internal affairs or to support counter-revolution, but because the proponents of continuing the war are also anti-Bolshevik, they are in reality drawn into supporting the Whites in the Russian Civil War.

1918

17 Feb.   France offers to give arms and money to the Bolsheviks if they fight on.

22 Feb.   The Central Committee votes, on Trotsky's advice, to accept Allied aid.

6 Mar.   A small number of British Marines land at Murmansk to protect the vast Allied warehouses and arms dumps from capture by the Germans or Finns. The Murmansk Soviet has requested Allied aid, and Trotsky approves it.

Mar.   France decides to help the Bolsheviks only if they resist the Germans. The Czech National Committee persuades the Bolsheviks to allow the Czech Legion to leave Russia via Murmansk.

May   Lenin condemns the Allied presence at Murmansk.

14 May   The Czech Legion, having been diverted to Vladivostok, clashes with Hungarian prisoners of war at Chelyabinsk on the Trans-Siberian Railway.

25 May   The 'Czech revolt' begins when the Legion refuse a Bolshevik order to surrender its weapons (see pp. 237–8).

8 Jun.   The Czechs occupy Samara. By the end of the month, they control most of the Trans-Siberian Railway, and are being used by the Allies and Whites to attack the Bolsheviks.

6 Jul.   President Wilson asks Japan to join America with 7,000 men in a landing at Vladivostok 'to aid the escape of the Czech Legion'.

24 Jul.   Lenin says that Soviet Russia is in a de facto state of war with the Allies.

Aug.   Britain causes a rift with Lenin by removing the Bolshevik authorities in Murmansk.

Aug.   Japanese forces start to arrive in Vladivostok, reaching no less than 70,000 by November. They show no interest in overthrowing the Bolsheviks or advancing westwards, but busy themselves in consolidating a Japanese enclave in Siberia.

11 Nov.   With the signing of the Armistice in the west, Lenin repudi-
ates the Treaty of Brest-Litovsk and the Supplementary Treaty.
Neither side had gained much from its efforts to exploit
the new Russian Republic. Germany had used brute force to
squeeze even more out of the Bolsheviks than given by Brest-
Litovsk, but subsequent military interference and occupation
of Russian territory diverted thousands of men from the
Western Front. Germany's resources were already too over
stretched to take advantage of the bounty that had fallen into
her lap. The Allies blundered into supporting the enemies
of the Bolsheviks in the unrealistic belief that the Eastern
Front could be re-opened. It would take them many months
and much gold to extricate themselves from the Russian
Civil War.

7.3 THE SPREADING CONFLICT

Bolivia	Broke off relations with Germany, 13 Apr. 1917.
Brazil	Broke off relations with Germany, 11 Apr. 1917. Declared war on Germany, 26 Oct. 1917.
Bulgaria	Declared war on Serbia, 14 Oct. 1915. Declared war on Romania, 1 Sep. 1916.
China	Broke off relations with Germany, 14 Mar. 1917. Declared war on Germany, 14 Aug. 1917. Declared war on Austria-Hungary, 14 Aug. 1917.
Costa Rica	Broke off relations with Germany, 21 Sept. 1917. Declared war on Germany, 23 May 1918.
Cuba	Declared war on Germany . . . 17 Apr. 1917.
Ecuador	Broke off relations with Germany, 8 Dec. 1917.
Greece	Declared war on Austria-Hungary, Bulgaria, Germany and Turkey, 27 Jun. 1917.
Guatemala	Declared war on Germany, 23 Apr. 1918.
Haiti	Declared war on Germany, 12 Jul. 1918.
Honduras	Declared war on Germany, 19 Jul. 1918.
Italy	Declared war on Austria-Hungary, 23 May 1915. Declared war on Turkey, 21 Aug. 1915. Declared war on Bulgaria, 19 Oct. 1915. Declared war on Germany, 28 Aug. 1916.
Japan	Declared war on Germany, 23 Aug. 1914. Declared war on Austria-Hungary, 25 Aug. 1914.
Liberia	Declared war on Germany, 4 Aug. 1914.
Montenegro	Declared war on Austria-Hungary, 5 Aug. 1914. Declared war on Germany, 8 Aug. 1914. Declared war on Bulgaria, 15 Oct. 1915.
Nicaragua	Declared war on Germany and Austria-Hungary, 8 May 1918.
Panama	Declared war on Germany, 7 Apr. 1917. Declared war on Austria-Hungary, 10 Dec. 1917.
Peru	Broke off relations with Germany, 6 Oct. 1917.
Portugal	Declared war on Germany, 9 Mar. 1916, and Austria-Hungary on 15 Mar. 1916.
Romania	Declared war on Austria-Hungary, 27 Aug. 1916. Capitulated to Central Powers, 7 May 1918. Re-joined the Allies, 10 Nov. 1918.
San Marino	Declared war on Austria-Hungary, 3 Jun. 1915.
Siam	Declared war on Germany and Austria-Hungary, 22 Jul. 1917.
USA	Declared war on Germany, 6 Apr. 1917. Declared war on Austria-Hungary, 7 Dec. 1917.
Uruguay	Broke off relations with Germany, 7 Oct. 1917.

WAR AIMS AND PEACE EFFORTS

INTRODUCTION

What are we fighting for? For the soldier going over the top, the wife dreading the postman's knock, the business man contemplating the ruin of his life's work or the monarch eyeing the collapse of an ancient dynasty, the question must have been rarely absent. Before the war, all states had national goals that might *eventually* be achieved. But apart from Austria's desire to tame Serbia, it is doubtful that any of them went to war in August 1914 in order to complete the national programme. But once war began, and particularly when it was going well, programmes were quickly drawn up to catalogue the fruits of victory. The vast cost in men and money seemed to legitimise calls for national recompense, while a lust to punish the hated enemy more than justified retaliatory stripping of his territory. The blood of soldiers and the sacrifice of civilians cried out for national aggrandisement and future security, although statesmen were very aware that too greedy demands would strain the loyalty of those millions who supported a just war of defence, but rejected a war of conquest.

8.1   THE WAR AIMS OF THE CENTRAL POWERS

Austria-Hungary

Austria-Hungary went to war to preserve the Empire, rather than to expand its territory. If Serbian territory was to be taken, this was seen as a security measure rather than a desirable addition to the Empire, but as the war went well, the possibility of making desirable economic and strategic acquisitions opened up. Conversely, as the tide turned after 1916, the Empire's principal war aim became to preserve what it had possessed in 1914.

Fundamental Austrian war aims

- *Russia*: To regain all lost territory, and to strengthen security through border annexations.
- *Italy*: Austria required minor frontier modifications to improve security.
- *The Balkans*: Austrian goals in the Balkans soon expanded from their initial intention to check the Serbian threat. On 7 January 1916, for instance, Burian suggested that Serbia should be reduced by half, Montenegro lose its coastline to the Empire, and Albania be made a Habsburg protectorate.
- *Poland*: Initially, Vienna wanted to expand its Polish territory. In March 1915, Burian proposed the 'Austrian solution', which entailed the linking of Russian and Austrian Poland (Galicia) in an autonomous kingdom

under Habsburg sovereignty. However, in August 1916, under the Vienna Agreements, Austria accepted an independent constitutional monarchy in Russian Poland after the war.

- *Modified Austrian aims 12 January 1917*: Because of the Empire's weakened state Ottokar Czernin recommended Austrian goals be restricted to maintaining the pre-war status quo, and minor frontier adjustments with Serbia, Montenegro and Romania.

Germany

Historians are divided about whether many German soldiers and politicians welcomed the war as an opportunity to achieve objectives that had been drawn up well in advance. Once war had begun, it did not take German politicians long to draw up their lists of demands, most of which had their antecedents in the programmes of the pre-war militarist and nationalist parties and pressure groups. Throughout the war, Germany stubbornly refused to modify these demands, whether it be to seduce neutrals into the war, to persuade Russia or France to sign a separate peace, or to further an overall negotiated peace.

The 'September Programme', 9 September 1914

Believing the war to be won, Bethmann Hollweg put his name, on 9 September, to a provisional plan for a western peace settlement. The package was discussed by Tirpitz, Rathenau and other business and military leaders and drafted by Bethmann's secretary Kurt Riezler. Most of its claims had been aired in the discussions and agendas of pre-war nationalist pressure groups. However, Bethmann later stressed that the programme was a provisional first draft, was a discussion paper rather than German government policy, and that its driving force was the need to obtain German security rather than economic exploitation. After Germany's defeat on the Marne it was overtaken by events.

- A '*central European customs association*': to include the Central Powers, Poland, Scandinavia and western Europe to 'stabilise' German ascendancy in central Europe.
- *Belgium and Luxemburg*: Liège and Antwerp would be annexed to form a corridor to link Antwerp with the German frontier. Belgium would be reduced to a 'vassal state', with her ports and coastline available to Germany whenever she wished. Luxemburg would be annexed.
- *France*: Germany would annex the western Vosges, the Longwy-Briey area, and perhaps a coastal area between Dunkirk and Boulogne. France would be disarmed, and a large war indemnity would make her economically dependent on Germany.
- *Africa*: A continuous belt of German colonies would be established at the expense of Belgium, France and Portugal.

Initial German war aims in the east

- *The Memorandum on German War Aims*, published by the Pan-German League on 28 August 1914 demanded greater annexation than envisaged by the September Programme in the west, and demanded large annexations at the expense of Russia. At the time the government tried to suppress it, but the manifesto reflected the views of important industrialists and politicians.
- *Poland*: After initially acquiescing to Austrian supremacy, Bethmann proposed in April 1916 a nominally independent Poland dominated by Germany.
- *The Baltic region*: Germany decided in September 1915 to establish a nominally autonomous but German-dominated duchy under a German prince, and in April 1916 said it would hang on to the region.

Expanding German ambitions

For the rest of the war Germany's claims in the west hardly varied, despite the pressure to make concessions to secure a separate peace with Russia and to conciliate the USA. Germany's leaders never shifted from their determination to take Longwy-Briey, and to hang on to Alsace-Lorraine. The work of making Belgium into a 'vassal state' continued, with the Kaiser approving in October 1915 indefinite German occupation of the Ostend–Zeebrugge–Bruges triangle. Germany made efforts to cultivate pro-German Flemish separatism, the Belgian economy was ruthlessly exploited, and Belgian workers shipped to Germany as forced labour.

The Petition of the Six Economic Associations (20 May 1915) An influential group of German industrialists opposed a premature peace, demanded annexation of the French northern coalfield, and peasant settlement in Russia's Baltic provinces.

The Petition of the Intellectuals (8 July 1915) This demanded 'the most ruthless humiliation of England' through an indemnity and the acquisition of overseas naval bases. Its 1347 signatories included 352 university professors; a rival, anti-annexationist, petition gained only 141 names.

Germany's reply to Professor Waxweiler (December 1915) Replying to peace-feelers by the envoy of King Albert of the Belgians, Berlin restated the aims of the September Programme with minor concessions.

Jagow's reply to French Initiatives (June 1916) Jagow told French politicians that Germany would keep Longwy-Briey, almost all of Alsace-Lorraine, and demand a large war indemnity.

Statement of War Aims by the German High Command (November 1916) before Bethmann's Peace Note to President Wilson (see below).

- No territorial cession whatever to France.
- Luxemburg must be annexed.
- The Belgian and Polish economies must be subordinated to Germany's and their railways placed under German control.
- The seizure of additional land on Poland's eastern border.

The maximum programme of the Central Powers, 1917

The February Revolution in Russia, the initial successes of the submarine campaign, and the need to bolster flagging Austro-Hungarian morale led to three meetings at Kreuznach in April–May 1917 in which the Central Powers increased their demands and redistributed the eventual spoils.

The Kreuznach programmes

- *Courland and Lithuania*: Germany would annex them and as much additional Baltic territory as possible.
- *Poland*: Germany would annex substantial Polish territory, and establish political, economic and military dominance over the rest.
- *Belgium* would remain under German military control until it was 'ready' for alliance with Germany, who would have permanent transit and occupation rights and control over its railways, and would occupy the Flanders coast and Liège for at least a century. Luxemburg would be annexed.
- *France*: Germany would keep Longwy-Briey and return only a token sliver of Alsace-Lorraine. (On 9 October 1917 the German Foreign Minister said Germany would never concede Alsace-Lorraine.)
- *Colonies*: Germany wanted a consolidated Central African empire, and a global chain of naval bases.
- *Austria-Hungary*: The Empire would retain its full territorial integrity.
- *Serbia, Montenegro, and Albania* would become Austro-Hungarian satellites.
- *Romania* would be in the Austro-Hungarian sphere of influence, but Germany would control its oil, railways, and Danube shipping lines.
- *Russian Poland* would be in the German sphere of influence.
- *The Ukraine* would come under German dominance in the event of Russia's collapse.

The Treaty of Brest-Litovsk (3 March 1918)

This was the most extreme statement of the ambitions of German nationalists and annexationists, but was also accepted in the Reichstag by all the German parties apart from the USDP.

- The signatories agree to refrain from any agitation or propaganda against each other, and Russia will cease all propaganda and agitation in the territories to be evacuated by her.
- Russia will lose all territories west of a line to be established by a Russo-German commission (see Map 7).
- Russia will refrain from all interference in the internal relations of these territories, the future status of which will be determined by Germany and Austria-Hungary.
- As soon as a general peace is concluded and Russian demobilisation is carried out completely Germany will evacuate the territory lying to the east of this line.

- Russia will evacuate eastern Anatolia and the districts of Erdehan, Kars and Batum and return them to Turkey.
- Russia will immediately demobilise her army including recently raised forces. Russian warships will either be disarmed or be confined to port until the final conclusion of peace.
- The barred zone in the Arctic Ocean will continue until the conclusion of a general peace.
- Russia will immediately conclude peace with the Ukrainian People's Republic and recognise the Peace Treaty between it and the Central Powers.
- Estonia and Livonia will be evacuated, and occupied by a German police force 'until security is ensured by proper national institutions and until public order has been established'.
- Finland will be evacuated, together with the Aaland Islands, from which Russian fortresses will be dismantled.
- Prisoners of war of both sides will be released.
- The signatories mutually renounce reparations for their war expenses.
- Diplomatic relations will be resumed immediately upon the ratification of the Treaty.
- The Treaty will be ratified within a period of two weeks.

8.2 THE WAR AIMS OF THE ALLIES

Apart from ensuring national survival, there was little consensus among the Entente partners about the ends for which they were pouring out their blood and treasure. When the US joined the war, this disunity of purpose became more glaring. Nonetheless, on 5 September 1914 the Allies adhered to the 'Pact of London' which bound them to make no separate peace, and not to offer peace conditions without previous agreement with each other. Until 1917, solidarity was maintained, with all of them making huge concessions to maintain the unity of the Alliance. However, in many areas – Poland, the Balkans, and the division of the colonial spoils – their goals *did* conflict, and in reality, most of their developing appetites for territory and economic advantage could only be satisfied at the expense of their allies.

Great Britain

Until late 1917 there was general consensus in Britain about war aims. There was a feeling right across the political spectrum that Britain was fighting a just war against German aggression, and unlike the continental powers, Britain had no territorial ambitions in Europe that might be furthered by the war. It was in the colonial sphere that Britain developed ambitions, and overall these did not arouse domestic opposition. Political crises arose because of the way the war was being run rather than why it was being fought. Believing public discussion would be divisive, governments avoided public debate, and it was not until the last year of the war that President Wilson's peace programme and the Russian Revolution stimulated public debate.

Fundamental British war aims

- *Reconstituting Belgium*: Asquith's Guildhall speech of 9 December 1914 spelt out Britain's basic war aim, for which she had entered the conflict. Britain would never entertain a peace settlement that did not include this. On 14 February 1916 Britain, France and Russia pledged in the 'Declaration of Sainte Adresse' to continue fighting until Belgium had regained economic and political independence and been compensated for the damage it had suffered.
- *Elimination of the German naval threat*: Politicians of both parties and service chiefs continued to cite this as a central British goal.
- *Stripping Germany of her colonies*: The Admiralty believed that it would be strategically dangerous for Germany to regain the colonies that had been captured early in the war by British and Dominion forces. There was little argument for retaining the colonies on economic grounds.
- *Eliminating the German economic threat*: At the Paris Allied Economic Conference in June 1916 the Allies put in place a raft of measures designed to weaken permanently German trading competition. However, British experts were divided about the advisability of this.
- *Smashing 'Prussian militarism'*: A common goal across the British political spectrum, this could only be achieved realistically by total victory and a dictated peace rather than a peace of compromise.
- *Punishing Germany* for violating international law, demonstrating that aggression did not pay.

Evolving British war aims

- *Memoranda on War Aims*: In response to a request by Asquith in August 1916, various leading figures submitted their ideas on British war aims. There was general agreement that France must regain Alsace-Lorraine, Belgium must be restored, and there should be at least an autonomous Poland. Although the First Sea Lord said Germany must lose her navy and colonies, the Board of Trade argued against ruining the German economy, and there was no call for large annexation of German territory.

Reports of the Imperial War Cabinet Committees

These were set up in the Spring of 1917, chaired by Lords Curzon and Milner, to discuss British war aims.

- *Milner's Report* argued against applying the anti-German economic measures of the Paris Economic Conference of 1916 and suggested that only small reparations be demanded.
- *Curzon's Report*, which was adopted by the Cabinet, said that Belgium and Serbia must be restored. The questions of Poland and Alsace-Lorraine should be settled according to the wishes of the inhabitants and the need

for a lasting peace. Germany should lose her colonies, and Palestine and Mesopotamia should be taken from the Turks.

The Labour Party Memorandum on War Aims (16 December 1917)

The Labour Party declared itself to be generally favourable to a peace based on a formula of 'no Annexations and Indemnities' as had been suggested in Lenin's Peace Decree of November 1917.

Lloyd George's Caxton Hall Speech (5 January 1918)

Reacting to the Bolshevik challenge to the Allies to open peace negotiations, which had been sympathetically received in Britain by the Labour Party and the Trade Unions, Lloyd George presented the following outline of British war aims to a gathering of Trade Unionists in Caxton Hall:

- Restoration and independence of Belgium.
- The restoration of Serbia and of the occupied lands of the Allies.
- The restoration of Alsace-Lorraine to France.
- 'Russia can only be saved by her own people'.
- An independent Poland.
- Self-government to the nationalities of Austria-Hungary.
- The union of all Italians to Italy.
- Justice for Romanians.
- Separate national conditions for the subjects of the Ottoman Empire.
- Self-determination for the German colonies.
- Reparation for injuries in violation of international law.
- The sanctity of treaties to be respected.
- An international organisation to limit armaments and reduce 'the risk of war'.

France

For the first two years of the war French war aims were driven by simple outrage against the second German invasion within two generations, and a determination to free the fatherland from foreign occupation. In August 1914, all political factions were united by this straightforward defensive patriotism, and all were reluctant to reopen old wounds by raising questions that went much beyond basic patriotic goals. However, there existed a right wing constituency of journalists, businessmen, and the nationalists of *l'Action française* and the *Ligue des Patriotes* who saw the war as an opportunity to address anti-German grievances that went back long before 1871. Many French industrialists represented in the *Comité des Forges* saw the war as an opportunity to turn back the tide of German economic competition. On the other hand, millions of French radical and socialist voters supported a war of national defence but not a war of annexation and imperialism. Until September 1917 there were socialist ministers in the government who agreed with them.

Fundamental French war aims

René Viviani's Statement to the National Assembly (December 1914) spelled these out:

- *France must regain Alsace-Lorraine*: This was a non-negotiable French objective. As the war progressed, it expanded to encompass regaining the border of 1814 and even 1790, which would include parts of the German Saarland.
- *Belgium must be restored to independence and prosperity*: During the war France made various efforts to persuade the Belgian government in exile to accept closer economic union with, and even to cede territory to, France.
- *Germany must pay indemnities to France* for the cost of her aggression. During the Paris Economic Conference of June 1916, France tried to win her Allies over, with little success, to a package of measures that would permanently weaken German trade and economic competitiveness.
- *'Prussian militarism' must be destroyed*: As the war progressed this vague objective crystallised into a programme to obtain French security through weakening German control over both banks of the existing Rhine frontier.

Evolving French war aims

The Meeting of 7 October 1916

Politicians and soldiers discussed France's long-term need for security against future German aggression. They agreed France needed a strategic frontier on the Rhine and several autonomous buffer States on its West Bank tied to France by a customs union. The General Staff wanted Germany to be broken up into nine independent States, and the left bank of the Rhine north of Alsace-Lorraine to be occupied until Germany paid off an indemnity.

The 'Cambon Letter' (12 January 1917)

A programme of war aims devised by the Ambassador to London Paul Cambon and his brother, the ex-Ambassador to Berlin, Jules.

- *Alsace-Lorraine* must be restored to the frontier of 1790, thus incorporating part of the German Saar.
- *The left bank of the Rhine* must be taken from Germany, and France should have 'the preponderant voice' over its future status.
- *Germany* must survive, but corralled by disarmament and loss of strategic border regions.
- *Austria-Hungary* must also survive, despite Cambon's original intention to recommend its break-up.

The Doumergue Agreement (8 March 1917)

The French minister won secret Russian support for a Rhine frontier, in return for France giving Russia a completely free hand to re-draw her western frontier with the Central Powers. It became another casualty of the February Revolution.

The Dumont Resolution

The French Chamber voted (467 to 52) to affirm that France was fighting for the liberation of invaded territories, the return of Alsace-Lorraine, and just reparations. It opposed conquest and subjugation of foreign peoples, but desired the overthrow of 'Prussian militarism', and a League of Nations to guarantee peace and the independence of all nations. Simultaneously in the Senate, Ribot approved the 'frontier of 1790' and a buffer state between France and Germany.

The Paris Conference (29 November–3 December 1917)

France unveiled a new war aim: to construct a *cordon sanitaire* of independent states in eastern Europe to block future German aggression. As a first step, she threw her weight behind the establishment of an independent Polish state.

Italy

Italy joined the war mainly because by the Treaty of London the Entente promised to satisfy all her national goals as the price of joining them. Subsequently, Italy expanded her demands to encompass a larger share of the apparently dying Ottoman Empire. Whether she would ever be able to cash these cheques depended first upon Allied victory, and then upon the Allies' ability to deliver the goods in the face of rampant South Slav and Turkish nationalism. (For the diplomacy of Italy's entry into the war, see Section 7.)

The Treaty of London (26 April 1915)

- Italy would take South Tyrol and the Trentino up to the Brenner Pass.
- Part of the Isonzo region, the Istrian Peninsula, Trieste, the entire Dalmatian Coast and its offshore islands, and northern Albania.
- The Dodecanese islands.
- A share in any future partition of the Ottoman Empire (see Treaty of St Jean de Maurienne, p. 220).
- A large British loan on favourable terms.

The Russian Empire

Russia went into the war believing that her national survival depended on resisting the aggression of the Central Powers. Realising their weakness, Russian political leaders set great store on maintaining the Alliance, and until November 1917 resisted the efforts of the Central Powers to tempt them into a separate peace. Nonetheless, Russia had very well-defined national goals, and she was not averse to playing upon Allied fears for her collapse to secure these. After the February Revolution of 1917, Russian leaders abandoned hopes of territorial gain in their desperation to escape the war's crippling domestic impact. But it was only the Bolsheviks who were prepared to carry the logic of 'no annexations' to its conclusion.

Fundamental Russian war aims

- Control of Constantinople and the Straits.
- Uniting all Poles under the Russian flag, as proclaimed by the Tsar on 14 August 1914.
- Gains in the Caucasus and Armenia at the expense of Turkey.

Sazonov's Thirteen Points (12 September 1914)

Summed up Russia's more specific objectives:

- Poland: A new (Russian-dominated) state would be constructed by the following annexations: the Lower Niemen basin, eastern Galicia, eastern Posen, southern Silesia, and western Galicia.
- Austria-Hungary should be divided into a tripartite monarchy comprising Austria, Hungary and Bohemia.
- Germany should be weakened by territorial losses, reparations, and a coercive alliance. She must restore the kingdom of Hanover, annexed by Prussia in 1866.
- Alsace-Lorraine to be returned to France, together with such bordering territory as France desired.
- Serbia should absorb Bosnia-Hercegovina, most of Dalmatia, and northern Albania.

The Straits Agreement (10 April 1915)

This fulfilled Russia's centuries-old ambition to control the entrance to the Black Sea, so long as victory was achieved.

- Russia would control zones of occupation on the northern shore of the Sea of Marmora and on both sides of the Bosphorus.
- Merchant ships of all nations would be guaranteed freedom of navigation through the Straits.
- Constantinople would become a Free Port.

Rethinking 'free' Poland

In March 1915 it was announced that the future Poland's armed forces, foreign policy, transport, and finance would remain under Russian control. In the Spring of 1916 Sazonov refused Allied requests to restate publicly the Tsar's promise of Polish autonomy, and on Christmas Day 1916 the Tsar admitted that Russia was *incapable* of conquering Prussian and Austrian Poland.

Russian war aims after the February Revolution

The change of regime in Russia resulted in a repudiation of Tsarist war aims. Those, like Miliukov, who wanted to hold on to them were soon swept away by moderate socialists who eschewed territorial gains, but were committed to defending the fatherland, and resisted leaving the war unilaterally. Their efforts to persuade the Allies to renegotiate their war aims failed.

- *Miliukov's Statement* The new foreign minister reaffirmed that Russia still expected to gain the territory promised to her under the Straits Agreement of 1915.
- *Declaration of support for an independent Poland* (29 March/16 March OS) This was to include parts of German and Austrian Poland, thus implying annexation of enemy territory.
- *The Manifesto to the Peoples of the World* (9 April/27 March OS) The Petrograd Soviet pledged support for the war effort, but demanded 'decisive action' to secure a peace without annexations of territory or war indemnities. It called on the peoples of the world to press their rulers to give up conquests. The 'Petrograd Formula' – 'Peace without Annexations and Indemnities' – became a rallying slogan for a world-wide drive by the Left to eliminate expansionist war aims.
- *The Declaration of the Provisional Government* (9 April/27 March OS) stated that the new Russian government would respect its alliance obligations but did not seek to gain territory. Miliukov's Covering Note was more equivocal, and he was forced by the Soviet to resign.
- *Lenin's April Theses* (17 April/4 April OS) demanded that all previous annexationist agreements be denounced (see p. 201).
- *Tereschenko's Circular* (13 June) informed the Allies that Russia wanted a general peace without annexations, and called for a conference to revise the coalition's war aims. The Allies rejected the recommendation of the French envoy Albert Thomas to take this opportunity for a re-think.

Colonial war aims of the Entente

The war presented the prospect of carving up Germany's colonies and legitimising long-held schemes to partition the Ottoman Empire. A web of Allied plans and agreements gradually emerged, many of them contradictory.

- *The Straits Agreements* (10 April 1915) Russia backed future British and French claims in the Ottoman Empire in return for the promise of Constantinople and the Straits (see above). Originally secret, the agreement was published by the Russians (with Allied consent) in December 1916.
- *The Treaty of London* (26 April 1915) Italy was promised a share of the Ottoman Empire (see p. 217).
- *The McMahon-Husain Letter* (24 October 1915) A vaguely worded letter in which the British High Commissioner in Cairo appeared to accept the predominance of Sharif Husain of Mecca over Arabia, Syria, Palestine and Iraq.
- *British recognition of Ibn Saud* (December 1915) This cut across British commitments to Sharif Husain.
- *The Sykes Picot Agreement* (16 May 1916) A secret agreement on the partition of the Ottoman Empire negotiated by the British diplomat Sir Mark Sykes and the French official George Picot. After the war France would receive Syria, the Lebanon, Celica and Mosul, and Britain would get Transjordan, Iraq and Northern Palestine.

- *The Treaty of St Jean de Maurienne* (19 April 1917) Italy was promised pre-dominance in the Smyrna and Konya regions of Turkish Anatolia, and a zone of lesser influence further north. On 18 August 1917 Italy confirmed her adherence to the various Allied agreements concerning the Ottoman empire. The new Russian Provisional Government was not included in the discussions.
- *The Balfour Declaration* (2 November 1917) The British Foreign Secretary supported a Jewish national home in Palestine. This had the dual advantage of securing world-wide Jewish support for the war and strengthening Britain's hand in Palestine.

The Allied Note of 10 January 1917

This was an agreed summary of Allied war aims communicated to President Wilson in response to his Note of 18 December 1916 asking the belligerents to state their terms for peace. They were expressed in sufficiently vague terms to encompass previous Allied arrangements to partition the Ottoman Empire and take Germany's colonies. France secured the return of Alsace-Lorraine and left the door open to further frontier gains at Germany's expense.

- The principle of a League of Nations was accepted.
- Belgium, Serbia and Montenegro must be restored to independence and compensated.
- France, Russia and Romania must be evacuated and receive 'just reparations'.
- All Italians, Slavs, and Romanians must be freed from 'foreign domination'.
- Turkey must be expelled from Europe and her subject peoples liberated.
- Territory previously taken from the Allies against the inhabitants' will, should be returned.
- International arrangements must safeguard land and sea frontiers against unjustified attack.

8.3   EFFORTS TO REACH A NEGOTIATED PEACE

Spiralling war aims made it far more difficult to achieve peace through negotiations. Disinterested efforts to find a negotiated settlement were rare, and most of the peace feelers of the belligerents were malicious attempts to manipulate one of one's enemies out of the war. When the Central Powers succeeded in achieving a separate peace with Russia (see Section 7) it encouraged them to close the door on President Wilson's efforts because they believed they could now *win.*

Austria-Hungary

On 21 November 1916, Karl I succeeded Franz Josef as Emperor of Austria. Karl is convinced that the Empire's interests are served by ending the war, and he initiates a series of meeting with the Allies, who believe that he is seeking a separate peace. Karl's new foreign minister Ottokar Czernin also believes in the need for peace, and conducts his own initiatives The two men have differing objectives, and the Emperor does not inform Czernin about some of his private diplomatic efforts.

- *The Mensdorff–Hopwood Affair* (February 1917) Czernin sends Count Mensdorff to Scandinavia to meet the British representative Sir Francis Hopwood, but Britain is only interested in Austria signing a separate peace, and the two never meet.
- *The Sixte Initiatives* (December 1916–June 1917) Emperor Karl I uses his wife's brother Prince Sixte de Bourbon-Parma, an officer in the Belgian army, to make advances to the French. Czernin is kept in the dark about these moves. On 24 March 1917, Sixte offers Paris a deal: Serbia would regain its independence, Belgium should be restored, and Austria would support French claims for the return of Alsace-Lorraine. The French take this as an Austrian attempt to secure a separate peace rather than the first move in a general negotiated peace, but Lloyd George is informed on 11 April 1917. Negotiations collapse when Italy refuses to make any territorial concession to Austria-Hungary and sticks to the letter of the 1915 Treaty of London.
- *The Bad Homburg Meeting* (3 April 1917) To persuade Germany to consider a negotiated peace, Karl offers Wilhelm II all Poland (including Galicia) if he agrees to return Alsace-Lorraine to France, and allows Austria dominance in Romania.

The Papal Peace Initiative (16 August 1917)

After preliminary discussions with Germany and Austria-Hungary the Vatican published the following suggestions for a negotiated peace:

- The belligerents should agree to disarm simultaneously.
- Disputes should be solved by international arbitration backed by sanctions.
- There should be freedom of the seas.
- Belligerents should pay their own war expenses.
- Germany should evacuate French and Belgian territory, and Belgian independence should be guaranteed.
- Germany's colonies should be returned.
- In territorial disputes the wishes of the population should be considered.

These aims were either unrealistic in the circumstances of war or ran counter to the war aims of both sides. The prestige of the Papacy made it incumbent on both sides to respond, but the initiative led nowhere.

International socialist conferences

At Zimmerwald in September 1915 and Kienthal in April 1916, Socialists from all the belligerent states tried to establish a basis for a just settlement without annexations and indemnities. However, they did not represent the majority of working people, who in all countries still supported the war. Their appeal was diluted by the efforts of Lenin and the Left Socialists to use the war to achieve social revolution.

The *Reichstag* 'Peace Resolution', 19 July 1917

This called for a 'peace of understanding and a permanent reconciliation of peoples'. It declared that 'forced territorial acquisitions and political, economic or financial oppressions are irreconcilable with such a peace' and it provoked a political crisis in Germany, but did not further the cause of a negotiated peace.

Lord Lansdowne's letter, 29 November 1917

In a letter to the *Daily Telegraph*, the distinguished ex-Foreign Secretary called for Britain to limit herself to minimum demands and to radically redefine Allied war aims 'in time to avert a world-wide catastrophe'. Similar arguments expressed by Lansdowne in a Memorandum to the Cabinet War Committee in 1916 had received short shrift from ministers and generals. The letter received little public support.

Initiatives of the Russian Provisional Government and Petrograd Soviet

- *The 'Petrograd Formula'* The Soviet's 'Manifesto to the Peoples of the World' called for peace without annexations or indemnities. *Izvestia* denounced secret diplomacy and called for a new revolutionary foreign policy.
- *The Compromise Declaration of 9 April* The Provisional Government called on the Allies to re-think their war aims to enable a negotiated peace.
- *Tereschenko's Circular* (13 June, 1917) proposing a conference to discuss the revision of war aims was ignored by the Allies.
- *The Proposal for a Stockholm Peace Conference* (15 May 1917) Socialists in the Provisional Government and the Petrograd Soviet took up an idea initiated by the International Socialist Bureau (22 April 1917). On 11 July another invitation was issued by the joint Russian–Dutch–Scandinavian Committee. The conference was opposed by Lenin, and by most belligerent governments, which refused to allow their nationals to attend.

The Bolsheviks: world peace through world revolution

Immediately after the October Revolution the Bolsheviks began an intense campaign to end the war. Until February 1918, their aim was a general negotiated peace. They needed to respond to the Russian people's overwhelming desire to end the war that had brought them to power, but Lenin and Trotsky believed that the Revolution in Russia could not survive in isolation. They were convinced that a unilateral and spectacular call for the war to end immediately would cause the masses in all countries to rise up and overthrow governments that were obstructing peace. For them peace was only a stepping stone to World Revolution.

- *The Decree on Peace* (5 November) called for a three-month armistice to enable the negotiation of an 'immediate democratic peace for all nations' without annexations and indemnities. On 9 November Britain and France rejected Lenin's call for a general armistice, reminding him of Russia's obligation under the Pact of London.
- *Publication of the 'secret treaties'* Trotsky, the new Commissar for Foreign Affairs, who is utterly opposed to the war, published the Allies' secret agreements as the first act of his revolutionary diplomacy.
- *Armistice negotiations* (3–5 December) The Russian delegation negotiated for a general armistice to include the Allies. They demanded that no German troops should be transferred to the west when fighting ceases on the Eastern Front, which it does on 15 December.
- *Direct appeals to the masses* In December 1917, Trotsky twice issued calls to the peoples of Europe to rise up against their rulers and demand immediate peace. On 1 January 1918, the Soviet appealed to the peoples of the Central Powers, claiming that their negotiators were not seizing the opportunity for peace. On 8 January 1918, the Soviet Congress published the *Declaration of the Rights of the Toiling and Exploited Masses* which the Allies regarded as an attempt to encourage uprisings in their colonies.

The Brest-Litovsk peace negotiations

Only representatives of the Bolsheviks and the Central Powers attended because the Allies refused to participate. The Bolsheviks continued to press for a general negotiated peace. Their Six Points were accepted by the Central Powers on Christmas Day 1917, but only if the Allies accepted them too, which they declined to do.

- Territory seized during the war to be given up. Immediate withdrawal from occupied territory.
- Restoration of the political rights of nations deprived of their independence.
- A right of referendum for the entire population of territories claiming national independence.
- Special protection and autonomy for national minorities within new states.
- No war indemnities, but compensation for private individuals from an international fund.
- The future of colonial peoples to be decided under points 1–4.

Trotsky's gamble (8 January–10 February 1918)

8 Jan.   Negotiations resumed at Brest-Litovsk, with Trotsky leading the Russian delegation. He demanded that the talks should be public, and adopted a confrontational and high-minded

223

tone, using the negotiations as a platform to spark 'World Revolution' rather than to conduct realistic negotiations. The Germans say that they will only accept a 'no annexation' clause as part of an overall peace settlement. However, the European masses stubbornly refused to revolt, and Russia, on 3 March, was forced to sign a separate peace with the Central Powers at Brest-Litovsk (see German war aims).

President Wilson's peace efforts

The diplomacy of Colonel House

Wilson was extremely keen to play a part in bringing about peace and setting up a new world order. In January 1915 he sent his unofficial aide Colonel House on a tour of belligerent capitals to sound out conditions for peace. In January 1916 House held a second round of discussions in Berlin but his discussions with German representatives made little progress. On 22 February 1916, House signed the Grey–House Memorandum with the British Foreign Secretary agreeing that President Wilson should propose a conference to end the war.

Wilson's peace note (18 December 1916)

Wilson asked all belligerents to declare upon what conditions they would be prepared to cease fighting. Germany replied negatively. The Allies formulated their war aims in the Declaration of 10 January 1917 (see above).

Peace without victory (22 January 1917)

Wilson outlined in the Senate his concept of a settlement based upon national self-determination, policed by a League of Nations.

Wilson's fourteen points (8 January 1918)

1. Open covenants of peace, openly arrived at.
2. Freedom of navigation upon the seas, in peace and in war.
3. The removal of all economic barriers and the establishment of equality of trade conditions among all the nations.
4. Adequate guarantees given and taken that national armaments will be reduced to the lowest point consistent with domestic safety.
5. A free, open-minded, and absolutely impartial adjustment of all colonial claims, based upon a strict observance of the principle that . . . the interests of the populations concerned must have equal weight with the equitable claims of the government whose title is to be determined.
6. The evacuation of all Russian territory.
7. Belgium . . . must be evacuated and restored.
8. All French territory should be freed and the invaded portions restored, and the wrong done to France by Prussia in 1871 in the matter of Alsace-Lorraine . . . should be righted.

9. Readjustment of the frontiers of Italy should be effected along clearly recognisable lines of nationality.

10. The peoples of Austria-Hungary should be accorded the freest opportunity of autonomous national self-determination.

11. Romania, Serbia and Montenegro should he evacuated; occupied territories restored; . . . and the relations of the several Balkan states to one another determined by friendly counsel along the lines of allegiance and nationality.

12. The Turkish portions of the present Ottoman Empire should be assured a secure sovereignty, but the other nationalities which are now under Turkish rule should be assured an undoubted security of life and an absolutely unmolested opportunity of autonomous development.

13. An independent Polish state should be erected which should include the territories inhabited by indisputably (sic) Polish populations, which should be assured of free and secure access to the sea, and whose . . . independence . . . should be guaranteed by international covenants.

14. A general association of nations must be formed under specific covenants for the purpose of affording mutual guarantees of political independence and territorial integrity to great and small states alike.

Final peace negotiations, 1918

14 Aug.	Accepting that the war is lost, Germany decides to approach the Allies to begin negotiations. No urgent approach is made because Ludendorff conceals the seriousness of Germany's military collapse.
1 Oct.	Ludendorff tells senior officers that the military situation is hopeless. He demands an armistice based on Wilson's Fourteen points (which he had never read).
3/4 Oct.	The new German Chancellor, Prince Max of Baden, appeals to President Wilson for an armistice based on the 'Fourteen Points'.
9 Oct.	Wilson's First Note. Without consulting his allies, Wilson asks if Germany accepts the Fourteen Points unconditionally, and is prepared to evacuate all occupied territory.
12 Oct.	Prince Max sends a noncommittal but favourable reply to Wilson, but simultaneously a U-boat sinks the liner *Leinster* with the loss of 200 lives, outraging Allied politicians and public.
14 Oct.	Wilson's Second Note demands an immediate end to submarine warfare, and immediate evacuation of occupied territory. It also calls for guarantees of 'constitutional change' implying that peace depends on the removal of the Kaiser. The High Command and the Kaiser reject this and suggest that Germany can fight on, but Prince Max replies to Wilson promising to stop attacks on civilian vessels and assures him that Germany now has a parliamentary government.

| 23 Oct. | Wilson's Third Note demands a promise not to resume hostilities after an armistice, and says that Wilson will only deal with the 'veritable representatives of the German people'. |
| 11 Nov. | Crippled by the collapse of her allies and growing civil unrest at home Germany accepts the Armistice. |

Terms of the Armistice

1. Terms to be effective six hours after signing.
2. Immediate evacuation of Belgium, France and Alsace-Lorraine, to be concluded within 14 days. Any troops remaining in these areas to be interned or taken as prisoners of war.
3. Surrender 5000 artillery pieces, 30,000 machine guns, 3000 trench mortars, 2000 planes.
4. Evacuation of the left bank of the Rhine, to a depth of 30 kilometres.
5. A neutral zone on the right bank of the Rhine 30–40 kilometres deep, to be evacuated within 11 days.
6. Nothing to be removed from the territory on the left bank of the Rhine. All factories, railways and plant to be left intact.
7. 5000 locomotives, 150,000 railway coaches, 10,000 trucks to be surrendered.
8. An Allied Army of Occupation to be maintained at German expense.
9. In the east, all troops to withdraw behind the boundaries of 1 August 1914.
10. The Treaties of Brest-Litovsk and Bucharest to be renounced.
11. Unconditional surrender of German colonies in East Africa.
12. Return of the property of the Belgian Bank, Russian and Romanian gold.
13. Return of prisoners of war without reciprocity.
14. Surrender of 160 U-boats, 8 light cruisers, 6 Dreadnoughts; the rest of the fleet to be disarmed and handed over to the Allies in neutral or Allied harbours.
15. Assurance of free trade through the Kattegat Sound; clearance of minefields and occupation of all forts and batteries, through which transit could be hindered.
16. The blockade to remain in effect.
17. Germany to remove all limitations by Germany on neutral shipping.
18. The Armistice to last 30 days.

EMERGENT NATIONS

INTRODUCTION

Before the war, it was difficult to imagine how the peoples of the great multinational Empires of Russia, Austria-Hungary and Germany could ever attain independent statehood. Most nationalist politicians favoured autonomy and equality *within* the existing structures, and few Czechs, Poles, or even Habsburg Slavs believed independence was possible or even desirable. However, the four years of war would turn these obscure advocates of independence into major political figures, and destroy all three Empires that stood in their way. As early as 17 September 1914 Russia's *Proclamation to the 'Peoples of Austria-Hungary* promising 'freedom and the realisation of your national strivings' revealed the war's potential for the subject peoples of Central Europe. However, it was not until the Versailles Declaration (3 June 1918) that the Allies gave their support to the dissolution of the Habsburg Empire and 'freedom' for Poles, Czechs and South Slavs.

9.1 YUGOSLAVIA

Before the war, the concept of a 'Yugoslav' state combining the existing Kingdom of Serbia with the various South Slavs living in the Habsburg Empire (Slovenes, Croats and Serbs) was only the dream of a few academics and intellectuals. Most Habsburg Slavs lived in the Magyar half of the Dual Monarchy, ruled repressively from Budapest. They wanted to shake off the Magyar yoke, but to achieve equality and autonomy within the Empire. For most of them, the ultimate goal was 'Trialism', an idea promoted by the heir to the Habsburg throne, Franz Ferdinand, by which they would be given equal weight with Germans and Magyars within the Empire. In contrast, nationalists in the independent Kingdom of Serbia wanted to incorporate all South Slavs in a Greater Serbia, dominated by Belgrade.

The effect of the war was to increase the influence of South Slav intellectuals and exiles, who were able to convert many Entente statesmen and journalists to the Yugoslav idea. On the other hand, Serbia's heroic resistance during the war greatly enhanced the prestige of Belgrade. In the end, the Yugoslav idea *was* achieved, but only under the dominance of Belgrade.

South Slav politics before the war

1903	A turning point in relations between the Habsburg Empire and the South Slavs: Emperor Franz Josef refuses even to meet a responsible Croat deputation wanting limited independence from Magyar rule.

1905	Delegates to the Dalmatian Diet at Fiume pass a resolution stating that 'Croats and Serbs are a single nation'. Later in the year, at Zadar, Serb delegates adopt the Fiume Resolution. In contrast, 40 Croatian deputies to the Hungarian Parliament call for a 'Kingdom of Croatia, Dalmatia and Slavonia' within the Habsburg Empire.
1912	The Hungarian governor of Croatia institutes a repressive regime, including compulsory use of the Magyar language in schools and public services.
1913	A Serbo-Croat Coalition wins an absolute majority in the Croatian parliament, posing a potential threat to Habsburg rule.

1914

28 Jun.	The Sarajevo Assassination is part of a campaign for a 'Greater Serbia'. The assassin Princip and his high-placed Serb sympathisers fear the 'Trialist' ideas of Archduke Franz Ferdinand as a danger to Serbian expansion.
22 Nov.	The Yugoslav Committee is established in Florence by Ante Trumbic, a Croatian deputy in the Austrian parliament. South Slav citizens of Austria-Hungary dominate the Committee, which aims to unite all South Slavs in one state. They are undecided about the form this should take. Both Belgrade and the Entente Powers initially regard the Committee as merely a useful propaganda organisation.
7 Dec.	The Niš Declaration. Serbia announces as a war aim the unification of all of the South Slavs in a single state.

1915

26 Apr.	The Treaty of London. To persuade her to enter the war, the Entente promises Italy territory at the expense of the South Slavs.
30 Apr.	In London, the Yugoslav Committee opposes the Treaty of London, and demands Habsburg territory. The Committee is becoming a focus of Slav aspirations, but Slavs within the Empire still support autonomy within it, rather than a new state.
7 May	Serbia complains to its allies that concessions to Italy are at the expense of its national aspirations.
12 May	The Yugoslav Committee's *Manifesto to the British Parliament and People* is published in the British Press.

1917

30 May	South Slav deputies in the Austrian *Reichsrat* call for South Slavs to be unified 'under the sceptre of the Habsburg dynasty'.

In return for their loyalty, they ask for a representative body within the Imperial constitution.

20 Jul.   The Corfu Declaration. After a month of discussion, the Yugoslav Committee and the Serbian Government in Exile agree that the eventual South Slav State will be ruled by the Serbian Karageorgevic dynasty. The languages, flags, alphabets (Latin and Cyrillic) of the three constituent peoples – Serb, Croat and Slovene – will be guaranteed equality. The balance of political power in the new state is ill defined, as are the rights of its *other* constituent nationalities – Bosnian Muslim, Albanian, Magyar, Macedonian and Greek.

1918

5–6 Oct.   The National Council of Slovenes, Croats and Serbs is founded by Slovenian and Croat politicians in the collapsing Austro-Hungarian Empire. It supports the creation of an independent state.

26 Oct.   Emperor Karl's Proclamation. Belatedly the Emperor offers to make the Austrian part of the Habsburg monarchy a federal state in which Slavs will be equally represented. This would have been welcomed earlier, but the process of South Slav nation building has now overtaken it.

29 Oct.   The Croatian *Sabor* declares independence, but devolves its powers to the National Council of the Slovenes, Croats and Serbs.

Nov.   Thousands of Albanians killed as the advancing Serbian army 'liberates' Kosovo (captured by Serbia from the Turks only 6 years previously).

2 Nov.   The Serbian army enters Belgrade.

9 Nov.   The Geneva Agreement. The Serbian government, the National Council, and the Yugoslav Committee accept that the National Council represents South Slavs in the Habsburg monarchy. The parties will form a government to represent all of the South Slav lands. Champions of an independent Croatia are ignored, and the Serbs begin to disregard the agreement almost immediately, and start to build a state dominated by Serbia and the Serbian minority in Croatia.

16 Nov.   The Dalmatian provincial government, fearing Italian incursions, asks to join the union.

24 Nov.   The leader of the Croatian People's Peasant Party, Stephan Radic, warns of the dangers of unconditional unification with Serbia. (In 1928, Radic and two other Croatian deputies are shot and killed in a meeting of the national parliament.)

231

25 Nov.	The Serbs of Vojvodina join the union.
26 Nov.	The national assembly of Montenegro (influenced by the presence of the Serb army) places itself under the Serbian monarchy.
1 Dec.	Crown Prince Alexander Karageorgevic of Serbia proclaims The Kingdom of the Serbs, Croats, and Slovenes. An uprising for a separate state of Croatia is put down by force.

The Treaties. By the Treaty of St Germain en Laye (10 September 1919) Austria recognised the independent Kingdom of the Serbs, Croats, and Slovenes. By the Treaty of Neuilly (27 November 1919) Bulgaria ceded parts of western Macedonia, and under the Treaty of Trianon (4 June 1920) Hungary ceded part of the Banat and Croatia-Slavonia.

9.2 POLAND

The 18th-century partitions of Poland had split the country three ways between Prussia (subsequently the German Empire) and the Russian and Habsburg Empires. In Austrian Poland (Galicia) the aristocracy had fully integrated itself into the Habsburg establishment and had a vested interest in remaining loyal to Vienna, while the peasantry (often Ukrainian speakers) were downtrodden and politically inert. The other two Empires were notorious for imposing programmes of 'Russification' and 'Germanisation' on their Polish populations. One of Austria's war aims was to take Russian Poland, which contained some of Russia's most important industrial resources, vital to her war effort. As the war unfolded, both sides tried to secure the loyalty of their Polish populations, and to subvert the Polish populations of the other side, by promising reform and autonomy after the war.

1914

31 Jul.	Germany promises to set up a Polish state after a German victory.
6 Aug.	Jozef Pilsudski, with the support of the Austrian government, enters Russian Poland in an unsuccessful attempt to incite an anti-Russian revolt.
8 Aug.	Polish deputies in the Russian Duma pledge loyal co-operation in the war effort. The armies of all three Empires contain many Poles, whose continuing allegiance is important to all of them.
14 Aug.	The Manifesto of Grand Duke Nicholas promises a unified Polish state under Tsarist rule after Russian victory.
16 Aug.	The Supreme National Committee is established by Pilsudski in Krakow. Special Legions are recruited to fight the Russians. Austria supports Pilsudski's action hoping that it will lead

to the eventual incorporation of Russian Poland into the Habsburg Empire, naively assuming that Pilsudski will spill Polish blood to extend Habsburg power.

25 Nov.   The Polish National Committee is set up in Warsaw to support the Russian war effort. Its leader, Roman Dmowski, holds extreme anti-Semitic and anti-German views, which he believes will best be served by a temporary alliance with Tsarist Russia.

1915

3 Apr.   Russia gives autonomy to urban areas of Russian Poland.

May–Jul.   Russian Poland is occupied in a series of offensives by the Central Powers: Lemberg (Lvov) falls to the Austrians (22 Jun.) and Warsaw to the Germans (5 Aug.). In occupied Poland, thousands of Poles are deported to Germany as forced labourers.

23 Jun.   German right wing politicians and industrialists draw up a programme of war aims which includes the annexation of Poland.

Mar.   Vienna proposes an 'Austrian Solution': Russian Poland would be unified with the Austrian Poles of Galicia in an autonomous kingdom under Habsburg sovereignty. Germany at first agrees to this.

Dec.   The Central National Committee founded by Polish left wing groups to win over the Central Powers by setting up a Polish Republic.

1916

25 Jul.   Pilsudski resigns his command because the Central Powers have not fulfilled their promise to set up a Polish state.

Aug.   The Vienna Agreements. Germany and Austria-Hungary commit themselves to establish an independent constitutional monarchy in Russian Poland after the war. Germany and Austria-Hungary would annex territory from it. In the east, it would incorporate as much Russian territory as possible. It would have no independent foreign policy. Germany would command its army, and its railways would be controlled by the Central Powers.

5 Nov.   Germany and Austria proclaim the future Kingdom of Poland. It fails in its main goal of persuading Poles to join the Austro-Hungarian army.

26 Nov.   The Central Powers appoint a Polish Regency Council and Council of State, with Pilsudski head of the military commission.

| 25 Dec. | The Tsar speaks of a free, united Poland if the Entente wins the war, but Russia secretly aims to push its border westward to absorb Polish inhabited land. |

1917

22 Jan.	President Wilson's 'Peace without Victory' speech calls for a 'unified, independent Poland'.
30 Jan.	Adoption of a Constitution in the 'Kingdom of Poland', reflecting the conservatism of the Central Powers' puppet Regency Council.
28 Mar.	The Petrograd Soviet denounces the historical partition of Poland, and recognises the right of Poles to have a unified and independent homeland.
30 Mar.	The Russian Provisional Government also accepts the principle of an independent Poland made up of 'territory where Poles are in a majority'. But it calls for Poland to continue fighting on Russia's side.
20 Apr.	The Polish Legions are put under German control.
May	The Russian army starts to transfer Poles into specifically Polish units, which will eventually comprise the three army corps that resist the Red Army in the Civil War.
30 May	Polish deputies in the Austrian *Reichsrat* unanimously demand a free and unified Poland, with an outlet to the sea.
5 Jun.	An army of 100,000 Polish refugees, volunteers and ex-prisoners of war is established in France.
2 Jul.	Pilsudski resigns from the Council of State in protest against German interference. Following this, most of the Polish officers and men in the German army renounce their oath of loyalty to Germany.
22 Jul.	Pilsudski is arrested and is imprisoned in the German fortress of Magdeburg.
15 Aug.	The Polish National Committee is established in Lausanne by Roman Dmowski. It is represented in the United States by Jan Paderewski, who persuades President Wilson to treat the Committee as the main representative of the Polish cause.
25 Aug.	The remaining members of the Polish Council of State resign in resentment at being treated as puppets of Germany.
22 Oct.	Poles in the United States join the Kosciuszko Army, recruited from Poles who are not subject to the US draft, to fight alongside American forces on the Western Front.
25 Oct.	The Germans appoint a Regency Council, with very limited powers, to replace the defunct Council of State.

1918

5 Jan.	Lloyd George's Caxton Hall Speech declares support for an independent Poland.
8 Jan.	Wilson's Fourteen Points. Article 13 calls for a free and independent Poland – with secure access to the sea.
9 Feb.	The Peace Treaty between Ukraine and the Central Powers cedes the predominantly Polish province of Chelm to Ukraine. The government of the 'independent' Kingdom of Poland resigns in protest.
15 Feb.	Many Polish soldiers desert the Austro-Hungarian army to join Polish units in Russia.
3 Mar.	Under the Treaty of Brest-Litovsk, Russia renounces all claims to Polish territory.
20 Mar.	The Polish army in France is placed under the control of Dmowski's Polish National Committee.
3 Jun.	The Versailles Declaration. The Allies recognise The Polish National Committee in Paris as an 'allied belligerent nation', and make the creation of an independent Polish state one of their war aims.
7 Oct.	The Polish Regency Council declares independence. In Berlin, Polish *Reichstag* deputies demand the incorporation of German Poland into the Polish state.
12 Oct.	The Polish National Committee becomes a virtual government in exile after Britain recognises its control over Polish forces on the Western Front.
15 Oct.	Polish deputies in the Austrian *Reichsrat* declare themselves citizens of an independent Poland. Austrians begin to hand over control to Polish officials.
19 Oct.	A Polish National Council is formed in Teschen, which has a large Czech population. Poles and Czechs agree to divide the region along ethnic lines and to await the verdict of the impending peace conference.
2 Nov.	The Ukrainians occupy Lvov, after fighting between Poles and Ukrainians for control of Galicia.
3 Nov.	The Polish Republic is proclaimed in Warsaw. A few days later Jozef Pilsudski triumphantly returns to Warsaw after his release from prison.

1919

28 Jun.	The Treaty of Versailles. The new Polish State is given most of German West Prussia, part of Pomerania, and Poznán (Posen) and a 'Corridor' to give it access to the Baltic. Danzig

(Gdansk) is declared a Free City, under a League of Nations High Commissioner. Later part of Upper Silesia is ceded to Poland after a plebiscite.

10 Sep.   Under the Treaty of St Germain en Laye Austria recognises Polish independence and cedes most of Galicia to Poland.

9.3 CZECHOSLOVAKIA

The Czech and Slovak lands (Bohemia and Moravia) comprised some of the richest and most developed parts of the Habsburg Empire. In 1914, it would have seemed unthinkable that within four years they would be thrust together, with Magyars, Poles, Ukrainians and a large and disgruntled German minority, in a single independent republic. Before the War, Czechs had succeeded in reducing the Austrian *Reichsrat* to chaos by their parliamentary tactics. However, they wanted equality with Germans inside a reformed Empire rather than independence outside it. As with other aspiring nationalities, the turmoil of war thrust forward new men who seized the opportunity to win the Great Powers over to what was, till very late in the day, a minority cause.

1915

6 Jul.   Tomas Masaryk calls for the dissolution of the Habsburg Monarchy and the creation of a new state, Czechoslovakia, as a homeland for the Czech and Slovak peoples. Masaryk, who went into exile in December 1914, was a Prague university professor and deputy in the Austrian parliament.

27 Jul.   The Czech Action Committee Abroad is founded in Paris. Representatives are sent to the Entente capitals to work for the liberation movement.

Sep.   A Czech and Slovak unit, the Družina, joins the Russian army under Russian command.

19 Oct.   Great Britain announces that Czechs and Slovaks are no longer regarded as enemy aliens.

22 Oct.   The Cleveland Agreement. Representatives of the Bohemian National Alliance and the Slovak League in the United States, call for union of Czechs and Slovaks in an independent federal state.

14 Nov.   The Manifesto of the Czech Action Committee Abroad, calling for the dissolution of the Habsburg Empire, which has failed to serve the interests of its 'minority' peoples, is published in Great Britain, France, Russia and the United States.

1916

3 Feb.   Tomas Masaryk meets French Premier Aristide Briand, who is sympathetic to the idea of Czech independence.

6 Feb.	The Czechoslovak National Council is founded as a virtual government in exile, with Masaryk as president, and Edvard Benes general secretary.
Sep./Oct.	Two Russian Foreign Ministry memoranda call for an independent Czechoslovakia.

1917

4 Jan.	Tsar Nicholas II finally agrees that freed prisoners of war can form a Czechoslovak brigade in the Russian army. The plan has been delayed for nearly a year, because the Tsar fears the implications for his own nationalities.
10 Jan.	Freedom of Czechs and Slovaks is included in the reply of the Entente to President Woodrow Wilson's Note of December 1916, asking the belligerents to define their war aims.
23 Mar.	The new Russian Provisional Government calls for an independent Czechoslovak state.
24 Mar.	The Provisional Government agrees to the formation of a Czech and Slovak brigade, but resistance within the army and among politicians delays it. Later in the month, a Czech Legion, commanded by its own officers, is set up.
30 May	The Austrian Parliament convenes in Vienna for the first time since 1914: Czech representatives immediately demand a new federal structure in which a united Czech and Slovak province will carry equal weight to German, Magyar and other national groupings.
23 Jun.	France agrees to transfer of 30,000 Czech and Slovak prisoners of war via Vladivostok to fight on the Western Front. Masaryk believes that fighting alongside the French and British armies will strengthen the Czech hand at the peace conference.
23 Jul.	Russia allows the Czech Legion to fight as an independent army because of its loyalty and effectiveness during the Brusilov Offensive.
18 Aug.	France provides a loan of 20 million francs to fund units of the Czechoslovak National Council fighting for Russia.
4 Oct.	A labour unit made up of freed Czech and Slovak prisoners of war joins the Italian army.
26 Dec.	On the Western Front, an autonomous Czecho-Slovak Legion is established. It is controlled by the Czechoslovak National Council, but subject to the strategic decisions of the French High Command.

1918

6 Jan.	The Epiphany Declaration. Czech representatives in the Vienna parliament and leading figures in the Austrian Czech

	community demand independence for the Czech lands and Slovakia.
8 Jan.	President Wilson's Fourteen Points states that the nationalities of Austria-Hungary should be free to develop autonomously. Allied politicians envisage self-government within a reformed Habsburg Empire rather than the dissolution of the Empire.
3 Mar.	The Treaty of Brest-Litovsk. The Bolsheviks agree to evacuate the Czecho-Slovak Legion via the Trans-Siberian Railway, and thence to the Western Front via Vladivostok.
24 May	A secret meeting of all the Slovak parties and organisations in Hungary resolves to work for an independent Czechoslovakia.
26 May	Along the Trans-Siberian Railway, fighting begins between units of the Czech Legion and local Soviets. By June the Legion, which is the best-quipped and trained force in Siberia, has taken control of hundreds of miles of the railway and numerous towns linked by it. Initially the Legion is only concerned with securing free passage out of Russia, but it finds itself allied with anti-Bolshevik forces and embroiled in the Russian Civil War.
30 May	Masaryk draws up the Pittsburgh Pact, which guarantees the Slovaks autonomy in a new Czechoslovakia.
22 Jun.	President Wilson amends Article X of the Fourteen Points, to call for the liberation of Slavs from Austro-Hungarian domination.
2 Jul.	The United States followed by Britain (3 August) recognises the Czech National Council as the provisional government of Czechoslovakia. A Czechoslovak National Committee is formed in Prague, and a Slovak National Committee in Budapest.
18 Oct.	Masaryk issues a Declaration of Czech Independence in Washington, in an attempt to pre-empt any move by the Allies to preserve the Habsburg Empire in the peace settlement.
21 Oct.	Germans, fearing for their security in a future Czechoslovak state, vote to join Austria when the war ends.
28 Oct.	The Czechoslovak Republic is declared by the Prague National Committee, which has taken control of Bohemia and Moravia and set up a provisional government.
30 Oct.	Slovak leaders agree to join the Czechs in a common State.
13 Nov.	Publication of a Provisional Constitution for the Czechoslovak Republic.
13–14 Nov.	Hungarian troops re-occupy most of Slovakia.
24 Nov.	In the first session of the National Assembly Tomas Masaryk is elected President.

1919

10 Sep.	Austria recognises the independence of Czechoslovakia under The Treaty of St Germain en Laye.

9.4 THE BALTIC STATES

By 1914, after centuries of Swedish, Polish and German domination, the future Baltic States of Latvia, Lithuania and Estonia were part of the Russian Empire. All three peoples had retained very strong linguistic and cultural identities, despite the efforts of the Tsarist regime to Russify them. Nonetheless, centuries of alien rule had blurred territorial boundaries. Their ethnic composition was far from homogeneous.

The Russian Revolution of 1905 provided the spark for Baltic nationalism and the First World War an unexpected opportunity to take advantage of the collision and collapse of their oppressors.

Lithuania

1905

Dec.	With Russia preoccupied by the Revolution, a congress in the Lithuanian capital Vilnius calls for all lands peopled by Lithuanians to be ruled as an autonomous province within the Russian Empire.
1915	As the Russian armies are pushed back, Lithuania is occupied by the German army. German military rule is established.

1917

18–22 Sep.	The Germans authorise a meeting of Lithuanian nationalists which calls for an independent Lithuanian state. A 20-member Council (*Taryba*) is elected.

1918

16 Feb.	The *Taryba* declares an independent Lithuanian state, which remains under *de facto* German occupation until the end of the war.
3 Mar.	Under the Treaty of Brest-Litovsk Germany assumes sovereignty of the Baltic States.
Nov.	The defeat of Germany leaves Lithuania exposed to the ebb and flow of the Russian Civil War.

1919

5 Jan.	The Red Army occupies Vilnius and installs a Soviet government.

Apr.	A Polish army dispatched by Marshall Pilsudski (whose family is partly Lithuanian) drives the Red Army out of Vilnius, but will not allow the Lithuanian government to return. By the end of the summer Soviet troops have been driven out, but **Poland** is now the barrier to Lithuanian national aspirations.

1920

12 Jul.	The Treaty of Moscow (Soviet-Lithuanian Treaty). The Russian Republic recognises the independence of Lithuania, having pushed the Poles out during of the Russian–Polish War. Vilnius is reoccupied by the Poles, and after a plebiscite in 1922 absorbed into the Polish Republic.
1922	The independence of Lithuania is recognised by international treaty.

Estonia

1905	The Estonian National Liberal Party meets in the capital Tallinn and votes for political autonomy for Estonia (27 Nov.). In December Russia declares martial law, leading to widespread violence and repression.

1917

12 Apr.	The Russian Provisional Government allows ethnic Estonian regions to be united into a single autonomous province.
14 Jul.	First meeting of the Estonian National Council (the *Maapäev*).
12 Oct.	A provisional Estonian government is set up headed by Konstantin Päts.
28 Nov.	The Estonian Diet decides to leave the Russian state.
8 Dec.	The Bolsheviks appoint a puppet government in Tallinn headed by Jaan Anvelt, who is unable to extend his power beyond the capital.

1918

24 Feb.	The *Maapäev* declares Estonian independence.
25 Feb.	German troops enter Tallinn and suppress the Estonian government.
3 Mar.	The Treaty of Brest-Litovsk. Germany takes over the Baltic States.
Nov.	After Germany's defeat, the Estonian Provisional Government re-affirms Estonian independence.

28 Nov.	Lenin declares the Brest-Litovsk Treaty void, and orders the Red Army to re-occupy Estonia.
29 Nov.	An Estonian Soviet Republic is proclaimed.

1919

Jan.	Backed by the Finns and a British naval squadron, Estonia begins an offensive against the Red Army.
1 Mar.	All Soviet forces are expelled from Estonian territory.

1920

15 Jun.	The Constitution of the Estonian Republic is adopted.
2 Feb.	Under the Soviet-Estonian Peace Treaty the Russian Republic recognises Estonian independence.

Latvia

1915

Sep.	After Latvia and Courland are occupied by Germany, Germany decides to eventually create an autonomous duchy under a German prince, joined to Germany by a common railway system, and military and customs agreements. Latvia will become a German satellite.

1916

Apr.	Germany states that the region will never be returned to Russia.

1917

Mar.	The Latvian National Political Conference in the Latvian capital, Riga, demands complete political autonomy after the overthrow of the Tsarist regime in Russia.
3 Sep.	The German army occupies Riga.
18–22 Nov.	Meeting in the territory occupied by the Germans, The Latvian People's Council proclaims independence. In the area held by the Russian army an alternative Latvian Socialist government favourable to the Bolsheviks is set up, but the whole country is soon occupied by Germany.

1918

3 Mar.	Under the Treaty of Brest-Litovsk Germany assumes sovereignty over the Baltic States.

| 9 Nov. | As the German Empire collapses, German aristocrats set up a 'Baltic Duchy' in an attempt to re-create their medieval dominance. |
| 18 Nov. | The Latvian People's Council, meeting in Riga, sets up a national government. |

1919

3 Jan.	The Red Army captures Riga and sets up a pro-Bolshevik Latvian government. The anti-Bolshevik government retreats to the port of Liepaja, under the protection of a British naval squadron.
22 May	German troops under General Rüdiger von der Goltz occupy Riga, but their advance is halted by combined Estonian–Latvian forces. (Britain and France have hitherto tolerated von der Goltz's activities because of his anti-Bolshevik credentials.)
Jul.	Under a British brokered armistice, the Red Army withdraws and the Latvian government returns.
8 Oct.	Von der Goltz's 'West Russian army', co-operating with anti-Bolshevik forces, again moves into the suburbs of Riga.
10 Nov.	The Latvian army and the Anglo-French naval squadron force the West Russian army out of Riga. Within a month, Latvia is cleared of foreign troops.

1920

| 1 May | The Latvian Constituent Assembly meets in Riga. Under the Treaty of Berlin, Germany recognises Latvian independence. By the Soviet-Latvian Peace Treaty, 15 February 1922, the Russian Republic renounces all claims. The Constitution of the Latvian Republic comes into force. |

SETTLEMENTS AND COSTS

10.1 GERMANY: THE TREATY OF VERSAILLES, 28 JUNE 1919

German territorial losses in the west

- Alsace and Lorraine were returned to French rule.
- The Saarland to be administered by the League of Nations until 1935. This coal-rich area was intended to compensate the French for the wanton destruction of French coalmines.
- Three small enclaves were given to Belgium.
- Northern Schleswig was ceded to Denmark after a plebiscite.

German territorial losses in the east

- Most of German West Prussia, part of Pomerania, and Poznán (Posen) were ceded to Poland.
- A 'Corridor' was delineated to give Poland access to the Baltic Sea (thus separating East Prussia from the rest of Germany).
- Part of Upper Silesia ceded to Poland after a plebiscite.
- Danzig (Gdansk) was declared a Free City, under a League of Nations High Commissioner.
- Memel, a German-populated town was placed under a French High Commissioner. It was seized by the Lithuanians in 1923.
- The Germans of Austria were forbidden to unite with Germany.

Germany's colonies

- All Germany's overseas colonies in Africa, China and the Pacific were taken over by Britain, the British Dominions, France and Japan.

Disarmament

- The west bank of the Rhine and a 30 mile strip of the east bank was declared a permanently demilitarised zone.
- An Allied army would occupy the left bank of the Rhine, until 1935, or until Germany had fulfilled her treaty obligations.
- Conscription was forbidden. The German army was restricted to 100,000 men, and deprived of a General Staff.
- Production of war-planes submarines, tanks, armoured cars and poison gas was forbidden.
- The German fleet was surrendered to Great Britain. In future, her navy was limited to 15,000 men and forbidden to have ships over 10,000 tons.

War guilt and reparations

Under Article 231, the 'War Guilt Clause', Germany was forced to admit responsibility for costs sustained by the Allies 'as a consequence of the war imposed on them by the aggression of Germany and her allies'. Following on from this forced admission of guilt, Germany was required to make reparations to the Allies, who were empowered to take punitive action if their defeated enemy failed to pay. The actual amount could not be computed at the time, but in 1921 a commission decided on the figure of 132 billion gold marks.

The League of Nations

* The Covenant of the League of Nations (to which Germany was denied membership) was incorporated into the Treaty.
* Members guaranteed each other's territorial integrity and independence.
* Economic sanctions would be applied against any member who resorted to war.
* Danzig, the Saar Basin, and ex-German colonies would be supervised by the League as 'Mandates'.
* Plans would be put forward to reduce armaments.
* A Permanent Court of International Justice and an International Labour Organisation were set up.

10.2 AUSTRIA: THE TREATY OF ST GERMAIN EN LAYE (10 SEPTEMBER 1919)

* Austria recognised the independence of Czechoslovakia, Poland, Hungary and the Kingdom of the Serbs, Croats and Slovenes (Yugoslavia).
* Eastern Galicia ceded to Poland.
* Trentino, Southern Tirol, Trieste and Istria ceded to Italy.
* Southern Carinthia remained part of Austria after a plebiscite.
* Sopron is ceded to Hungary after a plebiscite.
* Union with Germany was expressly forbidden without the consent of the Council of the League of Nations.
* The Austrian army limited to 30,000.
* The Austro-Hungarian navy to be divided among the Allies. Reparations were to be paid (none, in fact, ever were).
* Austria to accept laws protecting her ethnic minorities.
* The Covenant of the League of Nations was integrated into the Treaty.

10.3 BULGARIA: THE TREATY OF NEUILLY (27 NOVEMBER 1919)

* Western Thrace ceded to Greece.
* Dobrudja ceded to Romania.

- Parts of western Macedonia ceded to Yugoslavia.
- Army to be limited to 20,000 volunteers.
- Reparations set at 2.2 billion gold francs, to be paid within 37 years (75% later remitted).

10.4 HUNGARY: THE TREATY OF TRIANON (4 JUNE 1920)

- Slovakia, sub-Carpathian Ruthenia, and Bratislava (Pressburg) ceded to Czechoslovakia.
- Burgenland ceded to Austria.
- Transylvania and most of the Banat ceded to Romania.
- Croatia-Slavonia and the rest of the Banat ceded to The Kingdom of Serbs, Croats and Slovenes (Yugoslavia).
- Fiume ceded to Italy.
- Armed forces restricted to 35,000 men.
- Reparations: exact amount to be determined, but some payment to be made by 1 May 1921.
- Livestock was to be delivered to devastated pro-Entente neighbours.
- Yugoslavia was to be provided with free coal for five years.
- The Covenant of the League of Nations was integrated into the Treaty.

10.5 THE OTTOMAN EMPIRE: THE TREATY OF SÈVRES (10 AUGUST 1920)

- The Ottoman Empire was abolished.
- The independence of former Ottoman provinces in the Middle East confirmed.
- The Bosphorus and the Dardanelles ('The Straits') made into an international waterway.
- Smyrna, part of Western Anatolia and certain Aegean islands ceded to Greece.
- Armenia to became an independent state.
- Kurdistan to be autonomous.

The last four of these provisions were never implemented because of the resistance of Mustapha Kemal (Atatürk) and the Turkish nationalists. The Treaty of Lausanne (1924) ended almost all foreign occupation of the Turkish heartland.

10.6 CASUALTIES FROM WAR AND INFLUENZA

Military Casualties

Country	Mobilised	Killed	Wounded	Prisoners/ missing	Total
The Allies					
Belgium	207,000	13,750	44,000	67,750	57,750
The British Empire	7,459,000	908,500	2,090,250	191,750	2,998,750
Great Britain	5,397,000	702,500	1,662,750	170,500	2,365,250
The French Empire	7,500,000	1,385,250	2,675,000	446,250	4,060,250
			4,266,000[a]		5,651,250
Greece	230,000	5,000	21,000	1,000	26,000
Italy	5,500,000	460,000	947,000	530,000	1,407,000
Japan	800,000	250	1,000	0	1,250
Montenegro	50,000	3,000	10,000	7,000	13,000
Portugal	100,000	7,250	15,000	12,250	22,250
Romania	750,000	200,000	120,000	80,000	320,000
Russia	12,000,000	1,700,000	4,950,000	2,500,000	6,650,000
Serbia	707,250	127,500	133,250	153,000	260,750
USA	4,272,500	116,750	204,000	4,500	320,750
The Central Powers					
Austria-Hungary	6,500,000	1,200,000	3,620,000	2,200,000	4,820,000
Bulgaria	400,000	101,250	152,500	11,000	253,750
Germany	11,000,000	1,718,250	4,234,000	1,073,500	5,952,250
Turkey[b]	1,600,000	335,750	400,000	200,000	735,750

[a] There are wide variations in estimates of French casualties.
[b] Estimate: No official Turkish figures exist.

The Influenza Pandemic of 1918

Estimated world-wide deaths	27,000,000

Starting in March 1918, the epidemic, known at the time as 'Spanish Influenza', quickly spread throughout the world. The special conditions of war undoubtedly increased its impact. Millions were on the move between continents, or were weakened by hunger, run down by stress and depression, crammed together in barracks, factories and troop-ships. Accurate figures are only available for the developed world, and many more are probably unrecorded in remote parts of the Third World.

10.7   THE ECONOMIC COST OF THE WAR

Costing the war is extremely difficult, as the peacemakers at Versailles were to find. Inflation makes estimates accurate only at the time they are made. Many costs would have been incurred in peacetime anyway. Money spent on replacing sunken ships and producing munitions brought prosperity to factory owners and workers and re-circulated in the domestic economy, and peasants were enriched by state procurements to feed the armies. Manufacturers benefited from import substitution. In some parts of Europe, industrial and agricultural resources were devastated, but the soil of Germany, the US and Britain never saw a shot fired, while some of the richest parts of France, Belgium, Serbia and central Europe became battlefields. War debts represented a real long-term cost, but in the inter-war years, inflation made nonsense of accounting, and debts would be cancelled if they were large enough. Thus, the following tables are useful mainly in pointing out the *relative* expenditures of the belligerents. The true cost – human talent snuffed out, lives ruined, society fractured – cannot be shown by lists and tables.

Approximate Cost of the War (in US dollars, 1981)

Germany	37,775,000,000
Great Britain	35,334,012,000
France	24,265,583,000
United States	22,625,253,000
Russia	22,293,950,000
Austria-Hungary	20,622,960,000
Italy	12,413,998,000
Canada	1,665,576,000
Romania	1,600,000,000
Turkey	1,430,000,000
Australia	1,423,208,000
Belgium	1,154,468,000
Bulgaria	815,200,000
India	601,279,000
New Zealand	378,750,000
South Africa	300,000,000
Serbia	399,400,000
Greece	270,000,000
Japan	40,000,000

The Growth of National Debt

	1914	1922	Rise (%)
USA	1,338	23,407	1749
Britain	3,440	34,251	996
France	6,492	27,758	428
Italy	3,034	8,689	286
Germany	1,228	1,303	106

Redistribution of Gold Reserves 1914–19 (million £ sterling)

USA	+278.5
Japan	+183
Spain	+84
Argentina	+49
Holland	+41
Switzerland	+12.5
Uruguay	+10
Sweden	+10
Denmark	+9
Canada	+9
Norway	+4.5
Australia	+1
New Zealand	0
South Africa	−0.5
Finland	−0.5
Bulgaria	−1
Portugal	−1.5
Belgium	−4
Romania	−7
Italy	−19
France	−25
Great Britain	−42
Austria-Hungary	−55
Germany	−123

The Devastation of France

Agricultural land laid waste	8,000 sq. miles
Forest laid waste	1,875 sq. miles
Livestock lost	1,300,000
Buildings destroyed	250,077
Schools	1,500
Churches	1,200
Factories	1,000
Public buildings	377
Other buildings	246,000

The Crippling of the Russian Economy

	1913	1921
Coal (million tons)	29.0*	8.9
Electricity (million kilowatts)	1945	520
Pig iron (thousand tons)	4216	116
Steel (thousand tons)	4231	183
Textiles (million metres)	2582	105
Sown area (million hectares)	1500	90.3
Grain harvest (million tons)	80.1	37.6
Rail freight (million tons)	132.4	39.4

* In millions of 1926–27 roubles

Loss of Merchant Shipping

Country	Tonnage
United Kingdom	9,055,000
Norway	1,172,000
Italy	862,000
France	531,000
United States	531,000
Greece	415,000
Japan	270,000
Sweden	264,000
Denmark	245,000
Spain	238,000
Holland	229,000
Belgium	105,000
Brazil	31,000

251

BIOGRAPHICAL SKETCHES

Aehrenthal, Count Alois Lexa von (1854–1912) Foreign Minister of Austria-Hungary, 1906–12. The new assertiveness that Aehrenthal brought to Habsburg foreign policy after 1906 did much to destabilise the Balkans in the decade before the war. Aehrenthal believed that Serbian ambitions posed a mortal threat to the multinational Empire, and that Serbia served as a bridge for Russian expansion in the region. An aggressive policy by Vienna would not only crush Serbia, but also free the Empire from subservience to its German ally. As a first step, Aehrenthal proposed the annexation of the two provinces of Bosnia and Hercegovina, which still remained technically part of the Ottoman Empire, but had been administered by Austria since 1878. He persuaded the Russian Foreign Minister, Alexander Izvolski, to agree to this in return for vague promises of support for Russian goals in the Straits. However, when events dictated a premature announcement of the annexation, Russia and Serbia were outraged by what they saw as the under-handed absorption of Slav lands. Aehrenthal steadfastly resisted an international conference to resolve the issue, and, in February 1909, Russia was forced to accept Aehrenthal's *fait accompli* under the threat of military action by the Dual Alliance. A few weeks later, abandoned by her protector, Serbia yielded to an Austrian ultimatum and accepted the annexation. Aehrenthal's policy has been criticised for poisoning Austria's relations with Russia, and for driving Serbian nationalists down a path of violence that culminated in the Sarajevo assassination. Nonetheless, he consistently opposed calls for a preventive war against Serbia or Italy. After his death from leukaemia in February 1912, a group of his younger diplomatic 'disciples' were influential in stiffening Austria's hard-line stance during the July Crisis of 1914.

Asquith, Herbert Henry (1852–1928) British Liberal Prime Minister, 1908–16. A brilliant scholar and successful lawyer, Asquith entered the House of Commons for East Fife in 1886 and remained its member for 32 years. Asquith, together with Rosebery, Grey and Haldane, supported the Tories' policy during the South African War, forming a group known as the Liberal Imperialists to which Winston Churchill later adhered. In 1908 Asquith replaced Campbell-Bannerman as Prime Minister, coming into office at a time when his party faced major social, constitutional and international problems. In 1911 he succeeded in curbing the power of the House of Lords, but the hostility of anti-war radicals, industrial militancy and the intractability of the Irish question meant that he confronted the July Crisis of 1914 in the midst of domestic political strife. Asquith misjudged the seriousness of the Crisis, but went along with the judgement of his former Liberal Imperialist colleagues that Britain could not afford to remain neutral. Asquith's urbane and detached style made him an unlikely war leader, but the task of welding together the disparate factions of a party, many of whose members were deeply uncomfortable with war, would have taxed any politician's abilities. In May 1915, Asquith rebuilt his government on a coalition basis with Lloyd George Minister of Munitions and including Conservative ministers, but the war continued to go badly and pressure for him to move aside for a more ruthless leader mounted. In 1916 the Easter Rising in Dublin and the disaster on the Somme led to a Press campaign orchestrated by his enemies. In December, he resigned to be replaced by Lloyd George. For the rest of the war, he mounted a somewhat ineffectual challenge to Lloyd George, but the Liberals lost badly in the election of 1918, and he never regained office.

Berchtold, Leopold, Count von (1862–1942) Foreign Minister of Austria-Hungary 1912–15. Berchtold, a former Austrian Ambassador in St Petersburg, never exhibited the grasp and personality of his abrasive predecessor. During the last two years of peace he moved indecisively between the foreign policy doves and hawks in Vienna. He opposed war against Serbia in 1912 and 1913 and succeeded in blocking Serbia's access to the sea by the creation of an Albanian state, but many felt that he had allowed Austrian policy to be determined by international conference and allowed Serbia to get off the hook. After the assassination of Archduke Franz Ferdinand in June 1914, Berchtold, now bolstered by unconditional German support, followed an obstinately hard line, perhaps because he did not wish to be accused of allowing another chance to obliterate Serbia to slip by. His ultimatum to Serbia was intentionally unacceptable to a sovereign state. Berchtold seemed determined to punish Serbia even if it meant fighting the Russians as well. He resisted calls for restraint from London and Berlin. Unfortunately for him, Austrian attempts to move quickly before the world could react were frustrated by the army's lack of preparedness and the need to secure Magyar support. After Berchtold's attempt to punish Serbia spiralled into European war, he turned his mind to preventing Italy and Romania from joining Austria's enemies. In January 1915, his suggestions for concessions to Rome were interpreted as defeatistism, and he was forced into retirement.

Bethmann Hollweg, Theobald von (1856–1921) Imperial German Chancellor, 1909–17. When Bethmann Hollweg became Chancellor, the foreign policy of his predecessors had already achieved the seemingly impossible task of pushing Britain, France and Russia into an anti-German coalition. The continuing aim of Bethmann's diplomacy, both before and during the war was to prise this circle of enemies apart. However, his efforts were constantly undermined. The Kaiser's obsession with naval competition estranged Britain. German imperial ambitions in Africa cemented the Entente Cordiale. Punitive tariffs demanded by Prussian landowners alienated potentially pro-German Russian conservatives. In 1912, after his attempts to counteract the popularity of the Left through electoral and tax reform were rejected by the Emperor, he came close to resignation. During the Balkan Wars Bethmann's sensible diplomacy defused the international confrontation and established a working relationship with Britain, but as 1914 approached, he became increasingly pessimistic about Germany's international and domestic situation. He seems to have come to the reluctant conclusion that war might be preferable to inaction.

Bethmann was an enigmatic figure whose personal motives often remain obscure. Because of the destruction of his private papers, his actions during the July Crisis of 1914 must be viewed through the rather dubious diaries of his private secretary Kurt Riesler. We know that he gave unconditional support to Austrian aggression against Serbia, no doubt assuming that Vienna would act quickly to avoid international complications. We know that he must have been aware that his support for Serbia could lead to a European war, because military men had explained the consequences of Russian intervention to him. Thus, he warned Russia that the German High Command would take even their pre-mobilisation measures as an unacceptable military threat. Too late, and unaware that the timetables of the Schlieffen Plan were already coming into play, he tried to hold Austria back, and to keep Britain neutral by asking the army to switch its attack to the east. However, neither Bethmann nor the Kaiser felt able to order the generals to improvise an alternative to the Schlieffen Plan.

During the war Bethmann had to compete for the Kaiser's ear with the ever-growing influence of the High Command which intensified with the advent of the Third Supreme Command in August 1916. His 'September Programme' of 1914 defined war aims designed to give Germany permanent security, but the spiralling annexationist demands of the hawks undermined his diplomatic attempts to divide Germany's enemies, and sabotaged his efforts to keep the US out of the war by unleashing unrestricted submarine warfare. Despite this, in April 1917 Bethmann acquiesced in the High Command's extreme programme, believing, he said later, that it was unachievable. In domestic politics, Bethmann attempted to hold the balance between Left and Right and to bolster civilian support for the war by pursuing a 'diagonal' policy', but his promises of future reform got nowhere because the Kaiser and the conservative military class resented any move towards liberalisation. In July 1917, Bethmann was ousted by an unholy alliance between the Supreme Command, which held him in contempt as a liberal, and the Reichstag, which hated him as a reactionary.

Caillaux, Joseph-Marie-Auguste (1863–1944) French politician and Prime Minister. Caillaux was one of the most charismatic and controversial politicians of the French Third Republic, whose career was dogged by a catalogue of scandals and disputes from the time of his election to the Chamber of Deputies in 1898. As Minister of Finance, under Clemenceau from 1906–9 he made many enemies fighting a losing battle to persuade his countrymen to accept income tax. His efforts to use his business connections with Germany to negotiate a way out of the Second Moroccan Crisis as Prime Minister in 1911 led to accusations of treason and corruption from the nationalist right. Caillaux's methods were always obscure and Machiavellian, and when in July 1914 his wife went on trial for shooting the editor of *Le Figaro* for threatening to publish personal letters, the political establishment trembled at the prospect of damaging revelations. Mme Caillaux was acquitted, and war closed this particular file, but the affair had deprived the country of Caillaux's considerable talents and international contacts at a crucial time. At the end of 1917, with Clemenceau's purges in full swing, Caillaux again hit the headlines when his opposition to the war and alleged contacts with German agents led to a formal charge of treason. He was imprisoned in January 1918, and found guilty in a politically charged trial after the war, but bounced back to hold office again under Painlevé and become an influential member of the Senate.

Churchill, Winston (1874–1965) First Lord of the Admiralty, 1911–15; Minister of Munitions, July 1917; Minister of War, December 1918. Born at Blenheim Palace in 1874, into a privileged but by no means wealthy family, Churchill led an unconventional and adventurous early life, gaining a reputation for vigour, brilliance and eloquence, and also for unpredictability and opportunism. In 1911, as First Lord of the Admiralty he threw his abundant energy into finishing the reform programme of his predecessor Fisher, creating the Royal Naval Staff College and the Royal Naval Air Service, and encouraging the development of oil-fired warships. Churchill always displayed his best qualities in time of crisis. During the 1914 July Crisis, aware of the danger of a pre-emptive German strike against the Royal Navy the took it upon himself to keep the fleet concentrated, and then to withdraw it northwards away from danger. He supervised the transport of the British Expeditionary Force to France with great efficiency and without the loss of a single soldier. However, as the war unfolded, his strategic judgement was increasingly called into question. His appointment of Jellicoe as Commander of the Grand Fleet upset the naval establishment. His tendency to interfere with the decisions of local commanders meant he became personally associated in the public mind with the escape of the *Goeben* and *Breslau*, the British defeat at Coronel, and the flashy and ineffective intervention at Antwerp with a token force. After the recall of Fisher as First Sea Lord in late 1914 there were frequent recriminations and rows between these two forceful egotists. Churchill's enthusiasm for the Dardanelles expedition early in 1915 reflected both his revulsion at the carnage on the Western Front, and his belief that the war could be won by striking at what he later called the 'soft underbelly' of the enemy. Unfortunately, military expertise and resources did not match his imaginative conception. He overestimated the effectiveness of a purely naval operation, and underestimated the resilience of the Turks. When the Liberal government collapsed in May 1915 Churchill lost his post, to the delight of the military experts who had opposed him. In mid-November 1915 he gave up his minor government post in protest at the decision to terminate the Gallipoli adventure, but far from licking his wounds in some country retreat, he spent the winter of 1915–16 commanding the 6th Royal Scots Fusiliers on the Western Front. On 17 July 1917, despite the disapproval of the Conservatives, his friend Lloyd George recalled him to be Minister of Munitions. Approaching the job with typical vigour and imagination, he championed the use of the tank, and supported the development of military intelligence and code breaking, the importance of which he was typically quick to appreciate. Between 1923 and 1931 he wrote a six-volume work 'The World Crisis' which presented a fascinating interpretation of the war and the events leading up to it.

Clemenceau, Georges, 1841–1929. French Prime Minister 1906–9, 1917–20. In the half century before he became France's wartime leader Clemenceau had already left an indelible mark on France. As a radical politician and journalist he had participated in the Paris Commune, the founding of the Third Republic, and the affairs of Boulanger, Panama and Dreyfus. As Interior Minister he had made himself the bête noire of the left; as Prime Minister he had been an architect of the Entente Cordiale. As a novelist, academic writer, friend and supporter of Monet and Zola, he had made himself a force in the intellectual life of the Republic. As a journalist, he had used his newspaper *L'Homme Libre* to expose the inadequacies of military preparations; in defiance of the wartime censorship, transformed it into the even more acerbic *L'Homme Enchainé* to expose corruption, incompetence and treason.

Refusing ministerial posts in the governments of Viviani and Briand, Clemenceau used his position in the Senate to attack Joffre's running of the war, and the shortcomings in munitions and medical services. By the middle of 1916 his anger was focused on the failure of Interior Minister Malvy to stop pacifist agitation that was undermining morale. By 1917, the failure of the Nivelle Offensive, mutinies in the army, and proliferating scandals caused many patriots to look to Clemenceau as the only man, despite his advanced age, with the energy and determination to mobilise the nation for victory in the spirit of Danton and Gambetta.

Public tolerance of half measures and half-baked coalitions was exhausted. At the age of 76 Clemenceau took office in November 1917 and proceeded to fashion an administration in his own image. Over the next 18 months he galvanised the Chamber and the country with his aggressive rhetoric, ruthlessly purged critics of the war, and took steps to implement *La Guerre Intégrale* – Total War. With his excellent command of English, Clemenceau won over the reluctant British to accept Marshall Foch as supreme commander. The implacable optimism and drive of 'the Tiger' was a major factor in eventual Allied victory. The war's aftermath was rather less heroic: caught between the demands of French annexationists and President Wilson's idealistic visions, Clemenceau was accused of 'winning the War and losing the Peace'. He was defeated in the Presidential elections of 1920, and never again held office.

Conrad von Hötzendorf, Count Franz (1852–1935) Chief of Staff of the Austro-Hungarian Army 1906–17. Conrad is reputed to have called for war against Serbia on 25 occasions. His abrasive and bellicose personality was a major reason for the deterioration in the relations between Austria-Hungary and her neighbours in the decade before the war. Conrad believed that the Habsburg Empire could only survive if it vigorously confronted neighbours who were exploiting the presence of their nationals within the Empire's borders to undermine it. In 1911 he was temporarily dismissed because of his embarrassing calls for war against Austria's ally. In June 1914, the murder of Archduke Franz Ferdinand removed a restraining influence, and Conrad seized upon it as an opportunity to crush Serbia before it was too late. However, by focusing exclusively on his longed-for war with Serbia, he ignored the danger of Russian involvement, and closed his mind to his promises for an offensive in the north to help Germany. Furthermore, Conrad's army was incapable of launching the quick campaign to crush Serbia demanded by the situation. By the time Conrad accepted that Russia would attack him, he had already sent his Strategic Reserve southwards for the invasion of Serbia. In the resulting logistical chaos, his southern force was too weak to defeat Serbia, while in Galicia the Russians threatened to blow away his exhausted and under-strength northern armies. Some Austrians regard Conrad as the greatest general of the war, but although his strategies were often brilliant in conception, they were usually beyond the capacities of the troops on the ground. As he visited the Front on only three occasions, it is easy to see how these realities escaped him. As the war unfolded, the disparity between Austrian and German resources forced Conrad into a subordinate rôle that he deeply resented. The Gorlice–Tarnow Offensive of May 1915 was largely his idea, but its success depended upon German troops. His 'Black-Yellow Offensive 'later that year, far from proving Austria's capacity to act alone was a failure costing 300,000 casualties. In October 1915, the German General Mackensen took credit for Conrad's initiative to conquer Serbia. Conrad's Trentino offensive in the spring of 1916 was another strategically imaginative stroke, but it was abandoned because of Brusilov's breakthrough in Galicia. The advent of the Third Supreme Command in Berlin in August 1916 made it very difficult for him to pursue an independent line. From the start of the war, Conrad had contemptuously pushed politicians aside and sought to impose the army's influence in all areas of civilian life. His reluctance to concede power to the new Emperor Karl led to his dismissal at the end of February 1917. Appointed commander of the South Tyrol Army Group, he continued to urge an offensive strategy, blind to the obvious disintegration of the Austrian-Hungarian army.

Czernin, Count Ottokar (1872–1932) Foreign Minister of Austria-Hungary, 1916–18. A member of the Czech aristocracy, Czernin served as a member of the Bohemian Landtag before the war, opposing universal suffrage and embracing various conservative causes. He was an influential member of the clique surrounding the heir to the throne, Franz Ferdinand. From 1913 to 1916, Czernin served as Ambassador to Romania, failing to persuade that country to fulfil its commitments to the Triple Alliance or to stop its drift towards the Entente. In December 1916, he was made Foreign Minister by the new Emperor Karl, who employed his rather dubious diplomatic skills in a series of botched attempts to find a way for Austria-Hungary to leave the war. He was heavily criticised for failing to uphold the Empire's interests at the Brest-Litovsk peace negotiations in February 1918, and in April became a scapegoat of the failure of Emperor Karl's confused private diplomacy during the Sixtus Affair.

Delcassé, Théophile (1852–1923) Foreign Minister, 1899–1905, 1914–15; Minister of Marine, 1911–13; Ambassador in St Petersburg, 1914. Théophile Delcassé was the leading exponent of assertive French colonial policy, which has been blamed for hastening the division of Europe into two armed camps. After France's attempt to challenge Britain in the Nile Valley failed at Fashoda in 1898, Delcassé concluded that French interests were best served by co-operation with Britain. He played an important part in negotiating the Entente Cordiale of 1904, by which Britain conceded French dominance in Morocco. However, his attempt to achieve this met with unexpected German resistance (The First Moroccan Crisis) and he was forced to resign under German pressure in July 1905. Although France eventually won Morocco, the episode poisoned Franco-German relations and instigated an informal Anglo-French military alliance. Delcassé identified French weaknesses that led him as Minister of Marine (1911–13) to sign the Anglo-French Naval Agreement of 1912, which was an important consideration in Britain's decision to join the war. From 1913 he was French Ambassador in St Petersburg, where his combative style and hostility to Germany did little to modify Russia's hard line during the Liman von Sanders Affair. Just before the July Crisis he was replaced by the scarcely less pugnacious Maurice Palèologue.

Dimitrijevic, Dragutin (1876–1917) Head of Serbian Army Intelligence and a Serbian nationalist. Known as 'Apis' (Holy Bull) Colonel Dimitrijevic was the central figure of Serbian nationalism before the war. His influence spanned the army, legal national movements like *Narodna Odbrana*, and illegal ones like *Ujedinjenje illi Smyrt*, known by its enemies as the Black Hand. Physically huge and personally dominating, Dimitrijevic wielded influence far beyond his humble rank. The name of his pressure group and newspaper '*Pijemont*' epitomised his central belief that, like the little 19th-century Italian state of Piedmont, Serbia should become the catalyst of the South Slav 'nation'. Dimitrijevic opposed pan-Slavism, seeing it as a Trojan horse for Russian imperialism in the Balkans, and expressed prescient hopes for a third tier of small nations freed from Great Power interference. In 1903, he masterminded the brutal coup which brought Peter Karageorgevic to the Serbian throne, and thereafter used his personality and position on the General Staff to become a dominant figure in the army hierarchy. He called for Serbia to assert her own identity and free herself from economic dependence on Austria and sentimental dependence on Russia. Austria's annexation of Bosnia was a shattering blow. Thereafter he threw his weight behind revanchist nationalist organisations, and the diversion of the Russian-sponsored Balkan League towards the 'liberation' of historic Serb territory in Kosovo and Macedonia. In 1914 Dimitrijevic was engaged in a three-way power struggle with the Old Radicals of Prime Minister Pašic and the Russophile Crown Prince Alexander. Historians have spent lifetimes trying to clarify what part, if any, this internal struggle played in the assassination of Archduke Franz Ferdinand on 28 June 1914. What is certain is that Dimitrijevic initially supported the assassins and provided the means for them to obtain arms and enter Austrian territory. However, he seems to have realised late in the day the inappropriateness of provoking war at a time of Serbian military exhaustion, and tried to call it off. In May 1917 Dimitrijevic was tried in Salonika and executed for treason by his old rival Nikola Pašic. Yugoslavs are still undecided whether he was a heroic patriot or a traitor who condemned their country to 4 years of ruin. At a 'retrial' in Belgrade in 1953 Dimitrijevic was cleared of all the charges laid against him in 1917.

Falkenhayn, General Erich Von (1861–1922) Prussian War Minister July 1913–January 1915, German C-in C September 1914–August 1916; General on the Romanian, Palestine and Lithuanian Fronts 1916–18. In 1914, Falkenhayn was blamed by Moltke for the failure of the Schlieffen Plan. Nevertheless, he was chosen by the Kaiser in September 1914 as Moltke's successor. Falkenhayn was convinced that ultimate German victory could only come in the west, but in 1915 he reluctantly sanctioned campaigns by Hindenburg and Ludendorff on the Eastern Front. Falkenhayn's greatest triumph in 1915 was the conquest of Serbia, but his determination to limit the troops he would allow Ludendorff and Hindenburg to squander in the east brought lasting enmity down upon him. In 1916, he turned his attention again to the west, unveiling his brutal but apparently rational plan to force the French to commit military suicide at Verdun. However, by the end of the summer Germany had lost as many men at Verdun as the French. In common with all wartime commanders, he overestimated the power of his artillery, and underestimated the will and determination of the defender. The Verdun disaster was nectar to Falkenhayn's enemies, who now included Chancellor Bethmann Hollweg, who had previously seen him as an ally in the battle against unrestricted submarine warfare. The setbacks of the Brusilov offensive and Falkenhayn's failure to predict Romania's entry into the war provided the last nails in his coffin, and he was forced out of office on 29 August 1916. His brave decision to accept command of the 9th Army on the Romanian Front was crowned with success, but he was not able to repeat this in subsequent tours of duty in Palestine and the Baltic States.

Foch, Marshal Ferdinand (1851–1929) Commandant of the École de Guerre, 1908–11; Commander of the French Northern Army, October 1914 to December 1916. Allied Supreme Commander on the Western Front, April 1918; Head of the Armistice Delegation and senior military advisor to the Paris Peace Conference, 1919. Foch served in the Franco-Prussian War as a young officer and subsequently rose steadily through the ranks of the French army, gaining particular experience as an artillery officer. His interest in military theory and strategy led to a Professorship at the École de Guerre in 1895, and as its Commandant from 1908–11, he developed tactics tailored to his conception of the traditional qualities of the French soldier. His assumption that the French soldier was particularly suited to swift attacking warfare lay at the heart of Plan 17 of 1914 under which French armies would seize the initiative through a strategy of all-out offence. His observations of the Russian manoeuvres of 1910 convinced Foch that France must help Russia to modernise her army and speed up her mobilisation if she was to offer any realistic counter-weight to a German invasion of France.

The outbreak of war found Foch, a 63-year-old military theorist, who had never experienced combat, commanding the IX Army. He cleverly disrupted the German advance on his headquarters at Nancy, and refused to adopt a defensive strategy during the battle of the Marne. Between October 1914 and December 1916 as Commander of the French Northern Army, he succeeded through force of personality in establishing a good working relationship with British generals. In the wake of Joffre's fall in December 1916, he was demoted to a nebulous consultative and trouble-shooting rôle, and was sent to Italy after the Caporetto disaster in the autumn of 1917. His brilliant performance there as a leader and conciliator rebuilding morale and co-ordinating Allied efforts convinced Haig and Lloyd George to support him as Allied supreme commander on the Western Front. He took up his post on 14 April 1918.

By the end of the war Foch was widely perceived as the architect of Allied victory, co-ordinating Allied forces on all fronts. In reality his powers as 'Generalissimo', were severely limited, depending almost entirely upon force of personality. As head of the Armistice Delegation and senior military advisor to the Paris Peace Conference, Foch became extremely dissatisfied with Clemenceau's hard but pragmatic line. His military career had begun amidst the defeat and humiliation of 1870, and he was determined to impose a settlement upon Germany that would free his country forever from the threat of invasion. Despite the disappointments and recriminations of his final years, Foch's contribution to the winning of the war was immense. His military theories profoundly influenced the development of the French army, and his aggressive and charismatic personality made a massive contribution to the Allied war effort.

Franz Ferdinand, Erzherzog von Österreich-Este (1863–1914) Heir to the throne of the Habsburg Empire. With the death of the heir apparent, Archduke Rudolf at Mayerling in 1889, Franz Ferdinand became heir to the Emperor Franz Josef. He was a prickly and unpopular figure, who alienated his uncle the Emperor by marrying the comparatively lowly born Sophie, Countess von Chotek. For several years before the war, his court at the Belvedere Palace in Vienna became an alternative power centre, where Franz Ferdinand held court and developed complex plans for the future of the Empire. He was particularly hostile to the obstruction of the Hungarians, and his well-publicised scheme for diluting their power through a system of 'Trialism' to include the Slavs, made him a bête noire to Magyar nationalists. While he lived, Franz Ferdinand's powerful and articulate personality, and his position as Inspector General of the Army, acted as a curb to the aggressive anti-Serb schemes of Conrad von Hötzendorf and firebrands in the Viennese foreign service. In November 1912 and on several occasions in 1913, his moderating influence was decisive. Franz Ferdinand was a close friend of the German Kaiser, whose personal sense of disgust and dynastic outrage at the Archduke's assassination may have played a part in his decision to give Austria carte blanche to deal with Serbia as it saw fit.

Franz Josef I (1830–1916) Habsburg Emperor 1848–1916. Ruler of Austria-Hungary since 1867. The survival of the multinational Habsburg Empire until 1918 owed much to the qualities displayed by Franz Josef during his 68-year reign, and to the immense personal loyalty that his subjects felt towards him in his final years. The nationalist tensions of his early years, and defeat by Prussia in 1866, had convinced him that the Empire's survival depended on three principles: balancing the interests of its dominant German and Magyar nationalities; maintaining close alliance with Imperial Germany, and avoiding war at all cost. Thus, under the *Ausgleich* [Compromise] of 1867 he gave the Magyars equal power in the 'Dual Monarchy'. This shored up the Empire for half a century, but created future problems by excluding its Slav population from power and placing most of them under Magyar misrule. Slav, and particularly Serb, hostility was heightened by his decision to annex Bosnia in 1908, a disastrous aberration that went against one of his basic foreign policy principles – co-operation with Russia in the Balkans. Its other cornerstone, the Austro-German Alliance of 1879, forced him in 1914 to abandon, with disastrous consequences, the principle of keeping the Empire at peace. He resisted constant demands by the Austrian militarists for strong action against Serbia until the spring of 1914. But after the assassination of his heir Franz Ferdinand in June 1914, the Emperor abandoned his habitual restraining role: after obtaining the 'blank cheque' from his ally Germany, he withdrew to his summer retreat at Bad Ischl and allowed his ministers to go ahead with their disastrous plan to punish Serbia. Perhaps this latest family tragedy, following the suicide of his original heir Rudolf in 1889, and the assassination of his beloved wife Elizabeth in 1898, had convinced him that the Empire's long balancing act could no longer continue. 'If the Empire must go down', he said, 'it must do so honourably'. Austria had no choice, he believed, but to avenge the dynastic insult perpetrated by the Serbs and to remain loyal to her German ally. Once war began, the venerable Emperor played a vital role in holding the multinational Empire together. Events following his death in November 1916 made it clear that most of its inhabitants were loyal to the austere and dedicated Emperor rather than the ramshackle institutions that he represented.

French, Field Marshal Sir John (1852–1925) Commander of British Expeditionary Force, August 1914–December 1915. French's career as a dynamic and stylish cavalry officer in colonial wars in no way prepared him for the situation that confronted him as commander of the British army in France. His first experience of modern firepower at Mons convinced him that Britain's tiny regular army would face annihilation unless it was withdrawn from the line. French felt an enormous responsibility as the custodian of Britain's last line of defence, and he believed that the BEF was in danger of being sacrificed by uncommunicative French commanders who were quite prepared to leave him in the lurch. After the subsequent long retreat, he was only stopped from pulling the BEF out of the line and persuaded to participate in the battles of the Marne by a personal visit from War Minister Kitchener. During 1915, his endemic mistrust of the French and persistent conflicts with his subordinates culminated in an incompetent performance during the Loos–Artois offensives. He was replaced in December by Douglas Haig.

French was in many ways the victim of Britain's pre-war military planning. Committed to a war for which nothing in his previous experience had prepared him, he was given an army deficient in numbers and munitions, and ordered both to preserve Britain's last line of defence and to risk all in an ill-defined enterprise not of his making. French was quick to identify the remedy – a fundamental transformation of Britain's economy for large-scale war production. By the time these measures were instituted, he had become the sacrificial victim of forces beyond his control.

Grey, Sir Edward (1862–1933) Viscount Falloden, July 1916. British Foreign Secretary 1905–16. As a member of a Liberal Cabinet distracted by domestic crises, and showing only sporadic interest in foreign affairs, Grey was able to dominate British foreign policy between 1905 and 1914. Coming from the Liberal Imperialist wing of the Party, and strongly influenced by hard-headed Foreign Office officials, he presided over the development of an informal but close military relationship with France and Russia which ran counter to the views of the neutralist and pacifist majority in his party.

Grey remained suspicious of German intentions, but believed that by 1914 the two countries had established a working relationship, epitomised by their successful co-operation during the Balkan Wars. During the July Crisis of 1914, he suggested various compromise formulas, tried to convene an international conference, and sought to exploit his apparent diplomatic rapport with Germany. He has been accused of encouraging German aggression by not making clear that Britain would oppose it by force, but it was impossible for him to take such a line. He did not wish to destroy hopes of co-operation with Germany, which he regarded until late July as the best hope for peace. He did not want to encourage reckless behaviour by Russia and France by aligning Britain with them too closely. Above all, he did not have his party's support for issuing threats to Germany.

When it became obvious that mediation efforts were futile, Grey switched all his energy into convincing colleagues and country that stopping Germany dominating the continent was Britain's most vital national interest. The Cabinet was gradually won over to support France, and on 3 August Grey convinced the Commons that Britain's interests were best served by standing up against Germany. The German invasion of neutral Belgium swept away any lingering Liberal doubts. Grey was convinced Britain must fight, but he hated war, and was a mediocre wartime diplomat. He managed to get Italy into the war, but at a price that poisoned post-war relations, and

265

his misjudgements contributed to the defection of both Turkey and Bulgaria to the side of the Central Powers. He had little more success in his dealings with Greece and Romania. Grey was not included in Asquith's War Committee of 11 November 1915, and was replaced as Foreign Minister in Lloyd George's December government by Arthur Balfour. His diplomatic mission to Washington from 1919–20 did not persuade the USA to ratify the Versailles Treaty.

Haig, Sir Douglas (1861–1928) Commander of British 1st Army, 1915; British Commander in Chief, December 1915–November 1918. After serving as a cavalry officer in the Sudan and in the South African War, Haig became, in his capacity as Director of Military Training and Advisor to the War Minister, the architect of the British Expeditionary Force and the new General Staff. Commanding the British 1st Army from early 1915, he became a harsh critic of Sir John French's conduct of the war, using his contacts at Court and in the Establishment to spread his reservations about French's leadership. On 17 December 1915 he was appointed to succeed French as C-in-C, remaining in command until the end of the war.

Despite the costly failures of 1916 and 1917 on the Somme and in Flanders, Haig was convinced that victory could be won by means of a great offensive breakthrough in the west. Previous failures he ascribed to insufficient preparation and attacking vigour rather than misguided tactics. He accepted heavy casualties as the inevitable consequence of modern firepower, but believed the only alternative was to accept a passive 'live and let live' philosophy that could prolong the war for decades.

Haig outfaced his critics, the chief of which was the Prime Minister David Lloyd George, with a combination of political influence and imperturbable conviction in the correctness of his tactics. The events of 1918 somewhat vindicated his uncompromising realism: the German army *was* brought to the point of exhaustion by the relentless long-term attrition to which he had subjected it. The means to achieve a breakthrough – tanks, vast manpower reserves, immense stockpiles of artillery and shells – were now available to him.

In the last months of the war his undoubted organisational skills came into their own, as Germany was brought to the brink of collapse. Haig's methods have made him into an easy scapegoat for armchair historians, but the young victims of the Somme and Passchendaele died because until 1918, defensive weaponry ruled the battlefield. No other general solved the problem of breakthrough using the weapons then available, and all of them presided over similar carnage.

Izvolski, Alexander (1856–1919) Russian Foreign Minister, 1906–10; Ambassador to France, 1910–16. Unexpectedly chosen as Foreign Minister on 12 May 1906, Izvolski negotiated the Anglo-Russian Agreement of 1907, and went on to achieve substantial improvements in Russo-Japanese relations. The Bosnian Annexation Crisis of 1908–9 was a disastrous episode for him. He was out-manoeuvred by the Austrian minister Aehrenthal into accepting the Austrian annexation, while his quid pro quo of a re-negotiation of the

Russian naval rights in the Dardanelles was never addressed. Slav opinion was outraged, and he did not long survive the Tsar's disapproval.

The events of 1908–9 left Izvolski with a legacy of resentment towards Germany and Austria. As Russian Ambassador in Paris from 1910 he strove to strengthen the Triple Entente and secure French loans for Russian re-armament and strategic railway building. During the Balkan Wars he advo-cated a strong military response from Russia, and in the July Crisis of 1914 his dispatches contributed to the Russian decision to mobilise. Early in 1915, Izvolski helped negotiate the Treaty of Constantinople, whereby Russia was promised a dominant rôle in the Straits in order to strengthen her commit-ment to the Entente.

Joffre, Marshal Joseph (1852–1931) Chief of General Staff, July 1911; Com-mander in Chief of French armies, 3 December 1915–13 December 1916. Born in a small Pyrenean village, the eldest of 11 children, Joffre won his way into the prestigious *École Polytechnique*, where he achieved great academic success. As a young man, he was involved in the defence of Paris in 1870–1, an experience that was to have strong resonance for him when Germans were again at the gates of the capital in the autumn of 1914. Fortuitously absent on colonial service during the Dreyfus Affair, he emerged from it as one of the few senior officers untainted by political or religious bigotry. He became a general in 1905, joined the General Staff in 1910, and was appointed Chief of General Staff in July 1911, a post that gave him command of the French army in case of war.

Joffre's colonial experience and his faith in the historical attacking qualities of the French soldier convinced him that the only way France could counter German aggression was by adopting a strategy of all out attack. Over the next three years, he packed the officer corps with men who shared his offensive preconceptions, bombarded politicians with demands for increased military spending, and threw his support behind the ill-considered Plan 17. In 1911, he proposed that France should move into Belgium to pre-empt a German advance. During the July Crisis he failed to understand the need for caution, and pressurised the politicians into full mobilisation. The first weeks of the war shattered Joffre's illusions, but he stuck to pre-war plans to within an ace of disaster. But belatedly accepting reality, he kept his nerve, rallied the army, and emerged on the Somme as the 'Saviour of France' – a domineering and autocratic figure, calm, methodical and courageous in adversity,

For the next two years Joffre was constantly under attack from journalists and jealous subordinates for his lack of accountability and his determination to carry on with his costly 'nibbling' tactics in Artois and Champagne. It was the disaster at Verdun that finally stripped from Joffre the mantle of prestige that had so long protected the 'Victor of the Marne'. At last, in December 1916, his enemies succeeded in removing him. Created the first 'Marshal of France' he eked out the war with ceremonial and formal duties.

Karl I (1887–1922) Emperor of Austria and King of Hungary, 1916–19. The assassination of his uncle, Franz Ferdinand in June 1914 left Karl as heir to the Habsburg Empire. After his accession, in November 1916, Karl embarked on a series of changes in domestic and foreign policy that were marked more by good intentions than good judgement. Within a few months he dismissed Prime Minister Ernst von Körber, his domineering Commander in Chief, Conrad von Hötzendorf, and the powerful Hungarian Prime Minister Istvan Tisza. He then took personal control of the army, but his attempts to limit brutality in the conduct of war and to curb the army's interference in civilian life were destabilising rather than progressive. Well-meaning attempts to use the offices of his relative Prince Sixtus in a peace dialogue with the allies ended in humiliation when Clemenceau revealed them to the Germans, placing him even more under the thumb of the German Third Supreme Command. His apparent liberalism led him to hold discussions with aspiring national independence leaders, but he was not prepared to offer them what they wanted and only succeeded in raising expectations and infuriating conservatives. In the course of 1918, he became little more than an impotent spectator of the disintegration of his Empire. At the end, he refused to abdicate, but in April 1919, was deposed in exile by the parliament of the new Austrian Republic.

Kiderlen-Wächter, Alfred von (1852–1912) German Foreign Minister, 1910–12. Kiderlen is best remembered for his decision to send the gunboat *Panther* to Agadir to counter France's military interference during the First Moroccan Crisis. This precipitated a six-week international crisis, which Kiderlen is accused of making worse by not clearly stating Germany's intentions or ultimate goals, although what these actually were historians remain undecided upon. Was Kiderlen simply actively asserting Germany's legitimate interests? Was he testing the will of the Triple Entente? Was he trying to force France into concessions elsewhere in Africa; or putting pressure on Britain into making naval compromises? Whatever his motives, the style and tone of his diplomacy added to the impression that German policy was unstable and aggressive. The results for Germany of all this 'table thumping' were hardly commensurate with the disruption it caused. Under the Franco-German Convention of November 1911, Germany was given territory in the Congo in return for giving France a free hand in Morocco. This was thought inadequate in German imperialist circles, while liberal opinion claimed that his reckless and Machiavellian diplomacy had brought Europe to the brink of war. Kiderlen was dismissed by the Kaiser in 1912, and died later in the same year.

Kitchener, Horatio Herbert (1850–1916) British Secretary of State for War 1914–16. The most famous and successful British general of the imperial era, Kitchener was first brought before the public eye by the Madhi at the battle of Omdurman in 1898, thus avenging the death of General Gordon 10 years before. In the same year, at Fashoda (Kodok) on the Nile, he defused a potential war crisis between Britain and France by sensible on-the spot negotiations with the French commander. In November 1900 he took command of the British army in the South African War, and by ruthless and efficient measures eventually snatched victory out of potential imperial humiliation. As Commander in Chief in India his bitter struggle with the Viceroy, Lord Curzon, did nothing to diminish his immense popular prestige, and in 1911 he accepted the post of British Proconsul in Egypt.

It was Kitchener's extraordinary popularity and respect among the public, rather than his administrative ability that led Asquith to appoint him as War Minister on the outbreak of hostilities in August 1914. Promoted to Field Marshall, he at once shook the complacency of the Cabinet by announcing that he expected the war to last for three years, and would require every man that Britain could raise. Over the next 18 months his greatest contribution was to use his immense prestige as the most recognisable British soldier to campaign for volunteers for what became known as Kitchener's New Armies. His poster 'YOUR COUNTRY NEEDS YOU!' became one of the most striking recognisable icons of the 20th century. By August 1915, over 2 million men had answered his call. In the day-to-day work as War Minister, Kitchener was a disaster. Britain had not yet steeled herself for total war, and Kitchener did not have the political skills to win colleagues over to his conviction that direction of industry and conscription were now essential. His military experience had not fitted him to debate decisions, compromise easily or delegate responsibility. He often seemed contemptuous of cabinet colleagues and civil servants and frustrated by the slow processes of civilian politics. Kitchener had played an important rôle in September 1914 in stiffening the resolve of General French, and in making the hard decision in 1915 to call off the Dardanelles Expedition, but he was progressively frozen out of his rôle in strategic planning, and relieved of his responsibilities for co-ordinating the industrial war effort. However, such was his position in the public eye as a talisman and symbol of Imperial success that it proved impossible to remove him from his Cabinet post. In June 1916 fate accomplished what Kitchener's political enemies had failed to do when he was drowned when the warship conveying him on a mission to Russia sank in the North Sea.

Lenin, Vladimir Ilyich (1870–1924) Leader of Bolshevik faction of the Russian Social Democrats; opponent of the war; Chairman of the Council of People's Commissars 1917–24. When war broke out Lenin was an exiled and isolated figure. Over the previous ten years, his doctrinaire and authoritarian leadership had alienated him from the mainstream of the Socialist International. Taking refuge in neutral Zurich after escaping as an enemy alien from Austrian Galicia he quickly presented an analysis of why the International had so tamely supported an imperialist war. Socialists, he proclaimed, should seize the opportunity presented by this 'capitalist civil war' to work for the defeat of their respective nations. The imperialist war must be turned into a class war with the aim of bringing about socialism.

At the socialist conferences at Zimmerwald and Kienthal in 1915 and 1916, Lenin's defeatist message was swamped by the arguments of French and German socialists who carried the rivalries of the trenches into the conference hall. Lenin and his tiny band seemed more isolated than ever. In 1917, he acknowledged that it was unlikely that the revolution would occur in his lifetime. With the overthrow of the Tsar, Lenin's pessimism disappeared at a stroke. Unashamedly accepting the assistance of Germany, which he believed was more abhorrent than any other capitalist state, he arrived at the Finland Station in Petrograd along with 31 other exiles on 16 April 1917. Now that the very qualities that had so infuriated his fellow socialists – refusal to compromise with 'fellow-travellers', single-mindedness, an obsession with party discipline, a penchant for reducing complex ideas to simplistic slogans and unsubtle rhetoric – were to prove priceless assets in the battles to come.

His April Theses set out a clear blueprint for future action, at the centre of which was a determination to end the war and promise an immediate and uncompromising programme of social and economic transformation. Lenin placed an absolute taboo on any co-operation with the Provisional Government, and made it clear that he regarded non-Bolshevik members of the Soviet as being equally compromised. In the atmosphere of 1917 Lenin's slogan 'Land, Bread and Peace' had an overwhelming resonance for the demoralised masses. Support for the Provisional Government and the moderate socialists, who both felt some constraints in the promises they were prepared to make, rapidly withered away.

After a potentially disastrous premature coup in July, Lenin acted with enormous vigour to prod the Party into action once he judged that the power was his for the taking. He presented Trotsky with the task of preparing the mechanics of the October coup, which because the credibility of the Provisional Government had collapsed, was achieved with remarkable ease. In the aftermath, Lenin again demonstrated his formidable qualities of decisiveness and vision. Seeing the need for immediate and spectacular actions to excite the watching world, he immediately proclaimed Peace, Land Redistribution, Workers' Control and a mass of other freedoms. Lenin believed that the revolution would be doomed if confined to backward Russia, but once he realised that there was no immediate sign of revolution elsewhere, and that Trotsky's polemics at Brest-Litovsk had failed to undermine the will of the enemy, he again acted with great decisiveness. With threats of resignation, he dismissed 'Left-Bolshevik dreams of continuing the war as a national revolutionary struggle', and bulldozed the Central Committee into accepting the Treaty of Brest-Litovsk. It was an inevitable evil that would enable the Revolution to survive. Its impact on Russia's erstwhile Allies was none of his concern. Nine months later the Treaty was indeed cast into the dustbin of history. Lenin had survived, but adrift in a ruined country amidst a sea of hostile peasants and counter-revolutionaries.

Lloyd George, David (1863–1945) Chancellor of the Exchequer 1908–15; Minister of Munitions, May 1915; Minister of War, June 1916; Prime Minister, November 1916–October 1922. By 1914 David Lloyd George's early reputation as a fiery radical who had made his reputation by opposing the Boer War had been eclipsed by his achievements as a practical social reformer and foreign policy pragmatist. In 1911, briefed by military experts about the seriousness of Germany's ambitions, he had employed his famous talent as a platform speaker to issue a severe warning to Germany. During the July Crisis of 1914, although still considered a leading member of the Radical, anti-war wing of the Liberal Party, he played a crucial role influencing the Liberal Cabinet towards intervention, throwing his weight behind Grey and the Liberal Imperialists in what some said was an act of political opportunism. Certainly his political antenna proved far more sensitive to the militant public mood than some of his more principled but blinkered colleagues.

Lloyd George's first wartime budget established the principle of financing the war through taxation, while incidentally furthering his Welsh teetotal principles by controlling the sale of alcohol. Becoming critical of Asquith's languid leadership style, and of Kitchener's failure to encourage armaments production, he favoured the 'Easterners' strategy of 'knocking away Germany's props' rather than confronting her head-on on the Western Front. As Minister of Munitions after May 1915, he adopted a vigorous and interventionist approach, bringing millions of women into the workplace and breaking the monopoly of traditional arms suppliers by exposing them to the competition of energetic small firms.

In June 1916, after narrowly escaping joining Kitchener at the bottom of the North Sea, he replaced the drowned general as Minister of War. The failed Somme Offensive increased his suspicion of the generals and invigorated his quest for alternative strategies such as the Salonika expedition, and ruined his relations with the High Command over the next two years. In December 1916, after allying himself with leading Conservatives and press barons to oust his old leader, he became head of a new coalition in place of Asquith. Lloyd George's new five-man War Cabinet now took all major strategic decisions. Leading figures from industry headed streamlined ministries with extended powers, and the Press baron Lord Northcliffe was appointed in recognition of Lloyd George's awareness of the importance of propaganda. His relationship with the service chiefs was less successful. By a great effort of will, he bulldozed the navy into adopting the Convoy System, but he was unable to win over the generals to his ideas about tactics on the Western Front. After being seduced into supporting Nivelle's 'war-winning' offensive, he then found it impossible to deter Haig's equally futile 1917 efforts. When Lloyd George's attempts to remove Haig foundered against the General's powerful political connections, he turned his energies into controlling the commander through a Supreme War Council. He then successfully backed Foch's elevation as Allied Generalissimo in the wake of the Spring 1918 disasters. At the Peace Conference he was trapped between his realisation that treating Germany too harshly would 'strew Europe with new Alsace-Lorraines', and the demands of conservative colleagues and a vengeful electorate. Subsequent generations might have thanked him for more courageous statesmanship.

Ludendorff, General Erich (1865–1937) Architect of Germany's success on the Eastern Front; driving force behind the German war effort 1916–18. A professional soldier who had involved himself in politics before the war to further the army's interests, Ludendorff immediately thrust himself into the public

271

eye in August 1914 through his brave exploits in the capture of the Liège fortresses. On 22 August he took over as Hindenburg's Chief of Staff in the east, sharing his commander's triumph at Tannenberg and laying the foundations of a potent military myth. In November, the duo took command of Germany's entire war effort in the east. In the spring of 1915, Ludendorff's exceptional military gifts were again in evidence in the Gorlice–Tarnow victories and the subsequent thrust into Poland, although his subsequent claim that he was on the point of defeating Russia before Falkenhayn interfered have been treated by military historians with great scepticism. Ludendorff fought tooth and nail to subvert Falkenhayn's plan for the invasion of Serbia in 1915, and used his prestige and right wing connections in the campaign to oust the Commander in Chief in the summer of 1916. Although Hindenburg was appointed Commander in Chief in Germany's Third Supreme Command on 29 August 1916, Ludendorff wielded real power as 'Quartermaster General'.

It was Ludendorff's hand that lay behind the attempt to militarise Germany under the Hindenburg Programme, the insistence on total victory with massive increases in German territory and crushing reparations, and the dismissal of the relatively moderate Chancellor Bethmann Hollweg in July 1917. He supported the resumption of unrestricted submarine warfare, and the crushing treaties levied upon Russia and Romania, which were in the long run disastrous for Germany's interests. In 1918, Ludendorff still believed that he could win the war with a final onslaught using German resources freed by the closing down of the Eastern Front. But he vastly over-estimated the remaining strength of the exhausted German army and the implacable technical obstacles that still prevented a sustained breakthrough. By July, he was convinced that Germany could not win, and that negotiations must begin while she was still undefeated. On 29 September he demanded immediate peace and sought to saddle the civilian government with responsibility for surrender, while retaining his command to defend the German homeland. But on 26 October he was forced into resignation and exile in Sweden, where he worked assiduously to foster the legend of an undefeated Germany 'stabbed in the back' by the very politicians he had himself manipulated into power.

Moltke, Field Marshal Helmuth von (1848–1916) German Chief of Staff 1906–17 September 1916. Von Moltke believed himself unworthy of comparison with his uncle, Helmuth von Moltke the elder, hero of the wars of German unification. He decided to retain the over-ambitious German War Plan of his predecessor von Schlieffen, but he weakened Schlieffen's conception by abandoning the projected advance through Holland and weakening the all-important right wing. Moltke's relations with his Austrian ally were far from honest: he promised to support the Austrians with an offensive in the east that he had no intention of making, while in turn Conrad promised to concentrate his attention on Russia, while really planning for an attack on Serbia.

By 1914 Moltke believed that war was inevitable, and that Germany should wage it before the military balance worsened for her, but he was also convinced Germany's only hope of victory was for the Schlieffen–Moltke Plan to operate like clockwork. During the July Crisis he became deeply anxious. Russia was stealing a march by mobilising secretly. Conrad was reneging on his commitments. Civilians were dithering, when even a delay of 72 hours could unhinge his plan. Thus from 28 July 1914 he demanded immediate mobilisation, sent private messages to Vienna urging an attack on Russia, and presumptuously overstepped his authority by advising Berchtold to stop further diplomacy. His reaction to the Kaiser's last-minute effort to tear up the Schlieffen Plan and turn the German advance eastwards amounted to insubordination, and although he succeeded in frustrating the Kaiser, the scare had a permanent effect on his confidence and equilibrium. Subsequently the failure of the Schlieffen Plan was blamed upon Moltke's failings. Co-ordination of the vast campaigns of 1914 proved beyond his powers, especially when the realities of battle unhinged the bureaucratic precision of the plan. Moltke had imagined that his plan had been so refined that when battle commenced there would be little for the commander to do. But ensconced far behind the lines, he possessed neither the force of personality nor the means of communication to prevent his field commanders taking ill-judged initiatives, while he himself lost his nerve and unnecessarily transferred troops to the east. By the time the French counter-attacked on the Marne, Moltke had lost control of events, and on 14 September, he was replaced as Commander in Chief by Erich von Falkenhayn.

Nicholas II (1868–1918) Emperor of Russia, 1895–1917. Soon after his accession to the throne, Nicholas I set the tone for his reign by informing a liberal delegation that their hopes of participating in the work of government were 'senseless dreams'. A man of limited education and weak personality, his ruling conviction was that his God-given right to reign as an autocrat must be handed down totally intact to his heirs. In this he was abetted by his wife Alexandra, whose stubborn and reactionary views increasingly dominated him.

Forced by overwhelming circumstances to accept an elected Duma during the revolution of 1905, he never hid his contempt for it nor ceased his efforts to undermine it. The first two Dumas were dismissed as 'insubordinate'. He appointed and dismissed ministers according to personal whim or under the influence of his wife and the reactionaries and mystics that surrounded her.

Although he favoured Russian expansionism in the Far East and the Balkans, and wished to establish Russian power over Constantinople, Nicholas hated war, and did all he could to defuse the July Crisis of 1914 by delaying mobilisation and making personal appeals to his cousin Wilhelm II. Once war broke out, the temporary rallying of Russian patriots to Church and Tsar was soon swept away by defeat, revelations of incompetence, and the Tsar's stubborn refusal to allow the Russian bourgeoisie to participate in the war effort.

Nicholas continued to regard all critics, regardless of their patriotic motivation, as self-interested upstarts and manipulative conspirators. On 5 September 1915, he made the fateful decision to take command personally of

Russia's armed forces. Henceforth, although he actually played little part in decision-making, all military set-backs and civilian hardships were popularly laid at his door, while in St Petersburg the Tsarina was free to give full rein to the faith-healers, mystics and charlatans who now surrounded her. Able ministers were sacked and replaced at the behest of the Empress and her guru Rasputin, as the Court became fatally mired in scandal and corruption. Nicholas's response to the situation in St Petersburg on 8 March 1917 was to order the garrison commander to put them down by force, but things had gone much too far for this. Neither the Provisional Committee of the Duma nor the Petrograd Soviet with which it shared power were prepared to have further truck with Tsarism.

On 15 March Nicholas II renounced the throne and passed with his family into captivity, first in the palace of Tsarskoye Selo, and then at Tobolsk and Yekaterinburg in the Urals, where in April 1918 they met their deaths at the hands of Bolshevik Red Guards.

Palèologue, Maurice-Georges (1859–1944) French Ambassador to St Petersburg 1913–17. Palèologue played a vital role in the July Crisis of 1914, and has been blamed by some historians for aggravating the crisis. His revanchism and suspicion of Germany rivalled that of his predecessor Delcassé. He persistently strove to bolster the Franco-Russian alliance by assuring Russia of French support, and used French finance as a lever to encourage Russian rearmament. During the July Crisis the absence of President Poincaré and Foreign Minister Viviani, put Palèologue in a key position to influence events. Subsequent 'editing' of the French diplomatic documents make his exact rôle unclear, but he seems to have gone beyond his brief in pledging French support for Russian actions, and dragged his feet when Paris told him to urge moderation on Russia. However, it is doubtful that he deliberately kept Paris in the dark about the pace of Russian mobilisation, as was once thought. A better explanation is that he was forced to send his dispatches to Paris by a long and time-consuming route because Germany had broken the French diplomatic codes. This meant that Palèologue's dispatches were delayed, and messages from Paris trying to restrain Russia arrived too late to have any influence.

During the war, Palèologue did all he could to keep Russia in the war by trying to get Paris to agree to territorial concessions. His attitude to the February Revolution was equivocal, and later in the year he was relieved by the French Socialist Albert Thomas who was believed to be more sympathetic to the new regime. His memoirs published in 1921–2, provide a fascinating, if excessively self-justifying, account of the July Crisis and Russia at war.

Poincaré, Raymond (1860–1934) French politician; President of the Republic, 1913–20. After a long spell in the Senate and cultivating his private law practice, Poincaré became French Prime Minister in January 1912, and a year later President of the Republic. Although no warmonger, he believed war with Germany was inevitable, and was determined that when it came France would face it with strong allies. Thus he strove to strengthen French military ties with Russia, concluded an important naval agreement with Britain, and was a strong advocate of the Three Year Law which would eventually allow France to mobilise as many trained conscripts as Germany. From 15–29 July 1914, he was absent on a State visit to Russia, and on his return the July Crisis was almost beyond redemption, but his critics accused him of not doing enough to stop Russia's provocative mobilisation.

Poincaré was instrumental in forging the wartime *Union Sacrée*, and during the war was able to play a more significant rôle than was usually the lot of Presidents in the Third Republic. However, for two years his authority, as of all politicians, was usurped in the Zone of the Armies by the High Command. Neither Prime Minister Viviani nor his successor Briand proved of much use in curbing the pretentions of the generals, but things improved with the dismissal of Joffre in December 1919.

1917 was a disastrous year for the President. The failure of the Nivelle offensive and the collapse of the Ribot and Painlevé government in a storm of scandal, corruption and treason allegations forced him to abandon national consensus. In November, he asked his old enemy Clemenceau, who formed an aggressive government of national defence, based on the Right. During most of 1918 Poincaré had to take a back seat to his combative Prime Minister, who even usurped him as leader of the French Delegation at the Paris Peace Conference, where Poincaré supported Marshall Foch's demands for large annexations of German territory. He was twice more Prime Minister in the 1920s before retiring in 1929 to write his memoirs.

Princip, Gavrilo (1894–1918) Assassin of Archduke Franz Ferdinand, and Serbian national hero. The son of Bosnian Serb peasants, Princip joined the Serbian secret society *Ujedinjenje ili Smrt* (Union or Death) known as the Black Hand which was committed to uniting the South Slav peoples into a federal nation. Princip, together with his young associate Nedjelko Cabrinovic and several others chose the well-publicised visit of the Archduke and his wife to Sarajevo on 28 June 1914 as the occasion for their action. At the time Princip was a politically naïve 19-year-old with a romantic belief in the 'politics the deed' and no clear vision of precisely what would follow from it. Whether Princip was supported and facilitated by Serbian nationalist groups, and in particular by Dragutin Dimitrijevic, head of Serbian military intelligence is hotly disputed, and will probably never now be known. It is likely that encouragement was initially given but then withdrawn too late to stop the act from taking place. Greatly aided by the incompetence of Austrian security arrangements, Princip was presented with a second opportunity to kill the Royal couple after an initial bomb effort by Cabrinovic had failed. He was sentenced in October 1914 to 20 years' imprisonment, but died of tuberculosis in 1918 before giving a coherent account of his motivations or revealing whom, if anyone had backed him.

Sazonov, Sergei (1860–1927) Russian Foreign Minister, 1910–16. Sazonov's central belief was that it was Russia's historic mission, and essential to her economic survival, to stop the Balkans and Near East from falling under Austrian and German domination. He became Russian Foreign Minister in the aftershock of the Bosnian crisis, which had brutally demonstrated how Russia's defeat in the Russo-Japanese War had rendered her temporally incapable of military action.

Sazonov was convinced of the need for speedy and massive Russian rearmament, but meanwhile Russia's vital interests in the Balkans and Near East had to be protected by diplomacy. He quickly negotiated a détente between Russia and Germany at Potsdam, and set about constructing a Balkan League as a barrier to Austrian ambitions. However, like many Russian Foreign Ministers Sazonov's policy was undermined by quasi-independent ambassadors pursuing independent initiatives. The Balkan states saw the League as a means of driving Turkey rather than Austria out of the Balkans, and the resultant Balkan Wars left Russia dangerously committed to her protégé, Serbia. The Liman von Sanders Affair fed Sazonov's fears that Germany was planning to ally with Turkey to cut Russia's lifeline through the Black Sea Straits. During the July Crisis he judged Russia had no choice but to make a stand if she wanted to remain a Great Power. He bombarded the Tsar with demands to mobilise the army to support the Serbs and put pressure on Austria, and seems to have realised very late in the day that Germany could not allow Russia the luxury of armed diplomacy.

Sazonov's wartime diplomacy began in triumph, with Romania promising neutrality in October 1914 in return for a promise of Hungarian Transylvania, and in 1915 Britain and France presenting him with Constantinople and the Straits as an inducement to remain in the war. He was regarded, rightly, by the Entente partners as the chief barrier to Conservatives hankering after a separate peace, but his concessions to Italy at the expense of South Slavs, and his pledge to create an independent Poland after the war, made him more and more hated by Russian Conservatives. In July 1916, using their influence over the Empress, they were able to secure his dismissal. He became Russian Ambassador to London, where he remained after the February Revolution, acting as representative of anti-Bolshevik forces at the Paris Peace Conference.

Sukhomlinov, General Vladimir (1848–1946) Russian War Minister 1909–16. As Russian Minister of War, he presided over a huge expansion of Russia's armed forces from 1910 to 1914. Sukhomlinov was a Conservative who favoured an accommodation with Germany. He was suspicious of France, and resentful of her attempts to force Russia to shape her war plans to suit French interests. Although the Rearmament Law of 1910 and the 'Great Programme' of 1914 had made little impact by the time the war broke out, the threat of future Russian military might was enough to alarm the German High Command, and lead some Germans to think that a pre-emptive war was preferable to waiting for Russia to attain overwhelming superiority by 1917. Sukhomlinov was unfairly blamed for the chaos that beset the Russian war effort after 1914, and for the divisiveness that beset the High Command for much of the war. His career ended in disgrace when he was dismissed in 1916 and subsequently tried for treason.

Trotsky, Leon (Lev Davidovich Bronstein) (1879–1940) Theorist of Socialist Internationalism; prime organiser of the Bolshevik coup against the Provisional Government of the Russian Republic in October 1917; Commissar for Foreign Affairs during the Brest-Litovsk peace negotiations; Commissar for War in the Russian Civil War; architect of the Red Army.

Born in 1879, into a Russified Jewish farming family in the Ukraine, Trotsky became involved at an early age in underground revolutionary activities. He escaped from a Tsarist prison in 1902, met Lenin in London, and worked on the revolutionary newspaper *Iskra*. When the Russian Social Democrats split in 1903 Trotsky inclined towards the Menshevik faction. Imprisoned again for his activities during the Russian Revolution of 1905, he again escaped and worked as a journalist in Vienna. In the years before the war Trotsky became one of Lenin's severest critics, believing that Lenin's concept of a 'vanguard Party' contained the germ of dictatorship. Trotsky's observations of the Balkan Wars as a war correspondent made him one of the few people accurately to predict the nature of the coming conflict. In common with most Russian Social Democrats he opposed the Tsarist war effort, but hounded by security agencies, was forced to confine himself to supporting anti-war movements from Zurich, Paris and Spain.

News of the February Revolution reached him in New York, but it was two months before he was able to reach his homeland to add his weight to the critics of the Provisional Government. Within weeks, he had merged his *Mezraionski* group with the Bolsheviks, burying his differences with Lenin in a common desire not to miss the revolutionary moment. As chairman of the Military Revolutionary Committee in the days before the Bolshevik coup of October, Trotsky's formidable skills as an orator, motivator and organiser found their historical moment, and the day after the Bolshevik seizure of power he triumphantly addressed the first session of the Congress of Soviets. As Commissar for Foreign Affairs, Trotsky did not believe his rôle was to conduct 'foreign policy' in the traditional sense, rather to use a unilateral declaration of peace and the treaty negotiations that followed as a lever to bring the whole edifice of capitalism tumbling down. The driving force of Trotsky's Marxism was a belief in international revolution. He saw the events in backward Russia as merely a preliminary to the *real* revolutions that would shortly break out in advanced capitalist countries with large proletariats. Thus he set out deliberately to treat the rules of traditional diplomacy with contempt, throwing open the archives to the public, cancelling foreign debts, appealing to enemy soldiers to desert and enemy populations to rise. As leader of the Russian delegation at Brest-Litovsk, he refused to abide by the niceties of diplomatic behaviour, or to conduct 'negotiations' in a traditional sense at all. All his actions were aimed at the watching millions whom he confidently assumed to be on the brink of revolution.

Unfortunately for Trotsky his judgement proved to be recklessly optimistic: the strikes, mutinies and demonstrations of January 1918 were contained with relative ease by belligerent governments. The Central Powers persisted in annexationist demands that only grew harsher with Trotsky's stalling. On the Central Committee Trotsky found himself marooned between unrealistic demands for 'revolutionary war' and Lenin's pragmatic belief that Russia must bury her pride and take whatever the Germans chose to offer her. His formula 'neither war nor peace' proved merely a green light for an unopposed advance of the German armies. The subsequent *dictat* of Brest-Litovsk was the graveyard of Trotsky's ideals. His subsequent heroic rôles – organiser of the Red Army, opponent of Stalinism – may be seen as rearguard actions against the forces unleashed by his miscalculations in the winter of 1917.

Venizelos, Elephferios (1864–1936) Greek Prime Minister, 1910–15, 1917, 1924, 1928–30. The most significant Greek statesman of the twentieth century, Venizelos was born in Crete while it was still under Turkish occupation. He led an unsuccessful insurrection to secure union with Greece in 1897, and participated in the subsequent autonomous Cretan government under Great Power protection. Such was his prestige in Greek nationalist circles that he was invited to go to Athens to lead the newly formed Military League in 1909, and a year later became Prime Minister with its backing.

He revised the constitution, reorganised the civil and military administration and played a prominent part in the formation of the Balkan League that doubled Greece's population and territory through victory in the Balkan Wars. This was a triumph for Venizelos, but his ambition extended much further than this, encompassing the re-conquest of Constantinople and the Greek-populated areas of Anatolia from Turkish rule. The onset of the First World War provided the opportunity to fulfil this dream, and for two years Venizelos strove to persuade King Constantine, who inclined towards the Central Powers, to join the Entente.

In 1916 he began an anti-Royalist and pro-Entente insurrection in Macedonia and Crete backed by the Allies, and in 1917, with French and British assistance, he secured the abdication of King Constantine. As legal Prime Minister again, under the regency of Constantine's second son Alexander, Venizelos at last brought Greece into the war on the Allied side.

During the Paris Peace Conference, his charm, eloquence and command of languages built him the reputation of an international statesman. The treaties of Neuilly with Bulgaria (1919) and Sévres with Turkey (1920) fulfilled his ambitions in full measure. However, at the moment of his triumph, Venizelos was defeated in the Greek elections of 1920, and over the next two years the Hellenist dream in Anatolia was turned into a nightmare by the rejuvenated Turkish armies of Kemal Atatürk. Venizelos returned from voluntary exile to head the Greek delegation that was forced to settle for the much-reduced territorial gains at the Treaty of Lausanne (1923).

Wilhelm II, Kaiser (1859–1941) King of Prussia and Emperor of Germany, 1888–1918. The German Constitution granted the Emperor enormous scope for personal intervention in military matters and foreign affairs, and Wilhelm II bore a heavy responsibility for the situation in which Germany found herself by 1914. Wilhelm was a complex and unpredictable figure whose ill-considered and high profile interventions were apt to intensify crises, and to generate an impression that German foreign policy was aggressive, hectoring and unpredictable. Wilhelm's conviction that Germany must have a colonial Empire to become a truly Great Power led to inevitable confrontation with the existing Colonial Powers. His enthusiasm for building a great navy pushed Britain into settling her differences with France and Russia, thus thrusting Germany deeper into isolation. Although Wilhelm wanted Germany to be a great industrial nation, he would not accept that the new social classes that industrialisation spawned would demand political power. He hated the *Reichstag*, refused to contemplate constitutional reform, and was deeply disturbed by the victory of the Socialists in the election of 1912. The entourage of right wing industrialists, militarists and uncritical courtiers with which he surrounded himself reinforced his conservative views. Believing that Germany was the victim of a plot to encircle and destroy her, he dreamed of uniting the nation behind its Supreme War Lord and using a national crisis to strike down his enemies while it was still possible to do so.

On 5 July 1914, he unhesitatingly placed his country's destiny in the hands of the politicians in Vienna, before airily departing for a three-week cruise in the Baltic while the crisis deepened. Upon his return, he announced that he could see no reason for war now that Serbia had handed Austria a great diplomatic victory. His belated attempts to conduct dynastic diplomacy by telegraph got nowhere, and his 'Halt in Belgrade' compromise was obstructed by his own ministers, and ignored in Vienna. On 1 August the straightjacket of the Schlieffen Plan was brutally spelt out for him by his Commander in Chief, probably for the first time. With the outbreak of war, Wilhelm rode on a tide of popular popularity for the first time, but when parades turned into fighting the limited powers of the 'Supreme War Lord' became apparent. As the great tactical and strategic decisions of the land war passed into the hands of experts, Wilhelm became a spectator. He retained some influence on the war at sea, but used this to prevent his beloved battleships being used at all. His right to make appointments was curtailed by the need to promote men of quality, who soon slipped out of his control. Thus in August 1916 his appointment of Hindenburg as of Chief of Staff marked a sharp decline in influence, as the Third Supreme Command assumed powers that undermined the last vestiges of his authority. Increasingly Wilhelm became a rubber stamp for the decisions of an authoritarian military regime, acquiescing in the Hindenburg programme and the disastrous decision to wage unrestricted submarine warfare. Increasingly, he supported the extreme annexationists and the military-industrial Right, whose programme reached its apogée in the Brest-Litovsk and Bucharest Treaties of 1918. By the war's end, he could only acquiesce in decisions made by others about the future of the monarchy. He was not consulted about the abdication announced by Prince Max of Baden on 9 November 1918, and fled tamely to exile in the Netherlands where he lived long enough to witness the arrival of Hitler's forces in 1940.

Wilson, Thomas Woodrow (1856–1924) President of the United States, 1913–21. Wilson's childhood experience of the aftermath of the American

Civil War gave him a lifelong distaste for conflict and a belief in the need for international conciliation. After a successful academic career he was elected Democratic President in the election of 1912, and the next year embarked on an energetic programme of domestic reform. Wilson showed little interest or aptitude for foreign policy and when war broke out in Europe he was determined to remain neutral. His education and culture inclined him towards Britain and France, and America's growing economic stake in Allied victory made him willing to connive at Britain's blatant flouting of international law over neutral shipping after 1915. As the historical wealth and influence of Europe seeped away cross the Atlantic through loans and gold transfers, Wilson glimpsed an opportunity to put his mark on history by adopting the rôle of peacemaker and architect of a new international order. Despite his lack of experience in foreign affairs, he pursued a personal foreign policy using his aide Colonel House, by-passing the experienced diplomats and ambassadors who sought to enlighten him. When he tried to draw the belligerents into peace negotiations at the end of 1916, both sides fobbed him off, making it clear that only those who fought the war could expect to have a say in the way it ended. However, in April 1917, having won the presidency only six months before on a neutralist ticket, Wilson's hand was forced by Germany's gamble on unrestricted submarine warfare. America's lack of military preparation and Wilson's refusal to allow American troops to fight under British or French command meant that it was over a year before his army was able make a significant contribution.

Although Wilson continued his efforts for a negotiated peace with the publication of his Fourteen Points in January 1918, he increasingly believed that his brave new world could only be built on the rubble of German defeat. When in September 1918 Germany asked him to broker a peace based on the Fourteen Points, he pressed ruthlessly for the overthrow of the imperial system, and allowed the military to impose a crippling Armistice. The Paris Peace Conference was an enormous frustration for him. Despite America's overwhelming predominance, he soon found that his simplistic ideas of national self-determination were at odds with the complex ethnic intermingling and ancient rivalries of the old continent. Nonetheless, by the time he left Paris in June 1919, the war was over, the Treaty signed, and the principle of a League of Nations accepted. But within months, the President's well-meaning structures came crashing down: in September 1919, in the course of a nation-wide tour to sell the settlement to a sceptical American public, he suffered a stroke. Next year the Senate refused to ratify the Versailles Settlement, or to honour the treaty guaranteeing France against future German aggression. Wilson's most imaginative and constructive conception, the League of Nations, was boycotted by his own country. By the time he completed his second term in 1921 little remained of the of the new world order that he dreamed of when he brought America into the war.

BIBLIOGRAPHICAL SURVEY

CONTENTS

Journals cited

A.H.R.	*American Historical Review.*
B.J.I.S.	*British Journal of International Studies.*
B.S.	*Balkan Studies.*
C.E.H.	*Central European History.*
E.H.R.	*English Historical Review.*
H.J.	*Historical Journal.*
J.C.H.	*Journal of Contemporary History.*
J.M.H.	*Journal of Modern History.*
P.P.	*Past and Present.*
S.E.E.R.	*Slavonic and East European Review.*
T.R.H.S.	*Transactions of the Royal Historical Society.*

*Books in CAPITALS are referred to several times in different contexts

1. BACKGROUND: THE GENERAL EUROPEAN PERSPECTIVE

These books provide a context for more detailed studies of the war and its origins.

P. Catterall, and R. Vinen (eds) *Europe 1870–1914* (1994); R. Gildea, *Barricades and Borders. Europe 1800–1914* (1987); O.J. Hale, *The Great Illusion 1900–1914* (1971); E.J. Hobsbawm, *The Age of Empire* (1987); James Joll, *Europe Since 1870* (1973); J.M. Roberts, *Europe 1880–1945* (1967); and Norman Stone, *Europe Transformed 1878–1918* (1983). All these provide excellent introductions, but the following deserve special mention: Gildea, a clear and comprehensive account of the major themes in European history; Hobsbawm, a sparkling and provocative book guaranteed to ignite the reader's imagination; Joll, a sophisticated overview that gives needed weight to cultural and intellectual aspects of European history.

2. BACKGROUND: INDIVIDUAL STATES

The following books show how the First World War fits into the historical development of individual States and regions.

Austria-Hungary: Alan Sked, *The Decline and Fall of the Habsburg Empire 1815– 1918* (1989). **The Balkans:** Barbara JELAVIC, *A History of the Balkans* Vol. II (1983). **France:** Maurice ALGUHON, *The French Republic 1879–1992* (1993); P. Bernard and H. Dubief, *The Decline of the Third Republic* (1985); J.-M. Mayeur and M. Reberioux, *The Third Republic 1871–1914* (1987); Anthony Adamthwaite, *Grandeur and Decline: France 1914–1940* (1995). **Germany:** V.R. Berghahn, *Imperial Germany 1871–1914* (1994); G. Craig, *Germany 1866–1945* (1978); John Michael, *The German Empire* (1994); W.J. MOMMSEN, *Imperial Germany 1867–1918* (1995); H.-U. WEHLER, *The German Empire 1871–1918* (1985). **Great Britain:** G.L. Friedberg, *Weary Titan: Britain and the Experience of Relative Decline* (1988); D. Read *Edwardian England* (1972); D. Brooks, *The Age of Upheaval: Edwardian Politics 1899–1914* (1995). **Italy:** Christopher Seton Watson, *Italy from Liberalism to Fascism* (1967); Denis Mack Smith, *Modern Italy* (1997). **Russia:** O. Figes, *The People's Tragedy: Russian Revolution 1891–1924* (1998); R. Pipes, *The Russian Revolution 1899–1919* (1990); H. Rogger, *Russia in the Age of Modernisation and Revolution 1881–1919* (1983); B. Menning, *Bayonets Before Bullets: The Imperial Russian Army, 1861–1914* (1994) an outstanding account of the ambivalent place the army held in Russian society.

3. ORIGINS OF THE WAR: ESSENTIAL READING

The best starting point is James Joll, *The Origins of the First World War* (1984), which introduces the various schools of explanation with great clarity and conciseness. L.C.F. Turner's excellent and thought provoking little book *The Origins of the First World War* (1970) is an excellent summary, with particularly interesting insights into of the rôle of Russia. Geoffrey Martel, *The Origins of the First World War* (1987) is in the excellent Seminar Studies in History Series which provides an up to date overview of the historical debate and useful collections of illustrative documents.

Several edited collections usefully gather together articles by major historians of the War: R.W.J. EVANS and Harmut Pogge von Strandemann *The Coming of the First World War* (1988) includes contributions by von Strandmann himself on Germany, the Habsburg Monarchy (Evans), Europe on the eve of war (Howard), Britain (Brock), the Balkans (Zeman), France (Cobb), and Russia (Spring). Another valuable collection is Keith WILSON, *Decisions for War, 1914* (1995) which includes Wilson himself on Britain, Hinsley on war origins, Fellner on Austria-Hungary, Röhl on Germany, Neilson on Russia, and Keiger on France. Of particular value are chapters dealing with areas where information is not readily available – Cornwall on Serbia, Stengers on Belgium, Nish on Japan, and a rare examination of the Ottoman Empire and the war by F.A.K. Yasamee. Other useful collections are H. KOCH (ed.)

The Origins of the First World War (1972) and an invaluable symposium by F.H. HINSLEY, *The Foreign Policy of Sir Edward Grey* (1977). All these books, apart from Hinsley, are available in paperback.

4. ORIGINS OF THE WAR: NATIONAL PERSPECTIVES

Since 1970 the origins of the war have been studied from the standpoint of virtually every European country. The reader can view events from the perspectives of the various European capitals, and compares national perceptions of these events. Recent studies include Volker BERGHAHN *Germany and the Approach of War in 1914* (1973); Richard Bosworth, *Italy and the Approach of the First World War* (1983); Richard KEIGER, *France and the Coming of the First World War* (1983); Dominic LIEVEN, *Russia and the Origins of the First World War* (1983); Werner Schölgren (ed.) *Escape into War The Foreign Policy of Imperial Germany* (1990); Zara STEINER, *Britain and the Origins of the First World War* (1977); and Samuel R. WILLIAMSON, *Austria-Hungary and the Origins of the First World War* (1993).

5. INTERNATIONAL RELATIONS BEFORE THE WAR

A.J.P. Taylor's *The Struggle for Mastery in Europe* (1964) is a stimulating, opinionated and often amusing introduction, although some of its conclusions have been overtaken by more recent research. R. Albrecht Carrié *A Diplomatic History of Europe since the Congress of Vienna* provides a coherent (if exceptionally dull) diplomatic narrative. William Langer's two old but impressively detailed studies, *European Alliances and Alignments 1871–1890* (1950) and *The Diplomacy of Imperialism 1890–1902* (1965) still give the best account of the formation of the alliance systems. Luigi ALBERTINI'S stupendous three volume study *The Origins of the War of 1914* (1952–57) covers the build-up to the war in enormous detail and with a wealth of documentary material, but in an accessible and readable style. It has the merit of being written by a man who had first-hand experience of many of the events he describes. In comparison Richard Langhorne, *The Collapse of the Concert of Europe* (1981) is positively featherweight, but provides a very clear and helpful outline. Geoffrey Barraclough, *From Agadir to Armageddon* (1982) is a stimulating account of the last years of peace, that makes interesting links between colonial and Balkan crises.

6. THE ALLIANCE SYSTEMS

The Triple Alliance: WILLIAMSON and BERGHAHN both deal with the developing tensions between the partners. Norman Stone, 'Moltke and Conrad: Relations between the Austro-Hungarian and German General Staffs,

1909–1914', in Paul KENNEDY (ed.) *The War Plans of the Great Powers* (London, 1979) explores the differing goals and expectations of the two generals. Further insight is provided by Christopher Andrew, 'German world policy and the reshaping of the Dual Alliance' (J.C.H., 1966); Frank Bridge (ed.) *From Sadowa to Sarajevo: The Foreign Policy of Austria-Hungary 1866–1914* (1972); and Richard Bosworth, *Italy, the Least of the Great Powers: Italian Foreign Policy before the First World War* (1979).

Britain and the Triple Alliance: Right up till 1914 it was still possible that Britain might reach agreement with the Triple Alliance Powers. The following books explore the possibility of a détente between them. As always, STEINER provides the starting-point, while Paul Kennedy, *The Rise of the Anglo-German Antagonism 1860–1914* (1980) provides a long-term perspective. R.J. Crampton, *The Hollow Détente* (1979) examines the apparent thaw in Anglo-German relations after 1912. Peter Hatton 'Britain and Germany in 1914: The July Crisis and War Aims' (P.P., 1967) gives a concise and clear headed analysis of their relations on the eve of war. Britain's contacts with Vienna are traced in Frank Bridge, *Great Britain and Austria-Hungary 1906–1914* (1972).

The Triple Entente: Britain and France: The exact nature of their relationship (unclear even to the British Cabinet) has been studied by many historians, particularly STEINER and KEIGER. For specific aspects, Christopher Andrew, *Théophile Delcassé and the Making of the Entente Cordiale* (1968); C. Howard, *Splendid Isolation* (1967); G.W. Monger, *The End of Isolation 1900–1907* (1963); and Keith Wilson, *The Policy of the Entente: Essays on the Determinants of British Foreign Policy 1904–14* (1985). Samuel Williamson, *The Politics of Grand Strategy: Britain and France Prepare for War, 1904–14* (1969) looks at their ambivalent military relationship. Trevor Wilson, 'Britain's "moral commitment" to France in August 1914' (*History*, 1979) exposes the muddle which afflicted Britain and France even as they teetered on the brink of war.

The Triple Entente: France and Russia: KEIGER, and LIEVEN provide an excellent introduction. The origins and evolution of the Alliance are described in two books by George R. Kennan, *The Decline of Bismarck's European Order, Franco-Russian Relations 1875–1890* (1974) and *The Fateful Alliance: France, Russia, and the Coming of the First World War* (1984). A fascinating Russian perspective is provided by V.I. Bovykin, 'The Franco-Russian Alliance' (*History*, 1979).

7. PRE-WAR CRISES: THE BALKANS

M. Anderson, *The Eastern Question 1774–1923* (1966) is a masterpiece of compression and clarity, invaluable for understanding the roots of Near Eastern and Balkan history. It is a first port of call for those wishing to make sense of the crises that beset the region. Volume I of JELAVIC is essential for the roots of Balkan history, while Volume II *The Twentieth Century* examines the impact of the Balkan Wars and the First World War on the region. In *The Road to Sarajevo* (1966) Vladimir Dedijer uses the Serbian documents to present a detailed account of the relationship between Austria-Hungary and the South Slavs, and a fascinating, insight into the Black Hand conspiracy. I. Banac, *The National Question in Yugoslavia: Origins, History, Politics* (1984) places more emphasis upon the South Slav movement *within* the Habsburg Empire.

On the Balkan Wars, E. Helmreich, *The Diplomacy of the Balkan Wars* (1938) is still the only detailed history, whereas the interference of the Great Powers in the Balkans has been extensively covered. Douglas Dakin, 'The diplomacy of the great powers and the Balkan States 1908–14' (B.S., 1962) provides a clear overview, while German ambitions in the Balkans and Near East are exposed by Ulrich Trumpener, *Germany and the Ottoman Empire 1914–1918* (1968). M.B. Cooper looks at 'British Policy in the Balkans 1908–9' (H.J., 1964), and there are several chapters on British Balkan policy in HINSLEY. Russian objectives in the region are explored by LIEVEN, who exposes the 'insubordination' of Russia's Balkan diplomats. A. Rossos, *Russia and the Balkans: Inter-Balkan Rivalries and Russian Foreign Policy 1908–1914* (1981), and E.C. Thaden, *Russia and the Balkan Alliance of 1912* (1965) both provide illuminating insights into Russia's Balkan ambitions. Austria-Hungary's Balkan policies are dealt with by WILLIAMSON, who tellingly compares the Balkan crises of 1913 and 1914. Fritz Fellner (in WILSON) makes John Leslie's revelations about the militarist clique in Vienna on the eve of war available to English readers.

The Balkans on the eve of war are covered by R.J. Crampton's two articles, 'The Decline of the Concert of Europe in the Balkans 1913–14' (S.E.E.R., 1974) and 'The Balkans 1909–1914' (in HINSLEY). Z. Zeman 'The Balkans and the Coming of War' (in EVANS) are also valuable. The rôle of the Balkans in the 1914 Crisis is explored by Joachim Remak, '1914: the Third Balkan War' (J.M.H., 1971, and in KOCH). Mark Cornwall (in WILSON) describes the domestic chaos of Serbia on the eve of the assassination.

8. PRE-WAR CRISES: COLONIAL COMPETITION

The prospect of war breaking out over a colonial dispute had receded by 1914, but colonial competition had played an major rôle in dividing Europe into competing groups. General overviews of pre-war colonial competition include D.K. Fieldhouse, *Economics and Empire 1830–1914* (1973); V.G. Kiernan, *European Empires from Conquest to Collapse 1815–1960* (1982); A. Hodgart, *The Economics of European Imperialism* (1977); and R. Shannon, *The Crisis of Imperialism 1865–1915* (1974).

The French Empire: R. Aldrich, *Greater France* (1996) provides an excellent new account of Europe's second largest empire, to complement the only previous English works, H. Brunschwig, *French Colonialism 1871–1914* (1966) and J. Cooke, *New French Imperialism 1880–1910* (1973). Christopher Andrew and A.S. Kanya-Forstner, *France Overseas: The Great War and the Climax of French Overseas Expansion* (1981) gives an invaluable account of France and her empire at war.

The German Empire: W.O. Henderson, *The German Colonial Empire 1884– 1919* (1993), and W.D. Smith, *The German Colonial Empire* (1978) introduce this topic, that has been largely ignored by English writers. Immanuel Geiss's article 'The German Version of Imperialism: Weltpolitik' (in SCHÖLGREN), is a thoughtful appraisal, while the motives for Germany's belated push into Africa are analysed by H. Stoecker in *German Imperialism in Africa* (1986) and J. Mortimer 'Commercial interests and German diplomacy in the Agadir Crisis' (H.J., 1967).

The British Empire: Dennis Judd, *Empire: The British Imperial Experience from 1765 to the Present* (1998) is an exhaustive and measured account, while Lawrence James, *The Rise and Fall of the British Empire* (1994) provides an alternative perspective. P.K. O'Brien 'The Costs and Benefits of British Imperialism, 1846–1914' (P.P., 1988), and more recently by Avner Offer, 'The British Empire, 1870–1914: A Waste of Money?' (E.H.R., 1993), question Britain's wisdom in investing so much in colonial adventures.

Michael Dockrill, 'British policy during the Agadir crisis of 1911' (in HINSLEY) explores the effect of colonial competition on Anglo-German relations. The prospect that colonial horse-trading might oil the wheels of an Anglo-German rapprochement is assessed by Peter Hatton, 'Harcourt and Solf: the search for an Anglo-German understanding through Africa 1912–14' (E.H.R., 1971), and by J.D. Vincent-Smith, 'Anglo-German Negotiations over the Portuguese Colonies in Africa 1911–1914' (H.J., 1974).

9. THE DEBATE ABOUT GERMAN RESPONSIBILITY

Fritz Fischer's book *Germany's Aims in the First World War* (1967) claims that German militarists planned the war in advance to scupper German socialism and carry through a well-defined programme of expansion foreshadowing Nazi ambitions. It reopened a historical debate that many Germans hoped was closed for ever. The 49 volume *Gross Deutsche Politik*, published between the wars, had apparently undermined the claims of 'War Guilt' embodied in Article 251 of the Versailles Treaty (see TAYLOR's bibliography). The interwar consensus, summed up in Sidney Fay's *The Origins of the World War* (1930) was that no state bore *unique* responsibility for 1914: Nations had 'stumbled into war' – all of them victims of secret diplomacy, atavistic cultural forces, military determinism, and dynastic and imperialist ambition. Fischer's book reopened the academic debate in Germany with a vengeance, while his subsequent *War of Illusions* (1973) and *World Power or Decline* (1974) added fuel to the fire. Accessible summaries of 'Fischer's Thesis' are provided by three articles in KOCH: Fischer, 'World Policy, World Power and German War'; James Joll, 'The 1914 Debate Continues: Fritz Fischer and his Critics', and Imanuel Geiss, 'Origins of the First World War'. Geiss's book *German Foreign Policy 1871–1914* (1976) sets out the main arguments of the 'Fischer school'. Older German historians like Gerhard Ritter, argued that Fischer had grossly overstated his case. Others argued that Germany's 'war aims' (cited by Fischer as a mainspring of German aggression) were drawn up *after* hostilities had broken out. Karl-Heinz Janssen, 'Gerhard Ritter: A Patriotic Historian's Justification' (in KOCH) gives a flavour of the reaction by conservative German historians to Fischer's bombshell.

Fischer's books caused great excitement among younger German historians, provoking a series of studies that developed the seeds he had sown. The part played by domestic politics (*Innenpolitik*) in the making of German foreign policy is a particular theme of BERGHAHN, WEHLER and MOMMSEN. John Moses, *The War Aims of Imperial Germany* (1968), and *The Politics of Illusion* (1975) clarify the issues, as do John Röhl's synopsis *1914, Delusion or Design?* (1973), and David Kaiser's analytical article 'Germany and the Origins of the First World War' (J.M.H., 1983). W. Mommsen's 'The Topos of Inevitable War in Germany in the Decade before 1914' in V.R. Berghahn and M. Kitchen (eds) *Germany in the Age of Total War* (1981), and Mommsen's two articles for the Journal *Central European History*, 'Domestic factors in German Foreign Policy before 1914' (1973) and 'Public Opinion and Foreign Policy in Wilhelmian Germany, 1897–1914' (1991) provide stimulating contributions to the debate. The rôle of German Chancellor Theobald von Bethmann Hollweg's in the July Crisis has been re-assessed by Konrad Jarausch in *The Enigmatic Chancellor. Bethmann Hollweg and the Hubris of Imperial Germany* (1973).

10.   THE CLIMATE OF OPINION BEFORE THE WAR

In 1928 Caroline Playne, *The Pre-War Mind in Britain*, identified certain characteristics that predisposed people to 'desert the haven of Edwardian security to plunge towards the abyss'. Subsequently, a host of historians has striven to analyse the 'mood' of a continent on the brink of war.

Barbara Tuchman, *The Proud Tower* (1966) presents an evocative sketch of the pre-war world as seen through certain key events and movements. More weighty, is Modris Eksteins, *Rites of Spring: The Great War and the Modern Age* (1989) a brilliant study of the early 20th century, which reveals a society obsessed with perfectionism, race, violence and action. Daniel Pick's two books, *Faces of Degeneration: A European Disorder* (1989) and *War Machine* (1993) are profound and suggestive. On the same theme, Paul Kennedy and A.J. Nicholls (eds), *Nationalist and Racialist Movements in Britain and Germany before 1914* (1981), and R. Chickering, *We Men who feel Most German: A Cultural Study of the Pan-German League 1886–1914* (1984) throw light on the pre-war Right.

Popular literature is examined by J.M. MacKenzie (ed.), *Imperialism and Popular Culture* (1986), and Cecil D. Eby, *The Road to Armageddon: The Martial Spirit in English Popular Literature 1870–1914* (1987). Two pioneering studies of the Press are E.M. Carroll, *French Public Opinion and Foreign Affairs 1870–1914* (1931), and *Germany and the Great Powers, 1866–1914: A Study in Public Opinion* (1938). O.J. Hale, *Publicity and Diplomacy, 1890–1914* (1940) and John MacKenzie, *Propaganda and Empire: The Manipulation of British Public Opinion*

1800–1960 (1986) show how the Press manipulated public opinion to add fuel to international crises. As an antidote, Keith Robbins, 'Foreign policy, Government structure and public opinion', and 'Public Opinion, the Press and Pressure Groups' (in HINSLEY) cautions against sweeping conclusions based on press studies. Influences on British young people are examined by Geoffrey Best, 'Militarism and the Victorian Public School', in M. Bradley, and B. Simon (eds) *The Victorian Public School* (1975), and John Springhall, *Youth, Empire and Society: British Youth Movements 1883–1940* (1977).

11. DOMESTIC POLITICS AND FOREIGN POLICY

Many historians, notably FISCHER, have wondered whether decision-makers welcomed war as a diversion from internal crisis, and a means of unifying the population behind the flag. George Dangerfield, *The Strange Death of Liberal England* (1935) paints a fascinating picture of the interlocking crises of Edwardian England, but fails to demonstrate how they influenced Britain's decision to go to war. A.J. Mayer, 'Internal Causes and Purposes of War in Europe 1870–1956' (J.M.H., 1969) surveys the issues, while Michael Gordon, 'Domestic conflict and the origins of the 1st W War: the British and German cases' (J.M.H., 1974) adopts a comparative approach. Niall Ferguson, 'Public Finance and National Security: The Domestic Origins of the First World War Revisited' (P.P., 1994) opens up another angle to this debate. W. Mommsen, 'Domestic factors in German Foreign Policy before 1914' (C.E.H., 1973) looks at *innenpolitik* in Germany, and the link between naval expansion and politics in Germany is the subject of Volker Berghahn, *Germany and the Approach of War in 1914* (1973). Berghahn develops this theme in 'Naval Armaments and Social Crisis: Germany before 1914' in G. BEST and A. Wheatcroft, *War, Economy and the Military Mind* (1976). The debate is carried forward by G. Eley, 'Reshaping the Right: Radical Nationalism and the German Navy League 1898–1908' (H.J., 1978).

12. ARMAMENTS AND NAVAL COMPETITION

David G. Herrmann, *The Arming of Europe and the Making of the First World War* (1996) analyses the part the arms race played in pre-war international relations. The outstanding recent book on pre-war armaments competition is David Stevenson, *Armaments and the Coming of War in Europe* (1996), a work of comprehensive scholarship that throws light on military spending, logistics, manpower resources and loan politics. G. Krumreich, *Armaments and Politics in France on the Eve of the First World War* (1986) shows how France used her financial strength and arms industry to gain influence in Russia and the Balkans. The most comprehensive account of the Naval Race is still A.J. Marder, *From the Dreadnought to Scapa Flow* vol. 1 (1961). Robert Massie, *Dreadnought: Britain Germany and the Coming of the Great War* (1991) is informative and entertaining. Jonathan Steinberg, *Yesterday's Deterrent* (1965) shows how the relative cost of British and German naval spending was similar to that of the superpowers after 1945, and explores other aspects of Anglo-German naval competition in 'The Copenhagen Complex' (J.C.H., 1966), 'The Kaiser's Navy and German Society' (P.P., 1964) and 'The Novella of 1908: and the Anglo-German Naval Arms Race' (T.R.H.S., 1971). H. Herwig, *Luxury Fleet* (1980) and I. Lambi, *The Navy and German Power Politics* (1984) examine other aspects of naval competition. Radical opposition to naval spending in Britain is dealt with by H. Weinroth, 'Left-wing opposition to naval armaments in Britain before 1914' (J.C.H.; 1971).

13.   THE WAR PLANS OF THE POWERS

A.J.P. Taylor's provocative little book *War by Timetable: How the First World War Began* (1969) shows how inflexible war plans and mobilisation schedules made it *impossible* for statesmen to stop the war once the troop-laden trains had begun to roll towards the frontiers. Thirty years on, Taylor's brilliant if overstated exercise in military determinism has been thoroughly tested. John Gooch, *The Plans of War: the General Staff and British Military Strategy, 1900–1916* (1974) and Paul KENNEDY (ed.) *The War Plans of the Great Powers 1880–1914* (1980) analyse the contingency plans of all the pre-war General Staffs. The Schlieffen Plan is described in great detail by Gerhard Ritter *The Schlieffen Plan* (1958), and analysed vigorously in Arden Bucholz, *Moltke, Schlieffen and Prussian War Planning* (1991) and L.C.R. Turner, 'The Significance of the Schlieffen Plan' (in KENNEDY). The French Plan 17 is described by Douglas Porch, *The March to the Marne. The French Army 1871–1914* (1981), and by Samuel Williamson Jnr, 'Joffre Reshapes French Strategy, 1911–1913' (in KENNEDY). The convoluted war plans of Russia and Austria are entertainingly dissected by Norman Stone, *The Eastern Front, 1914–1917* (1975) and by L.C.F. Turner, 'The Russian Mobilisation in 1914' (in KENNEDY). Contradictions between German and Austro-Hungarian military goals is exposed in Norman Stone's article 'Moltke and Conrad: Relations between the Austro-Hungarian and German Chiefs of Staff' (H.J., 1966, and KENNEDY). A recent work by B. Tunstall, *Planning for War Against Russia and Serbia* (1993) has contributed greatly to our understanding of pre-war planning in the eastern theatre.

Great Britain's confused pre-war military posture is elegantly dissected by Michael Howard, *The Continental Commitment* (1972). Aspects of Britain's defence planning are addressed by the following writers: Keith Wilson, 'British War Plans and the Military Entente with France before the First World War' (B.J.I.S., 1977); David French, *British Economic and Strategic Planning 1905–15* (1982); and P. Haggie, 'The Royal Navy and War Planning in the Fisher Era' (KENNEDY).

The question of whether the rival High Commands knew what their enemies had in store for them is addressed by Ernest May, *Knowing One's Enemies* (1984). This includes contributions by Jan Karl Tannebaum, *French Estimates of Germany's Operational War Plans*, and Christopher Andrew, *France and the German Menace*. The German secret service is addressed by U. Trumpener, 'War Premeditated? German Intelligence Operations in July 1914' (C.E.H., 1976). Douglas Porch, *The French Secret Services* (1997) shows how the French High Command persistently ignored warnings about the Schlieffen Plan. Preconceptions about a future war are examined entertainingly by I.F. Clarke, *Voices Prophesying War, 1763–1914* (1970). More academic approaches are L. Farrar, *The Short War Illusion* (1973) and John Gooch, 'Attitudes to War in Late Victorian and Edwardian England' in Bond and Roy, *War and Society* (1975). The obsession with offensive tactics is studies by J. Snyder, *The Ideology of the Offensive: Military Decision-Making and the Disasters of 1914* (1984), and by Steven Evara, *Military Strategy and the Origins of the First World War* (1991). In two fascinating studies, *Supplying War, Logistics from Wallenstein to Patton* (1979) and *Technology and War from 2000 BC to the Present* (1991), Martin van Crefeld throws light on these important but under-researched topics.

14. THE JULY CRISIS OF 1914

The most comprehensive account is the third volume of ALBERTINI, while I. Geiss, *July 1914* (1967) traces the unfolding crisis through the original diplomatic documents. William Jannen Jnr, *The Lions of July: Prelude to War, 1914* (1997) displays an outstanding mastery of the complex issues and an ability to make them interesting and understandable. Barbara Tuchman's *The Guns of August* (1962) if rather outdated, is still a stimulating introduction. George Malcolm Thomson, *The Twelve Days* (1964) is based upon the accounts of those who experienced the crisis. The first few chapters of Cameron Hazlehurst, *Politicians at War: July 1914–May 1915* (1971) present a compelling account of the British Cabinet's relentless slide into intervention. BERGHAHN, KEIGER, LIEVEN, STEINER and WILLIAMSON allow the reader to contrast the ways the unfolding crisis was perceived in different capitals. Memoirs, biographies and diaries of the protagonists provide an extraordinary insight into how statesmen and generals reacted during these heated and exhausting few days. (See 21 Biographies and memoirs.)

15. THE WAR: GENERAL HISTORIES

Until recently, no general history of the war of any significance had been published since the 1970s. Since Basil Liddell Hart's iconoclastic *A History of the First World War* (1930), the overviews of the war had been short, stimulating surveys: A.J.P. Taylor's scintillating *The First World War: An Illustrated History* (1963), and Cyril Falls's masterly summary, *The First World War* (1960). Marc Ferro's survey *The Great War 1914–18* (1973) emphasises political and social themes, and looks at the war from a French rather than an Anglo-Saxon perspective (a viewpoint recently carried to extremes by ALGUHON, who contrives to ignore the existence of France's allies almost entirely).

However, a spate of excellent new books has been prompted by the 80th anniversary of the war. Hew Strachan's *Oxford Illustrated History of the First World War* (1998), provides a concise and up to date analysis of the war by experts in the field illustrated by well-chosen and evocative images. John Keegan, *The First World War* (1998) is a balanced and comprehensive narrative which avoids the facile 'general-bashing' that comes easily to those who sit at desks. Holger Herwig, *The First World War: Germany and Austria-Hungary* (1997) makes available to English readers a quarter of a century of research by German and Austrian scholars, and is presented with the author's characteristic vigour and piquancy. It gives due weight to the titanic events of the Eastern Front, and is a mine of information about the Austro-German home-fronts. Niall Ferguson, *The Pity of War* (1998) will disappoint those seeking accounts of battles, generals, or even 'campaigns. It is not a history of the war in the conventional sense at all, but nonetheless a stimulating read for those who relish assaults upon historical clichés. Ferguson uncovers a wealth of challenging information about the financing and economics of the war, and asks many provocative and disorientating questions: Should Britain have stayed out altogether? Why did the Entente get so little military success for its greatly superior expenditure? Did some soldiers positively embrace the joy of battle, and make it a way of life. Finally, for denizens of second-hand bookshops who are prepared to seek out the full eight volume set, there is *Purnell's History of the First World War* (1969–71) edited by Barrie Pitt and P. Young, a cornucopia of maps, tables, photographs, art-work, and articles by distinguished scholars.

16. THE WAR: EXPERIENCE OF INDIVIDUAL STATES

France: Most general histories of France provide an extraordinarily superficial and uncritical account of the nation rushing enthusiastically off to war. The traditional mythology of 'sacred union' is challenged by Jean-Jacques Becker, whose detailed studies of the French people at war is now available in English as *The Great War and the French People* (1985). Becker's chapter in Patrick Fridenson (ed.) *The French Home Front 1914–18* (1992) is another antidote to the cherished myths of patriotic historians. Fridenson's collection gives us valuable insights into the social and economic aspects of France at war, including Gerd Hardach on industrial mobilisation, Mathilde Dubesset *et al.* on female munition workers and John Horne on the labour market.

Germany: The relevant chapters in CARR, CRAIG and WEHLER provide excellent introductions. Several HERWIG chapters are extremely informative about life behind the lines. Arthur Rosenberg *Imperial Germany: The Birth of the German Republic 1871–1918* (1931/1964) is an account of wartime German politics by a man who himself played an intimate part in them. L. Moyer, *Victory Must Be Ours* (1995) gives a detailed account of the German people at war, and of the increasing privations of everyday life. The impact of the war on the economy is examined by G. Feldman, *Arms, Industry and Labor in Germany,*

1914–18 (1966). Roger Chickering, *Imperial Germany and the Great War, 1914–1918* (1998) provides a well-structured synthesis of the latest research on this subject.

Russia: Writing about Russia at war is often distorted by teleological judgement or pro- or anti-Bolshevik polemics. In the chaotic aftermath of 1917 accurate figures and objective analysis were rare commodities. Between the wars, an army of exiles strove to justify their actions, and Soviet historians soon found themselves in the headlock of Stalinism. ROGGER, FIGES and PIPES have chapters on the war, and STONE deals with Russian finances and civil military relations. Raymond Pearson, *The Russian Moderates and the Crisis of Tsarism, 1914–17* (1977) describes the doomed attempts of Russian Liberals to get some say in the defence of their country. Leonard Schapiro's *1917: The Russian Revolution and the Origins of Present-day Communism* (1984) is a lucid introduction, and Allan K. Wildman, *The End of the Russian Imperial Army: The Old Army and the Soldiers' Revolt (March–April 1917)* (1980) describes the military collapse of 1917.

Great Britain: The British Home Front has attracted great interest from historians. A.J.P. Taylor *English History 1914–45* (1965) and John Stevenson, *British Society 1914–45* (1984) provide perspective and context. The following deal with more specific themes: Paul Guinn, *British Strategy and Politics, 1914–18* (1965); Arthur Marwick, *The Deluge: British Society and the First World War* (1991); J.M. Bourne, *Britain and the Great War, 1914–1918* (1989); and John Turner, *British Politics and the Great War* (1992). Several recent books are deserving of particular attention. J.M. Winter *The Great War and the British People* (1985) is a sensitive survey of the war's impact on lives of ordinary people. In Stephen Constantine (ed.) *The First World War in British History* (1995), various specialists look at the war's impact on industry, agriculture, the trade unions, science and technology, society, women and culture. Gerard DeGroot, *Blighty: British Society in the Era of the Great War* (1996) takes a refreshing new look at some of the sacred cows of British social history, and challenges some of the doctrinaire assumptions of recent social historians. British reluctance to convert her entire economy onto a war footing is described in David French, *British Economic and Strategic Planning, 1905–1915* (1982). Keith Grieves, *The Politics of Manpower, 1914–1918* (1988) looks at the difficult choice of whether to direct men to war production or send them to the Front. R.J.Q. Adams and I. Poirier, *The Conscription Controversy* (1987) examines the jettisoning of one of Britain's most cherished shibboleths – a voluntary army. L.M. Barnett, *British Food Policy during the First World War* (1985) describes how Britain came to accept, with surprising enthusiasm, a form of war-socialism. In the wake of Arthur Marwick's pioneering study *Women at War, 1914–1918* (1977), Gail Braybon, *Women Workers in the First World War* (1981) and C. Tylee, *The Great War and Women's Consciousness* (1990) have cast much-needed light on women's wartime experience.

Austria-Hungary: The history of the Habsburg Empire at war is not easily accessible to those who do not read German, but HERWIG has recently made available a wealth of German and Austrian research. The latter chapters of SKED provide an excellent overview, and Z.A.B. Zeman, *The Break-up of the Habsburg Empire, 1914–1918: A Study in National and Social Revolution* (1961) while showing its age, is still one of the few books to deal with civilian issues. J. Galantai, *Hungary in the First World War* (1989) describes the impact of the war upon the Magyar half of the Empire, while Leo VALIANI. *The End of Austria-Hungary* (1973) shows how the nations of the Empire seized the opportunity to push for statehood.

17. STRATEGY AND TACTICS

The incompetence, lack of imagination and cold-heartedness of First World War generals has become one of the great historical clichés. The stereotype of the purple-faced staff-officer quaffing fine wines far behind the lines was already well-established by the mid-twenties, and it has been embedded even more deeply in popular consciousness by productions like *Oh What a Lovely War!* and *Blackadder.* Carnage on this scale cries out for explanation and scapegoats. Why did so many First World War generals ignore the murderous implications of modern firepower in their planning, and after the experience of the battlefield? The lessons of recent conflicts in South Africa, Manchuria and the Balkans were there for all to see, as Shelford Bidwell and Dominic Graham, *Fire Power* (1982), and J.B.A. Bailey *Field Artillery and Firepower* (1989) make plain. The question of the mentality and culture of military elites is addressed by Norman F. Dixon, *On the Psychology of Military Incompetence* (1994), Jay Luvaas, *The Education of an Army: British Military Thought, 1815–1940* (1964), Andrew Wheatcroft, 'Technology and the military mind: Austria 1866–1914' (in BEST).

In the early 1960s starting with Alan Clark, *The Donkeys* (1961) and Corelli Barnett's *The Swordbearers* (1963) another wave of historians charged over the top against the long-dead generals. John Laffin, *British Butchers and Bunglers of World War One* (1988) helpfully sets out his conclusion before the reader even opens the book. There followed the most ferocious assault upon Douglas Haig's reputation yet seen, Denis Winter's *Haig's Command* (1991). What was the alternative strategy? That was the problem for the generals, and remains so for their modern critics. Attempts to outflank the Western Front led to the disastrous Gallipoli and Salonika campaigns, exposed the generals to an even more ferocious roasting, made hotter by the importance of these episodes as founding myths of Antipodean nationalism (see below The Gallipoli Campaign, and, E.M. Andrews, *The Anzac Illusion: Anglo-Australian Relations during World War I* (1994). Attempts to escape stalemate by technological innovation is the theme of John Terraine's stimulating *White Heat: The New Warfare, 1914–18* (1982). Donald Richter, *Chemical Soldiers: British Gas Warfare in World War One* (1992) describes a weapon so crude that a change in the wind would decimate one's own ranks. Hubert C. Johnson, *Breakthrough: Tactics, Tanks, Technology and the Search for Victory* (1994) describes the wasting of a potentially war-winning innovation, not least by the supposedly innovative

German High Command, much praised by Bruce L. Gudmundsson, *Stormtroop Tactics: Innovation in the German Army, 1914–18* (1995). However R. Asprey, *The German High Command at War* (1991) and Martin Kitchen, *The Silent Dictatorship: The Politics of the German High Command under Hindenburg and Ludendorff* (1976) show that German decision-making was not always the well-oiled process that many writers believed it to be. The Allies won the war because their generals *did* hold their nerve and adapt their tactics. In a recent counter-attack against critics of the British High Command, both Tim Travers *The Killing Ground* (1987) and *How the War Was Won* (1992) and Paddy Griffith, *Battle Tactics of the Western Front* (1992) and *Forward into Battle* (1990) redressed the balance of eighty years of excoriation.

18. BATTLE FRONTS AND CAMPAIGNS

GILBERT describes, and KEEGAN analyses the fighting on all Fronts, and John Terraine, *The Western Front* (1964) presents a well-organised overview. For the **Western Front**, Barbara Tuchman, *August 1914* (1965) possibly too well-written to be taken seriously by military historians, gives an excellent account of the first weeks of the war. E. Spears, *Liaison 1914: A Narrative of the Great Retreat and Prelude to Victory* (1939) describes the almost unbelievable lack of communication between the British and French High Commands, a topic also dealt with in William Philpott's excellent *Anglo-French Relations and Strategy on the Western Front* (1996). Martin Middlebrook, *The First Day on the Somme* (1971) and Alistair Horne, *The Price of Victory* (1962) are classic accounts of the great battles of 1916. Martin Middlebrook, *The Kaiser's Battle* (1978) tells of the German onslaught in the spring of 1918 that nearly won the war. In comparison, writing in English about **The Eastern Front** is surprisingly sparse in quantity but not quality. STONE's study is a magnificent piece of pioneering scholarship, still indispensable for the fighting in the east and for its account of civil–military relationships in the eastern empires. HERWIG gives an enormous boost to our understanding of the great events in the east, while D. Showalter, *Tannenberg* (1991) throws a much wider light than its title would suggest. On the **Italian Front** HERWIG is again indispensable, while Cyril Falls, *Caporetto* (1966) gives a sympathetic account of the temporary collapse of the Italian army in 1917. The **Balkan Fronts** have been treated very badly in English, with no specific account of the heroic defiance of the exhausted and diseased Serbian army. John Reed, *War in Eastern Europe: Travels through the Balkans in 1915* (1916) conveys something of the flavour of this. Alan Palmer, *The Gardeners of Salonika* (1965) succeeds in the seemingly impossible task of explaining the Salonika landings, the Macedonian Front, and even the complexities of Greek politics.

    The Gallipoli Expedition has attracted a disproportionate amount of historical attention for such a costly and misconceived fiasco. Alan Moorehead led the way with his beautifully crafted *Gallipoli* (1956), followed closely by Robert Rhodes James, *Gallipoli* (1965). G. Cassar, *The French and the Dardanelles*

(1971) reminds us that the unfortunate episode was not just a Commonwealth affair. Recently there have been three more excellent accounts, Philip Haythornethwaite, *Gallipoli, 1915* (1991), Nigel Thomson and Peter Hart, *Defeat at Gallipoli* (1994), and Michael Hickey, *Gallipoli* (1995). The complex issues surrounding the Allied Intervention in Russia are disentangled in Evan Mawdsley, *The Russian Civil War* (1989) and C. Ellis, *The Transcaspian Episode* (1963).

The War at Sea is surveyed by P.G. Halpern's excellent book, *A Naval History of World War I* (1995). John Terraine describes the German submarine war in his usual readable and authoritative fashion in *Business in Great Waters* (1989). The Battle of Jutland, during which huge British and German fleets blundered around in the North Sea to little effect, has attracted abundant attention from historians. John Keegan, *Battle at Sea* (1993) makes the battle one of his key naval engagements of history. A. Gordon, *The Rules of the Game* (1996) and Geoffrey Bennett, *The Battle of Jutland* (1999) have recently re-examined the affair.

19. THE SOLDIER'S EXPERIENCE

No other war has had its sights, sounds, smells and emotions so exhaustively described. Malcolm Brown, *The Imperial War Museum Book of the Western Font* (1993) uses the diaries and letters of ordinary soldiers, many of whom died in the war, to provide a vivid account of its everyday reality. John Keegan, *The Face of Battle* (1976) a comparative study of Agincourt, Waterloo and the Somme, gives us an unforgettable insight into the actuality of the battlefield in all its facets. Peter Simkins, *Kitchener's Army* (1988) helps us to understand why nearly two million young Britons *chose* to fight for their country without being compelled to do so. In *Chronicles of the Great War*, Simkins and David Gibbon give us a vivid insight, in the words of the soldiers themselves, into the daily routines of soldiers at the front. *Realities of War* (1920) by the ex-war correspondent Philip Gibbs, was one of the earliest books to expose the horror of the battlefield. Denis Winter, *Death's Men; Soldiers of the Great War* (1978), John Toland *No Man's Land* (1980) and E. Leed, *No Man's Land: Combat and Identity in World War I* (1979) help us to envisage its sufferings. Trevor Wilson, *The Myriad Faces of War* (1986) deals with experiences of the families left behind. Other descriptions of the miseries of British soldiers are Denis Winter, *Death's Men: Soldiers of the Great War* (1978), John Laffin, *On the Western Front* (1985), Peter Liddle, *The Soldier's War 1914–1918* (1988) and Samuel Hynes, *The Soldier's Tale: Bearing Witness to Modern War* (1998). The experiences of other belligerent soldiers are described by Hugh CECIL and Peter Liddle (eds), *Facing Armageddon* (1986). It includes Stéphane Andoin-Rouzeau, 'The French soldier in the trenches', whose later book *Men at War, 1914–18: National Sentiment and Trench Journalism in France during the First World War* (1992) provides a rich insight into the mentality of the ordinary *poilou*. D. Englander's 'The French Soldier, 1914–18' (*French History*, 1987) gives another excellent account. The French army is still reluctant to release information about the great mutinies of 1917. Guy Pedroncini, *Les Mutineries de 1917* (1967) remains the only book of any substance on the affair.

The German soldier's war is described in R. Whalen, *Bitter Wounds: German Victims of the Great War* (1984), and by John Horne, '1914: The Evidence of German Soldiers' Diaries' (J.M.H., 1994). B. Gammage, *The Broken Years: Australian Soldiers in the Great War* (1974) and Myles Dungan, *They Shall Not Grow Old: Irish Soldiers and the Great War* (1997) exemplify the extraordinary variety of material now available to us. Finally, there is Lyn Macdonald's extensive and fascinating record of battlefield experiences, built up in over twenty years of interviews and research: *They Called It Passchendaele* (1978), *The Roses of No Man's Land* (1980), *Somme* (1983), *1914: The Dawn of Hope* (1987), *1914–1918: Voices and Images of the Great War* (1988), *1915: The Death of Innocence* (1993) and her most recent book, *To the Last Man: Spring 1918* (1998). (See also the soldiers' memoirs in Section 21.)

20. WARTIME DIPLOMACY

David Stevenson, *The First World War and International Politics* (1989) is a comprehensive overview that makes comprehensible and interesting the interweaving complex of war aims and peace negotiations. Z.A.B. Zeman, *A Diplomatic History of the First World War* (1971) is an old but still very readable and clear account. **The Quest for Allies:** Both sides expended huge energy trying to persuade others to join them, usually to the detriment of both pursuer and pursued. Feroz Yasammee (in WILSON) describes Germany's triumphant seduction of Turkey. W.A. Renzi, 'Italy's neutrality and entrance into the Great War: a re-examination' (A.H.R., 1967–8) analyses the tortuous efforts of both camps to buy Italian support, while J.A. Thayer, *Italy and the Great War: Politics and culture, 1870–1915* (1964) describes the deep divisions opened up by the question of intervention. Bulgaria's decision to join the Central Powers is examined by STEVENSON and ZEMAN, while R.J. Crampson, *A Short History of Modern Bulgaria* (1987) explains the decision from the Bulgarian point of view. The dilemma faced by Greece is outlined by PALMER, and treated in more detail by George B. Leontaritis, *Greece and the First World War, 1917–1918* (1980). America's decision is analysed by J.A.S. Grenville, 'Diplomacy and War Plans in the United States, 1890–1917' (in KENNEDY). Thomas A. Bailey and Paul B. Ryan, *The Lusitania Disaster an Episode in Modern Warfare and Diplomacy* (1975) describe the impact of German submarine warfare upon American opinion, and Barbara Tuchman, *The Zimmermann Telegram* (1959) the more disastrous impact of this episode on US–German relations. Germany's triumphant manoeuvring of Russia out of the war is described with academic detachment by STEVENSON, and with anti-Leninist zeal by PIPES. **War Aims:** The following historians have studied this topic: Barry HUNT and Adrian Preston, *War Aims and Strategic Policy in the Great War 1914–1918* (1977); Hans Gatzke, *Germany's Drive to the West: A*

Study of Germany's Western War Aims during the First World War (1966); David French, *British Strategy and War Aims, 1914–1916* (1986); J. Gooch, 'Soldiers, Strategy and War Aims in Britain, 1914–1918' (in HUNT); Roy A. Prete, 'French military war aims, 1914–1916' (H.J., 1985); John Moses, *The War Aims of Imperial Germany* (1968) and by J.A.S. Grenville (in KENNEDY).

21. BIOGRAPHIES AND MEMOIRS

Thousands of participants have recorded their experiences of the war, so the few examples below must serve to whet the reader's appetite. **Civilian Memoirs:** Winston S. Churchill, *The World Crisis* (5 vols, 1923–31) was written as a history of the period, but it is saturated by the writer's personal involvement in events. Sir Edward Grey, *Twenty-Five Years* (1925) conveys the statesman's strange mixture of honesty and evasive inarticulateness. David Lloyd George, *War Memoirs* (2 volumes, 1938) is a masterly piece of self-justification. Other memoirs that evoke the atmosphere of the July Crisis are Sir Horace Rumbold, *The War Crisis in Berlin, July-August 1914* (1940), Prince Max Lichnowsky, *Heading for the Abyss, Reminiscences* (1918), and Theodor Wolff, *The Eve Of 1914* (1935). **Civilian Biographies:** Essential reading includes Kenneth Morgan, *Lloyd George* (1974); Keith Robbins, *Sir Edward Grey: A Biography of Grey of Fallodon* (1971); Martin Gilbert, *Winston S. Churchill, The Challenge of War, 1914–1916* (1971); John Röhl, *The Kaiser and His Court* (1994); Lamar Cecil, *Wilhelm II, Vol. 2, Emperor and Exile* (1996); Dominic Lieven *Nicholas II; Twilight of the Empire* (1994); David Watson, *Georges Clemenceau: A Political Life* (1974); Gregor Dallas, *At the Heart of a Tiger: Clemenceau and his World 1841–1929* (1993); Arthur S. Link *Woodrow Wilson: Revolution War and Peace* (1979); and Thomas J. Knock, *To End All Wars: Woodrow Wilson and the Quest for a New World Order* (1992).

Soldiers' Biographies: The sympathetic interpretation of John Terraine, *Haig, the Educated Soldier* (London, 1963) is challenged by Gerard De Groot's critical study, *Douglas Haig* (1988). Other English generals are written about by Philip Magnus, *Kitchener* (1959); R. Hohnes, *The Little Field Marshal* (1981) which deals sympathetically with Sir John French; and David R. Woodward, *Field Marshal Sir William Robertson* (1998). Two excellent biographies, now very old but still of great merit, are Basil Liddell Hart, *Foch: Man of Orleans* (1931), and J. Wheeler-Bennett, *Hindenburg: The Wooden Titan* (1936). D. Goodspeed, *Ludendorff* (1966) studies the other constituent of the German High Command. The American commander is described in Donald Smythe, *Pershing General of the Armies* (1986). **Classic accounts:** Vera Brittain, *Testament of Youth, An Autobiographical Study of the Years 1900–1925* (1933) presents a rich portrait of how the war brought personal tragedy to a comfortable middle-class existence. The early chapters of Sybylle Bedford, *Jigsaw* (1999) paint a vivid picture of the privations of rural Germany before and during the war. For the first time, educated and articulate volunteer officers experienced privations normally endured only by voiceless rankers. The following accounts are well known, but familiarity does nothing to diminish the extraordinary impact. Guy Chapman, *A Passionate Prodigality* (1933–4); Robert Graves, *Goodbye to All That* (1929); Siegfried Sassoon, *Memoirs of an Infantry Officer* (1930); Paul Maze *A Frenchman in Khaki* (1934); Ernst Junger, *The Storm of Steel: From the Diary of a German Storm-Troop Officer on the Western Front* (translated by Basil Creighton, 1928).

22. REFERENCE AND ATLASES

The Macmillan Dictionary of the First World War edited by Stephen Pope and Elizabeth-Anne Wheal (1995) is a magnificent work of reference that provides clear and accessible information on all facets of the war. Malcolm Brown, *The Imperial War Museum Book of the First World War* (1993) and John Laffin, *The Western Front Companion, 1914–1918* (1997) are informative and beautifully produced. Randall Gray, *Chronicle of the First World War* (1991) provides a day-by-day overview of the various theatres, and contains a compendium of useful if somewhat eccentrically chosen information and biographical sketches. Anthony Livesey, *The Viking Atlas of World War I* contains an excellent selection of campaign maps produced with modern cartographic techniques, while the recently republished Arthur Banks, *A Military Atlas of the First World War* (1999) makes up in the detail of its historical explanation for its rather outdated presentation. Martin Gilbert *First World War Atlas* suffers from a tendency to oversimplify, but is excellent on war aims and territorial rearrangements.

Section Thirteen

GLOSSARY

13.1 GLOSSARY OF TERMS

Agadir Crisis   Another name for the *Second Moroccan Crisis* of 1911.

Algeçiras Conference (1906)   This settled the *First Moroccan Crisis* that had begun in 1905. France was granted limited rights in Morocco, leaving many Germans feeling that their country had been unfairly outwitted and denied proper respect as a *Great Power*.

Allies   The wartime coalition against the *Central Powers*. The USA termed itself an 'Associated Power'. (*See Entente*)

Alsace-Lorraine   The area incorporated into the German Empire after France's defeat by Germany in 1871. The loss of territory was a major strategic and economic blow to France. Germany's determination to hold on to it, and France's unswerving commitment to regain it stood in the way of Franco-German rapprochement before the war and peace negotiations during it. The Provinces were returned to France under the Versailles Treaty.

Amiens Despatch   A critical article in the London *Times* on 30 Aug. 1914 that revealed the pessimism of the British High Command about the military situation in France.

Anglo-French Naval Agreement (Nov. 1912)   Britain undertook to protect the west coast of France in return for reciprocal French commitment in the Mediterranean. Sometimes called the *Grey–Cambon Correspondence*.

Anglo-Russian Entente (1907)   A settling of colonial disputes that partially improved relations between these long-standing imperial rivals. Germany regarded it as another link in the chain of '*Encirclement*'.

Anglo-Russian Naval Agreement   Although Sir Edward Grey's denied it, this was about to be signed in the summer of 1914. It increased German feelings of '*Encirclement*', and undermined Anglo-German diplomacy to resolve the July Crisis by destroying Bethmann's Hollweg's trust in Grey.

Antwerp, Siege of   The unexpected resistance of the fortified Belgian port for several weeks in 1914. Although of brief duration, it undermined the *Schlieffen Plan* by diverting four German divisions and wasting vital time.

Armand-Revertera Conversations (Aug. 1917)   An abortive attempt to negotiate Austria-Hungary's exit from the war.

Athens Landing   The repulse by Greek Royalist troops of a mainly French force which had landed at Piraeus in December 1916 as part of the campaign to force the Greek monarchy to support the Entente.

Austria-Hungary   The official name of the state established under the constitutional compromise (*Ausgleich*) of 1867, which gave Austria and Hungary separate but equal status within the territory ruled by the Habsburgs. The state is also variously described as the *Habsburg Empire*, the *Austro-Hungarian Empire*, the *Austro-Hungarian Monarchy*, the *Dual Monarchy*, and sometimes merely *Austria*.

Austro-German Alliance (1879)   The earliest and most long lasting of the pre-war international groupings.

Balance of Power   An 18th century concept much favoured by the British foreign office which held that European harmony was based upon equilibrium between the five 'Great Powers'. Cynics said that Britain only applied this static and simplistic principle when her world hegemony was threatened by the appearance of a continental competitor.

Balfour Declaration (2 Nov. 1917)   A letter to Lord Rothschild from the British Foreign Secretary, Arthur Balfour, pledging support for an eventual Jewish homeland in Palestine. This had the effect of rallying Jewish support to the Allied side.

Bessarabia   Now part of the Moldovan Republic, this territory had been disputed for centuries between Russia and the Ottoman Empire. In 1914 it was ruled by Russia but coveted by Romania because of its mainly Romanian population.

Björköe Agreement   A blueprint for a defensive alliance agreed between Russia and Germany in July 1905. If ratified it would have reversed the pre-war alliance systems, but the existing commitments of the two countries meant that it came to nothing.

Black Hand   A popular name for the Serbian secret society, *Ujedinjenje ili Smrt* (Unity or Death) formed by Serb army officers in May 1911 to absorb into a greater Serbian Kingdom all South Slavs under Austro-Hungarian rule. The group organised the assassination of the heir to the Habsburg throne on 28 June 1914.

Black Yellow Offensive   Code-name for the disastrous Austrian offensive in Eastern Galicia in the summer of 1915. The failure of the offensive, which was partly intended to assert the ability of Austria-Hungary to act independently of its German ally, further diminished Vienna's standing.

Blank Cheque   A term used to describe the reply given on 5 July 1914 by the German Kaiser to an Austrian request to support strong action against Serbia for the assassination of Archduke Franz Ferdinand.

Bolsheviks   The faction led by Lenin that split from the Russian Social Democratic Workers Party in 1903. Central to Lenin's belief was internationalism, disciplined organisation and refusal to compromise with liberal parties. Leon Trotsky, for long a critic, joined the group in 1917.

Bonnet Rouge, Le   A French pacifist newspaper which tried to maintain war-time contacts with Germany, leading to accusations of treachery.

Bosnia-Hercegovina   A Balkan region that was part of the Ottoman Empire from the 14th century until 1908. Despite a large Muslim population, it was regarded by Serbian nationalists as part of their historic homeland. Under the Treaty of Berlin of 1878, the Habsburg Empire was allowed to occupy and administer the provinces, which remained technically under Ottoman sovereignty. In 1908, their annexation by Austria stimulated a violent anti-Austrian backlash in Serbia leading to the assassination of Franz Ferdinand in the Bosnian capital in June 1914.

Bosnian Crisis (1908–9)   This was provoked by Austria-Hungary's decision to bring Bosnia and Hercegovina under direct rule. Although Russia was warned (*see Buchlau Meeting*) the annexation provoked fury in Russia, Serbia and brought Europe to the point of war. Germany's decision in March 1909 to issue threats to Russia and Serbia to support Austria's action caused a serious deterioration in Russo-German relations.

Bosphorus   A narrow strip of water running from the Black Sea to the Sea of Marmora.

Brest-Litovsk, Treaty of   A punitive settlement forced upon the Russian Bolshevik regime by the Central Powers on 3 March 1918.

British Expeditionary Force (BEF)   A small British force (five regular divisions) created after 1905, specifically earmarked for action on the European continent.

Brotfrieden   (German: 'Bread Treaty') Signed between the Central Powers and the new Ukrainian Republic on 9 February 1918.

Brusilov Offensive   The most successful Russian offensive of the war launched in the summer of 1916.

Bucharest Treaty of (10 Aug. 1913)   This reduced Turkey to a small European enclave and greatly increased the size of Greece and Serbia. It was a disaster both for Austria-Hungary, because its enemy Serbia doubled its territory, and for Bulgaria, which was stripped of its wartime gains.

Bucharest, Treaty of (7 May 1918)   Forced upon Romania by the Central Powers in the wake of Russia's withdrawal from the war, it was repudiated in October 1918.

Buchlau Meeting   A private conference in 1908 between the Austrian Foreign Minister Aehrenthal, and his Russian equivalent, Alexander Izvolski. (*See Bosnian Crisis*)

Bundesrat   The un-elected Upper House established by the Constitution of 1871 to represent the 25 states that comprised the German Empire.

Bürgfrieden (Fortress peace)   The pact agreed by all German Parties to support the war effort because they accepted the justice of Germany's cause.

Caillaux Affair (Mar.–Jun. 1914)   A scandal caused by the shooting of the editor of *Le Figaro* newspaper by the wife of the French Radical leader Joseph Caillaux. Caillaux' enforced resignation, and the subsequent trial of Madame Caillaux distracted France on the eve of the war.

Calais Conference   An Anglo-French meeting on 4 December 1915, at which the British tried, with ultimate lack of success, to persuade the French to abandon the *Salonika Expedition.*

Cambon Letter (12 Jan. 1917)   A programme of war aims that became France's bottom line for ending the war.

Caporetto, Battle of   The defeat and disintegration of the Italian army in October 1917.

Carnet B   A list of potential anti-war activists who were to be arrested on the outbreak of hostilities. In the event, no action was taken because of the positive response to the war by the French Left.

Central Powers   The wartime alliance of Germany, Austria, Hungary, Turkey and later, Bulgaria.

Central Working Association Agreement (15 Nov. 1918)   German trade unions and employers combine to isolate the extreme left and forestall a communist revolution.

Chantilly Conference (Dec. 1915)   One of many meetings between British and French commanders at the French HQ at Chantilly, at which the main British Somme offensive of 1916 was first mooted.

Chatalja Lines   The fortifications that protected Constantinople (Istanbul) during the Balkan Wars. The huge casualties incurred in Bulgarian assaults on them pre-figured the costly offensives of the First World War.

Committee of Union and Progress (CUP)   *See Young Turks.*

Conrad-Moltke Conversations   A series of pre-war meetings between German Army Commander Helmuth von Moltke and his Austrian counterpart Conrad von Hötzendorf, aimed at co-ordinating their military plans.

Corfu Declaration (27 July 1917)   An agreement between Serbia, Croatia, Slovenia and Montenegro to set up a unified Yugoslavian state after the defeat of Austria-Hungary.

Courland   A mainly Latvian-inhabited region of the Russian Empire that was incorporated into independent Latvia in 1918.

Cruiser Rules   A naval convention, sometime called 'Prize Rules', whereby warships allowed the passengers and crew of civilian vessels time to abandon their ship before sinking it. (*See Unrestricted Submarine Warfare*)

Curragh Incident (20 Mar. 1914)   British army officers stationed at the Curragh army base in County Kildare, Ireland, threatened to disobey orders because they opposed the government's intention to compel the Province of Ulster to be included in its scheme to grant Home Rule to Ireland. The affair diverted attention from international affairs and led German strategists to doubt the loyalty and capacity of the British army.

Czech Legion   A force of Czech and Slovak captives of the Russians freed to fight against the Central Powers on the Eastern Front. While attempting to reach Vladivostok for evacuation in the summer of 1918, the Legion came into confrontation with Red forces, and became part of the anti-Bolshevik coalition in the Russian Civil War.

Czechoslovak National Council   A body set up in London and Paris in 1916 by Tomas Masaryk and Edvard Benes to campaign for independence from Austria-Hungary.

***Daily Telegraph* Interview**   Speaking to a journalist of the London *Daily Telegraph* in October 1908, Kaiser William II's indiscreet remarks about his rôle in German foreign policy irritated British public opinion and provoked a political crisis in Germany, leading to the resignation of Chancellor Bernhard von Bülow.

Dardanelles   Often called '*the Straits*'. A series of narrow channels bordered by Turkish territory that joins the Sea of Marmora to the Aegean and Mediterranean Seas, which controlled the exit of Russian ships from the Black Sea.

Dardanelles Commission   A British enquiry into the failure of the *Dardanelles Expedition.*

Dardanelles Expedition   Abortive Allied attempt in 1915 to land troops on the Turkish mainland.

Dilution   A British term for the temporary acceptance of workers without formal qualifications into hitherto closed trades for the duration of the war.

Dogger Bank Incident (21 Oct. 1904)   The sinking of a British trawler by the Russian Baltic fleet on its way to the Far East during the *Russo-Japanese War.* Russia's subsequent apologetic and conciliatory response did much to win British public opinion over to the *Anglo-Russian Entente* of 1907.

Dogger Bank, Battle of the (24 Jan. 1915)   The sinking by the Royal Navy of the German cruiser *Blücher* during a sortie to bombard British coastal towns.

Dreadnought   A British battleship launched in 1906 that was faster and more heavily armed than any yet built, thus making all existing battleships redundant, including those of Britain. *Dreadnought* triggered a naval race in which all naval powers sought to gain a technical head start over their competitors. Subsequently used as a generic term for *all* comparable battleships.

Dual Alliance   A term used to describe both the *Austro-German Alliance* (1879) and the *Franco-Russian Alliance* (1894).

Dual Monarchy   *See Austria-Hungary.*

Dual Power   The de facto sharing of power between the Russian *Provisional Government* and the *Petrograd Soviet* between March and November, 1918.

Duma   The parliament granted by the Tsar of Russia in response to the Revolution of 1905.

Easter Rising   An uprising in Dublin in April 1916 that sought to take advantage of British involvement in the First World War to secure immediate Irish independence.

Eastern Front   The line of confrontation between the armies of the Central Powers and those of the Russian Empire running from the Baltic Sea to the Carpathian Mountains. Fighting ebbed and flowed hundreds of miles eastwards and westwards in a war of movement totally unlike the stalemate in the west.

Easterners   'Strategists' like Churchill and Lloyd George, who believed the stalemate on the Western Front could be broken by switching resources to attack the 'soft underbelly' of the Central Powers on the Gallipoli, Salonika and Italian Fronts.

Encirclement   A common German belief that the Reich was surrounded by hostile Powers bent upon its destruction.

Entente   The initial wartime alliance of Britain, Russia, France and Belgium. (*See Allies*)

Entente Cordiale (1904)   The agreement that that solved virtually all the outstanding colonial disputes between Britain and France. It was not an 'alliance', there being nothing in it to oblige the signatories to assist each other if attacked. Late 20th-century commentators would describe it as a 'détente'.

Ersatz   Substitute products developed in Germany to replace materials that had become unavailable because of the allies' wartime blockade. From the German *ersetzen*, to substitute.

Fashoda Crisis   A confrontation in 1898 between General Kitchener, fresh from his great victory at Omdurman, and a small French force that had occupied a fort on the White Nile to assert French interests in the region. Overwhelming British numbers compelled France to accept a humiliating withdrawal, but the Crisis began a gradual improvement in Anglo-French relations, culminating in the *Entente Cordiale*.

Fatherland Party   A right wing German movement founded in 1917, financed by the *Third Supreme Command*, and headed by the former naval minister Alfred von Tirpitz. Eventually claiming 1.2 million members, the Party attacked those seeking to end the war, called for authoritarian policies at home, and for massive annexations of enemy territory.

Faustschlag   The German offensive of February 1918 which pushed the disintegrating Russian army back 250 miles and forced the Bolsheviks to accept the draconian *Treaty of Brest-Litovsk.*

February Revolution (8 Mar. 1917)   The uprising that overthrew Tsar Nicholas II of Russia, so named because it began on 23 February of the Old Style (Julian) Calendar, 13 days behind its Western (Gregorian) equivalent. The Tsarist regime was replaced by a *Provisional Government* drawn from liberal members of the *Duma*, most of whom wanted to continue the war to protect Russia's territory, fulfil her treaty obligations, and achieve her war aims. The parallel authority based in the *Petrograd Soviet* was convinced that Russia must negotiate to end the war as soon as possible.

First Balkan War (Oct. 1912–May 1913)   Serbia, Bulgaria, Greece and Montenegro combined to eject Turkey from her remaining provinces in Europe. (*See Second Balkan War*)

Fischer Thesis   A revisionist interpretation of the origins of the war first propounded in 1959 by the German historian Fritz Fischer. He argued that German militarists had a well-defined programme of territorial objectives that foreshadowed those of the Nazi period, and had planned the war well in advance in response to intractable international and domestic problems. His books caused great resentment in German academic circles and the Press.

Fleet in Being   The naval strategy in which the enemy is intimidated merely by the *possibility* that one's warships might undertake an aggressive sortie. (*See also Risk Theory*, and *Luxury Fleet*)

Four-Minute Men   A body of 75,000 speakers recruited to tour the USA after April 1917 to give four-minute addresses encouraging US citizens to support the war effort by buying War Bonds, eliminating waste, and helping the men in uniform.

Fourteen Points   A programme presented to the US Congress by President Wilson on 8 January 1918 laying out the principles for which he claimed the US to be fighting, and presenting a blueprint for peace negotiations.

Franco-Russian Alliance (1894)   A series of diplomatic and military undertakings committing the signatories to support each other if attacked by Germany. The Alliance fed German fears of '*encirclement*'.

French army mutinies   A wave of discontent in the French army on the Western Front in May–June 1917. Soldiers refused to fight in protest about leave, rations and pay, and bitterness about the callous demands made upon them during the *Nivelle Offensive*, rather than opposition to the continuance of the war. Once their concerns were addressed by the more humane General Pètain, they loyally resumed the fight. The Germans were unaware of the disarray in the opposing trenches.

Galicia The northern province of Austria-Hungary that abutted the Russian Empire, now split between Poland, the Slovak Republic and the Ukraine.

Galician Offensive (1917) *See Kerensky Offensive.*

Gorlice–Tarnow Offensive The first of a series of outstandingly successful offensives by the Central Powers that the drove the Russians out of Austrian Galicia in May–June 1915.

Grand Fleet The main component of the British Royal Navy based at Rosyth and at Scapa Flow in the Orkney Islands. Its rôle was to enforce the naval blockade of Germany and to protect Britain from invasion.

Great Powers States that were traditionally deemed to be of global significance by virtue of their military power and economic substance. In 1914, Great Britain, Germany, France, the United States, Russia, and Austria-Hungary were generally accepted to be Great Powers, although the latter clung to the status because of her past achievements. Italy, Japan and the Ottoman Empire considered themselves members of the club.

Great Programme A massive catalogue of military spending agreed by the Russian *Duma* in June 1914. This, the last of a series of Russian rearmament measures since 1909, was intended to give Russia overwhelming military superiority by 1916–17. It strengthened the hand of German leaders who wanted a *Preventive war.*

Great Retreat (German) The withdrawal of the German armies in the Autumn of 1914 after French victories on the Marne had thwarted the *Schlieffen Plan.* The retreat ended in the entrenched line of confrontation that scarcely changed until the last weeks of the war.

Great Retreat (Russian) The hasty 200 mile withdrawal of the Russian army from Poland in the summer of 1915. The retreat was successful in that the Russian army escaped from its German and Austrian pursuers, but it resulted in the loss to Russia of invaluable agricultural and industrial resources.

Great Retreat (Serbian) The flight of the Serbian army and administration from Kosovo to the Adriatic coast in November 1915, following an invasion by the Central Powers and their new partner Bulgaria.

Grey–Cambon Correspondence *See Anglo-French Naval Agreement.*

Habsburg Empire *See Austria-Hungary.*

Haldane Mission A British delegation to Berlin in February 1912 that tried to negotiate an end to the *Naval Race* based on the establishment of a fixed ratio of battleships. It failed because Germany would only agree to limit her programme if Britain gave a pledge of neutrality in a future European war. (*See also 'Luxury Fleet'*)

High Seas Fleet The main German battle-fleet of 27 *Dreadnoughts* confronting the Royal Navy in the North Sea. (*See Risk Theory*)

Hindenburg Line A complex system of fortifications behind which the German army on the Western Front withdrew in the winter of 1916–17. It withstood numerous Allied offensives was not breached until the last few weeks of the war. (*See also Siegfried Line*)

Hindenburg Programme An over-ambitious attempt to mobilise the German economy for total war by the German *Third Supreme Command* after 1916. It failed to boost production in an economy already stretched to its limits, and by diverting resources from civilian needs, contributed greatly to the disaffection of the masses and the growth of opposition to the war.

L'Homme Enchainé The wartime newspaper of George Clemenceau, which criticised many aspects of the French war effort. Formally called *l'Homme Libre*.

Hellenism A variety of Greek nationalism that aspired to bring all Greek people and all areas that had been historically associated with Ancient, Byzantine and Modern Greece under Greek rule again. (*See Megali Idea*)

Honved The territorial army of Hungary.

Innenpolitik, der Primat der A phrase coined by the historian Eckhart Kehr to describe his theory that German foreign policy was dominated by domestic political concerns. Its converse, *Der Primat der Aussenpolitik* espoused by traditional historians like Ranke, held that statesmen conducted international relations according to ostensibly objective considerations, such as the '*Balance of Power*'.

International Socialist Bureau The executive of the *Second International*, set up in Brussels in 1891.

International Socialist Commission Set up by the Left-Socialists at the the *Zimmerwald Conference* to rival the *International Socialist Bureau*.

Irredentism An Italian term that came to be universally applied to the desire to reunite national groups cut off from the main body of the nation.

July Crisis A rather misleading term for the crisis that began with the assassination of Archduke Franz Ferdinand on 28 June and ended with the outbreak of war in early August. (*See Sarajevo Crisis*)

July Days A protest demonstration led by Bolsheviks in St Petersburg against the failed *Kerensky Offensive* which began on 16 July 1917 (3 July OS) Although temporally crushed, the Bolsheviks increased their popularity by showing that, unlike the *Provisional Government* and the moderate socialists, they were committed to ending the war.

July Offensive (1917) *See Kerensky Offensive.*

Jutland, Battle of (31 May–1 Jun. 1916) The principal naval engagement of the war The British *Grand Fleet* lost more ships, but the battle is generally regarded as a British victory, since the German *High Seas Fleet* was confined to its bases until the end of the war.

Kadet   The Russian Constitutional Democratic Party, or a member of it. From the Russian letters, K.D.

Kaiserschlacht (Kaiser's Battle). The opening phase of the great German offensives of 1918.

Kerensky Offensive   A disastrous Russian operation on the Eastern Front launched on 1 July 1917 (18 June, OS), it quickly collapsed because most Russian soldiers were no longer willing to fight. Although it was intended by the Minister of War, Aleksandr Kerensky, to rally the Russian people behind the *Provisional Government*, the subsequent *July Days Uprising* showed how unpopular the war had become.

Kiel Canal   The 61 mile German waterway built between 1887 and 1895 to connect the North Sea with the Baltic. By 1914 it had been widened and deepened to allow passage to the latest German *Dreadnoughts*.

Kienthal Conference (Apr. 1916)   An anti-war gathering in Switzerland at which Lenin's revolutionary slogan: 'Transform the Imperialist War into Civil War!' was rejected in favour of the more unambiguous formula but rather less snappy 'Immediate Peace without Annexations or Indemnities and the Right of the Peoples to Self-Determination'.

Kindermord   The slaughter of thousands of idealistic young German volunteers, mainly students, in ill-considered infantry assaults during the first few weeks of the war.

Kitchener's New Armies   The vast British volunteer force that responded to general Kitchener's patriotic call in August 1914. Over two million joined up within eighteen months.

Kluck's Turn   The premature change of direction by General Alexander von Kluck, commander of the German 1st Army, during the German advance of 1914 into France. Kluck's decision to wheel inward north of Paris, rather than south-west of the city as envisaged in the *Schlieffen Plan* has been blamed for the subsequent German defeat in the Battle of the Marne.

Kornilov Rebellion   An attempted putsch against the Russian *Provisional Government* at the end of August 1917 by its Army Commander General Lavr Kornilov. The *Bolsheviks* gained popularity by thwarting it, and were able to justify the subsequent *October Revolution* by citing the threat of militarist counter-revolution.

KRA   The ineffectual organisation charged in 1914 with matching German industrial production to the needs of the army. It disappeared in 1916 with the introduction of the *Hindenburg Programme.*

Kriegszielmehrheit   The 'War-Aims Majority' in the German *Reichstag* that supported the war till 1917.

Kruger Telegram   A communication that caused a rift in Anglo-German relations in 1896. Kaiser Wilhelm II congratulated President Kruger of the Transvaal for repulsing a raid into his territory by British freebooters ('the Jameson Raid').

Landtag   An assembly representing one of the 25 states of the German Empire. Collectively, they comprised the *Bundesrat.*

Lansdowne Letter   (19 Nov. 1917)   A plea for moderation by the ex-British Foreign Secretary, published in the *Daily Telegraph.*

Liman von Sanders Affair   A crisis in 1913 that soured Russo-German relations, when General Liman von Sanders was made director of a German military mission in Turkey.

London, Pact of   (5 Sep. 1914)   Britain, France and Russia agreed not to sign a separate peace with the Central Powers.

London, Treaty of   (30 May 1913)   The treaty that ended the First Balkan War. The Ottoman Empire lost most of its remaining European territory. Macedonia was divided between Serbia, Greece and Bulgaria. Albania gained its independence.

London, Treaty of   (26 Apr. 1915)   The secret treaty by which Italy agreed to join the *Entente* and declare war within 30 days in return for promises of territorial gain after the war.

Longwy-Briey   A French enclave on the German border, rich in iron-ore, possession of which became an important German war aim.

Louvain Atrocity   Maltreatment of the civilian population and burning of a priceless medieval library by advancing German troops in 1914. It provided rich material for Allied propaganda.

Lusitania   British passenger liner sunk by a German submarine on 7 May 1915, drowning 1198 people (including 128 US citizens).

Luxury Fleet   Phrase used by Winston Churchill In 1912. He claimed that the German fleet was completely unnecessary for her national interests as a land power, whereas Britain's was essential for her survival as a maritime trading nation.

Magyar   Another word for Hungarian.

Magyarisation   The imposition of Magyar culture and language upon the Slav, Romanian and Italian populations in the Magyar-ruled half of *Austria-Hungary.* A major reason for the growth of *irredentism* among these ethnic groups.

Mansion House Speech   An address by David Lloyd George at the height of the second *Moroccan Crisis* in July 1911, in which he issued a strong public warning to Germany. His words carried extra weight because of his previous rôle as a vocal critic of assertive British foreign policies.

313

Maurice Debate An exchange of 9 May 1918 in the British House of Commons in which Lloyd George fought off a Liberal claim that he had misled the country about troop numbers in France.

Megali Idea The most extreme statement of Greek nationalism, entailing the 're-conquest' of former Byzantine territory and the incorporation of all Greek people into the Hellenic Kingdom.

Military Service Act A British law of January 1916 that brought in conscription (the Draft) to replace the voluntary service that had been in place since August 1914.

Mittelafrika Long-standing German ambition to establish a contiguous Central African Empire, mainly at the expense of Portugal.

Mitteleuropa A long-standing German project for a European economic zone to counter-balance the existing World Powers. Friedrich Naumann's book *Mitteleuropa* became a best seller in Germany in 1916.

Mittelmeerdivision The German Mediterranean Squadron, elements of which were 'sold' to Turkey when they arrived in Constantinople in August 1914, having eluded the Allied fleets.

Moroccan Crises Two international crises, in 1905–6 and in 1911, that poisoned the atmosphere of pre-war international relations and increased the probability of a general European war. Both stemmed from France's determination to colonise Morocco and Germany's determination to assert its international status by preventing this.

Narodna Odbrana (National Defence) A left wing Serbian nationalist organisation that was committed to *irredentism* and the principle of a 'Greater Serbia'.

National Schism The split over whether Greece should join the Allies or remain neutral.

Naval Holiday Winston Churchill's proposal in 1912 for Britain and Germany to halt the ruinous expenditure of the *Naval Race* by agreeing to a fixed ratio of warship construction.

Naval Race The competition in warship construction that was the chief reason for Anglo-German antagonism before the war. It began with the German Naval Law of 1898 and 1899, and was given impetus by the launch of *Dreadnought* and the '*Naval Scare*' of 1909. Other 'naval races' took place between Italy and Austria-Hungary in the Adriatic; and Russia and the Ottoman Empire in the Black Sea.

Naval Scare A British panic in 1909 about claims Germany was secretly building more battleships than revealed in her published estimates. The Press demanded that Britain lay down eight Dreadnoughts instead of six ('We want eight and we won't wait!') forcing the government to build the extra ships. (*See Naval Race*)

Navy League   A pre-war German pressure group campaigning for a strong navy.

Neuilly, Treaty of   Signed between Bulgaria and the victorious Allied powers in November 1919.

Nivelle Offensive   The disastrous *Allied* Spring offensive 1917, based on French Commander Robert Nivelle's claim that it could end the war in 48 hours. It failed completely, the Germans having withdrawn, aware of Nivelle's plans, to the *Hindenburg Line*. The *French army mutinies* a month later were a direct result of the 350,000 casualties suffered in this misconceived endeavour.

Novi Bazar, Sanjak of   A strip of territory of great strategic importance separating Serbia from Montenegro. The Austrians occupied it in 1878 to prevent the union of the two Slav states, and to stop Serbia, or even Russia, using Montenegro's narrow strip of coastline as an Adriatic naval base. Austria evacuated the territory after the *Bosnian Crisis* of 1908, and could not prevent the merging of Serb and Montenegrin armies during the Balkan wars.

October Revolution (6–7 Nov. 1917/24–25 Oct. OS)   The removal of the Russian *Provisional Government* engineered by the Bolsheviks in the name of the All Russian Congress of Soviets.

Octobrists   Conservative Russian party, dedicated to implementing the Tsar's October Manifesto of 1905.

Open Door   The principle formulated by the US in 1899, that all powers should have economic access to China.

Order No 1 (14/1 Mar. 1917)   A decree of the *Petrograd Soviet* widely blamed for undermining the discipline of the Russian army.

Ottoman Empire   The vast multinational Empire ruled from Istanbul (Constantinople) that until 1913 stretched from the Adriatic Sea to the Persian Gulf. Often loosely called Turkey.

Pact of London   An agreement of 5 September 1914, whereby the Entente partners undertook not to sign a separate peace with the Central Powers.

Parécchio   Italian *'a lot'*, *'much'*: what the Italian politician Giovanni Giolitti said Italy could gain by remaining neutral. His published letter of 2 February 1915 added fuel to the bitter debate over intervention.

Paris Gun   A German 210-millimetre cannon which bombarded Paris from 68 miles in 1918.

Paris Peace Settlement   Often used as an alternative to '*Versailles Settlement*'.

Patriotic Service Law (Dec. 1916)   German decree for recruiting all able-bodied men and certain categories of women to work in selected industries that were vital to the war effort.

Peace Offer, German A speech by German Chancellor Bethmann Hollweg, 12 December 1916, which raised the prospect of peace negotiations without making any specific offers or assurances.

Peace Resolution (19 Jul. 1917) A vote by the German calling for a peace of understanding and reconciliation.

Pénétration pacifique Informal colonisation through trade, loans and missionary activity, that does not lead to direct rule. Examples include Britain in China, France in Morocco, and all the Powers in the Ottoman Empire.

Petrograd The traditional wartime name assumed by St Petersburg, capital of the Russian Empire.

Petrograd Soviet of Workers' and Soldiers' Deputies The elected council representing the working people of the Russian capital which ruled in parallel with the *Provisional Government* between March and November 1917. (*See* '*Dual Power*')

Plan 17 The French plan for war against Germany. It ignored the obvious intention of the Germans to invade France through Belgium, and gambled all on an invasion of Germany through Lorraine.

Plan 19 The Russian war plan for an immediate invasion of East Prussia to take advantage of the German army's concentration in the west attempting to carry out the *Schlieffen Plan.*

Pless Convention (6 Sep. 1915) A military convention obliging Bulgaria to join the *Central Powers* in an invasion of Serbia within 35 days.

Polish National Committee Set up in 1914 by Roman Dmowski, it operated as a de facto Polish administration under Russian protection.

Porte Shorthand for the Ottoman Foreign Ministry.

Potsdam Meeting (1910) A conference between Tsar Nicholas II and Kaiser Wilhelm II that raised false hopes of a Russo-German rapprochement after the *Bosnian Crisis.*

Preparedness Movement An American campaign, in which ex-President Theodore Roosevelt was prominent, to increase US military capacity and to press for that US to join the Entente.

Preventive war A widely held belief in Germany that it would be better to have a war sooner rather than later because of the long-term threat of the Russian *Great Programme*, the French *Three Year Law*, and the *Anglo-Russian Naval Convention.*

Provisional Government The body that ruled Russia between the February and October revolutions of 1917. Initially dominated by Liberal patriots determined to continue the war, it soon passed under the control of moderate Socialists who repudiated Tsarist war aims but still wished to defend Russian soil. Its resistance to popular demands for peace was the main reason for its overthrow by the Bolsheviks in the *October Revolution*.

Quai 'd'Orsay   Shorthand for the French Foreign Ministry.

Raccognigi Agreement (Oct. 1909)   A Russo-Italian accord based on the dissatisfaction of both countries at their treatment during the *Bosnian Crisis*.

Radiant May   The intense national debate that preceded Italy's entry into the war in 1915.

Race to the Sea   The leap-frogging attempts of each side to outflank each other as they competed to establish themselves on the Channel coast at the end of 1914.

Rapallo Conference (5 Nov. 1917)   Emergency Allied meeting to discuss responses to the Italian collapse at *Caporetto*, at which it was decided to set up a *Supreme War Council*.

Red Army (*Krasnaya Armiya*)   The Russian 'Workers' and Peasants Army' set up on 28 January (15 Jan. OS), to replace the defunct Imperial Russian Army. It fought briefly against the *Central Powers* until March 1917, and thereafter against the *White Armies* in the Russian Civil War.

Reichsrat   The parliament of the Austrian part of the Habsburg Empire, which met in Vienna.

Reichstag   The Lower House of the Imperial German Parliament established in 1871. Outwardly a democratic body elected by universal male suffrage and the secret ballot, by 1914 it did not accurately represent existing social forces of Germany. It had little control over foreign policy and the armed forces, but its agreement was required to obtain war credits.

Reichstag Peace Resolution   A motion passed in the German Parliament on 19 July 1917, calling for a negotiated peace with no territorial gains.

Revanchism   The sentiment, at times a political movement, stirred up in France by annexation of Alsace and Lorraine by Germany in 1871. It was at its height in the 1870s but revived just before the war.

Reveil National, Le   A patriotic upsurge in pre-war France that was characterised by a revival of '*revanchism*' and a preoccupation with the great events of French history.

Risk Theory   The basis of German naval strategy before the war, by which German planners hoped that Britain, with her world-wide commitments, could be forced to recognise Germany's interests by the mere threat of a German fleet concentrated in the North Sea. (*See 'Fleet in Being', 'Risk Theory'*)

Rome Congress (Apr. 1918)   A meeting sponsored by the Italian government at which representatives of national groups within the *Habsburg Empire* planned their post-war independence.

317

Room 40   Shorthand for the Royal Navy Intelligence Department. The capture of German Code Books in August 1914 enabled it to break the German naval codes and forewarn the Admiralty of German future ship movements. Its greatest triumphs were to predict the German breakout before *Jutland*, and to decipher the *Zimmermann Telegram*.

Russo-Japanese War (1904–5)   A struggle for control of Manchuria in which Russia was comprehensively defeated, precipitating the Revolution of 1905 and weakening Russia's military capability for a decade. (*See also Tsushima*)

Salonika Expedition (Oct. 1915)   Joint Anglo-French occupation of an enclave in northern Greece intended to support Serbia and deter Bulgaria from entering the war. Despite its failure to achieve either objective, 400,000 Allied soldiers remained there until 1918, making little contribution to the Allied effort until the last few weeks of the war.

Sarajevo Crisis   *See July Crisis.*

Schlieffen Plan   Germany's contingency plan for a European war, which committed Germany to an immediate attack in the west even in the case of a quarrel with Russia, and necessitated the invasion of neutral Belgium and Luxembourg. Germany had no alternative plan.

Second Balkan War (June–August 1913)   Bulgaria, unhappy with the result of the *First Balkan War*, attacked Serbia and Greece. After Romania and Turkey joined in, she was quickly defeated and lost most of her wartime gains.

Second International   A loose federation of trade unions and socialist parties founded in Paris in 1889. Before 1914, the International advocated compulsory courts of international arbitration and the reduction, and eventual elimination of armaments. The majority of members rejected the use of a general strike to obstruct mobilisation, and in 1914 only the Serbian and Russian sections upheld its anti-war principles. The decision of most socialists to rally behind their respective governments caused the movement to split, and over the next four years, only a minority supported active resistance to the war.

September Programme   A list of territorial demands drawn up by the German Chancellor Bethmann Hollweg in September 1914 when he was convinced that Germany was about to win the war. An important component of the *Fischer Thesis*.

Sèvres, Treaty of   The initial settlement between Turkey and the Allies signed on 10 August 1920. It was not accepted by Kemal Pasha's nationalist movement and superseded by the Treaty of Lausanne in 1923.

Shell Scandal (May 1915)   A crisis that brought about the replacement of the Liberal government in Britain by an all-party coalition. It was provoked by a Press campaign, claiming that the failings of the *BEF* were explained by munition shortages.

Side-Shows   A derogatory term for operations, like the *Gallipoli* and *Salonika Expeditions*, that diverted resources from the *Western Front*. (*See Westerners and Easterners*)

Siegfried Line   A section of the *Hindenburg Line*.

Sixtus Affair (sometimes, 'Sixte Affair')   An abortive attempt, in 1917, by Austria-Hungary to conduct peace negotiations with the Allies and the US.

Smuts-Mensdorff Conversations (18/19 Dec. 1917)   Abortive negotiations between Britain and Austria-Hungary.

Social Darwinism   A theory popularised by the British writer Houston Stewart Chamberlain that found great favour with Kaiser Wilhelm II and General Ludendorff. It applied Darwin's concept of 'natural selection' to the struggle between races and nations, inferring that that war was a natural mechanism for ensuring the survival of 'the fittest races'.

Socialist International   See *Second International.*

Sonderweg, der Deutche   A controversial theory that German history has followed a unique path marked out by Germany's peculiar geographical and historical circumstances.

Sovnarkom   The Council of People's Commissars, Lenin's government after the October Revolution.

Splendid Isolation   A phrase of Lord Salisbury's that embodied a common 19th-century British belief that the Empire was strong enough to stand alone. The weaknesses revealed by the South African War led to its abandonment.

Straits Agreement (10 Apr. 1915)   Britain and France agreed to Russian control of Constantinople and the Straits after the war, in return for Russia allowing them a major share of the Ottoman Empire.

St Germain, Treaty of   The Treaty between Austria and the victorious *Allies* signed on 10 September 1919. It recognised the independence of Czechoslovakia, Poland, Hungary, and the Kingdom of the Serbs, Croats, and Slovenes (Yugoslavia) thus confirming the break-up of the *Habsburg Empire.*

St Jean de Maurienne, Treaty of (19 Apr. 1917)   An agreement between Britain, France and Italy for the post-war dismemberment of the *Ottoman Empire.* The new Russian *Provisional Government* was not invited to participate. (*See Sykes Picot Agreement*)

Stockholm Conference   An attempt by the *International,* and the *Petrograd Soviet* in July and August 1917 to convene a gathering of socialist and anti-war forces to seek a way to end the war. It did not take place because most belligerent governments refused to allow their nationals passports to attend.

Summer Offensive (1917)   See *Kerensky Offensive.*

Supreme War Bureau   An organisation headed by General Groener that controlled the distribution of materials under the *Hindenburg Programme*.

Supreme War Council (9 Nov. 1917)   A committee set up by the *Allies* at the *Rapallo Conference* to co-ordinate their military operations.

Sykes Picot Agreement (9 May 1916)   A secret convention signed between the British diplomat Sir Mark Sykes and the French official Georges Picot for the post-war partition of the Ottoman Empire. (*See Treaty of St Jean de Maurienne*)

Tangier Incident (Mar. 1905)   The visit of Kaiser William II to Tangier aboard his private yacht at a time when France was attempting the annexation of Morocco. The Kaiser's support for Moroccan independence precipitated the *First Moroccan Crisis*.

Third Supreme Command (Aug. 1916)   The quasi-dictatorial system established in Germany under Hindenburg and Ludendorff in an attempt to galvanise Germany's war production. It marked the eclipse of Kaiser Wilhelm as a political force, and adoption of a much more aggressive programme of German war aims.

Three Year Law (7 Aug. 1913)   A French attempt to match Germany's larger number of men of military age by increasing the length of military service. In the short term it weakened the French army, but its long-term threat encouraged German advocates of *Preventive War*.

Transylvania   A region in the east of *Austria-Hungary* with a large Romanian population. The *Magyarisation* policies of the Budapest government caused many ethnic Romanians to seek unity with Romania, causing great tension between Austria-Hungary and Romania. In 1916, Romania launched a short-lived invasion of the province, which was given to her under the *Treaty of Trianon*.

Trialism   Archduke Franz Ferdinand's blueprint for the future of the Habsburg Empire, under which the Slav inhabitants of the Empire would be given equal weight with the Germans and Magyars.

Trianon, Treaty of (4 Jun. 1920)   Signed in the Trianon Palace at Versailles between representatives of Hungary and the victorious Allies.

Triple Alliance (1882)   The military agreement between German, Austria-Hungary and Italy renewed every 5 years.

Triple Entente   The pre-war combination of France, Russia and Britain.

Tsushima, Battle of (27–8 May 1905)   The destruction of the Russian Baltic fleet by the Japanese navy.

Turnip Winter   Popular name for the shortages in Germany in the winter of 1916–17.

Two Emperors Manifesto (5 Nov. 1916)   Proclamation promising an independent Poland after the war comprising territory conquered from Russia.

Union Sacrée   The 'political truce' in France that lasted until 1917.

Unrestricted Submarine Warfare   A policy adopted by Germany at various times during the war, but most resolutely in February 1917, whereby U-boats sank civilian vessels without surfacing or giving warning. (*See 'Cruiser Rules'*)

Verdun, Battle of (Feb.–Dec. 1916)   A battle launched by Germany against the great French fortress of Verdun on the River Meuse. It was intended to 'bleed the French Army white' defending a symbol of French resistance, which national pride would not allow to be surrendered.

Versailles Declaration (3 Jun. 1918)   The first Allied document supporting the dissolution of the Habsburg Empire and 'freedom' for Poles, Czechs and South Slavs.

Versailles, Treaty of (28 Jun. 1918)   The settlement between the Allies and Germany, which is often wrongly used to describe the entire post-war settlement of 1919–20, which comprises the *Treaties of Versailles, Neuilly, Trianon, Sèvres,* and *St Germain.*

Vesenkha   The Supreme Council of the National Economy established by Lenin in November 1917.

Voie Sacrée, La   Popular name for the road from Bar-le-Duc to the beleaguered fortress of Verdun along which men and supplies flowed at enormous cost to sustain French resistance during 1916.

War Council (8 Dec. 1912)   A meeting at Potsdam of the German Kaiser and his immediate advisors at which proponents of the *Fischer Thesis,* claim the German military élite made a calculated decision to go to war, and to initiate a programme of military and diplomatic preparation for it. Other historians play down its significance, saying that nothing was decided and no important policy changes flowed from it. (*See Preventive war*)

Weltpolitik   A policy pursued after 1897 by Kaiser Wilhelm II, Admiral Tirpitz and Chancellor Bernhard von Bülow. It was based on the belief, expressed by Max Weber, that if Germany was 'not to become another Switzerland' she must cease to be a mere European Power and become a World Power. This would entail the building of a great navy, the acquisition of overseas colonies and bases, and the assertion of Germany's rights all over the world. All of these inevitably brought Germany into conflict with the existing world powers, Britain, France, Russia and the USA.

Western Front   Line of confrontation between the armies of Germany and the Entente stretching 466 miles from Nieuwpoort on the Belgian coast to the Swiss frontier.

Westerners   Allied strategists like Haig and Foch, who believed the only way to win the war was to concentrate all efforts on the Western Front. (*See also 'Easterners'*)

Willy–Nicky Correspondence   A series of telegrams between Kaiser Wilhelm II and his cousin Tsar Nicholas II at the height of the *July Crisis*, in which the two monarchs tried in vain to find a way out of the impending disaster.

Wilson's Peace Note (18 Dec. 1916)   An invitation by the US President for the belligerents to state their war aims.

Young Turks (*Jöntürkler*)   A combination of reforming groups that took power in Turkey between 1908 and 1913 with the aim of replacing the ramshackle *Ottoman Empire* with a modern secular state. In 1914, they joined the war on the side of the *Central Powers*, whom they judged to be the most likely winners and the least likely to pursue colonial ambitions at Turkey's expense.

Yugoslav Committee (Apr. 1915)   A body founded in Paris and London to work for a South Slav state comprising Serbs, Croats, Slovenes, Montenegrins and Bosnians.

Zabern (Saverne) Incident (Nov. 1913)   An episode in which a German officer mishandled French inhabitants in German occupied Alsace. French patriotic outrage was matched by anger among German Liberals at military high-handedness.

Zimmermann Telegram   The document that precipitated American entry into the war. Published in the American Press on 1 March 1917, this was a message from German Foreign Secretary Alfred Zimmermann to the German embassy in Mexico, suggesting that if Mexico entered an alliance with Germany she might regain territories conquered by the US in the 19th century. The message was deciphered by *Room 40* and passed to the US Ambassador in London.

Zimmerwald Conference (Sep. 1915)   An international socialist conference that called for an immediate halt to the war and the initiation of peace negotiations based on the principle of 'no annexations, no indemnities'.

13.2 CHANGING PLACES

Adrianople/Edirne	Now in Turkey
Agram [A-H]	Now Zagreb [Croatia]
Altenburg [A-H]	Now Magyarorszag [Hungary]
Belgrade/Beograd	Now in Yugoslavia
Bozen [A-H]	Now Bolzano [Italy]
Breslau [Germany]	Now Wroclaw [Poland]
Brixen [A-H]	Now Bressanone [Italy]
Brody [A-H]	Now in Ukraine
Brunn [A-H]	Now Brno [Czech Republic]
Cattaro [A-H]	Now Kotor [Croatia]
Cilli [A-H]	Now Celje [Slovenia]
Constantinople/Istanbul	Now in Turkey
Corfu/Kerkyra	Now in Greece
Czernowitz [A-H]	Now Černivtsi [Ukraine]
Danube/Dunaj	River Danube
Danzig [Germany]	Now Gdansk [Poland]
Dorpat [Russia]	Now Tartu [Estonia]
Dubrovnik/Ragusa	Now Dubrovnik [Croatia]
Dulcigno/Ulcinj	Now in Albania
Durazzo/Drac [A-H]	Now Durrës [Albania]
Edirne/Adrianople	Now in Turkey
Erivan/Yerevan	Now in Armenia
Esseg/Eszék	Now Osijek [Croatia]
Fiume [A-H]	Now Rijeka [Croatia]
Franzensbad [A-H]	Now Frantigkovy Lazile [Czech Republic]
Görz/Gorica	Now Gorizia [Italy]
Gumbinnen [Germany]	Now Gusev [Kaliningrad, Russia]
Helsingfors [Russia]	Now Helsinki [Finland]
Hermannstadt/ Nagyszeben [A-H]	Now Sibiu [Romania]
Insterburg [Germany]	Now Chernyakhovsk [Kaliningrad, Russia]
Jassy/Iassy	Now in Romania
Königsberg [Germany]	Now Kaliningrad [Russia]
Karfreit/Kobarid/Caporetto	Now in Italy
Kishinev [Russia]	Now Chişinâu, Moldovan Republic
Kolozsvar [A-H]	Now Cluj Napoca [Romania]
Komdrom/Kornorn	Now in Hungary
Königgrätz [A-H]	Now Hradec Králové [Czech Republic]
Konopischt [A-H]	Now Konopigte [Czech Republic]
Kovno [Russia]	Now Kaunas [Lithuania]
Krakau [A-H]	Now Krakow [Poland]
Kremsier [A-H]	Now Kromeriz [Czech Republic]
Kronstadt/Brasso [A-H]	Now Brasov [Romania]
Kronstadt/Kolosvar [A-H]	Now Cluj [Romania]

323

Laibach [A-H]	Now Ljubljana [Slovenia]
Langemarck	Now Langemark [Belgium]
Libau [Germany]	Now Liepaja [Latvia]
Lissa [A-H]	Now Vis [Croatia]
Louvain/Leuven	Now in Belgium
Luck/Lutsk	Now in Poland
Lvov/Lemberg [A-H]	Now Lviv [Ukraine]
Marburg [A-H]	Now Maribor [Slovenia]
Marienburg [Germany]	Now Malbork [Poland]
Memel [Germany]	Now Klaipeda [Lithuania]
Meran [A-H]	Now Merano [Italy]
Moldau River [A-H]	Vltava River [Czech Republic]
Monastir [Turk]	Now Bitola/Bitolj [Macedonia]
Neusatz/Újvidék [A-H]	Now Novi Sad [Yugoslavia]
Niemen [Germany]	Now Nemunas [Lithuania]
Nish/Niş	Now in Yugoslavia
Oedenburg	Now Sopron [Hungary]
Olmütz [A-H]	Now Olomouc [Czech Republic]
Ortelsburg	Now Swzytno [Poland]
Peterwardein/Petrovaradin	Now Pétervására [Hungary]
Philippopolis/Plovdiv	Now in Bulgaria
Pilsen [A-H]	Now Plzen [Czech Republic]
Pless [A-H]	Now Psczyna [Czech Republic]
Pola [A-H]	Now Pula [Croatia]
Posen/Pozsony [A-H]	Now Poznan [Poland]
Prague/Prag	Now Praha [Czech Republic]
Pressburg/Pomony [A-H]	Now Bratislava [Slovakia]
Raab	Now Gyor [Hungary]
Ragusa/Dubrovnic [A-H]	Now Dubrovnik [Croatia]
Rastenburg [Germany]	Now Ketrzyn (Poland)
Reichstad [A-H]	Zekupy [Czech Republic]
Reval [Russia]	Now Tallinn [Estonia]
Rovno [Russia]	Now Rivne [Ukraine]
Salonika/Thessaloniki	Now in Greece
Scutari/Shkodër/Skadarsko	Now on border of Montenegro and Albania
Skopje [S-C] Uskub [A]	Now in Macedonia
Smyrna/Izmir	Now in Turkey
Spalato [A-H]	Now Split [Croatia]
St Petersburg/Petrograd	Now in Russia
Stalluponen [Germany]	Now Nesterov [Poland]
Strassburg/Strasbourg	Now in France
Szeged/Szegedin	Now in Hungary
Tannenberg [Germany]	Now Stebark [Poland]
Tarnopol [Poland]	Now Ternopol [Ukraine]
Temesvar [Hun]	Now Timisoara [Romania]

Teschen[A-H]	Now Cieszyn [Poland] and Cesky Tešin [Czech Republic]
Theiss River [A-H]	Tisza River [Hungary]
Tiflis/Tbilisi	Now in Armenia
Trient [A-H]	Now Trento [Italy]
Tripoli	Now Libya
Troppau [A-H]	Now Opava [Czech Republic]
Valona/Vlora; Vlone	Now Vlore [Albania]
Vienna/Wien	Now Austria
Vilna [Russia]	Now Vilnius [Lithuania]
Vlora/Valona	Now in Albania
Volhynia	Volyn [Ukraine]
Weichsel River	Vistula River [Poland]
Zabern	Now Saverne [France]
Zara [A-H]	Now Zadar [Croatia]

13.3 COMMON ABBREVIATIONS

AEF	American Expeditionary Forces
AFSR	Armed Forces of South Russia
AIF	Australian Imperial Force
AMC	Armed Merchant Cruiser
ANZAC	Australia New Zealand Army Corps
ARCS	All-Russian Council of Soviets
ASW	Anti-submarine warfare
BEF	British Expeditionary Force
CC	Central Committee of the Bolshevik Party
CEC	Central Executive Committee of the All-Russian Council of Soviets
CEF	Canadian Expeditionary Force
CGT	*Confédération Générale du Travail.* General Confederation of Labour (France)
CID	Committee of Imperial Defence (GB)
CIGS	Chief of the Imperial General Staff (GB)
C-in-C	Commander-in-Chief
CM	Committee on Public Information (US)
CUP	Committee of Union and Progress ('Young Turks')
C3	Men unfit for active overseas service, under the Military Service Act 1916 (GB)
Cheka	*Chrezvychainaya Kommissiya* (Extraordinary Commission for Fighting Counter-Revolution and Sabotage)
DMI	Director of Military Intelligence (GB)
DMO	Director of Military Operations (GB)
DNI	Director of Naval Intelligence (GB)
DORA	Defence of the Realm Act (GB)
DVP	*Deutsche Vaterlandspartei.* German Fatherland Party
EEF	Egyptian Expeditionary Force (1916–19)
EPD	Excess Profits Duty (GB 1915)
KuK	*Kaiserlich und Königlich,* Imperial and Royal (armed forces of Austria-Hungary)
FANY	First Aid Nursing Yeomanry Corps (GB)
GHQ	General Headquarters
GQG	*Grand Quartier Général* (French General HQ)
HMG	His Majesty's Government (GB)
HMS	His Majesty's Ship (GB)
KRA	*Kriegsrohstoffarbteilung* (German Department of War Raw Materials)
Kadet	Constitutional Democrat (Russian)
MP	Member of Parliament (GB)
MI5	Military Intelligence, section 5 (British Counterintelligence Agency)

MI6	Military Intelligence, section 6 (British Intelligence and Espionage Agency)
NCO	Non-Commissioned Officer
NUR	National Union of Railwaymen (GB)
NZEF	New Zealand Expeditionary Force
OHL	*Oberst Heeresleitung*, German Supreme Command
RA	Royal Artillery
RAF	Royal Air Force
RAMC	Royal Army Medical Corps
RAN	Royal Australian Navy
RCAF	Royal Canadian Air Force
RFC	Royal Flying Corps
RFP	Retail Food Price Index (100 in July 1914, GB)
RIC	Royal Irish Constabulary
RM	*Reichsmark*
RM	Royal Marines (GB)
RMLE	*Régiment de Marche de la Légion Étrangère* (French Foreign Legion)
RN	Royal Navy
RNAS	Royal Naval Air Service
RND	Royal Navy Division
RNR	Royal Naval Reserve
RSFSR	Russian Socialist Federative Soviet Republic (1918–24)
SDP	*Sozialdemokratische Partei Deutschlands* (German Social Democratic Party)
SFIO	*Section Française de l'Internationale Ouvrièr*. The largest French Socialist Party
SR	Socialist Revolutionary Party (the party of the Russian peasants)
STAVKA	Russian Supreme HQ
TUC	Trades Union Congress (GB)
USDP	*Unabhängige Sozialdemokratische Partei Deutchlands*. German Independent Social Democratic Party
USN	US Navy
USW	Unrestricted Submarine Warfare
U-boat	*Unterseeboot*
VSNKh	Supreme Council for the National Economy (Russia, 1917)
WL	Women's Legion (GB)
WLA	Women's Land Army (GB)
WRAF	Women's Royal Air Force (GB)
WRNS	Women's Royal Naval Service ('Wrens', GB)
WSPU	Women's Social and Political Union ('Suffragettes', GB)
WVR	Women's Volunteer Reserve (GB)

13.4 SOME WARTIME SLANG

'Abdul'	A Turk
'About Turn'	*Hèbuterne*
'Alleyman'	A German (*Allemand*)
''Arf a mo', Kaiser!'	Popular catch phrase from a 1914 recruiting poster
'Asiatic Annie'	Heavy Turkish gun at the Dardanelles
'Ballyhooly'	*Bailleul*
'Battle Bowler'	British steel helmet
'Battle-bag'	Naval airship
'Big Bertha'	A huge Krupp gun
'Blighty one'	A light wound (but serious enough to be sent home)
'Blighty'	Britain
'Boche'	French term for Germans
'Cherry Nobs'	British Military Police ('red-caps')
'Coffee cooler'	Shirker (US)
'Comic cuts'	Intelligence summaries
'Compo'	Pay
'Cook's tour'	A VIP visit to the trenches
'Cooshu'	Sleep (*coucher*)
'Digger'	Australian or New Zealand soldier
'Do an alley'	To go off (*aller*)
'Doughboys'	US soldiers
'Flaming onion'	German anti-aircraft shell
'Fly boys'	English who evaded conscription by crossing to Ireland
'Funky Villas'	*Fonquevillers*
'Gas bag'	Airship
'Hairy'	Large British draught horse
'Hazy Brook'	*Hazebrouck*
'Hommes forty'	French railway carriage (from their capacity)
'Japan'	Bread (*du pain*)
'Johnny'	A Turk (dating from Crimean War)
'Kapai'	A New Zealand soldier (Maori, *'Very good'*)
'Khakis'	German slang for British troops
'Landowner'	Dead man
'Lazy Eliza'	A long-range large shell
'Lousy Wood'	*Leuze* Wood
'Moo-Cow Farm'	*Mouquet* Farm, near Thiepval
'Mouth organ'	Stokes mortar
'Oofs'	Eggs (*oeufs*)
'Pill-box'	Concrete German blockhouse
'Plug Street'	*Ploegsteert*, near Armentières
'Pork and beans'	British nickname for Portuguese troops
'Pronto'	'Hurry up' (US phrase from Mexican War)
'Pudding basin'	British steel helmet

'Quakers'	Conscientious objectors
'Quick Dick'	British gun on Western Front
'Sally Booze'	*Sailly la Bourse*
'Sammies'	Early British nickname for US soldiers
'San Fairy Ann'	'It doesn't matter' (*'Ça ne fait rien'*)
'Sausage Hill, Go to'	To be captured by the Germans
'Shocks'	*Choques*, near *Bethune*
'Silent Susan'	A German high-velocity shell
'Sister Susie'	British woman doing army work
'Stink bomb'	A mustard gas shell
'Suicide Club'	Undertaking risky duties
'They've opened another tin'	'Someone new has arrived in the Line'
'Tommy'	A British soldier (from 'Thomas Atkins', the model name on Army forms)
'Umpty poo'	Just a bit more' (*'Un petit peu'*)
'Up the Jigger'	In the trenches
'Weary Willie'	A long-range shell passing overhead
'Whistling Percy'	A large German naval gun at Cambrai
'White Sheet'	*Wytschaete*, Flanders
'Whizz-bang'	Type of German shell
'Woolly-bear'	German shrapnel shell trailing brown smoke

INDEX